HYDERABAD
GAZETTEER

HYDERABAD GAZETTEER

By

MIRZA MEHDY KHAN

WITH CONTRIBUTIONS FROM
E. VREDENBURG (GEOLOGY) AND
LIEUT.-COL. PRAIN (BOTANY)

COSMO PUBLICATIONS

2001 INDIA

HYDERABAD GAZETTEER
First COSMO Print 2001

ISBN 81-7755-112-4

Published by
MRS. RANI KAPOOR
for COSMO PUBLICATIONS Div. of
GENESIS PUBLISHING PVT. LTD.
24-B, Ansari Road, Darya Ganj,
New Delhi-110 002, INDIA

Printed at
Mehra Offset Press

PREFACE

THE articles in this volume were drafted by Mirza Mehdy Khān. When the drafts had been finished, the Districts into which the State is divided were rearranged; and it has not been found possible to deal completely with the Districts as now constituted, though revised statistics have been included so far as available. Materials were largely collected by District officers and heads of departments; and sections on technical subjects have been contributed by Mr. E. Vredenburg (Geology) and Lieut.-Col. Prain, C.I.E. (Botany). Mirza Mehdy Khān also received valuable assistance from Major Haig, I.A., and Mr. C. Wilmott, formerly Assistant Financial Secretary in Hyderābād.

TABLE OF CONTENTS

PROVINCIAL GAZETTEERS OF INDIA

HYDERABĀD STATE

Hyderābād State[1].—A Native State better known as the Dominions of His Highness the Nizām, lying between 15° 10′ and 20° 40′ N. and 74° 40′ and 81° 35′ E., with an area of 82,698 square miles. It forms a polygonal tract occupying almost the centre of the Deccan plateau. Berār and the Central Provinces touch it on the north, and the Khāndesh District of the Bombay Presidency on the north-west; on the south it is bounded by the Kistna and Tungabhadra rivers, which separate it from the Guntūr, Kurnool, and Bellary Districts of Madras; on the west it is bounded by the Ahmadnagar, Sholāpur, Bijāpur, and Dhārwār Districts of Bombay; and on the east by the Wardhā and Godāvari rivers and the Kistna District of Madras. The State is equal in area to the Madras Presidency, minus the Coromandel Coast and Coimbatore, or a little more than two and a half times the area of Ireland, or one and two-fifths of the combined areas of England and Wales.

Physical aspects. General outline of the State, its dimensions and boundaries.

The country is an extensive plateau, with an average elevation of about 1,250 feet above the level of the sea, but with summits here and there rising to 2,500 and even to 3,500 feet. It is divided into two large and nearly equal divisions, geologically and ethnically distinct, separated from each other by the Mānjra and Godāvari rivers. The portion to the north and west belongs to the trappean region, that to the south and east being granitic and calcareous. There is a corresponding agreement between the two ethnical elements. The trappean region is inhabited by speakers of Marāthī and Kanarese, the granitic country by speakers of Telugu. The

Natural divisions.

[1] In 1905 the administrative units of the State, from Divisions to *tāluks*, were completely reconstituted. The text generally refers to their constitution before the rearrangement, but the main changes are explained in the paragraph on Administration and in the individual articles.

trappean or black cotton soil country is a land of wheat and cotton; while Telingāna, or the granitic region, is a land of rice and tanks. The difference between these two tracts is very marked. The trap or black cotton soil region is covered with luxuriant vegetation, with cliffs, crags, and undulating hills. The soil resulting from the decomposition of trap is of a dark colour, and very fertile; and, being argillaceous, it retains its moisture for a considerable time. In the granitic and calcareous region, on the other hand, the hills are bare of vegetation, but the plains are covered with scattered brushwood of every description; dome-shaped hills and wild fantastic boulders and tors abound in many parts, giving the region a gloomy aspect. The soil derived from the decomposition of the granite is sandy, and does not retain moisture. Consequently the rivers in this region run dry during the hot season, and this gives rise to the necessity of storing water in artificial reservoirs, known as tanks, with which the whole of the Telingāna tract is studded. The surface of the country has a general slope from north-west to south-east, the main drainage being in this direction; the country to the extreme north-west corner near Aurangābād has an average altitude of about 2,000 feet above sea-level, falling imperceptibly to near 1,200 feet at Raichūr and to between 800 and 900 feet near Kurnool.

Hill system and mountain ranges.

The following are the chief hill and mountain ranges in the State. The Bālāghāt (*bālā* = 'above,' *ghāt* = 'a mountain pass') is a range of hills which extends almost east and west from the Biloli *tāluk* in the east of Nānder District, through Parbhani, till it reaches Ashti, in Bhīr District, with a length in Hyderābād of 200 miles and an average width of about 4½ miles. A spur of this range branches off through tracts lying between the Sīna, Mānjra, and Kāgnā rivers, extending from Ashti in Bhīr District through Osmānābād, and terminating in Gulbarga District. A spur of the Bālāghāt runs between the Godāvari and Mānjra rivers, and passing southwards from the west of Biloli in Nānder reaches Kaulās in Indūr District.

The Sahyādriparvat range runs along the north, from Nirmal in Indūr District in the east, and passing through Parbhani District and the province of Berār reaches Ajanta, and proceeding farther in a westerly direction enters the Khāndesh District of Bombay. Its total length within the State is about 250 miles, for about 100 miles of which it is styled the Ajanta Hills.

Another range, known as the Jālna hills, starts from

Daulatābād fort in Aurangābād District, and proceeds eastward as far as Jālna in the same District, and thence passes into Berār, having a length of 120 miles.

The Kandikal Gutta range, 50 miles in length, extends from Warangal District in a north-westerly direction through the Chinnūr *tāluk* of Adilābād. It is also called the Sirnapalli range.

The principal rivers are the GODĀVARI and the KISTNA, with their tributaries the TUNGABHADRA, the PŪRNA, the PENGANGĀ, the MĀNJRA, the BHĪMA, and the Māner. There are, besides these, many smaller streams, such as the MŪSI, the Windi, the Munair, and others. **River system.**

The Godāvari enters the State at Phultamba in Aurangābād District, flows through it and the Districts of Parbhani, Nānder, Indūr, and Adilābād for a distance of 500 miles, and changing its course at the north-east corner of Elgandal, continues in a south-easterly direction for about 170 miles, forming the eastern boundary of Elgandal and Warangal Districts, until at Pāranthpalli, in the latter District, it enters the Godāvari District of Madras. It is joined by the Mānjra, which rises in the Pātoda *tāluk* of Bhīr, after a course of 387 miles through Bhīr, Osmānābād, Bīdar, Medak, Nānder, and Indūr Districts.

The Kistna crosses the border of the Bijāpur District of Bombay at Echampet in Lingsugūr, and taking a south-easterly course traverses the Districts of Lingsugūr, Raichūr, Mahbūbnagar, Nalgonda, and Warangal, forming the southern boundary of the last three Districts and consequently of the State. Its tributary, the Bhīma, enters Hyderābād at Urchānd in Gulbarga District from the Sholāpur District of Bombay, flows through Gulbarga and Raichūr, and falls into the Kistna in the latter District. The Tungabhadra, another tributary of the Kistna, touches Lingsugūr District at Madlāpur, and flows in a north-easterly direction until it reaches Raichūr District, whence it flows due east until its confluence with the Kistna near Alampūr in the same District. The Tungabhadra separates Lingsugūr and Raichūr from the Bellary and Kurnool Districts of Madras.

The Pengangā rises in the Sahyādriparvat and runs east along the north of Hyderābād, separating Parbhani, Nānder, and Sirpur Tāndūr (now Adilābād) Districts from the southern parts of Berār. In Sirpur Tāndūr it flows along the western and northern borders until it falls into the Wardhā river, north of the Rājūra *tāluk*.

Scenery.

This wide expanse of country presents much variety of surface and feature. In some parts it is mountainous, wooded, and picturesque; in others flat or undulating. The champaign lands are of all descriptions, including many rich and fertile plains, much good land not yet brought under cultivation, and numerous tracts too sterile ever to be cultivated at all. Aurangābād District, besides its caves at AJANTA and ELLORA, presents a variety of scenic aspect not met with elsewhere. The country is undulating in parts, with steppe-like ascents in some places and abrupt crags and cliffs in others.

Lakes and tanks.

Properly speaking there are no natural lakes in the State, but some of the artificial sheets of water are large enough to deserve the name. These are reservoirs formed by throwing dams across the valleys of small rivulets and streams, to intercept water during the rains for irrigation purposes, and they number thousands in the Telingāna tract. The largest and most important is the PĀKHĀL LAKE in the Narsampet *tāluk* of Warangal District, the dam of which is 2,000 yards long, and holds up the water of the Pākhāl river. Its area is nearly 13 square miles, and its length and breadth are respectively 8,000 and 6,000 yards.

Geology.

The geological formations of Hyderābād State are the recent and ancient alluvia, laterite, Deccan trap, Gondwāna, Kurnool and Cuddapah, and Archaean. Those mo largely developed are the Deccan trap and the Archaean, covering immense areas in the north-western and south-eastern portions of the territory respectively. The Gondwāna rocks extend for a distance of 200 miles along those portions of the valleys of the Godāvari and Pranhitā which form the north-eastern frontier of the State. Though the main area of the Cuddapah and Kurnool formations lies in the Madras Presidency, south of the Kistna, they are found in the valley of that river along the south-eastern frontier for 150 miles, and again in the valleys of the Kistna, the Bhīma, and their tributaries in the south-west.

Archaean series.

The oldest formation, the Archaean, consists largely of massive granitoid rocks, particularly well developed round Hyderābād, which extend eastwards past Khammamett as far as the eastern corner of the State, where they become more varied and schistose, containing mica and hornblendic schists, beds of magnetite, metamorphic limestones, and other rocks. Again, a great series of schistose rocks occurs between the Kistna and Tungabhadra in the south-western Districts, which has been mapped and named as the Dhārwār system.

This consists of hornblendic, chloritic, and argillaceous schists, epidiorites, and beds of quartz, associated with varying amounts of hematite and magnetite, representing a highly metamorphosed sedimentary and volcanic series. Except the groups mentioned above, the Archaean formation has not been studied in sufficient detail to define the character and boundaries of its component petrological types. The long narrow bands forming the Dhārwār schist outcrops in the last-mentioned region constitute deeply folded and faulted synclines, embedded within older crystalline schists and gneiss, and injected by later granitoid intrusions. They are intersected by auriferous veins, of great economic importance, leading in the past to considerable mining activity, which is now being resumed. Innumerable basic volcanic dikes occur throughout the Archaean area, some of which are epidiorites, probably of the Dhārwār period, while others, consisting of augite-dolerite or diabase, with micro-pegmatitic quartz of a later period of volcanic activity, are connected with the lavas of the Cuddapah group.

Cuddapahs.

The outcrop of the Cuddapah series north of the Kistna river, consisting of quartzites, slates or shales, and limestones, has been divided into several unconformable groups, of which the upper groups principally occur in this State. The Kurnool series, which is unconformable to the Cuddapah, consists of quartzites, limestones, and shales, which are not so altered and indurated as those of the Cuddapah. Both these have long been known as the diamondiferous sandstones of Southern India. The gems occur principally towards the base of the Kurnools. A portion of the Cuddapahs corresponds with the Bījāwārs of Central India, while the Kurnools are closely related to the Vindhyas. The main area of the Cuddapahs and Kurnools terminates near Jaggayyapet, north of the Kistna. A considerable outcrop of the Cuddapahs follows the south-western border of the Godāvari, its former connexion with the main area being indicated by a series of elongated outliers, the largest of which lies east of Khammamett. The largest continuous spread commences north-east of Khammamett, forms the Pākhāl hills, and extends to within a short distance of the Godāvari and Māner confluence. The beds reappear north of the Godāvari, and continue north-west up to the frontier of Hyderābād, where they disappear beneath the basaltic lavas of the Deccan trap. The Cuddapahs of this area are unconformably overlaid by a vast series of quartzites and conglomerates with a few slaty beds, known as the Sullavai series, which possibly represent the Kurnools. Another outcrop of the Cuddapahs, locally known as the Kalādgi series, occupies a large area in the Belgaum and Dhārwār Districts of Bombay, the eastern extremity of which lies within Hyderābād. Farther to the north-east is another belt of the Kurnool strata, intercalated between the Archaean gneiss and the Deccan trap, and locally named after the Bhīma river, which flows through their outcrop.

Gondwānas.

The Gondwāna rocks, containing the coal-measures, and occupying an enormous area in the valleys of the Godāvari and Pranhitā, are divided into the Chikiāla, Kota-Māleri, Kamptee, Barākar, and Tālcher groups. The first two belong to the Upper and the rest to the Lower Gondwānas. The boundaries of this area are mostly faults, as in most of the Indian coal-fields, which accounts for their straightness and parallelism. The Tālchers consist of fine buff sandstones, often of a greenish tinge, overlying greenish-grey slaty shales and sandstones, beneath which lies the well-known boulder-bed. The glacial origin of this latter formation has been thoroughly confirmed by the remarkable section in the Pengangā near the village of Irai, not quite a mile above the Wardhā confluence, where not only do the boulders exhibit glacial striations, but the surface of the underlying Cuddapah limestones is deeply furrowed and grooved by ice-action, as is commonly seen in glacial regions.

The Barākars are not more than 250 feet thick, but they are of great economic importance, owing to the coal-seams which they include. They consist of coal-beds, sandstones, and shales, with a few impure thin carbonaceous layers. The coal-beds are of great thickness, the Singareni thick coal averaging 56 feet.

The Kamptees rest unconformably on the Barākars and contain no coal. They consist of clays, conglomerates, and especially sandstones, many of them highly ferruginous, others calcareous, and a few manganiferous. Their principal outcrop lies west of the Godāvari, below the confluence of the Pranhitā, extending almost as far as the delta.

The Lower Gondwānas are principally upper palaeozoic in age. The Upper Gondwānas contain mesozoic fossils. Some of the most interesting are those of the Kota-Māleri group, including several species of fishes and reptiles which occur in limestone beds associated with clays. Abundant red and green clays and clayey sandstones form the most distinctive petrological feature of these beds, which rest unconformably on the Kamptees, occupying vast areas to the west of the Godāvari and Pranhitā. The Chikiāla beds, resting on the Kota-Māleri, and consisting of highly ferruginous glassy-looking sandstones and iron bands, are unfossiliferous. Their connexion with the Gondwānas is doubtful.

The Deccan trap, consisting of bedded lava-flows of basalt and dolerite, with occasional intercalations of fresh-water deposits, known as intertrappeans, covers the western part of the State, and extends all along its northern frontier. Deccan trap.

Ancient alluvial gravels and clays, sometimes of considerable thickness, occur at various parts in the valleys of the Godāvari, Kistna, Tungabhadra, and some of their tributaries, indicating geographical conditions differing from the present ones. Their vast antiquity is shown by their containing the remains of extinct mammalia of pleistocene or upper pliocene age. The surface of the rocks is often concealed by laterite, which is a peculiar form of rock-weathering special to tropical regions. Rocks rich in iron, like the Deccan trap, are particularly liable to this form of decomposition. In the absence of laterite, the weathering of the Deccan trap produces the well-known fertile black soil, which may be in parts contemporaneous with the trap, while in the large river valleys it must have been formed or reconsolidated within a (geologically speaking) recent period, judging from the palaeolithic or even neolithic stone implements found in it. Recent alluvial flats cover considerable areas of the large river valleys, especially along the Godāvari below the Pranhitā confluence down to the delta. Alluvium and surface formations.

The principal mineral products of the Dominions are diamonds, gold, and coal. The first occur in the Kurnool series; the gold in the Dhārwār system in Lingsugūr; and the coal in the Barākar, in the Godāvari-Pranhitā-Gondwāna system, which is worked at Singareni. Rich iron ores occur in the Chikiāla sandstones, and in the Dhārwār schists. These products will be more fully described in dealing with Minerals. Minerals.

Much of the land in the Hyderābād State is level, and a large portion of it is under cultivation, though there are tracts where arable soil has never been broken or cultivated, or where cultivation has lapsed. But wherever the ground is left uncultivated for a year or two, it becomes covered with a low jungle, consisting chiefly of *Cassia auriculata* and *Zizyphus microphylla*. Other level tracts also exist where the ground is quite unfit for cultivation. The forests contain, among the larger species, *Tectona grandis*, *Diospyros tomentosa*, *Boswellia serrata*, *Anogeissus latifolia*, *Terminalia* Botany.

tomentosa, *Dalbergia latifolia*, *Ougeinia dalbergioides*, *Schreibera swietenioides*, *Pterocarpus Marsupium*, and *Adina cordifolia*, with smaller species like *Briedelia retusa*, *Lagerstroemia parviflora*, *Woodfordia floribunda*, *Zizyphus*, *Morinda*, *Gardenia*, *Butea*, *Acacia*, *Bauhinia*, *Cochlospermum*, *Grewia*, and *Phyllanthus*. When ground once occupied is allowed to go out of cultivation for a short time, a similar forest speedily asserts itself, containing, besides the trees already mentioned, a considerable number of the semi-spontaneous shrubs and trees that are frequently found in the neighbourhood of Indian dwellings, such as *Bombax*, *Erythrina*, *Moringa*, *Cassia Fistula*, *Anona reticulata*, *Melia Azadirachta*, *Crataeva Roxburghii*, *Feronia Elephantum*, *Aegle Marmelos*, and various species of *Acacia* and *Ficus*.

In the hilly tracts the hills are often covered with forests, not as a rule containing much large timber, the leading constituent species being the same as those that grow in the level tracts and arable lands, but stunted and deformed. Throughout the whole State scattered trees of *Acacia arabica* and *Acacia Catechu* and toddy-palms (*Borassus flabellifer* and *Phoenix sylvestris*) are common; the latter two are extensively cultivated on account of their sap, which, when drawn and allowed to ferment, produces an intoxicating beverage largely consumed in the Telingāna tract. The soils of this area are also favourable to the growth of the coco-nut, which cannot be grown even with the greatest care in the Marāthā region. Around villages, groves of mango (*Mangifera*), tamarind, *Bombax*, *Ficus bengalensis*, *F. religiosa*, and *F. infectoria*, and similar species exist. The tamarind does not flourish in the Marāthā region to the same extent as in Telingāna.

auna. A greater variety of wild animals and feathered game is not to be met with in any other part of India, excepting perhaps Mysore State. Tigers and leopards are found everywhere, while bison and occasionally elephants are met with in the immense jungle about the Pākhāl Lake. The high lands are resorted to by spotted deer (*Cervus axis*), *nīlgai* (*Boselaphus tragocamelus*), *sāmbar* (*Cervus unicolor*), four-horned antelope, hog deer, and 'ravine deer' or gazelle. Wild hog are found in the jungles, and innumerable herds of antelope in the plains. Hyenas, wolves, tiger-cats, bears, hares, jackals, &c., are in great abundance. Of the varied species of the feathered tribe in Hyderābād, may be mentioned the grey and painted partridge, blue rock and green pigeon, sand-grouse, quail, snipe, bustard, peafowl, jungle-fowl, wild duck, wild geese, and teal of various descriptions. The florican and flamingo are occasionally seen on the banks of the Godāvari and Kistna.

The climate is not altogether salubrious, but may be considered as in general good, for it is pleasant and agreeable during the greater part of the year. The country being partially hilly, and free from the arid bare deserts of Rājputāna and other parts of India, the hot winds are not so keenly felt. There are three marked seasons: the rainy season from the beginning of June to the end of September, the cold season from the beginning of October to the end of January, and the hot season from early in February to the end of May. Climate.

The mean temperature of the State is about 81°. The following table gives the temperature for the three stations where observations have been taken regularly:— Temperature.

Station.	Height of Observatory above sea-level in feet.	Average temperature (in degrees Fahrenheit) for the ten years ending with 1901 in							
		January.		May.		July.		November.	
		Mean.	Diurnal range.	Mean.	Diurnal range.	Mean.	Diurnal range.	Mean.	Diurnal range.
Raichūr	1,326	75·7	23·0	91·3	24·0	81·5	17·0	76·9	19·0
Hyderābād *	1,690	72·1	25·8	91·9	23·2	80·4	14·4	73·5	22·1
Hanamkonda †	871	75·1	23·3	93·2	22·0	82·4	13·0	75·6	21·8

* The figures for January, May, and July are for ten years, and for November for eleven.
† The figures for January are for three years and the rest for four.

The annual rainfall is estimated at from 30 to 32 inches, principally received during the south-west monsoon between June and October. The north-east monsoon brings between 4 and 7 inches of rain. The rainfall in 1901 was 32 inches, but in 1900 the total fall amounted to only 15 inches or less than half the normal. Westerly winds blow generally from the beginning of June to the end of September; during the next five months, from October to February, the wind blows from the east; and in March, April, and May north-easterly winds are frequent. The following table gives the rainfall at three stations:— Rainfall.

Station.	Average rainfall (in inches) for the twenty-five years ending with 1901 in												
	Jan.	Feb.	March.	April.	May.	June.	July.	August.	Sept.	Oct.	Nov.	Dec.	Total of year.
Raichūr	0·02	0·18	0·30	0·84	1·00	3·70	5·01	5·60	6·27	3·91	1·02	0·10	27·95
Hyderābād *	0·11	0·21	0·61	0·91	0·96	4·43	6·14	6·98	6·62	3·58	1·45	0·37	32·37
Hanamkonda	0·25	0·27	0·74	0·50	0·76	4·58	8·36	7·43	6·93	2·51	1·20	0·26	33·79

* The figures for August are for twenty-four years only.

History. Early period.

In prehistoric times the great Dravidian race occupied the southern and eastern portions of the State together with the rest of Southern India. The Telugu-speaking division of this race constitutes the most numerous section even to the present day. The Rāmāyana and the Mahābhārata contain traditions of Dakhshinapatha (Deccan), which forms the central portion of the State. The visit of Rāma to Kishkindha, identified with the modern Vijayanagar and Anegundi, is familiar to all students of ancient literature.

Asoka.

It is uncertain when the invasion of the Deccan by the Aryans occurred, but the dominions of the Buddhist king Asoka (272–231 B.C.) covered the whole of Berār and a considerable portion of the north-western and eastern tracts of the State. Among the list of conquered nations in Asoka's inscriptions occurs the name of the Pitenikas, who inhabited the city and country of Paithan, on the upper Godāvari in Aurangābād District.

Andhras.

The Andhras were the next kings who ruled the Deccan. They are mentioned in Asoka's inscriptions, but their rise to power dates from about 220 B.C. Gradually extending their sway from the Kistna delta, they soon possessed an empire reaching to Nāsik; and towards the close of the first century of the Christian era were contending with the Sakas, Pallavas, and Yavanas of Mālwā, Gujarāt, and Kāthiāwār. Pulumāyi II, who succeeded about A.D. 138, and married a daughter of Rudradāman the Western Satrap, is mentioned by Ptolemy. He was defeated by his father-in-law and thus lost the outlying portion of his dominions. About a hundred years later the dynasty came to an end, but little is known of the reasons for its collapse. It is possible that the Pallavas who ruled south of the Kistna then extended their power into Hyderābād.

Chālukyas.

The next dynasty of importance is that of the Chālukyas, who rose to power in Bijāpur District about 550, and founded a kingdom spreading east and west across the Peninsula with their capital at Kalyāni. Pulikesin II (608–42) ruled practically the whole of India south of the Narbadā, and even came into contact with Harshavardhana of Kanauj. Throughout their period of supremacy, however, the Chālukyas were at war with the Pallavas, and their fortunes and dominions varied, though they continued to rule a large portion of Southern India to the middle of the eighth century, when they were displaced by the Rāshtrakūtas of Malkhed in Gulbarga District. About 973, the Chālukyan dynasty was restored, and for nearly 200 years maintained its position, in spite of fierce struggles with the Cholas and Hoysalas of Dorasamudra. The Chālukya power fell about 1189 to the Hoysalas and Yādavas, the latter of whom established themselves at Deogiri (Daulatābād). The Yādavas were the last great Hindu rulers of the Deccan, for the Vijayanagar kingdom, which was founded half a century after the advent of the Muhammadans, never acquired much sway in the Deccan proper.

Muhammadan conquest. Alā-ud-dīn Khiljī led the first Muhammadan expedition into the Deccan, in 1294, against the Yādava ruler of Deogiri and coerced him into submission. In 1296 he assassinated his own uncle and seized the throne, and sent an expedition to Deogiri. His first expedition was dispatched in 1303 against the Kākatīyas of Warangal, who had been established there since the middle of the twelfth century. This having failed, he sent a second under Malik Kāfūr in 1309, which resulted in the submission of the Rājā and a promise to pay tribute. Ulugh Khān, who afterwards ruled at Delhi as Muhammad bin Tughlak, conducted a later campaign against Warangal, and finally broke the Kākatīya power in 1321, though not without a prolonged struggle. In 1310 Malik Kāfūr was sent against the Hoysala Rājā of Dorasamudra (Halebīd in Mysore), who was made a prisoner and lost his capital, the spoils consisting of 600 elephants, 96,000 maunds of gold, quantities of jewels and pearls, and 20,000 horses. In 1318 Harpāl, the Deogiri ruler, rebelled, but was taken prisoner and executed, and with his death ended the Yādava dynasty, after a rule of about 130 years. When Muhammad bin Tughlak ascended the throne of Delhi in 1325, the Muhammadans were masters of the Deccan from north to south, the chief Rājās of Telingāna acknowledging their sway and paying tribute. He changed the name of Deogiri to Daulatābād and made it his capital. A few years later the imperial governors of the Deccan revolted. Their rebellion resulted in the alienation of the Deccan provinces and the establishment of the Bahmani dynasty.

Bahmani kings. Zafar Khān, who styled himself, according to some historians, Alā-ud-dīn Hasan Shāh Gangū Bahmani, or, according to a contemporary inscription, Alā-ud-dīn Bahman Shāh, founded this line; and having taken possession of the Deccan provinces, including Bīdar and Gulbarga, he made the latter place his capital and commenced to reign in 1347. The Bahmani kingdom extended from Berār in the north to the left bank of the Tungabhadra in the south, and from Dābal on the west coast to the Telingāna tract in the east. Muhammad Shāh, who succeeded his father Alā-ud-dīn in 1358, waged wars with

Vijayanagar (1366) and Warangal (1371), and acquired great booty from both. It is said that 500,000 Hindus were slain during his reign. He died in 1375 and was followed by his son, Mujāhid Shāh, whose uncle, Daud Shāh, three years later, murdered and succeeded him, but was assassinated in the same year (1378). Muhammad[1], the grandson of Hasan Gangū, was proclaimed king and ruled peacefully to the time of his death in 1397. His son, Ghiyās-ud-dīn, reigned only two months when he was blinded and deposed by Lālchīn, a discontented slave, who proclaimed the king's brother, Shams-ud-dīn. Fīroz Khān and Ahmad Khān, the grandsons of Bahman Shāh, who had been married to Ghiyās-ud-dīn's two sisters, rose against Shams-ud-dīn, and, forcing their way into the *darbār*, made the king and Lālchīn prisoners. Fīroz was proclaimed king in 1397; Shams-ud-dīn was blinded after a reign of five months, and Lālchīn was put to death. Fīroz marched against the Vijayanagar Rājā, who had invaded the Raichūr Doāb in 1398, and defeated him, bringing back much plunder. In 1404 the Rājā of Vijayanagar advanced to Mudgal and war broke out between the two kingdoms; the Rājā was defeated and sued for peace, which was granted on the condition that he gave his daughter in marriage to the king, besides presenting a large sum of money, and pearls and elephants, and ceding the fort of Bankāpur as the marriage portion of the princess. In 1417 the king invested the fortress of Pāngal, and the Rājās of Vijayanagar and Warangal and other chiefs advanced to its relief at the head of a large force. Although Fīroz's army had been decimated by a pestilence which broke out among his troops, the king gave battle, but suffered a severe defeat. The Musalmāns were massacred, and Fīroz was pursued into his own country, which was laid waste with fire and sword. These misfortunes preyed on his mind and he fell into a lingering disorder, which affected both his spirits and intellect, so that he finally abdicated in 1422 in favour of his brother, Ahmad Shāh. Ahmad Shāh marched to the banks of the Tungabhadra and defeated the Rājā of Vijayanagar; peace was, however, concluded on the latter agreeing to pay arrears of tribute. In 1422 Ahmad Shāh sacked Warangal and obtained much plunder. He founded the city of Bīdar in 1430, and died there in 1435. In 1443 there was again war between the Vijayanagar Rājā and the Bahmani king Alā-ud-dīn II, in which the latter was defeated. Alā-ud-dīn was succeeded in 1458 by his son

[1] Wrongly styled Mahmūd by Firishta, whose error has been unfortunately followed by many modern historians.

Humāyūn, 'the cruel.' Soon after his accession, he marched to Nalgonda to quell a rebellion which had broken out in his Telingāna provinces. Hearing of an insurrection at Bīdar, he left his minister to carry on the campaign and returned to Bīdar, and, after putting to death thousands of innocent persons of both sexes, his cruelties ended only with his own death after a reign of three and a half years. He was succeeded by his eldest son, Nizām Shāh, who died two years afterwards (1463), when his younger brother, Muhammad Shāh III, was crowned. The reign of this prince is notorious for the execution of the great minister, Mahmūd Gāvān. The king died in 1482, and was succeeded by his son, Mahmūd Shāh, who gave himself up to pleasure and dissipation; and the governors of provinces, seeing this state of affairs, acted independently, so that only Telingāna and adjacent districts of Bīdar remained in the king's possession.

Kāsim Barīd now became minister, and induced the king to make war against Yūsuf Adil Khān, who had taken Bijāpur and declared his independence. The Bahmani forces were defeated and the king returned to Bīdar. In 1504 Kāsim Barīd died, and his son, Amīr Barīd, becoming minister had the king completely in his power. About this time (1510) Yūsuf Adil Khān died, and Amīr Barīd attempted to reduce Bijāpur. After a reign of constant vicissitude and trouble, Mahmūd Shāh died in 1518. Though he was succeeded by his son, Ahmad Shāh, Amīr Barīd remained all-powerful. Ahmad Shāh died after a reign of two years, and his son, Alā-ud-dīn, was assassinated by Amīr Barīd. Two other kings, Walī-ullah Shāh and Kalīm-ullah Shāh, followed one another in the course of five years, the latter dying in exile at Ahmadnagar in 1527; and with him ended the great Bahmani dynasty, which had reigned first at Gulbarga and then at Bidar for more than 180 years.

The Barīd Shāhi kingdom.

Amīr Barīd assumed sole charge of the affairs of the kingdom; and after many vicissitudes and constant wars with the rulers of Bijāpur and Berār, he died at Daulatābād (1538), and was succeeded by his son, Alī Barīd, who was the first to assume the title of Shāh. In 1565 he, with the other Deccan kings, marched against the Vijayanagar Rājā, and the memorable battle of Tālikotā was fought, which sealed the fate of the kingdom of Vijayanagar. Alī Barīd died in 1582, and was succeeded by three other kings, the last of whom, Alī Barīd II, was expelled by a distant relation, Amīr, who continued to rule for some time after 1609, but it is not known exactly when and how his reign ended.

The Kutb Shāhi kingdom.

Kutb-ul-mulk, Sultān Kuli, a Turk of noble family, who was governor of the Golconda province under the Bahmanis, took advantage of the distracted state of the kingdom under Mahmūd Shāh and declared his independence, establishing the Kutb Shāhi dynasty, which reigned here from 1512 to 1687. Sultān Kuli waged wars with the Vijayanagar and Kammamett Rājās, and extended his kingdom in the north to the banks of the Godāvari. He defeated the Bijāpur forces near Koilkonda, and later on took Medak, Kaulās, and other forts from the Barīd Shāhi king of Bīdar. He was assassinated in 1543 at the age of ninety, while kneeling in prayer in the chief mosque at Golconda, at the instigation of his son Jamshid Kuli, after ruling for sixteen years as governor and thirty-one as king. He was succeeded by Jamshid Kuli (1543), Subhān Kuli (1550), and Ibrāhīm Kuli (1550). The last of these allied himself with the Ahmadnagar king against the ruler of Bijāpur, who had sought the alliance of Vijayanagar. In 1564 he proposed the alliance against the Vijayanagar kingdom, which led to the battle of Tālikotā. He died in 1581, and was succeeded by his son Muhammad Kuli. In 1603 Shāh Abbās, the king of Persia, sent an ambassador to Hyderābād with valuable presents. Muhammad Kuli was succeeded in 1612 by his nephew and son-in-law Muhammad II, who died about 1635, and was succeeded by his son Abdullah.

Mughal invasions.

When the Mughals invaded the Deccan, the local rulers formed an alliance against them; but after defeating the invaders, they fell out among themselves, thus enabling the imperial troops gradually to subdue the country. Shāh Jahān, after rebelling against his father, fled from Burhānpur and was welcomed at Golconda by Abdullah Kutb Shāh. In 1635 Shāh Jahān, who had then become emperor, sent a *farmān* to Golconda which was well received; the *khutba* was read in the name of the emperor in the chief mosque, and coins were also struck in his name. Mīr Jumla, the king's minister, appealed to Aurangzeb for help against his master in 1655, and this afforded a pretext for Aurangzeb to invade the territory. Hyderābād was plundered, but Abdullah sued for peace and paid arrears of tribute. He died in 1674, and was succeeded by his nephew Abul Hasan, also called Tāna Shāh. After the fall of Bijāpur in 1686, Aurangzeb turned his attention to Golconda, which was taken in the following year. Tāna Shāh was made prisoner and sent to Bīdar, and thence to Daulatābād, where he died in 1704, and with him ended the line of the Kutb Shāhi kings.

The house of the present Nizāms was founded by Asaf Jāh, a distinguished general of Aurangzeb, of Turkomān descent. After long service under the Delhi emperor, distinguished alike in war and political sagacity, he was appointed Sūbahdār or viceroy of the Deccan in 1713 with the title of Nizām-ul-mulk, which has since become the hereditary title of the family. The Mughal empire at this period was on the verge of decline, owing to internal dissension and attacks from without. Amid the general confusion, Asaf Jāh had little difficulty in asserting his independence against the degenerate and weak occupants of the throne of Delhi, but he had to repel the inroads of the Marāthās who were harassing the west of his newly acquired territory. His independence was the cause of much jealousy at Delhi, and the court party secretly instructed Mubāriz Khān, the governor of Khāndesh, to oppose him by force of arms. A battle was fought at Shakarkhelda (Fathkhelda) in the Buldāna District of Berār in 1724, when Mubāriz Khān was totally defeated and lost his life. This battle established the independence of Asaf Jāh, who annexed Berār, and fixed his residence at Hyderābād. At the time of his death in 1748 he was fairly established as independent sovereign of a kingdom co-extensive with the present State, including the province of Berār. **The Nizāms.**

After his death, Nāsir Jang, his second son, and Muzaffar Jang, his grandson by one of his daughters, strove for the succession. At this time the English and the French were contending for supremacy in the East, and each of the claimants secured the support of one of these powers; Nāsir Jang's cause was espoused by the English, while Muzaffar Jang was supported by the French. The latter, however, fell a prisoner to his uncle, but, on the assassination of Nāsir Jang, Muzaffar Jang was proclaimed the sovereign. Dupleix, the French governor, became the controller of the Nizām's authority. Muzaffar Jang was killed by some Pathān chiefs, and the French then selected Salābat Jang, a brother of Nāsir Jang, as ruler. Ghāzi-ud-dīn, the eldest son of Asaf Jāh, who, it was alleged, had relinquished his claim at first, now appeared as a claimant, supported by the Marāthās, but his sudden death put a stop to further struggles. The English and the French were now contesting power and influence in the Deccan; but the victories of Clive in the Carnatic caused the latter to turn their attention to their own possessions which were threatened, and to leave Salābat Jang to shift for himself. Nizām Alī Khān, the fourth son of Asaf Jāh, at this juncture obtained the **French and English.**

support of the English on the promise of dismissing the French from his service. Salābat Jang was dethroned in 1761, and Nizām Alī Khān was proclaimed ruler.

Cession of the Northern Circārs. In 1766 the Northern Circārs were ceded to the British, on condition that the Nizām was to be furnished with a subsidiary force in time of war, and should receive 6 lakhs of rupees annually when no troops were required, the Nizām on his part promising to assist the British with his troops. This was followed by the treaty of 1768, by which the East India Company and the Nawāb of the Carnatic engaged to assist the Nizām with troops whenever required by him, on payment. In 1790 war broke out between Tipū Sultān and the British, and a treaty of offensive and defensive alliance was concluded between the Nizām, the Marāthās, and the British. Tipū, however, concluded peace, and had to relinquish half of his dominions, which was divided among the allies. In 1798 a treaty was concluded between the Nizām and the British Government, by which a subsidiary force of 6,000 sepoys and a proportionate number of guns was assigned to the Nizām's service, who on his part agreed to pay a subsidy of 24 lakhs for the support of the force. On the fall of Seringapatam and the death of Tipū Sultān, the Nizām participated largely under the Treaty of Mysore (1799) in the division of territory, and his share was increased because of the Peshwā's withdrawal from that treaty.

Ceded Districts. In 1800 a fresh treaty was concluded between the Nizām and the British, by which the subsidiary troops were augmented by two battalions of infantry and one regiment of cavalry, for the payment of which the Nizām ceded all the territories which had accrued to him under the treaties of 1792 and 1799, known as the Ceded Districts of Madras. The Nizām on his part agreed to employ all this force (except two battalions reserved to guard his person), together with 6,000 foot and 9,000 horse of his own troops, against the enemy in time of war.

Marāthā War. About 1803 Nizām Alī Khān's health was in a precarious condition, and Sindhia and Holkar, disappointed by the reinstatement, by the British, of Bājī Rao, the last of the Peshwās, prepared to resort to arms. To meet the preparations made by the Marāthās, the subsidiary force, consisting of 6,000 infantry and two regiments of cavalry, accompanied by 15,000 of the Nizām's troops, took up a position at Parenda on the western frontier of the Nizām's Dominions. General Wellesley was ordered to co-operate with this force in aid of the Peshwā, with 8,000 infantry and 1,700 cavalry. But before the arrival of General Wellesley at Poona, Holkar had left, and on his way to

Mālwā had plundered some of the Nizām's villages, and levied a contribution on Aurangābād. On hearing of this, Colonel Stevenson advanced towards the Godāvari with the whole force under him, and was joined by General Wellesley near Jālna. The next day (September 23) the memorable battle of Assaye was fought by General Wellesley, followed shortly afterwards by the battle of Argaon, which completely crushed the Marāthās, and secured the Nizām's territories.

Sikandar Jāh. Nizām Alī Khān died in 1803, and was succeeded by his son, Sikandar Jāh. In 1822 a treaty was concluded between the British and the Nizām, by which the latter was released from the obligation of paying the *chauth* to which the British had succeeded after the overthrow of the Peshwā in 1818.

Nāsīr-ud-daula. On the death of Sikandar Jāh in 1829, his son Nāsīr-ud-daula succeeded. In 1839 a Wahhābi conspiracy was discovered at Hyderābād, as in other parts of India. An inquiry showed that Mubāriz-ud-daula and others were implicated in organizing the movement against the British Government and the Nizām. Mubāriz-ud-daula was imprisoned at Golconda, where he subsequently died. Rājā Chandū Lāl, who had succeeded Munīr-ul-mulk as minister, resigned in 1843, and Sirāj-ul-mulk, the grandson of Mīr Alam, succeeded him. In 1847 a serious riot took place between the Shiahs and the Sunnis, in which about fifty persons lost their lives. Sirāj-ul-mulk, who had been removed in the same year, was reinstated as minister in 1851. As the pay of the Contingent troops had fallen into arrears, a fresh treaty was concluded in 1853, and Districts yielding a gross revenue of 50 lakhs a year were assigned to the British. The Districts thus ceded consisted, besides Berār, of Osmānābād (Naldrug) and the Raichūr Doāb. By this treaty the British agreed to maintain an auxiliary force of 5,000 infantry, 2,000 cavalry, and four field batteries; and it was stipulated that after paying the Contingent and certain other charges and interest on the Company's debt, the surplus was to be made over to the Nizām. The Nizām, while retaining the full use of the subsidiary force and Contingent, was released from the unlimited obligation of service in time of war; and the Contingent ceased to be part of the Nizām's army, and became an auxiliary force kept by the British Government for the Nizām's use. A week after the conclusion of this treaty Sirāj-ul-mulk died and Nawāb Sālār Jang, his nephew, was appointed minister.

Afzal-ud-daula. Nāsir-ud-daula died in May, 1857, and was succeeded by his son, Afzal-ud-daula. This was a critical period for Hyderābād, as the Mutiny which convulsed Northern India affected this

State also. It was feared that, if Hyderābād joined the revolt, the whole of Southern India as well as Bombay would rebel. But though His Highness was urged by some of his reckless advisers to raise the standard of revolt, he listened to the good counsels of his faithful minister, Sālār Jang, and cast in his lot with the British with unshaken loyalty. After the storm of the Mutiny had subsided, the British Government, in recognition of the services rendered by the Nizām, modified the treaty of 1853. By a treaty made in 1860 Osmānābād (Naldrug) and the Raichūr Doāb, yielding a revenue of 21 lakhs, were restored, and a debt of 50 lakhs was cancelled, while certain tracts on the left bank of the Godāvari were ceded and the Assigned Districts of Berār, yielding a revenue of 32 lakhs, were taken in trust by the British for the purposes specified in the treaty of 1853. Presents to the value of £10,000 were bestowed upon His Highness, and his minister and other noblemen were also rewarded. Afzal-ud-daula was made a G.C.S.I. in 1861.

Mīr Mahbūb Alī Khān. The present Nizām, Mīr Mahbūb Alī Khān Bahādur, succeeded on his father's death in 1869. Being only three years old, a regency was constituted for the administration of the country, with Sir Sālār Jang I as regent and Nawāb Shams-ul-Umarā as co-regent, the Resident being consulted on all important matters concerning the welfare of the State. On the death of the co-regent in 1877, his half-brother Nawāb Vikār-ul-Umarā was appointed co-administrator; but he also died in 1881, Sir Sālār Jang remaining sole administrator and regent till his death in 1883.

Reforms in administration. Not being fettered in any way, the great minister pursued his reforms with untiring effort. The four Sadr-ul-Mahāms or departmental ministers, who had been appointed in 1868, managed the Judicial, Revenue, Police, and Miscellaneous departments under the guidance of the minister, who, besides instructing them in their work, had direct control over the Military, *Mansab*, Finance, Treasury, Post, Mint, Currency, and State Railway departments. Transactions with the British Government, His Highness's education, and the management of the *Sarf-i-khās* domains also received his personal attention. A revenue survey and settlement were taken in hand and completed in the Marāthā Districts, civil and criminal courts were established, stamps were introduced, the Postal department was placed on a sound basis, and the Municipal, Public Works, Education, and Medical departments received their due share of attention. Thus almost every department of the British administration was represented in the State, and worked with creditable efficiency under the guiding spirit of the great minister. In particular, the finances of the State, which had become greatly involved, were much improved.

Instalment of the present Nizām.

In 1884 His Highness Mīr Mahbūb Alī Khān, having attained his majority, was installed by Lord Ripon. Sir Sālār Jang II was appointed minister, and was followed in 1888 by Sir Asmān Jāh. In 1892 a code, known as the *Kānuncha-i-Mubārak* ('the auspicious code'), was issued for the guidance of the minister, and this was followed by the establishment of a Council composed of all the ministers of the State. In the following year Sir Vikār-ul-Umarā became minister, and several changes were effected in various departments of the administration. Mahārājā Sir Kishen Prasād Bahādur, the Peshkār, was appointed minister in 1901, and still holds that office.

Berār.

In November, 1902, the Assigned Districts of Berār were leased in perpetuity to the British Government at an annual rental of 25 lakhs, a most important event in the history of the State.

Archaeology.

Many objects and places of historical and archaeological interest are found scattered throughout the State. Among the most noteworthy are the caves of ELLORA, AJANTA, AURANGĀBĀD, and OSMĀNĀBĀD (Dhārāseo). Of the numerous forts may be mentioned those at GOLCONDA, GULBARGA, WARANGAL, RAICHŪR, MUDGAL, PARENDA, and NALDRUG. Besides these, Hindu temples of various descriptions are found in every part of the State, some of them of great antiquity, such as the 'Thousand Pillars' temple at HANAMKONDA, and the temples at TULJĀPUR and AMBAJOGAL.

Architecture.

The oldest type of architecture is of a religious character, and is represented by the caves already mentioned, which belong to Buddhist, Jain, and Brāhmanical styles of architecture. Numbers of other caves are found at places of less importance. The temple at Hanamkonda, the temple and its ruined courtyard in the fort of Warangal, and numerous others, are good specimens of Hindu religious architecture. Among the most remarkable specimens of Musalmān architecture may be mentioned the mosque in the old fort of Gulbarga; the Mecca and Jāma Masjids, the Chār Minār, the Chār Kamān, the Dār-ush-Shifa (hospital), and the old bridge over the Mūsi, all in the city of Hyderābād; the tombs of the Kutb Shāhi kings near Golconda; the tombs of the Bahmani and Barīd Shāhi kings near the city of Bīdar, and that of Aurangzeb's wife at Aurangābād. Besides these, there are numerous other examples of both Hindu and Musalmān architecture, now in ruins, such as the palaces of Golconda, Bīdar, Gulbarga, and Daulatābād.

Population. Density. The population returned at the Census of 1901 was 11,141,142. The total area is 82,698 square miles, and the average density of population is thus 135 persons per square mile; but excluding the capital it falls to 129. The density ranges from 184 to 141 in the thickly populated Districts of Bīdar, Medak, Gulbarga, Nalgonda, Nānder, Elgandal, and Raichūr; from 139 to 125 in Lingsugūr, Osmānābād, Indūr, Parbhani, and Atrāf-i-balda; and from 117 to 54 in the sparsely populated Districts of Aurangābād, Bhīr, Mahbūbnagar, Warangal, and Sirpur Tāndūr. Table I (p. 82) shows the distribution of population in 1901.

Towns and villages. The State contains 79 towns and 20,010 villages; and of the total population 1,132,109, or 10 per cent., were enumerated in urban areas. The chief city is HYDERĀBĀD, with a population of 448,466. The State contains four places with a population ranging between 20,000 and 50,000, 16 towns of 10,000 to 20,000, and 58 towns of 5,000 to 10,000. Of villages with a population of 2,000 to 5,000, there are 514; in 1,862 villages the population ranges from 1,000 to 2,000; 4,344 villages have a population between 500 and 1,000, and 13,290 villages have less than 500 inhabitants. Some of the places classed as towns, from the fact of their having 5,000 or more inhabitants, are really overgrown rural villages, while on the other hand many *tāluk* head-quarters, with decided urban characteristics, are reckoned as villages, from the accident of their falling short of that standard.

Character of villages. The average population of a village is about 500. *Garhīs* or walled villages are found all over the State, testifying to the necessity that existed, up to the beginning of the nineteenth century, of affording security against the depredations of marauders, and the constant fear of civil wars in those troublous times. The houses are usually built of mud with thatched roofs.

Movement of population. The population of the State, according to the two previous enumerations, had been (1881) 9,845,594 and (1891) 11,537,040. At the Census of 1891 it was found that the number had risen in all Districts, with the single exception of Nānder, where there was a small decline. The total increase during the decade amounted to 17·18 per cent.; but the six Districts of Lingsugūr, Raichūr, Gulbarga, Mahbūbnagar, Nalgonda, and Warangal showed abnormal increases, ranging from 29 to 26 per cent. The first three Districts had suffered most severely from the famine of 1876-8, and were recovering from their depressed state when the first Census was taken in 1881; while the other three Districts had also been affected by the same cause.

The Census of 1901 showed a net decrease from the population of 1891 of 3·45 per cent., due to the famines of 1897 and 1900, and to the abnormally high mortality from plague and cholera during the latter half of the decade, notably in the Districts of Bīdar, Aurangābād, Bhīr, Nānder, Parbhani, and Osmānābād, in which the loss varied from 13 to 20 per cent. Elgandal, Indūr, and Raichūr suffered less severely, the decrease ranging from less than one per cent. to about 5 per cent. In the remaining Districts of Atrāf-i-balda, Nalgonda, Warangal, Medak, Mahbūbnagar, Sirpur Tāndūr, Gulbarga, and Lingsugūr, population rose by about 10 per cent., including Hyderābād city.

Age statistics.

The age statistics show the usual tendency to omit from enumeration females of ages ranging between 6 and 20. As elsewhere in India, girls exceed boys in number up to the age of 5. But after that age there is a fall in the number of females up to the age of 20, when the females again preponderate over the males. After the age of 30 a sudden fall is observed in the number of females, which continues up to the age of 60 and over, when the proportion of females again exceeds that of the males. Apart from the omission above alluded to, there is probably a real deficiency of females between 5 and 20 due to deaths caused by early marriage and childbirth. Another tendency exists, especially among the Hindus, to understate the age of unmarried girls after they have attained the marriageable age. The effects of famine may, however, be clearly traced in the age statistics, imperfect as they are. Thus, the Census of 1901 showed the number of children under the age of 5 to be less than that of children in the age periods 5-10 and 10-15.

Vital statistic

No reliable vital statistics are available, though the police *pātels* are supposed to record births and deaths regularly. The effect of the famine of 1900 on the birth-rate has already been alluded to, and infant mortality must have been very great during the period of stress.

Diseases.

The most common ailment is fever, which accounts for half the total deaths. Diarrhoea, dysentery, and other bowel complaints, as well as small-pox, are the next commonest causes of death. Cholera and small-pox sometimes carry off many persons. The people do not, as a rule, appreciate the advantages of vaccination, but its value is gradually becoming known.

Plague, and measures taken to combat it.

When plague invaded the State, the measures first adopted to stamp out the disease or arrest its progress consisted in evacuating infected houses and villages, and in disinfecting them. Camps were subsequently established at some frontier railway stations, where passengers were inspected and detained, and travellers from infected areas were kept under observation after leaving the camps.

Sex statistics.

Out of the total population in 1901, males numbered 5,673,629 and females 5,467,513. There were thus 964 females to every 1,000 males. The only Districts in which females exceed males are Nānder and Indūr, with 1,006 and 1,005 females respectively to every 1,000 males.

Civil condition.

As regards civil condition, out of every 16 persons, roughly speaking, 8 are married, 5 unmarried, and 3 widowed. Of the male population, 46, 49, and 5 per cent. are single, married, and widowed respectively; while among females the proportions are 31, 50, and 19 respectively. These figures show that the married males and females are almost numerically equal, the difference being an excess of only 43,223 married males over married females. The unmarried males, however, number half as many again as the unmarried females, while widowed females are about four times as numerous as widowed males. From the evenness of the proportions of married males and females it is obvious that, as a rule, polygamy does not exist, though allowed by the two main religions. On the other hand, the large number of widowed females leads to the conclusion that a strong prejudice exists against widow remarriage, shared by even the inferior castes of Hindus, who in this matter follow the practice of the Brāhmans. Among the agricultural castes, however, widow remarriage is largely practised, being called *mohtūrat* or *mārmanu*.

Distributing the population of either sex in each main age period by civil condition, it is found that unmarried boys under the age of 10 years form 97 per cent., while among females

	1891.			1901.		
	Persons.	Males.	Females.	Persons.	Males.	Females.
Unmarried .	4,232,492	2,573,236	1,659,256	4,311,525	2,604,439	1,707,086
Married . .	6,038,260	3,055,266	2,982,994	5,502,367	2,772,795	2,729,572
Widowed .	1,259,910	242,151	1,017,759	1,327,250	296,395	1,030,855
Unspecified .	6,378	2,476	3,902	..	..	..
Total	11,537,040	5,873,129	5,663,911	11,141,142	5,673,629	5,467,513

of the same age the percentage of single girls is 89. In the next age period 10–15, the percentage of unmarried boys and girls is 86 and 40 respectively. Between 15 and 40, however, 71 per cent. of the males and 78 per cent. of the females are married. The table at the foot of the previous page shows the population according to sex and civil condition.

Language. Telugu is spoken by 46 per cent. of the population, followed by Marāthī, which claims 26 per cent. Next come Kanarese and Urdū or Hindustāni, spoken by 14 and 10 per cent. respectively, so that these four languages claim between them nearly 97 per cent. of the total population. The Mārwārī dialect is spoken by 57,777 and Hindī by 28,767 persons, the former being the language of bankers and traders from Mārwār, and the latter that of emigrants from Northern India. The Tamil-speaking population number 24,475, who mostly come from the Madras Presidency. Gondī is spoken by 59,669 and Koya by 15,895. The Gipsy dialects are spoken by 125,070 persons, the Lamānī (Lambādī) or Banjārā alone claiming 120,394. Of the European languages, English was returned by 7,907 persons.

Language.	Persons.	
	1891.	1901.
Chief vernaculars of the State :—		
Urdū	1,198,382	1,158,490
Marāthī	3,493,858	2,895,864
Kanarese	1,451,046	1,562,018
Telugu	5,031,069	5,148,056
Other languages	362,685	376,714
Total	11,537,040	11,141,142

Hindu castes. The main groups of Hindu castes represented in Hyderābād are 21 in number, divided into a large number of sub-castes. The Kāpus or Kunbīs, the great agricultural caste of the State, number 2,953,000 persons, or 26 per cent. of the whole population. Next to the Kāpus in numerical strength are the Mālas or unclean castes, who number 1,584,000, or 14 per cent. of the total. The main group Māla includes the Mālas or Dhers and the Mādigas of Telingāna, corresponding to the Mahārs and the Māngs of the Marāthā tract; and though they occupy a very low position in the social scale, they play a most important part in the village economy. The other numerically strong castes are the Gollas (Dhangars) or shepherds, 832,400; the Brāhmans, 692,800; the Vaisyas or trading castes, 548,000; the Korwas, 533,600; the Sālas (weavers), 424,900; and the Gaundlas or toddy-drawers and liquor-vendors, 284,600. The Lamānis (Lambādis) or Banjārās, who are grain-carriers, number 172,300. Of the important aboriginal tribes, Gonds number about 55,000 and Bhīls 9,600.

Religions. The population comprises people of various religions, but only two, Hinduism and Islām, have any appreciable following, comprising 88·6 and 10·4 per cent. respectively of the entire population of the State. The followers of other religions are: Animists (65,315), Christians (22,996), Jains (20,345), Sikhs (4,335), and Pārsīs (1,463).

The Hindus have lost 4·3 per cent. since 1891, and it may be observed that the Hindu population has been steadily decreasing for the last twenty years. In 1881 they formed 90·3 per cent. of the population; in 1891 the percentage was 89·4; while in 1901 it was only 88·6. Unlike the Hindus, the Musalmāns are steadily increasing in numbers. During the last decade there was an increase of 17,084 persons, or 1·5 per cent. In 1881 Musalmāns formed only 9·4 per cent. of the total population, while they formed 10·4 per cent. in 1901.

Like the Musalmāns, the Christians have risen in numbers. During the last decade they increased by 2,567, or 12·6 per cent. The Jains lost 7,500 persons, or 27 per cent., in the same period. A large increase was recorded between 1881 and 1891, which may be explained by the fact that some of them were returned as Hindus in the Census of 1881. During the last decade the Sikhs also decreased, while the Pārsīs showed a marked tendency to increase; their numbers, however, are still small.

The increase among the Musalmāns is partly due to proselytizing and partly to their fecundity; while the rise in the Christian population is chiefly due to the efforts of missionaries, and in a less degree to the influx of Eurasians in the army and the civil service or in the mercantile class. Europeans decreased by 914, numbering 4,347 in 1901, compared with 5,261 in 1891. The number of Eurasians rose from 2,507 in 1891 to 3,292 in 1901, while native Christians increased from 12,661 to 15,357. The table on the next page shows the variation in the population classified by religion.

Christian missions. The first English public school in Hyderābād was founded by a clergyman of the Church of England about 1834, and was followed shortly after by another school opened by the Roman Catholic missionaries. Since then the latter mission has gradually progressed, with the result that it now has several schools and convents in various parts of the State. In 1901 the Catholic adherents were returned at 11,649. The Church of England supports two schools, and in 1901 had 6,813 followers. Among other missions working in the State may be mentioned the Wesleyans and the Baptists, with 1,468 and 885 adherents respectively. The former mission was established in 1880; and, as opportunity offered, its operations have been extended in the Districts lying principally to the north and north-east of Hyderābād city, with stations at Aler, Karīmnagar, Siddipet, Indūr, Medak, and Kandi. The mission carries on medical, educational, and evangelistic work, the principal medical establishments being at Medak, where there is a well-equipped hospital for women and children, with two branch dispensaries. With a few exceptions, all the schools in connexion with this mission are primary. Lace-making is taught at Secunderābād, Karīmnagar, and Siddipet, embroidery at Medak, weaving at Siddipet, and cabinet-making at Indūr. The mission has 11 schools in various Districts, 6 of which are for boys. The American Baptist Telugu Mission commenced work at Secunderābād in 1875, and since then branches have been opened at Hanamkonda, Mahbūbnagar, Nalgonda, Suriapet, Jangaon, and Gadwāl. In 1902 a hospital was completed at Hanamkonda. The work of this mission is chiefly among the Telugu population, and none of its schools is of a higher grade than lower secondary.

Religion.	Persons.	
	1891.	1901.
Hindus	10,315,249	9,870,839
Musalmāns	1,138,666	1,155,750
Christians: Native	12,661	15,357
Christians: Others	7,768	7,639
Others	62,696	91,557
Total	11,537,040	11,141,142

Of the total population, 5,132,902, or 46 per cent., are supported by agriculture. About 32 per cent. are landholders and tenants, 9 per cent. agricultural labourers, and 5 per cent. growers of special products. These figures exclude those who are partly agriculturists, numbering 250,000. Personal, household, and sanitary services support 655,870 persons, or nearly 5·9 per cent. of the population; and the provision of food, drink, and stimulants supports 536,016 persons, or 4·8 per Occupations.

cent. Commerce provides a living for 427,974 persons, or 3·8 per cent. The preparation of textile fabrics and dress comes next, supporting 301,729 persons, or 2·7 per cent.; while the care of animals maintains 284,304 persons, or 2·5 per cent. Earthwork and general labour provide a livelihood for 1,434,259 persons, or 13 per cent.; and those leading an independent life number 410,394, or 3·7 per cent.

Food. The staple food of the poorer classes consists chiefly of cakes of *jowār* and *bājra*, though in the Telingāna Districts rice is also used to a large extent. Along with the cakes are eaten curries made of vegetables and pulses, onions, oil or *ghī*, seasoned with tamarinds or chillies or both. Musalmāns and Hindus alike eat goats' flesh. The Musalmāns in the country tracts, out of respect to the feelings and prejudices of their Hindu neighbours, do not indulge in beef; but the Musalmān inhabitants of towns and large cities have no such scruples. The Mālas, including Dhers, Chamārs, Mahārs, and Māngs, will eat the flesh of cattle which have died a natural death.

Dress. The ordinary form of dress for a villager is a *dhotī* or waist-cloth, a short jacket or coat of cotton, a turban of red or white colour in the Marāthā Districts and always white in Telingāna, and a *kammal* or blanket which he almost always carries. The women wear a *sārī*, which is a piece of cloth 5 or 6 yards long and 4 feet broad, one end being fastened round the waist, while the other is carried over the head and shoulders and covers the rest of the body. In addition to the *sārī*, the women wear a *cholī* or a short bodice. The dress described above is worn by Hindus and Musalmāns alike; but Musalmān women often wear a *lahnga* or petticoat, with a *cholī* and *dupatta*, the last covering the head and the body. Gond and Waddar females discard the *cholī* altogether, but wrap the end of the *sārī* round the upper part of the body.

Houses. The home of the common cultivator consists of three or four small rooms, the walls being of mud and the roof tiled or thatched, the rooms being built round a *bhavanti* or court-yard. The Dhers and other low castes, and the poorer classes of villagers, live in huts made of reeds and hurdles, plastered over with mud and cow-dung.

Disposal of the dead. Hindus of the higher castes, such as Brāhmans, Rājputs, and Baniās, burn their dead, while the lower castes usually bury them. Among Musalmāns the dead are always buried.

Amusements and games. There are very few amusements in which the cultivators indulge. In the evenings they gather at the village *chauri* and join in gossip or pass the time with their families, discussing the topics of the seasons and the crops. Occasionally they go to neighbouring markets or visit places of pilgrimages and fairs in the neighbourhood. Sometimes they enjoy the performance of mountebanks or strolling actors, and the recitation of religious poems is very popular.

Festivals.

The ordinary Hindu festivals are the Holī, the Divāli, the Dasara, the Nāgapanchamī, the Rāmnaumi, the Pitrapaksha, and the Sivarātrī. The Pola festival is celebrated everywhere, when the cattle are garlanded and decorated, and led through the village, accompanied by their owners. The Musalmān festivals are the Muharram, the Bakr-Id, the Id of Ramzān (feast after fasting month), the Shab-i-barāt, the Duāzdahum-i-sharif (anniversary of the Prophet's death), and the Yāzdahum. The Nau-roz or Persian New Year's Day is also celebrated as a State holiday.

The joint family system.

Among Hindus the joint family system prevails everywhere, but in most cases it is not maintained beyond one generation.

Nomenclature.

In the Marāthā Districts the name of a person is usually followed by the name of the village to which he originally belonged, as for example Dāda Korlekar, which means 'Dāda of the Korla village.' But in Telingāna the name of the village precedes the personal name, as Mātūr Yenka, which means 'Yenka of Mātūr village.' Marāthās and Brahmāns usually have three names, the first being the person's own name, the second his father's, while the third is the name of his family or village.

Agriculture. General conditions of soils and conformation of surface.

The soils of the Hyderābād State may be divided into two main divisions. Those of all the Telingāna Districts may be classed generally under three kinds, black, red, and sandy; and those in the Marāthā Districts may be similarly classed in three divisions, black, red, and a mixture of the two. Locally, a number of varieties are distinguished in Telingāna. Thus, *utcha regar* is dark in colour and plastic when wetted, and consists chiefly of alluvium, with a good supply of lime and little silica. *Katta regar* is a stiff loam, containing less lime than *utcha regar* and little soluble matter. *Raura* is a good garden soil, containing 7 per cent. of lime in a pulverized state. *Rauti zamīn* is also a garden soil, containing only 5 per cent. of lime. *Sola zamīn* is greyish in colour, and resembles *rauti zamīn*. It is used for the *ābi* rice crop, and is manured by herding cattle, goats, and sheep on it. *Chunaka regar* is a rough aluminous soil, containing 12 per cent. of lime, and is best suited for *jowār* and pulse. *Chauka regar* or *milwa* is a mixture of red and black soils, with very little lime. *Chalka* or *reva zamīn* is a finely pulverized reddish soil, with sand and traces of lime, and is well suited for rainy season crops. *Yerra chauka* is similar in every respect to *chalka zamīn*, but not so finely powdered. The Marāthwāra soils are called *regar* (black), *masab* (red), or *milwa* (mixture). The soils of the higher tracts are heavy and rich in alumina, while those found on the plains are light and loamy; but neither is of very great depth. Broadly speaking, they are derived from the disintegration of basalt and amygdaloid wacke, the former giving rise to the stiff black soil, and the latter forming a friable earth. But when the black soil is mixed with the light friable earth, the result is a rich loam, which is more retentive of moisture than the others.

Climate and rainfall.

The climate of the Marāthā Districts is generally hot and dry from March to the end of May, and temperate during the remaining months; while that of Telingāna is hot and damp from March to the end of September, and temperate for the rest of the year. More than three-fourths of the total rainfall, or about 23 inches, is generally received between June and September, the remainder falling between October and November.

System of cultivation.

Yellow *jowār*, *bājra*, sesamum, cotton, *tuar* and other pulses form the *kharīf* or monsoon crops; and gram, barley, cotton, and linseed are the chief *rabi* or cold-season crops. The total area of Government lands cropped in 1901 was 30,240 square miles, of which 94 per cent. was devoted to 'dry crops,' and 6 per cent. was irrigated.

In the Marāthā country only two crops are raised, the *rabi* and the *kharīf*; while in Telingāna there are five crops, the *ābi* and *tābi* for rice, and the *kharīf*, *rabi*, and *māghi* for 'dry crops,' the last being intermediate between the *kharīf* and *rabi*.

As regards Marāthwāra, the extent of the *kharīf* and *rabi* crops depends upon the rainfall. If the monsoon commences in June, *kharīf* crops are largely sown at the beginning of the season; but if the rains are late and the time for the *kharīf* sowing has passed, then more land is reserved for the *rabi*. In Telingāna, where there is a smaller extent of *rabi* lands, the *kharīf* sowing proceeds as late as July, closely followed by the *māghi* sowing. Certain kinds of rice may be sown in the *ābi* as late as the beginning of August, if the rains are late; and the *tābi* or hot-season rice crop is sown from December up to the end of February.

The cultivator begins preparing his land for the *kharīf* sowings in December or January, and for the *rabi* during the monsoon, whenever there is a break in the rains. The *regar* is ploughed with the large plough or *nāgar*, drawn by eight bullocks, only once in seven or eight years, the *bakkhar* or harrow being considered sufficient in intermediate years. The Telingāna soils, being mostly sandy and finely divided, require only slight ploughing and harrowing. The land is ploughed first in one direction, and the second ploughing is done at right angles to the first. The ploughing is repeated till the soil is perfectly pulverized and clean. Tillage.

The land thus prepared is then ready to receive the seed; and after the first shower or two, on the breaking of the monsoon in June, *kharīf* sowings are commenced. In Telingāna, after a few good showers have fallen, the land for rice cultivation is ploughed by buffaloes and left for a few days. The seed, which has been soaked beforehand and has sprouted, is now sown broadcast in the fields and ploughed in. But in fields irrigated from large tanks, the preparation of the 'wet' lands begins even before the monsoon. For the *rabi* sowings, the land, which has been ploughed during the breaks in the rainy season, is sown in September or October, as at this time there are usually autumn showers which help the germination of the seed. For the *tābi* or hot-season rice crop, the land is first soaked with water from tanks and wells. The sowings proceed for two and even three months, from the beginning of December to the end of February.

The Marāthā cultivator has his *kharīf* and *rabi* crops weeded three or four times during the season; the Telingāna ryot, on the other hand, is generally careless, weeding both crops only once or twice. His attention is chiefly devoted to the rice crop, which pays him best, and he weeds that three or four times during the season.

Yellow *jowār*, *bājra*, and the rainy season rice ripen about December; and white *jowār*, gram, wheat, barley, and the hot-season rice ripen from April to the end of May.

Cotton is extensively raised in all the black-soil Districts, as well as in Telingāna, wherever there is a suitable soil for its production. The short-stapled variety is the only kind which the cultivator grows, as he finds it easiest to produce. In the Districts served by railways, cotton-ginning and pressing factories are taking the place of the old system of hand-ginning; and within the last four years several of these factories have been opened in those Districts, the railway having made it possible for the machinery required to be conveyed to parts where it was impossible to transport it in carts. Railway extension has also given an impetus to the cultivation of cotton and superior cereals.

Population engaged in, and dependent on, agriculture.

Of the total population of the State in 1901, 5,132,902, or 46 per cent., were supported by agriculture. Of these, 58,858 were landholders or rent receivers, 3,454,284 were rent payers, 186,671 were farm-servants, and 836,972 were field-labourers.

Principal crops.

The principal crops in the Marāthā country consist of *jowār*, *bājra*, wheat, cotton, linseed, and pulses; and those in Telingāna are rice, yellow *jowār*, *bājra*, castor-seed, sesame, and pulses. The staple food of the people of Marāthwāra consists of *jowār*, *bājra*, and, to some extent, wheat; while in Telingāna, rice, *jowār*, and *bājra* are consumed. Pulses and inferior grains of many kinds are grown everywhere. Oilseeds include linseed, sesame (gingelly), *karar*, and castor-seed, the two last being grown very largely in the Telingāna Districts. Besides cotton, *san*-hemp and *ambāri* are the principal fibre-plants, while aloes and *bhendi* fibre are not unknown. Large quantities of chillies are grown everywhere, and *zira* (caraway) and *ajwain* (*Ligusticum Ajouan*) are also grown in the Districts of Bīdar, Atrāf-i-balda, and Sirpur Tāndūr.

In 1901 the areas occupied by the several important crops and their percentages to the total area cropped were as follows:—

Jowār	12,531 square miles, or	41·4 per cent.
Cotton	3,226 ,,	10·7 ,,
Bājra	2,487 ,,	8·2 ,,
Rice	1,358 ,,	4·5 ,,
Til (*Sesamum orientale*)	1,263 ,,	4·2 ,,
Wheat	914 ,,	3·0 ,,
Castor-seed	883 ,,	2·9 ,,
Gram	768 ,,	2·6 ,,
Linseed	622 ,,	2·0 ,,
Tuar	561 ,,	1·9 ,,
Karar	531 ,,	1·7 ,,
Maize	484 ,,	1·6 ,,
Rāla or *kangni*	425 ,,	1·4 ,,
Mūng (*Phaseolus Mungo*)	307 ,,	1·0 ,,
Kodro (*Paspalum scrobiculatum*)	177 ,,	0·6 ,,
Chillies	149 ,,	0·5 ,,
Tobacco	125 ,,	0·4 ,,

Average yield.

The yield per acre of different crops varies so much that it is difficult to give a fair average; the weight of rice, for instance, ranges between 3 cwt. and 23 cwt. per acre. An attempt, however, has been made to give an average from figures obtained from the several Districts. Raw sugar, $18\frac{1}{2}$ cwt.; rice, $10\frac{1}{4}$ cwt.; *jowār*, $2\frac{1}{2}$ cwt.; wheat, $2\frac{1}{2}$ cwt.; *bājra*, $2\frac{1}{4}$ cwt.; *sāwān*, $2\frac{1}{4}$ cwt.; *kulthi*, 2 cwt.; castor-seed, 2 cwt.; gram, $1\frac{3}{4}$ cwt.; sesame, $1\frac{1}{2}$ cwt.; linseed, $1\frac{1}{3}$ cwt.; and cotton, 641 lb.

Manures and rotation of crops.

All the rice and sugar-cane fields are manured, the latter very heavily. The manure generally used is that obtained from the village cattle, and the sweepings from the village, and from leaves and branches of trees. *Jowār* and wheat in the *regar* receive no manure. Rotation of crops in the Telingāna Districts is followed in the inferior kinds of soils called *chalka*. When waste lands are first prepared, oilseeds are sown for the first year; the next year yellow *jowār* is grown, and in subsequent years they are put under *sāwān* (*Panicum frumentaceum*) and *kodro* (*Paspalum scrobiculatum*). In lands of a better description, if the soil has become exhausted, *jowār* is followed by cotton. Yellow *jowār*, being a very exhausting crop, is never grown for two successive seasons on the same land. Where new land is of better quality, such as *regar* and *milwa*, and is suited for *rabi* crops, it is usual first to sow *kulthi* (*Dolichos biflorus*), *lākh*, or castor-seed. These are followed in the next year by *kulthi*, gram, or peas. In the third year *jowār* is grown, mixed with linseed or *kardi* gram; after that, *jowār* and *kulthi* are sown every alternate year. In rice lands no regular rotation is followed, but sugar-cane and betel-leaf are sometimes raised. In the Marāthā Districts the rotation is as follows. When waste land is prepared for the *kharīf* sowing, it is first put under *bājra* or cotton; and for two or three years afterwards only *bājra* is raised. Then, successively, *mūng*, *urd*, *matt*, or *san*-hemp is grown; and when the land is in a fit condition for being ploughed, a *tuar* crop follows. The roots of this crop strike deep into the soil and loosen it, thereby making ploughing easy. When waste land is prepared for *rabi* cultivation, *jowār* or *kardi* is sown first, followed by wheat or *jowār* for the next four or five years. In 'wet' cultivation sugar-cane is followed by rice in the next year.

Fruit and vegetables.

Oranges are extensively grown in and around Aurangābād, Osmānābād, Parbhani, and Nirmal, but at Hyderābād and other places they are found only in private gardens. Ordinary mangoes are produced everywhere, but very superior grafted mangoes are grown in gardens around Hyderābād. During the rainy season, country vegetables are raised in all parts, but English vegetables are grown only at Hyderābād, its suburbs, and Secunderābād, and also at some District head-quarters. Excellent grapes were formerly grown at Daulatābād, and an attempt is being made to revive their cultivation.

Extension of cultivation and agricultural improvements.

The area under cultivation has considerably increased during the last twenty years. Large tracts of unoccupied cultivable land are still to be found in the Sirpur Tāndūr, Mahbūbnagar, Warangal, Elgandal, and Indūr Districts of Telingāna. In the Marāthā Districts the whole of the cultivable land has been taken up. The ryots have taken no interest in improving the quality of their crops by selection of seed, or by the cultivation of new varieties, or by introducing improved agricultural implements.

Implements.

In the Marāthā tract a large heavy plough is used for breaking up the hard black soil, which is drawn by four or five yoke of cattle, but in Telingāna a light plough is employed. Other implements are bullock hoes, the *bakkhar* (harrow), and the *tippan* (seed-drills). The ordinary *mot* or leathern bucket is the most common water-lift, and is worked by a pair of bullocks. On the banks of rivers and streams, the *yātam* or *bhudki* (a lever-like contrivance) is used by one or two men.

Miscellaneous.

There is no agricultural department in the State at present. The duties of a department of Land Records are performed by the Revenue department. Advances for the construction of wells are given by the State in times of scarcity and famine. The well and field are assigned as security, and the loan is repaid by instalments, with interest at 6 per cent. per annum. The cultivators are often largely indebted to the money-lender, and frequently become tenants of their creditors. Money is usually advanced by professional money-lenders, but wealthy agriculturists also lend money. Agricultural banks established on sound principles would probably succeed and would be beneficial to the cultivators. The ordinary rate of interest on money advanced is nominally 25 per cent. for the season. The money-lender advances a loan on the security of the future crop, and at harvest time receives 25 per cent. as interest in cash or in kind, at prices ruling at the time, so that the real interest is about 50 per cent. per annum.

Cattle, ponies, sheep, and goats.

With the exception of the white cattle of Eastern Telingāna, the Khammamett and Devarkonda cattle, and the small bullocks of Adilābād and the Amrābād *tāluk*, no special breeds are to be found in the State. The white cattle are indigenous to the country, and are a hardy stock, with black-tipped tails. The Khammamett and Devarkonda breeds are much stronger than the white cattle, and resemble the Mysore breed.

The Sirpur Tāndūr and Amrābād bullocks are of small size, but are fast trotters. The waste lands and forests of the Telingāna Districts form the pasture grounds where they are bred. Horses adapted for military and general purposes were formerly reared in large numbers, but the importation of Arabs and Australian horses has diminished the demand. The Government maintains a few Arab sires in some of the Marāthā and Telingāna Districts, and it is believed that the result has been satisfactory. The Deccan ponies are still noted for their surefootedness, hardiness, and powers of endurance. The other animals, such as buffaloes, goats, and sheep, are all of the ordinary type. The Marāthwāra buffaloes are very superior milch cattle, and fetch double or treble the price of the buffaloes of Telingāna. Sheep and goats of the ordinary kind are bred everywhere. In most of the Marāthā districts, goats of the Gujarāt breed are reared, which generally yield a good supply of milk. The price of cattle varies from Rs. 40 to Rs. 150 or even Rs. 200 per pair; that of ponies from Rs. 15 to Rs. 150 each. Milch buffaloes in Telingāna are worth from Rs. 30 to Rs. 45, but in the Marāthā Districts they fetch from Rs. 50 to Rs. 150. Sheep and goats are sold at from Rs. 2 to Rs. 3–8 per head, and milch goats at from Rs. 7 to Rs. 20 or Rs. 25.

The last famine caused great mortality among cattle in the famine-stricken Districts. Grazing lands have been set apart, but in dry seasons the grass in them is very poor. *Kadbi*, or *jowār* stalks, form the chief fodder supply, of which more than sufficient is raised in good years, and large quantities are stacked to meet requirements in times of scarcity.

Fairs. Until recently (1897), a great horse fair was held annually at MALEGAON, in Bīdar District, at which a large number of horses and cattle were sold; but for several years past the fair has not taken place owing to the prevalence of plague. At Hyderābād city there is an extensive horse mart. In every District weekly or monthly horse and cattle fairs are held.

Irrigation. The Marāthā country being composed of black soil, there is not so much necessity for irrigation as in Telingāna; the black soil has the power to retain moisture, which is further supplemented during the cold season by a copious deposit of dew, which supplies the crops with moisture sufficient for their growth and maturity. Where rice, sugar-cane, and garden produce are raised, the chief sources of supply are wells. The Telingāna soils being sandy, it becomes of paramount importance to store water; and for this purpose advantage has been taken of the undulating character of the ground. Dams have been thrown across the valleys of streams and gorges between hills, and rain-water which falls over a large catchment basin is thus collected, and made available for purposes of irrigation by means of sluices.

Besides the tanks and *kuntas* or ponds, irrigation is carried on by means of wells generally, and by means of canals and anicuts in certain Districts. For rice, sugar-cane, and turmeric the land is constantly watered as long as the crops are standing, while *bāghāt* or garden lands require only occasional irrigation. Wheat and barley are usually sown near wells, and are watered from them once a week. Across the Tungabhadra, in Lingsugūr District, a series of anicuts have been constructed to hold up the water, which is directed into side channels and is used for supplying tanks and fields along the banks of the river. There are several anicuts in a length of 30 miles on the Tungabhadra, the principal one being at Kuragāl, which extends completely across the river. All of these anicuts were built many years ago, and no statistics are obtainable regarding their cost. A new project is now under construction for taking water from the Mānjra river in Medak District for irrigation purposes and the supply of tanks.

Tanks. The water from Government tanks is utilized for irrigating the 'wet' lands, which pay a water tax. There are altogether 370 large tanks and 11,015 *kuntas* or ponds, besides 1,347 channels, in the State. The large tanks are maintained by the Public Works department, while the smaller ones, as well as the *kuntas*, are in charge of Revenue officers; but since the introduction of the *dastband* system, *zamīndārs* and local officials and others have taken up some of the breached tanks, receiving a certain percentage for their maintenance after reconstruction. These, however, are mostly tanks of no very large size.

Most of the tanks—such as the Husain Sāgar, the Ibrāhīmpatan, the Mīr Alam, the Afzal Sāgar, the Jalpalli, and many other large tanks, as well as irrigation channels—were constructed by the former rulers or ministers of the State. The minor tanks are the work of *zamīndārs*. No complete record is available as to the actual capital outlay, but those constructed in recent years will be described in dealing with Public Works.

Wells. The land served by wells is irrigated by the primitive method of lifting the water by means of large buckets drawn by bullocks. The total number of wells in the State is 123,175. Where any supply channels from a river or a perennial stream are constructed to carry water to tanks, the ryots sometimes bail out water on either side of the channel by means of hand-buckets called *bhurki* or *guda*, and so get a constant flow. Masonry wells cost between Rs. 400 and Rs. 600, and those lined with stone without any mortar between Rs. 200 and Rs. 300; such wells have two bullock runs and two buckets, and are capable of irrigating 4 to 5 acres of rice or sugar-cane and 10 acres of garden land.

Rents, wages, and prices. Rents.

As *ryotwāri* is the prevailing revenue system throughout Hyderābād, the sum paid by the cultivator represents the land revenue, which will be dealt with later. In the case of deserted villages, which have been leased by the State, the holder is free to charge his tenants what rent he pleases, provided the rates do not exceed those previously paid to the State. The *pattadārs*, or ryots who hold directly from the State, sometimes sub-let the whole or a part of their lands or take partners called *shikmīdārs*. The latter cultivate land in partnership with the *pattadārs*, and divide the produce and expenses in proportion to the cattle employed by each, the *pattadār* receiving from his co-sharer a proportionate amount of the State dues. If he sub-lets, the occupant frequently receives from his sub-tenant an enhanced rental for the land in money or in kind. *Ināmdārs* and non-cultivating classes usually let their lands. The non-cultivating occupant, if he be a money-lender and has purchased the occupancy right of the land, generally obtains a larger rent or share from his sub-tenant than the *ināmdār*, who, having no cattle of his own, is obliged to let his land for a small share. The money-lender, on the other hand, supplies his sub-tenant with funds to purchase cattle and implements, and either charges interest or lets his land at rates far higher than he himself pays to the State. The latter system is very common in the Marāthā Districts, where land has acquired a much higher value since the settlement, and where the non-cultivating classes, mostly comprising money-lenders, form a much larger proportion of the population than in Telingāna.

Wages.

No official returns of the prevailing rates of wages are available. Agricultural labourers and domestic servants may be taken as types of unskilled labour, and carpenters, blacksmiths, and masons as those of skilled labour. The former are paid from Rs. 30 to Rs. 36 per annum, besides receiving one meal a day and a blanket and a pair of sandals every year. Sometimes the labourer borrows two or three years' wages from his employer for marriage expenses and undertakes to serve for a stipulated period at a reduced rate, the reduction representing the amount of interest on the sum borrowed. Wages are sometimes paid partly in cash and partly in kind. To persons hired by the day, wages are generally paid in grain, but in the case of cotton-picking the labourer gets a certain proportion of the quantity picked. Village artisans are usually paid in kind, and in some few instances partly in cash and partly in grain. When grain is dear, cash wages are substituted by the employer.

In the vicinity of towns cash wages are the rule; and wherever cotton-ginning and pressing factories are established, or mining industries developed, such as coal-mining and stone-quarrying, or railway and road construction are started, high cash wages are demanded, varying from Rs. 7 to Rs. 10 per month.

In times of scarcity wages fall considerably below the average, owing to the large number of labourers thrown out of employment. The favourable rates of assessment introduced since the last settlement have been conducive to much agricultural activity and a greater demand for labour, whereby wages have risen, and the labourer who got Rs. 30 per annum now demands Rs. 36. The same may be said of all other labourers, artisans, and domestic servants. The higher prices of food-grains have also contributed towards enhancement in the rates of wages.

Prices

In the absence of any regular record of prices, information specially collected has been embodied in Table III (p. 84). No records exist of prices prior to the construction of railways; but it is certain that prices were then much lower than now, because, owing to the absence of means of transport, only a small quantity of the grain produced was exported. The railways have made prices of grain uniform over large tracts; and in times of famine and scarcity in the neighbouring Provinces the surplus grain of the country is exported, thus causing a rise in prices. During the famines of 1897 and 1899–1900 prices of grain were extraordinarily high, though, while grain was being imported for the relief of the affected areas, it was being largely exported from the other parts of the State to Provinces where large profits were probable. During the famine of 1899–1900, *jowār* sold at 5 seers per rupee in Aurangābād, at $3\frac{3}{4}$ seers in Bhīr and Nānder, at $4\frac{1}{4}$ seers in Parbhani and Osmānābād, and at $5\frac{1}{4}$ seers in Bīdar. In Table III the price of salt is given for Hyderābād city only, the prices in the country being almost the same.

Forests.

A total area of nearly 18,000 square miles is under forests, which are divided into three classes: the 'reserved' (5,184 square miles), the protected (4,408 square miles), and the open or unprotected (8,387 square miles). In the 'reserved' and protected forests, trees are under the control of the Forest department; but in the open forests only sixteen species are 'reserved', namely, sandal (*Santalum album*), teak (*Tectona grandis*), *shīsham* (*Dalbergia Sissoo*), ebony (*Diospyros melanoxylon*), satin-wood (*Chloroxylon Swietenia*), *eppa* (*Hardwickia binata*), *nallāmadi* (*Terminalia tomentosa*), *bījāsāl* (*Pterocarpus Marsupium*), *batta-gunam* (*Stephegyne parvifolia*), *somi* (*Soymida febrifuga*), *dhaura* or *tirmani* (*Anogeissus latifolia*), *kodsha* (*Cleistanthus collinus*), *sandra* (*Acacia Catechu*), *bhandāra* (*Adina cordifolia*), *mokab* (*Schrebera swietenioides*), and *chinnangi* (*Lagerstroemia parviflora*). The forests form six divisions—Warangal, Indūr, Nirmal, Mahbūbnagar, Aurangābād, and Gulbarga—the two last being in Marāthwāra, and the remainder in Telingāna. Each division is under an Assistant Conservator. The management of this department is guided by the Forest Act of 1899, which empowers the Conservator to exercise full control over 'reserved' and protected forests, and 'reserved' species of trees in open forests. Timber is supplied to purchasers at prescribed rates, while cultivators receive free timber and fuel for agricultural implements and domestic purposes. Minor produce, such as grass, branches, and leaves, &c., is likewise granted free to the local ryots. Free grazing is also permitted, under certain restrictions. After meeting the local demand, timber of various kinds is exported to different parts of the State. Local railways and the military workshop are also supplied with timber, exploited and transported departmentally. No use is made of elephants nor are floating operations resorted to.

No special fuel and fodder Reserves are maintained, but the grazing in the 'reserved' and protected forests is regulated by the department, and fees are collected either departmentally or through contract agency. Grazing rights in the open forests are auctioned annually by the Revenue department. In years of scarcity cattle are sent to the forests, which are then thrown open to free grazing. Measures are adopted to prevent the destruction of trees for leaf fodder, and some attempts have been made to store fodder. Edible fruits, roots, and flowers are utilized during famines by the destitute and starving poor. Some of the valuable forests are protected from fire by making regular fire lines, prohibiting the carrying of inflammable materials, closing areas to grazing, and by the appointment of patrols and guards.

There are no special plantations of any economic value in

the State. The following table shows the area of each class of forest in each Forest division in 1901:—

Forest Divisions.	Area in square miles.			
	Reserved.	Protected.	Open.	Total.
Warangal	2,368	...	2,000	4,368
Indūr	907	644	2,980	4,531
Nirmal	700	3,307	2,000	6,007
Mahbūbnagar	800	322	547	1,669
Aurangābād	288	69	600	957
Gulbarga	121	66	260	447
Total	5,184	4,408	8,387	17,979

As the forest survey and demarcation have not been completed, the areas shown above are only approximate, and it is possible that as much as one-third of the total is really cultivated. The forests are not equally distributed in all parts, the two Districts of Osmānābād and Bhīr having no forest at all, while the forests in Karīmnagar (Elgandal), Warangal, and Adilābād (Sirpur Tāndūr) occupy half the area of the State lands. The Marāthā Districts are far less wooded than the Telingāna country.

The figures given below show the average revenue, expenditure, and surplus of the Forest department for a series of years:—

	Average for ten years ending 1890.	Average for ten years ending 1900.	1901.	1903.
	Rs.	Rs.	Rs.	Rs.
Revenue	1,02,546	2,02,004	3,45,445	3,69,511
Expenditure	72,360	1,14,904	1,44,369	1,47,125
Surplus	30,186	87,100	2,01,076	2,22,386

The practice of shifting cultivation in forests, or *pode*, which was very common some years ago, is now strictly prohibited; but illicit clearances for temporary cultivation are sometimes made, and, when found out, departmental punishment is inflicted on the offenders.

Several grasses are known to possess economic properties. The fibres of *mannakopri* and *modian* are extensively used for making ropes, stringing cots, and various agricultural uses. If properly treated, these might also prove suitable for manufacturing paper. Among other minor products, *mahuā* flowers are of importance as being generally used for distilling country liquor.

Mines and minerals. Coal.

The Hyderābād State is rich in minerals, chief among which may be mentioned the extensive coal-measures of WARANGAL and the gold-mines of LINGSUGŪR. The coal-field of Singareni was discovered by Dr. King of the Indian Geological Survey so far back as 1872. Active operations were, however, delayed till 1886, when the Hyderābād (Deccan) Company obtained a concession and opened the mine at Singareni, which is the only mine profitably worked at present. Four distinct seams have been discovered in the Singareni field. The first varies in thickness from 30 to 50 feet, and is composed of alternating layers of coal and carbonaceous shale, the former being of tolerably good quality and supplying a fair steam coal. The second seam, lying about 100 feet below the first, consists of shaly coal. Similarly, the third seam, which is about 30 to 40 feet below the second, consists of a hard shaly coal; and as the coal these two contain gives 30 per cent. of ash, they have been abandoned as being of no commercial value. The fourth seam, called the King seam after its discoverer, consists of the most valuable coal, being semi-bituminous hard coal which does not coke but yields a good gas for lighting purposes. This is the seam which is now being worked. Its thickness is from 3 to 7 feet and its area about 9 square miles, and at the average thickness of 5 feet it is computed to contain no less than 47,500,000 tons of coal. The royalty paid to the State varies from 8 annas to R. 1 per ton. In 1896 the total royalty realized was Rs. 1,25,000. The output of coal from the Singareni coal-field rose from 3,259 tons in 1887 to 144,668 in 1891 and 421,218 in 1901, and was 419,546 tons in 1904.

Gold occurs in Lingsugūr District, in the rocks of the transition series, in the Muski, Bomanhāl, and Sāgar formations. The total area of gold-bearing rocks in this territory, as proved by the Geological Survey of India and by the prospecting operations of the Hyderābād (Deccan) Company, is about 1,240 square miles. The first band of rocks lies between the Tungabhadra and Kistna rivers, and is composed essentially of a schistose black hornblendic trappoid. This band was actively prospected in 1896–7 by the Hyderābād (Deccan) Company, and a subsidiary company has since been formed to work the quartz. The average yield here, it is alleged, has been an ounce to the ton, and certain specimens have yielded as much as 20 oz. to the ton, but this is rare. Want of water for working the stamps has hampered operations, but this difficulty has been got over by the construction of an artificial reservoir. The next band is at Bomanhāl, extending from the left bank of the Kistna west of Sūrāpur for about 20 miles, and disappearing under the black cotton soil between the Bhīma and the Kistna. This band is not more than Gold.

3 miles in width and is chiefly composed of hornblendic schists. Undoubted traces of old workings have been found in this locality, and from this it is inferred that the band may yet prove profitable. The third band, that of Sāgar between Sāgar and Sūrāpur, is not of much importance.

Iron. Innumerable deposits of iron ore of varying quality are widely distributed over the lateritic and granitic tracts of the State, while similar deposits have been discovered in the sandstone formations in the Godāvari and Wardhā valleys. In the tract situated between the Kistna and Tungabhadra rivers hematite occurs in considerable quantities. The rocks of the Kamptee series, which are extensively developed between the Godāvari and Wardhā valleys, abound in hard ferruginous pebbles and clay iron ores, and are worked in the Chinnūr *tāluk* of Adilābād District. Jagtiāl, Nirmal, Warangal, Yelgarab, and other places are noted for their cast-steel cakes or disks, which were once largely exported to distant parts.

Diamonds. From ancient times diamond mines have been worked in the alluvial deposits round about Partyāl, near the Kistna, as well as in other localities in the alluvial tract of the same river. The Partyāl diamond-bearing layer is about 10 to 16 inches thick, and is concealed by black cotton soil. Trials made in recent years by the Hyderābād (Deccan) Company, involving a considerable outlay, proved unsuccessful; only stones of very small size were found, the gangue having been worked out by the old miners.

Miscellaneous. Among other minerals found in the country may be mentioned mica in the Khammamett *tāluk* of Warangal; fine specimens of corundum and garnets in the Pāloncha *tāluk* of the same District; and a small deposit of graphite in the vicinity of Hasanābād in Karīmnagar (Elgandal) District. A copper lode has recently been discovered at Chintrāla in Nalgonda District, which promises to be remunerative. Excellent limestone is quarried at Shāhābād, between the Wādi junction and Gulbarga on the Great Indian Peninsula Railway. These quarries are extensively worked on both sides of the line for a considerable distance. The limestone is of two colours, black and grey, the latter being the more abundant of the two, and taking a polish almost equal to marble. An extensive industry has been carried on, and the stone is not only being widely used for flooring purposes, but is exported outside the State also in large quantities for building purposes. In addition to the minerals already mentioned, red chalk and saline deposits are found.

Cotton-weaving is carried on in almost every *tāluk*; and *sārīs*, *dhotīs*, and coarse cloths called *khādis* are woven by hand in every large village and used largely by the people, who find these, though coarse and unattractive in appearance, more durable than the goods made in mills. *Sārīs* of silk and other silk stuffs are made in Nalgonda, Raichūr, Mahbūbnagar (Nārāyanpet *tāluk*), Lingsugūr, Aurangābād, Indūr, Elgandal, and other Districts, some of these being of extra fine quality and very durable, and fetching very high prices. In late years the silk-cloth industry in Nalgonda has improved, where the Sālīs, a caste of silk-weavers, are doing good work. Their example is being followed by others of their caste in the adjoining Districts. Aurangābād and Paithan have both been noted from olden times for their embroidery and their gold and silver lace-work. *Kamkhwāb*, or cloth woven with silver and gold of superior quality, was once made at Paithan; but the manufacture is now practically confined to Aurangābād, where about a dozen looms are at work. Lately, the *himru* industry has considerably increased and patterns have been improved. This cloth is a mixture of silk and cotton producing different patterns, and the new varieties include imitations of Kashmīr shawls. The great advantage of this stuff is that it is washable. Other stuffs such as *elaicha* and *mashrū* are still made, the demand for these being very great. Muslin of a very fine texture is made in Nānder and Amarchinta, but this industry is unfortunately dying out for want of support. **Arts and manufactures.**

Brocades of coloured silk and gold and silver thread of very fine quality are made at Aurangābād and Vaijāpur. *Tasar* silk is largely used for making scarfs, *sārīs*, and other silk fabrics. The *tasar* cocoons are gathered in the jungles of the southern and eastern Districts, the silk is made in exactly the same way as that obtained from cultivated cocoons, and a very durable silk cloth is manufactured from it at Warangal, Mathwāda, and Hasanparti in Warangal District, at Nārāyanpet in Mahbūbnagar, and Kosgi in Gulbarga. In the vicinity of the Pākhāl Lake this silkworm abounds in the jungles, but the best description of *tasar* silk is manufactured at Nārāyanpet and at Mahādeopur in Elgandal District.

Warangal was formerly noted for its woollen and silk carpets and rugs, samples of which have been sent to European exhibitions, where they commanded a good sale. The use of aniline dyes, however, has caused much injury to the trade, owing to the fading of the colours. *Shatranjīs* of very good quality are made in the Gulbarga and Warangal Central jails, as also at many District head-quarters.

Aurangābād is noted for its silver-ware and silver ornaments. Bedstead legs, spittoons, *pāndāns*, and other silver articles used in marriages by the wealthy natives are manufactured there in large quantities. Fine filigree and wire-work is done both in Aurangābād and Karīmnagar (Elgandal), some specimens showing exceedingly delicate workmanship.

Bidri ware—so named from Bīdar town, where it is manufactured—consists of an alloy of zinc, copper, tin, and lead; and after the vessels, &c., are made, the surface is inlaid with silver and sometimes with gold, and finely turned and polished. The articles made are ewers, jugs, wash-hand basins, bedstead legs, *pāndāns*, betel-nut boxes, *hukkas*, spittoons, cups, and other kinds of vessels. Sometimes sword and dagger handles are also made of *bidri* ware. The work is very neat, delicate, and highly artistic, and the patterns are exceedingly good.

Sword-blades and other weapons were once extensively made at Hyderābād, Wanparti, Gadwāl, Kolhāpur, Jagdeopur, and other places; but they were not of so good a quality as those imported from Persia, which commanded high prices. The industry is dying out from the circumstances of the age. Inferior smooth-bore muskets were formerly made in the city factory for the use of the police and irregular troops, but the factory has now been abolished. Daggers and knives used by the Arabs and other irregulars were formerly produced at Gadwāl, Jagdeopur, and other places near Hyderābād from Nirmal steel, but they are rarely made now.

The factory industries consist of ginning and pressing factories at Aurangābād and Jālna in Aurangābād District, Māzalgaon and Parlī in Bhīr, Raichūr and Yādgīr in Raichūr, Lātūr in Osmānābād, Udgīr in Bīdar, and also in Warangal, Indūr, Parbhani, and Nānder Districts.

There are three spinning and weaving-mills in the State, employing 2,712 hands: namely, those of the Hyderābād (Deccan) Spinning and Weaving Company, near Hyderābād; the Gulbarga Mahbūb Shāhi Mills Company, at Gulbarga; and the Aurangābād Spinning and Manufacturing Company, at Aurangābād city. The first of these mills commenced work in 1877, while the others were opened in 1886 and 1889. Together they represent a capital of 31 lakhs. The table on the next page shows the statistics of progress.

Commerce and trade. Regular statistics of trade are not maintained, but a general guide to the nature and direction of trade is obtained from the customs and railway returns. The principal exports are food-grains, cotton, linseed, sesamum, ground-nuts, castor-seed, indigo, oils, timber, cotton cloth, hides, cattle, and coal; while the chief imports are mill-made cloth, yarn, raw silk, salt, refined sugar, dried fruits, betel-nuts, horses, cattle, silver and gold, copper and brass in sheets and utensils, iron, timber, mineral oil, and opium. Exports and imports.

	1880-1.	1890-1.	1900-1.
Number of mills	1	3	3
Number of looms	169	443	459
Number of spindles	14,958	50,713	49,465
Hands employed	583	2,236	2,490

The State is divided, for the purpose of levying customs duties on articles entering or leaving the country by the ordinary trade-routes, into nine customs divisions, five of which—Naldrug, Jālna, Lingsugūr, Rājūra, and Kodār—deal exclusively with road-borne trade, while the remaining four—Hyderābād, Secunderābād, Warangal, and Gulbarga—deal with both rail-borne and road-borne traffic. Besides the places already mentioned, the following distributing centres are important: Aurangābād, Nānder, Parbhani, Hingoli, Parlī, Sūrāpur, Koppal, Lātūr, Raichūr, Seram, Shāhābad, Nārāyanpet, Sadāseopet, Siddipet, Indūr, Karkeli, Khammamett, and Edlābād. Complete statistics showing the quantities of exports and imports at each of these places are not prepared by the Customs department, as articles comprised in the Customs tariff are alone registered. The railway returns show only the weight of rail-borne traffic. Chief trade centres.

In the absence of reliable statistics, it is impossible to estimate the amount of the internal trade of the State, but there is no doubt that it far exceeds the foreign trade. For the purpose of export, the produce of the country is collected from the interior at certain important centres. There is also a large interchange of commodities of local growth and production between adjoining Districts. The same agency that is employed for collecting the produce for export also performs the office of distributing imported articles to distant parts by means of carts and pack-bullocks. The trading castes are represented by the Jain Vānīs in the Marāthā Districts, by Lingāyat Vānīs in the Carnatic, and by Komatis in Telingāna, while Mārwāri traders are to be found in all the large villages. The village Baniā is a general tradesman, being grain-dealer, cloth-vendor, and banker. He it is who advances to the ryot Internal trade.

the amount to enable him to meet the land revenue, and at harvest time takes charge of the produce, which he passes on to the agents of wholesale exporters at large centres or the nearest railway station.

External trade.

Goods and commodities imported from British territory are brought in either by rail direct to important stations in the State, or in the case of frontier Districts, where there are no railways, by means of carts and pack-bullocks from commercial centres outside Hyderābād, such as Bārsi, Sholāpur, Ahmadnagar, Kurnool, Adoni, Bellary, Bijāpur, Jaggayyapeta, Bezwāda, Bhadrāchalam, Rājahmundry, and Chandarpur. The rail-borne imports are mostly from Bombay, and to a smaller extent from Madras. With regard to exports, the produce of the frontier Districts finds its way to the same centres, but that of the interior is carried to the nearest railway station, whence it is either sent to Hyderābād or consigned to Bombay or Madras. The chief channels of trade are the Great Indian Peninsula Railway in the west and the south, and the Madras and East Coast Railways in the south and east. These are connected with the Nizām's Guaranteed State Railway, which traverses the State from Wādi in the west to Bezwāda in the east. The Hyderābād-Godāvari Valley Railway, which passes through the central and north-western Districts, connects the capital with Manmād in the Nāsik District of Bombay. Numerous feeder-roads in the interior convey commodities to and from the various stations on the State Railway. The principal exports to Bombay in 1903 consisted of linseed (46,466 tons), castor-seed (45,090 tons), other seeds (29,550 tons), hides and skins (527 tons), and miscellaneous including raw cotton (123,443 tons); the exports to Madras in the same year were linseed (5,233 tons), castor-seed (14,095 tons), other seeds (5,094 tons), hides and skins (3,136 tons), and miscellaneous (26,845 tons). The imports from Bombay consisted of cotton twist and yarn (7,541 tons), cotton piece-goods (5,194 tons), grain (13,632 tons), kerosene oil (8,522 tons), fruits and provisions (7,110 tons), iron (7,391 tons), tobacco (25 tons), and salt (33,848 tons); and from Madras, yarn (240 tons), piece-goods (451 tons), grain (47,688 tons), tobacco (2,062 tons), and fruit and provisions (1,703 tons); while from stations outside these two Presidencies the imports consisted only of grain (4,731 tons). The total exports by rail in 1901 amounted to 113,340 tons, and the total imports to 122,345 tons; and in 1903 they were 300,679 and 152,334 tons respectively. These figures are exclusive of the coal exported, the figures and value of which are shown below:—

1891 . .	81,882 tons . .	Rs. 7,66,270
1901 . .	343,945 " . .	Rs. 18,61,940
1903 . .	291,499 " . .	Rs. 17,58,444

The south-western corner of the State is crossed for 137 miles by the broad-gauge line from Bombay to Madras. About 120 miles of this line belong to the south-eastern section of the Great Indian Peninsula, while the remainder is part of the north-western branch of the Madras Railway, the junction being at Raichūr. From Wādi on the Great Indian Peninsula Railway, the Nizām's Guaranteed State Railway runs east to Warangal and then south-east towards Bezwāda on the East Coast section of the Madras Railway. The total length of the main line is 310 miles, while two branches from Husain Sāgar to Hyderābād and from Dornakal to the Singareni coal-fields add 20 miles. The Hyderābād-Godāvari Valley Railway (metre gauge) runs for 391 miles north-west from Hyderābād city to Manmād on the north-eastern section of the Great Indian Peninsula Railway. The State thus contains 467 miles on the broad gauge, all built before 1891, and 391 miles on the narrow gauge, opened between 1899 and 1901. Means of communication. Railways. General.

The Nizam's Guaranteed State Railway is owned and worked by a company under a guarantee from the Hyderābād State, and the same company works the metre-gauge line, capital for which was raised by the issue of redeemable mortgage debentures. Method of working.

The total capital expenditure on the Nizām's State Railway to the end of 1904 was 4·3 crores, and in that year the net earnings were nearly 28 lakhs, or about 6½ per cent. on the outlay. The Hyderābād-Godāvari Valley Railway has cost 2·6 crores, and earned 7·7 lakhs net in the same year, or nearly 3 per cent.; but in 1901 and 1902 the earnings had been about 3¼ per cent. Financial results.

With the exception of some roads in the immediate vicinity of Hyderābād city, none of the roads in the State can be considered as equal to roads described as first-class in British India, and even these are gravelled rather than metalled. Prior to 1868 there were trunk roads leading from Hyderābād to Sholāpur, Gulbarga, Kurnool, Masulipatam, Hanamkonda, and Nāgpur, some of which were originally constructed by the British military authorities to facilitate the movements of troops. They were eventually made over to the State about 1867. Roads.

The following are the principal roads: The Hyderābād-Nāgpur road runs due north, leaving the State at Pullara in Principal routes.

Adilābād (Sirpur Tāndūr) District, 195 miles from the capital. This road is partly bridged and well maintained, and is passable at all seasons. The Hyderābād-Jālna road is 265 miles long, and proceeds via Bīdar, Udgīr, and Gangākher. Up to Bīdar, the road is good and practicable at all seasons, but beyond it is only a fair-weather road. A bridged road connects Hyderābād, via Homnābād and Naldrug, with the Sholāpur railway station, and is 180 miles long. Before the extension of the Great Indian Peninsula Railway beyond Sholāpur, this was the main road from Hyderābād to the Bombay side. The Hyderābād-Kurnool road is passable at all seasons and is 136 miles long. A branch from Jedcherla to the Kistna river, 60 miles in length, was constructed between 1879 and 1882. Another branch road starts from the sixty-ninth mile and proceeds by Makhtal to the Kistna station on the Great Indian Peninsula Railway, 42 miles, while a third extends to Raichūr, 55 miles. This last forms a part of the Hyderābād-Bellary road, with a total length of 158 miles. The Hyderābād-Masulipatam road, partly bridged and passable at all seasons, has a length of 116 miles in the State. From the sixtieth mile of this road the old Madras road branches off. A made road connects Hyderābād city with Warangal, 91 miles, and proceeds thence to Mangampet on the Godāvari, 72 miles. The former section was constructed in 1868–71 and the latter in 1871–6.

The other principal roads are Hyderābād to Medak, 54 miles; Aurangābād to Nāndgaon on the Great Indian Peninsula Railway, 54 miles, 43 of which lie in the State; Aurangābād to Jālna, 39 miles; Aurangābād to Toka, 25 miles; Aurangābād to Bhīr, 72 miles; Bhīr to Ahmadnagar railway station, 70 miles, and then south via Parenda to Bārsi Road station; Naldrug to Gulbarga, 52⅓ miles; Naldrug to Osmānābād (Dhārāseo), 32½ miles; Gulbarga to Sūrāpur, 60 miles; Raichūr to Lingsugūr, 55 miles, being part of the old road from Kurnool to Dhārwār; the Bhongīr-Nalgonda road, 40 miles long; and the branch road from Homnābād to Gulbarga railway station, 36 miles. Many of these roads now serve as feeders to railway stations.

Feeder-roads. After the extension of the Great Indian Peninsula Railway beyond Sholāpur in the direction of Gulbarga and Raichūr, 13 feeder-roads were constructed with a total length of 382 miles; and when the Nizām's Guaranteed State Railway was opened from Secunderābād to Wādi in 1874, seven more feeder-roads were completed, totalling 97½ miles. Eleven years later the railway was extended from Secunderābād to Warangal, and thence to Dornakal, necessitating the construction of 13 new roads to serve as feeders to this section of the railway. Subsequently, at the request of the railway company, 15 roads, with a total length of 109 miles, were constructed as feeders to the Hyderābād-Godāvari Valley Railway.

In 1891 there were 1,241 miles of road under maintenance, costing 3 lakhs, while in 1901, 1,614 miles were maintained at a cost of 5½ lakhs. The Local fund roads are not included in these figures. Improvements in the method of maintenance accompanied the increased grants in 1901, and portions of roads and bridges have been reconstructed.

Carts.

In the interior of the State the only means of transport are pack-bullocks and the ordinary two-wheeled country cart drawn by a pair of bullocks. The majority of the carts are crude in appearance, but are constructed of well-seasoned wood by the village carpenter and blacksmith, and are very serviceable. They consist of a framework of wood, placed across a log, through which passes an iron axle, while the bullocks are yoked to a long pole attached to the log at right angles, below the framework. In the two longer side pieces are fixed uprights 2 feet high, secured by another piece of wood on top. The wheels have tires made from country iron.

Post office.

The Hyderābād State maintains its own postal system for internal communications and issues stamps. State correspondence was conveyed by contractors for a stipulated amount from 1856 to 1869, in which year the State undertook the carriage of mails on a system devised by Sir Sālār Jang I. The *ghungru* service, or express post, seems also to have been introduced at the same time, but was abolished in 1902 because of its cost, since at least two runners had to be kept at every stage.

When the State took over the direct management of the department in 1869, District and *tāluk* post offices were immediately established, numbering 125. The net income and expenditure in the first year were Rs. 16,100 and Rs. 2,45,000 respectively. The number of post offices was gradually increased, so that in 1892 they numbered 195, and the receipts and expenditure rose to Rs. 1,27,300 and Rs. 2,60,500 respectively. By 1901 the number of post offices had risen to 239 and the receipts were Rs. 1,57,700, while the expenditure had increased to Rs. 2,99,200. The receipts do not include income from the carriage of service covers, which are carried free of all postal charges. The amount which would have been realized from the conveyance of these during 1901 was estimated at Rs. 3,67,500. In 1901 mails were carried by runners over

3,882 miles of post lines, and by railways over 1,076 miles. The number of persons employed in 1881, 1901, and 1903 was 1881, 2,177, and 2,140 respectively.

The following table gives statistics of the operations of both State and British post offices in 1902–2 :—

	State post.	British Indian post.
Number of post offices	248	38
Number of letter boxes	289	64
Number of miles of postal communication	4,910¼	1,308
Total number of postal articles delivered	6,683,718	6,461,073
Letters	5,612,302	3,235,177
Post-cards	1,033,560	1,920,735
Packets (including unregistered newspapers)	...	525,807
Newspapers (registered as newspapers in the Post Office)	...	734,954
Parcels	37,856	44,400
Value of stamps sold to the public . Rs.	99,245	84,715
Value of money orders issued . Rs.	...	43,32,662
Total amount of savings bank deposits . Rs.	...	9,01,150

Famine. The Nizām's Dominions, in common with other parts of India, are subject to periodical visitations of famine of a more or less severe character. It is recorded that 1629, 1659, and 1685 were famine years, while in the eighteenth century there were famines in 1713, 1747, and 1787. In the nineteenth century famine or scarcity was experienced at eleven periods: namely, 1804, 1813, 1819, 1846, 1854, 1862, 1866, 1871, 1876–7, 1896–7, and 1899–1900. There are no records of famine relief measures prior to 1876. In that year the rains failed, and the Districts affected were Lingsugūr, Raichūr, Gulbarga, Bhīr, and Osmānābād (Naldrug); in the Districts of Nalgonda and Mahbūbnagar (Nāgar Karnūl) there was no famine, but the distress caused by scarcity was severe. The whole of the State, in fact, suffered, as prices of food rose very high, and famine-stricken people migrated from the affected Districts. Relief works were started in October, 1876, and were finally closed in November, 1877. During this period 6¼ million units were provided with work, and 2 millions were relieved in poorhouses. The cost of this famine, excluding remissions of land revenue, was 13¼ lakhs. In 1890 the rains again failed in parts of the southern Districts, in which relief was given by opening works and remitting revenue.

1896-97. A more severe famine appeared imminent in 1896, but was fortunately averted by good rains in November, which saved the standing *rabi* crops. Although there was no famine, the distress was very severe in some parts, owing to heavy exports of grain to adjoining British famine-stricken territory, and to a local failure of crops. The whole of the Districts of Raichūr and Lingsugūr, and parts of Gulbarga, Osmānābād, and Bhīr, comprising an area of 10,278 square miles with a population of 1½ millions, were involved in distress. In July, 1897, the affected area increased to 17,835 square miles, with a population of 2,400,000, but a sufficient fall of rain in August averted famine. The total expenditure on relief was 7¾ lakhs.

1899–1900.

In 1899 the rainfall received was only 15½ inches, or less than half the usual quantity. In the Aurangābād and Gulbarga Divisions the later rains failed entirely, and the area affected in 1900 was 23,007 square miles with a population (1891) of 3,573,651. In addition to this, scarcity was felt in an area of 51,541 square miles with a population of 6,512,379. The *kharīf* harvest in the famine Districts was estimated at 25 per cent. of the normal, and in the *rabi* harvest the largest food-crop yielded not more than 12 per cent. The Census of 1901 showed a net decrease of 394,898 persons; and if a normal rate of increase be assumed, the total loss must have been nearly 1½ million persons, in spite of an expenditure on relief of more than two crores. In 1899 the Government of India lent two crores to the State, for expenditure on famine relief.

Tract subject to famine.

Raichūr, Gulbarga, and Lingsugūr are the Districts which are generally the first to suffer from a failure of rains, and are more liable to famine than any other part of the State. Failure of the monsoon rains means the failure of the *kharīf* harvest, which provides about half the staple food-grains of the people; and if the late or autumn rains fail, the *rabi* crops also suffer, which means that besides his linseed and wheat the cultivator loses the whole of the white *jowār*, which forms the largest food-grain crop of the State.

Famine warnings.

The first indications of famine are a sharp rise in the prices of grain. If the crops fail in the neighbouring Districts or Provinces, there is a sudden influx of immigrants in search of work. Sometimes sufficient grain is produced for the local needs; but if there be famine outside the country, grain is largely exported, resulting in high prices. This was actually the case in 1899–1900. The rains failed in 1899, and grain began to be exported largely to the Bombay Presidency, where 90,000 persons were on relief works by November 1, 1899.

Prevention of famine.

The system of land assessment in the Marāthā or 'dry-crop' Districts was based on that of the Bombay Presidency, and no remissions are ordinarily given for a failure of crops. The famine of 1900 so affected the people that special orders were given for extensive remissions in this tract, and the total loss to Government under this head was not less than 45 lakhs. For the Telingāna Districts extensive irrigation schemes have been prepared, while in Marāthwāra the protective measures include the extension and maintenance of roads and the construction of wells. In times of famine food and rations are given to those able to work, and poorhouses are established for the infirm and decrepit. Loans are advanced to the ryots to enable them to purchase cattle, and cheap grain shops are opened for the relief of others.

Administration. The Minister and Council. The present form of administration was prescribed by the original instructions issued by the Nizām in the *Kānūncha* (edict) of 1893, subsequently modified in some respects. According to these, the *Madār-ul-Mahām* or Minister is the chief controlling authority in the State. To assist him in the work of administration there are four Assistant Ministers: namely, Financial, Judicial, Military, and Miscellaneous, known as *Muīn-ul-Mahāms*. All questions of importance are referred to the Council, which is composed of the Minister as president and the *Muīn-ul-Mahāms* as members. Matters on which there is a difference of opinion between the Minister and an Assistant Minister may also be referred to the Council. Business disposed of by the Council is immediately reported to the Nizām, and the orders of the Council are carried out without awaiting his sanction unless he is pleased otherwise to direct.

Distribution of work. The work is distributed as follows: The Financial Assistant Minister has charge of the departments of finance, mint, railways and mines, and stud. The Judicial Assistant Minister has under him the judicial department, jails, registration, medical, post office, and religious institutions. The Military Assistant Minister disposes of the work of the regular and irregular and the Imperial Service troops; and the Miscellaneous Assistant Minister has under him police, public works, education, municipalities, and sanitation. The Revenue department is directly under the Minister, who exercises control over the departments of land revenue, revenue survey and settlement, *inām*, customs, excise and *ābkāri*, forests, agriculture and commerce, and local funds. The Secretaries are responsible for the work of their departments, both to the Minister and to the Assistant Ministers concerned. The number of Secretaries at present is as follows: (1) financial; (2) two joint for revenue work; (3) judicial, police, and general departments; (4) public works; (5) military secretary; and (6) the private secretary to the Minister. The financial department has charge of the accountant-general's office and the audit branch; and the public works department is under a Secretary with two Superintending Engineers for the Irrigation and the General Branches as executive officers. The other departments are as follows: the judicial, under the High Court, consisting of a Chief Justice and five Puisne Judges; the District police and jails, under an Inspector-General; the city police, under a Kotwāl; customs, under a Commissioner; education, under a Director; stamps and mint, under a Superintendent; forests, under a Conservator; postal, under a Postmaster-General; and medical, under a Director.

Administrative divisions.

Until lately the whole State, excluding the *Sarf-i-khās* or Crown District of Atrāf-i-balda, was divided for administrative purposes into four *Sūbahs* or Divisions, 15 Districts, and one *Amaldāri* or sub-District. In 1905 certain changes were made in the constitution of the Districts; and though the number of *Sūbahs* remains the same, one District (Lingsugūr) has been broken up, and the *Amaldāri* has been made a District, so that there are still 15 Districts. Each *Sūbah* or Division is under a Sūbahdār (Commissioner), and each District under a First Tālukdār (Collector). The latter officers have two or more assistants, known as Second and Third Tālukdārs. At the head of each *tāluk* is a *tahsīldār*. There are now 101 *tāluks*, managed by Government, instead of 117 prior to the recent changes. Excluding the Atrāf-i-balda or Crown District, but including all the *jāgīrs* and *samasthāns*, each of the four *Sūbahs* had an average area of 19,825 square miles and an average population of 2,567,993 in 1901. Exact details of the areas as reconstituted are not available, and the following particulars are based on the statistics of 1901. The average District area and population were 4,956 square miles and 641,998 persons respectively. These were subdivided into 117 *tāluks*, with an average area of nearly 678 square miles and 87,794 persons. The *tahsīldār* has charge of the revenue and the magisterial work of his *tāluk*, with a *peshkār* (assistant) and a *girdāvar* (revenue inspector) to assist him in his work. The last class of subordinates is found only in the Telingāna Districts, where remissions are given on 'wet' cultivation in case of excessive or scanty rainfall, or breach of tanks, it being the duty of the revenue inspector to verify and report the extent of the injury thus caused.

Village officers.

The headman of the village is called *pātel* and the village accountant *patwāri*, *karnam*, or *kulkarni*; there are generally *pātels* in villages the revenues of which exceed Rs. 500, the *māli* or revenue *pātel* and the police *pātel*. Up to 1870, the *pātels* and *patwāris* enjoyed *ināms* or grants of land in payment for their services; but since that year the *ināms* have been resumed and cash payments introduced, the *inām* lands, after assessment, remaining in their possession as before.

Estates.

Besides the ordinary territory of the State, large areas are held as estates, known as *samasthāns* or *jāgīrs*. The most important *samasthāns* are those of GADWĀL, AMARCHINTA, WANPARTI, JATPOL, and PALONCHA; the smaller are Gopālpet, Nārāyanpur, Anegundi, Gurgunta, and the Medak *samasthāns*. These are scattered all over the southern half of the State. The largest *jāgīrs* are those of Nawāb Sālār Jang, the three *paigah* nobles, Mahārājā Sir Kishan Prasād Bahādur, Nawābs Hisām-ul-mulk and Fakhr-ul-mulk Bahādur, Mahārājā Sheorāj, and Rājā Rai Rayan Bahadur. The *jāgīrs* are dispersed in all parts of the State. Besides these large *jāgīrs*, there are numerous smaller ones containing from one village to 60 villages. In 1901 *jāgīrs* and *samasthāns* covered an area of 24,400 square miles, with a population of 3,259,000. Separate articles explain the constitution of the PAIGĀH ESTATES, the SĀLĀR JANG ESTATE, and the *samasthāns*.

Legislation. History of legislation.

In 1870 Sir Sālār Jang I, then Minister, appointed a committee of Muhammadan lawyers to frame laws for the State on the model of those enacted in British India. Later on, the Council of State, composed of the principal nobles, with the Nizām as president, became a Legislative Council also; and to supplement its labours, and prepare drafts of bills for its consideration, a special committee was nominated. In 1890 a Law Commission, with a president and a secretary, was appointed. The president was required to tour in the State, and lay his notes of inspection before the Commission, to enable it to prepare and submit drafts of laws required, in such form as to admit of their being finally cast into a code. Reports were to accompany these drafts, explaining the existing laws, the defects observed in their working, and the proposals for removing those defects. The High Court was also directed to submit, for the information of the Commission, the drafts of any laws it might have under consideration, and to communicate any matters for which, in its opinion, new laws or amendments of existing laws were necessary. Other officers also were requested to communicate to the Judicial Secretary their opinions as to any reforms they might consider necessary in existing laws.

History of the Legis-

His Highness's attention having been directed to the desirability of establishing a Legislative Council for the purpose of making laws, orders for its establishment were promulgated in 1893. Under these orders the Council was to consist of the Chief Justice, a Puisne Judge of the High Court, the Inspector-General of Revenue, the Director of Public Instruction, the Inspector-General of Police, and the Financial Secretary. In 1884 Act I of 1304 Fasli received the Nizām's sanction, recognizing the right of the people to share in the work of framing laws and to representation. In 1900 this Regulation was re-enacted with certain modifications as Act III of 1309 Fasli, and is still in force. lative Council.

Constitution of the Legislative Council.

The Legislative Council consists of 19 members, of whom, besides the president and vice-president, 11 are official and 6 non-official members. The Minister is the president, and the Assistant Minister, whose department is concerned with a bill before the Council, is vice-president for the time being. Of the 11 official members, the Chief Justice, the Judicial Secretary, and the Legal Adviser are *ex-officio* members, the remaining 8 official members being nominated by the Minister for two years. Of the 6 non-official members, 2 are elected by the *jāgīrdārs* and landowners, 2 by the pleaders of the High Court, and the remaining 2 are nominated by the Minister from among the residents of the State, of whom one must be nominated from the *paigāh ilāka*. The non-official members are appointed for two years, but retiring members are eligible for re-election.

Public criticism.

To ensure facilities for ascertaining public opinion, the Council Regulation provides that bills, with the statements of objects and reasons, shall be published in the *State Gazette* in such language as the Council directs. Bills are based on Muhammadan jurisprudence, the Hindu Shāstras, special laws binding on a particular community, or customs and usages having the force of law. In addition to these sources, laws in force in British India and elsewhere are consulted.

Principal Acts.

In 1304 Fasli (1894) Act I already referred to was passed. In 1305 Fasli (1895) five Acts were passed, Act II being the Gambling Act. In 1307 Fasli (1897) six Acts were passed, relating to Oaths, Criminal Tribes, Succession Certificates, Court Fees, Court of Wards, and Labour Contracts. The six Acts passed in the following year dealt with amendments to the District Police and Stamp Rules, General Clauses, Public Demands Recovery, Opium, and Legal Practitioners. Of the thirteen Acts of 1309 Fasli (1899), the Army, the Local Cess, the Game Preservation, the Post Office, the Finger Impressions, the Land Acquisition, the Inventions and Designs, the Forest, and the Counterfeit Coins Acts are the more important. The principal Acts of 1310 Fasli (1900–1) were the Census, the Weights and Measures, and the Limitation Acts. In 1903–4 the Hyderābād Criminal Procedure Code, the Evidence Act, and an Act for Prevention of Cruelty to Animals were passed. The most important of the six Acts passed in 1904–5 were amendments to the High Court Regulations and to the Stamps Act, the Ferries Act, and an Act for inquiry into the behaviour of public servants.

Civil and criminal justice. For the administration of justice there are 123 civil and 271 criminal courts, including the High Court. *Tahsīldārs* can try suits up to a limit of Rs. 100, but only seventy-nine *tahsīldārs* and five *naib-tahsīldārs* exercise these powers; where Munsifs are appointed, the *tahsīldārs* have no civil jurisdiction. There are fifteen Munsifs who try suits up to Rs. 500, while the Nāzim-i-Dīwāni or District Civil Judge and the Judicial Assistants to the First Tālukdārs can try suits up to Rs. 5,000, except in the Medak *Sūbah* (Division), where the limit is up to Rs. 10,000. Only five First Tālukdārs exercise civil powers, and they can try suits without any limit to the amount involved. The Nāzim-i-Sūbah or Divisional Judge tries suits of Rs. 5,000 and upwards. Appeals from the *tahsīldārs* or Munsifs lie to the Nāzim-i-Dīwāni, or to the First Tālukdārs wherever they have civil jurisdiction; and those from the Nāzim-i-Dīwāni or First Tālukdārs lie to the Nāzim-i-Sūbah. There being no Divisional court in the Medak *Sūbah* (Division), the appeals from the District civil courts lie to the divisional bench of the High Court. In the city of Hyderābād, the Small Cause Court tries suits up to Rs. 5,000 and hears appeals from the Subordinate Judges of the same court up to Rs. 500. All appeals from the City Small Cause Court and from the Nāzim-i-Sūbah or Divisional Judge lie to the divisional bench of the High Court. In civil cases up to a value of Rs. 300, in which the District court agrees with the decision of the subordinate court, there is no appeal and the decision is considered final, but revision is permissible on points of law. Similarly, in suits up to Rs. 500 decided by the Subordinate Judges of the Small Cause Court, and upheld by the Judge of that court, there is no appeal, but the judgements are subject to revision on the original side of the High Court.

In criminal cases the *tahsīldārs* and the Second and Third Tālukdārs exercise, respectively, third and second-class magisterial powers, and the First Tālukdārs, being the chief magistrates of the District, are first-class magistrates. Appeals from the *tahsīldārs* and the subordinate Tālukdārs lie to the

First Tālukdār, and from his decision to the Nāzim-i-Sūbah or Divisional Judge. In criminal cases, except trials for murder, if the fines inflicted do not exceed Rs. 500, the decision of the Nāzim-i-Sūbah is considered final, but revision on points of law is allowed. In all other cases appeals lie to the divisional bench of the High Court, and its decision is final. Appeals from cases in which subordinate magistrates in the city have given sentences not exceeding three months' imprisonment or a fine up to Rs. 100 are heard by the Chief City Magistrate; but appeals from cases in which imprisonment or fine above those limits have been inflicted are heard by the High Court. On its original side the High Court exercises the powers of a Sessions Judge. The divisional bench has power to sentence up to fourteen years, but sentences of imprisonment for life are sent by the High Court to the Minister for confirmation. Sentences of death are submitted to the Nizām. Many of the holders of large *jāgīrs* and *samasthāns* exercise judicial powers, both civil and criminal, within their respective domains, and are required to submit periodical returns regarding their judicial work to the Judicial department of the State.

Progress of litigation.

No extraordinary increase has been observed in civil suits, but in years of famine and scarcity their numbers decrease. On the other hand, criminal cases increase in proportion to the severity of the season. Regular statistics began to be collected in 1885, and judicial reports were published from that year. The table on the next page shows what particulars are available.

The increase in the number of offences against special and local laws is due to the fact that, almost up to the close of 1890, municipal cases were not heard by the criminal courts.

Registration.

A registration department was established in 1889, and placed under the High Court, and an Act was passed in the same year to regulate operations. From 1890 to 1895 the department was supervised by the Excise Commissioner, after which it was again made over to the High Court. In 1897 an Inspector-General of Registration and Stamps was appointed, and the department was placed under his charge. In 1899 paid registrars were appointed in the Districts of Aurangābād, Bhīr, Osmānābād, Atrāf-i-balda, Raichūr, and Gulbarga; but in the other Districts and *tāluks* revenue and judicial officers were entrusted with the work, who receive a moiety or two-thirds of the fees. The work in Hyderābād city is in charge of a city registrar.

In 1891 there were 18 registrars and 107 sub-registrars, and the number of documents registered was 16,956. The average number of documents registered in the decade ending 1900 was 18,465. In 1901 there were 20 registrars' and 121 sub-registrars' offices, the number of documents registered being 15,826. In 1903 there were 20 registrars' and 122 sub-registrars' offices, and the number of documents registered was 12,033.

CIVIL JUSTICE

Classes of suits.	Average for six years ending 1890.	Average for ten years ending 1900.	1901.	1905.
Suits for money and movable property	12,855	12,787	11,913	11,076
Title and other suits	1,535	2,441	2,280	2,436

CRIMINAL JUSTICE

	Average for six years ending 1890.	Average for ten years ending 1900.	1901.	1905.
Number of persons tried:				
(*a*) For offences against person and property	7,373	6,062	6,276	6,660
(*b*) For other offences against the Indian Penal Code	36,043	31,882	29,599	16,356
(*c*) For offences against special and local laws	742	4,347	7,632	6,762

Finance. Revenue.

The statistics of revenue and expenditure, shown in Tables V and VI (p. 86) and discussed in this article, do not extend to the *Sarf-i-khās* or Crown lands, or to the *paigāhs* and *jāgīrs*, which together make up a third of the whole area of the State. Subject to this limitation, the total revenue averaged 327 lakhs between 1881 and 1890, 383 lakhs between 1891 and 1900, and was 417 lakhs in 1901 and 469 lakhs in 1904. The chief source, as usual, is land revenue, which in 1904 yielded 243 lakhs, or 51 per cent. of the total. Customs (56½ lakhs), excise (58 lakhs), and railways (36 lakhs) are also items of considerable importance. The last of these, which entailed a net loss in the twenty years ending 1900, now yield a profit. The rise in revenue, in spite of unfavourable years, points clearly to the improvements which have been made in many branches of the administration.

While the revenue has expanded, the expenses of the State have also increased largely, amounting to an average of 316 lakhs between 1881 and 1890, 402 lakhs in the next decade, 411 lakhs in 1901, and 450 lakhs in 1904. Charges in respect of collection include refunds of various classes; part of the salaries of District officers and their establishments, the remainder being debited to law and justice; survey and settlement; the *inām* department; payments to village headmen and accountants; *dastband* or payments for the maintenance of irrigation tanks; and the cost of establishments for collection of customs and forest dues, excise and opium fees, manufacture and vend of stamps, and registration. These charges amounted to 56 lakhs in 1904. **Expenditure.**

The item 'general administration' includes the salaries of the Minister and the Assistant Ministers, the cost of establishments in all the head-quarter offices, and the pay and establishment charges of the four Sūbahdārs. A considerable increase has been made in the allotments for law and justice (including jails), police, education, and medical charges. The expenditure on pensions includes a variety of charges, most of which are decreasing, though the head 'service pensions' is responsible for an increase, due to the improvement in the position of officials of the State. The miscellaneous charges include expenditure on famine relief, and have thus risen largely. The loan of two crores, already referred to, together with interest at 4 per cent., is being gradually paid off, partly from the State balances and partly by appropriation of a portion of the rent paid by the British Government for Berār.

The current coin of the State is known as the *Hālī sikka*, and the quantity in circulation has been reckoned at about 10 crores. The issue of the *Hāli sikka* began in 1854, when the first Sir Sālār Jang was Minister, and has continued with occasional interruptions. Free coinage was allowed in the mint up to 1893, but after that date comparatively little silver was coined. The stock of rupees in circulation became somewhat depleted; and the rate of exchange between the State rupee and the British rupee, after fluctuating violently in 1901 and 1902, has since remained fairly steady, the former exchanging at about 8 per cent. above its bullion value. In 1904 an improved coin of a new design was minted, known as the *Mahbūbia* rupee, representing on one side the famous Chār Minār building, which stands in the centre of Hyderābād city; since this new rupee was issued, the supply has been regulated so as to prevent serious fluctuations of exchange Currency.

value. The rate now stands at between 115 and 116 to 100 British rupees. The copper coins issued by the State were till recently oblong pieces of about 2 pies in value. Since 1905, however, copper coins of a better pattern have been issued from the Hyderābād mint representing the same value. Half-anna coins are also being made. The old coins are still in use, and will remain in circulation until a sufficient quantity of the new coins has been produced.

Land revenue settlement.

The common system of land tenure throughout the State is *ryotwāri*. All the nine Districts of Marāthwāra and four of the Telingāna Districts have been surveyed and settled according to this system; they are Aurangābād, Bhīr, Nānder, Parbhani, Gulbarga, Osmānābād, Raichūr, Lingsugūr, Bīdar, Nizāmābād (Indūr), Medak, Mahbūbnagar, and Warangal. Of the remaining four Districts, Karīmnagar (Elgandal) and Nalgonda have been surveyed and partly assessed. Adilābād (Sirpur Tāndūr) and the Crown District of Atrāf-i-balda have not yet been surveyed. In the earlier settlements the period of settlement was for thirty years, while those surveyed later were settled for fifteen years. Revision work has been commenced in some of the latter class, where the terms have expired or are about to expire.

Ryotwāri tenure.

Under the *ryotwāri* system each field is considered a holding, which the ryot holds directly from the State, and the holder or occupant of the field is called the *pattadār*. The right of occupancy depends on the regular payment of the assessment by the *pattadār*, and in case of failure to meet the demand he forfeits his right. In such a case the land reverts to the State, and the right of occupancy is sold by auction to satisfy the demand for arrears. The period of holding is nominally one year, but if the holder pays the assessment and dues regularly, he may retain his land indefinitely. A *pattadār* may relinquish his land by giving due notice of his intention, or he may sell or transfer his right if he wishes to do so. Reference has already been made, in dealing with rents, to the practice of subletting or taking partners (*shikmīdārs*).

Other tenures.

The other systems of tenure are known as *jāgīr*, *inām*, *makta* or *sarbasta*, *peshkash*, *agarhār*, and *ijāra*. A *jāgīr* is a free grant of one or more villages, and the tenure may be classed under four heads: *al-tamghā* or *inām-al-tamghā*, which are grants of an hereditary or permanent nature; *zāt jāgīrs*, or personal grants for the maintenance of the grantees; *paigāh jāgīrs*, or grants to the nobles of the State for maintaining troops for the Nizām; *tankhwāh-i-mahallāt*, or grants in lieu of certain local payments that were binding on the State. The *inām* lands are granted for service or charitable purposes, either free of revenue or subject to a quit rent. *Makta* or *sarbasta* resembles the *jāgīr* tenure, except that the holder has to pay a certain fixed proportion of the revenue to the State; it is also known as *pālampat* in the Marāthā Districts. Under the *peshkash* tenure villages are granted on a fixed assessment, like the *zamīndāri* tenure in Northern India; all the *samasthāns* in the State are held under this tenure. *Agarhār* is a free grant of one or more villages for the upkeep of Hindu temples. *Ijāra* is a lease granted for a whole waste village for a term of thirty or forty years. The *ijāradār* or lessee pays no rent for the first three or five years; after that he begins to pay a fraction of the full assessment, varying from one-tenth to one-fifth, and increased every year till the full assessment is reached, which is paid till the lease expires.

Classification of villages. In 1901 there were 13,039 *ryotwāri*, 2,904 *jāgīr*, 664 *makta* or *sarbasta*, 681 *peshkash*, 415 *ijāra*, 309 *agarhār*, and 1,006 deserted villages in the State; and the revenue derived from the *ryotwāri*, *makta*, and *peshkash* villages was 191 lakhs, 6·7 lakhs, and 139 lakhs respectively.

Method of assessment. The assessment was originally based on the quantity of grain sown in a field or on its produce, of which a certain share was taken by the State as revenue. On 'dry crops' the share was about one-fourth of the produce, and on 'wet' lands, irrigated from tanks and wells, the State received half and two-fifths respectively of the produce. When payment in kind was commuted to cash payment, the amount thus fixed became the revenue of the field. A *tāluk*, after it has been surveyed, is divided into groups of villages for the purpose of classification and assessment. The fertility and depth of the soil, the absence or presence of sand, limestone nodules, saline efflorescences and other defects in it, proximity of the group to, or its distance from, centres of trade or railways, and easy means of communication are all factors which are considered in determining the assessment. A standard maximum rate per acre is fixed for the group, and varying rates to be applied to all land in the group are calculated on the basis of its advantages or defects.

Former demands. No records exist to show what the revenue demand was in early times, but the revenues under Musalmān rule seem to have been generally farmed out. Traces of settlements made by the Bahmani kings and by the Adil Shāhi and Kutb Shāhi rulers have been found in some of the Districts; but it was not until Akbar's annexation of Berār in 1596, and Malik Ambar's rule in Aurangābād, that regular settlements were introduced. The *Sūbah* of Berār under the Mughals was more extensive than it is now, as it included portions of Sirpur Tāndūr, Elgandal, Indūr, Nānder, Parbhani, and Aurangābād Districts, which now fall within the boundaries of the Nizām's Dominions. Under Akbar's famous settlement, the assessment was fixed by measuring the arable lands, and making a careful estimate of the produce. Each *bīgha* was then rated at one-fourth the estimated produce, and the total demand on a village was termed its *tankhwāh* or standard rent-roll. In 1600 the province was assessed at 161 lakhs, and during the time of the first Nizām at 120 lakhs.

Telingāna during the reign of Abul Hasan, the last of the Golconda kings, yielded a total revenue of 166 lakhs, but the boundaries of the Golconda kingdom then extended as far as the sea-coast, including the Northern Circārs. It has been estimated that the present revenue is about equal to the cash assessments at the beginning of the seventeenth century. During the eighteenth century the State suffered from the inroads of the Marāthās; and when order was restored, the revenues of the State were farmed out to bankers and to Arab and Pathān soldiers, who extorted as much money as they could from the cultivators. The farming system was abolished by Sir Sālār Jang immediately after his appointment as Minister, and from that date the prosperity of the people has increased.

Size of holdings and incidence of revenue.

The average area of a holding in the whole State is $20\frac{2}{3}$ acres, varying from $28\frac{1}{2}$ acres in Marāthwāra to $12\frac{1}{2}$ acres in Telingāna. In the Marāthā Districts the Government assessment on 'dry' lands ranges from Rs. 3-0-1 to R. 0-10-2 per acre, the average being R. 0-12-9, while for 'wet' and *bāghāt* (garden) lands the average is Rs. 4-5-6 per acre, the maximum being Rs. 15 and the minimum Rs. 1-2. In the Telingāna Districts the average assessment on 'dry' lands is R. 0-13-5 (maximum Rs. 4, minimum R. 0-1), and on 'wet' lands Rs. 9-4-2, the maximum and minimum being Rs. 24 and Rs. 3 respectively. The average rate per acre for the whole State is Rs. 1-3-8, but for Marāthwāra and Telingāna it is R. 0-14-3 and Rs. 1-13-10 respectively, the high rate of assessment and the smallness of holdings in Telingāna being due to the prevalence of 'wet' cultivation. No reliable figures are available to show the gross produce, and it is impossible to say what proportion the land revenue demand bears to it. No difficulty is experienced in collecting the revenue, and there is very little resort to coercive measures.

The general principle of assessment is to take half the net profits, after paying cost of cultivation, &c., as the State share.

Suspensions and remissions. In times of scarcity or famine, the demand is suspended and recovered in the following year; and remissions are also granted when distress is severe or when the ryot has lost his cattle. In Marāthwāra and in the settled Telingāna Districts, remissions are not granted for 'dry' land, as the assessment is very light. But in the unsettled Telingāna Districts, remissions are given on 'dry' lands affected by bad seasons, including excessive rain; and on 'wet' lands for want of water, including breach of tanks and decay of wells. These remissions are granted in ordinary years. Remissions are also given for 'wet' lands in settled Districts when the water-supply fails.

In the settled Districts the ordinary rates of assessment apply to the whole extent of the holding; but in the unsettled Districts only the cultivated area of a holding is assessed, and the revenue of the uncultivated portion is remitted on both 'wet' and 'dry' lands. Special rules have been made for encouraging ryots to plant mango groves, and land is given at 10 annas per acre for this purpose.

The ryot is free to transfer or sell his right of occupancy, and in this way much land has been acquired by professional money-lenders in the Marāthā Districts. The Telingāna ryot is just beginning to realize the value of occupancy rights.

Miscellaneous revenue. Under Miscellaneous Revenue are included opium and drugs, customs, excise, and stamps.

Opium and drugs. In accordance with the terms of an agreement made with the Government of India, the cultivation of poppy was prohibited in 1881, and all opium for consumption has since been imported from Mālwā under passes issued by the Opium Agent. The duty levied amounts to Rs. 15 per seer, of which Rs. 10 is paid on issue of the pass and the balance on the arrival of the opium. Contracts for the monopoly of retail vend are sold in each District and in the city circle. The right to sell hemp drugs (*gānja* and *bhang*) is also sold by auction.

	Average, 1882-90.	Average, 1891-1900.	1901.	1903.
	Rs.	Rs.	Rs.	Rs.
Opium	2,19,730	3,15,232	4,25,590	5,16,001
Gānja and *bhang* and other intoxicating drugs	...	...	64,328	74,949
Total	2,19,730	3,15,232	4,89,918	5,90,950

The number of chests of opium, containing 70 seers each, imported in 1901 was 249. The gross value of the opium imported during the decades 1881–90 and 1891–1900 (averages) and in 1901 was Rs. 2,49,630, Rs. 1,60,898, and Rs. 1,86,830 respectively. The net revenue realized from opium and hemp drugs since 1882 is given in the table on the preceding page.

Customs. Customs duty is levied on imports and exports at the rate of 5 per cent. *ad valorem*, which is the maximum fixed by treaty with the Government of India. British gold, silver, and copper coins, vegetables, certain seeds, wool, books and maps, building stone (except Shāhābād stone), dry and green grass, and firewood are all exempt from both export and import duty. Since 1885 the duty on bar silver has been raised to 10 per cent., to check its import for illicit coinage. Salt is imported from Bombay and Masulipatam by railway, and a duty of Rs. 2 per *palla* or three maunds (120 seers) is collected by the Customs department. The total quantity of salt imported and consumed in 1881–90, 1891–1900 (averages), and 1901 was 41,840, 43,910, and 46,810 tons respectively; and the consumption per head in 1881, 1891, and 1901 was 9½, 8½, and 9½ lb.

The following table shows the customs receipts for 1901 and 1903, including the duty on salt:—

	1901.	1903.
	Rs.	Rs.
Import duties	18,07,528	19,43,324
Export duties	25,32,100	28,13,552
Octroi*	1,92,372	2,39,719
Salt	8,73,782	8,59,760
Duties on wines and spirits	37,523	17,276
Miscellaneous	20,437	24,192
Total	54,63,742	58,97,823

* This duty is levied at Hyderābād, Secunderābād, and Bolārum on produce and manufactures of the State brought into these towns, the tariff being the same as for Customs duty.

Excise. The excise revenue is farmed at auction, by contracts for periods ranging from three to ten years. The chief sources of income are country spirits, toddy, and *mahuā* flowers. In the Districts country spirits are manufactured in out-stills, and there is no restriction as to the quantity or strength of liquor. At Secunderābād there is a State distillery. Contracts for drawing and selling of toddy are sold by *tāluks* in the Districts, while in the city circle, including Secunderābād and Bolārum, similar arrangements are made, besides which a *nazarāna* is levied on toddy shops, and a duty of 4 annas per pot of 20 seers. The duty on *mahuā* flowers is Rs. 16 per *palla* or three maunds.

The total receipts from excise for 1901 and 1903 are shown in the following table:—

	1901.	1903.
	Rs.	Rs.
Country liquor	6,37,592	10,83,730
Toddy	19,61,366	18,43,355
Mahuā flowers	7,10,251	9,70,804
Secunderābād contract . .	4,19,000	4,60,000
Total	37,28,209	43,57,889

Licences are granted for the sale of European liquor on payment of Rs. 30 a month. A private distillery has been licensed at Chādarghāt for the manufacture of rum after European methods from raw sugar and treacle.

Toddy is largely consumed in the Telingāna Districts, where the two kinds of toddy-palm (*Borassus flabellifer* and *Phoenix sylvestris*) are cultivated. In the Marāthā Districts the palm is rare, and the people use *mahuā* liquor to a much greater extent. There is a growing taste for European liquor in the city and suburbs and some of the District head-quarters. No special efforts have been made to restrict the consumption of intoxicants, though their increased cost, owing to better methods of administration, has had some effect. The incidence of excise revenue per head of population for the years 1901 and 1903 was respectively R. 0–5–7 and R. 0–6–3.

Postage and other stamps, post-cards, embossed envelopes, and stamp paper are all made at the Hyderābād Stamp Office. A discount of 5 per cent. is given to the vendors of all kinds of stamps. Until recently all the stamp paper used in Berār was also supplied from the Hyderābād Stamp Office, but since 1902 this has been discontinued. Most of the large *jāgīrdārs* who have their own courts are supplied with stamp paper at 25 per cent. of the full value of the stamp. Up to 1892 there were separate judicial and non-judicial stamps, but since that year all the stamps have been marked 'revenue.' Bad seasons affect the sale of stamps in a marked degree. The table on the next page shows the net revenue derived from the sale of stamps since 1881. Stamps.

In 1887 a cess of one anna per rupee of land revenue was imposed. It was at first levied only in settled Districts, but was subsequently introduced into Warangal District, in anticipation of settlement. An Act was passed in 1899 to legalize the levy of other cesses, such as lighting and cart and carriage tax; but these cesses have not yet been imposed. Local boards.

The Local Board department was first created in 1887, and was placed under a Central board at Hyderābād, composed of high officials. This *Sadr* or Central board was, however abolished in 1894, and the Sūbahdārs were empowered to sanction works up to Rs. 5,000, the general control being vested in the then Revenue Board, with powers to sanction up to Rs. 10,000, while estimates exceeding that amount were referred to the Minister.

	Average for ten years ending 1890.	Average for ten years ending 1900.	1901.	1903.
	Rs.	Rs.	Rs.	Rs.
Stamp paper	8,77,493	14,96,809	9,84,866	6,35,937
Postage stamps	31,008	46,671	57,696	58,913
Stamped envelopes	8,888	16,127	23,965	28,926
Post-cards	...	4,055	8,322	11,406
Hundi paper	...	5,212	4,839	2,630
Summons stamps	...	27,313	35,893	42,158
Receipt stamps	...	4,823	16,543	17,785
Hundi stamps	...	2,579	22,153	38,870
Total	9,17,389	16,03,889	11,54,277	8,36,625

Number and constitution of boards. In 1901 there were 13 District and 70 *tāluk* boards, consisting of 182 and 560 members respectively. The District board generally has the First Tālukdār as president and thirteen members, of whom seven are non-officials, selected from among the *zamīndārs*, respectable tradesmen, and pleaders; the official members, besides the president, are the revenue assistant at head-quarters, the District Engineer, the Superintendent of police, the District medical officer, the *tahsīldār* at head-quarters, and the head schoolmaster. The *tāluk* boards are subordinate to the District board, and are composed of two official members, the Second or Third Tālukdār in charge of the *taluk* and the *tahsīldār*, and three non-official members. The *tāluk* boards control the expenditure on work connected with their *tāluks* and sanctioned by the District board, and keep detailed accounts of such expenditure. The District boards have power to sanction works up to Rs. 2,000.

Objects of expenditure. The local cess provides funds for the construction and maintenance of roads, schools, dispensaries, resthouses, and other works calculated to benefit the inhabitants of the District. It is collected with each instalment of revenue paid by the cultivators and is credited in the accounts as follows: village police fund, 4 pies; educational fund, 2 pies; road fund, 2 pies; medical, 1 pie; and general improvement fund, 3 pies. The village police fund is credited to the State, which meets the cost of the village police, and the educational fund is controlled by the Educational department.

The work undertaken by these boards since they have been in effective existence has been of the following classes: repairs to local roads at the head-quarter towns, construction of roads to *tāluk* head-quarters, bridges, causeways, approaches to ferries, dispensaries, *chaurīs*, resthouses, *dharmsālas*, *sarais*, markets, drinking wells and gardens, expenditure on municipal conservancy, lighting, sanitation, town police, and local board schools. Vaccination and cattle disease have also received attention. During famines many new wells were dug and old wells cleaned and repaired. In fact, all local works are entrusted to the boards which are likely to promote the general health and convenience of the people. All these works are carried out by the local board engineers and are not in charge of Public Works officers. Working of the boards.

The following table shows the income of the boards:— Income.

	Average, 1891–1900.	1901.	1903.
	Rs.	Rs.	Rs.
Provincial rates	40,864	40,093	42,920
Interest	...	549	108
Education	1,42,868	1,36,620	1,96,117
Medical	36,566	68,154	98,064
Miscellaneous	3,68,535	5,20,291	5,47,333
Public works	3,87,493	3,77,670	4,97,465
Ferries	23,701	27,309	22,470
Total	10,00,027	11,70,686	14,04,477

'Provincial rates' here means toll tax and fees collected at fairs and places of pilgrimage. Under 'miscellaneous' are included refunds, fines, school fees, income from public gardens, district municipalities, and deposits. 'Education' and 'medical' represent the two pies and one pie set apart from the local cess for these purposes.

The following table shows the expenditure:— Expenditure.

	Average, 1891–1900.	1901.	1903.
	Rs.	Rs.	Rs.
Education	1,70,868	93,592	1,73,501
Medical	6,478	43,877	67,023
Miscellaneous	3,10,852	2,31,685	7,22,519
Public works	4,17,758	3,62,151	4,41,357
Total	9,05,956	7,31,305	14,04,400

The tables of income and expenditure refer to the whole

State, except the Districts of Karīmnagar (Elgandal), Nalgonda, Adilābād (Sirpur Tāndūr), and the Crown District of Atrāf-i-balda. The allotments for education and medical are both spent through the General departmental Secretary on the establishments of the Educational department, the normal school, and the secretariat, and the travelling expenses of the inspectors of schools, house rent, scholarships, prizes, and repairs to buildings, and in the medical department for allowances to establishments and vaccinators. Under 'miscellaneous' are included the pay of the police, the *pātels'* salaries, health officers' allowance, the upkeep of public gardens, the planting of roadside trees, &c.

Municipal government. The city and suburbs.

Municipal administration was first introduced in Hyderābād in 1869, when the city proper was divided into four, and the suburbs into five, divisions for municipal purposes, the whole management being placed under a municipal superintendent. In 1881 the suburban area was handed over to a separate officer, both the officers being thenceforward designated secretaries to the two municipalities of Hyderābād city and Chādarghāt. In 1903 the two municipalities were amalgamated and placed under a special officer, styled the secretary to the committee. The members of the committee, who are called municipal commissioners, number twenty-seven. The president and some of the members are officials, the remainder being selected from the *vakīls* of the High Court, bankers, representatives of the *Sarf-i-khās* and *paigāh* departments, and other persons not in State service.

Other municipalities.

Sanitation and conservancy were also provided for in the Divisional, District, and *tāluk* head-quarters; but regular arrangements and the appointment of committees were effected only after the establishment of local boards and the levy of the one anna cess, from which municipal expenditure is met, as well as that of the District and local boards. The members of the local boards are also members of the municipal committees at the Divisional and District head-quarters. Excluding the city, there were 21 municipalities in the State in 1901. In 14 of these the population ranged from 10,000 to 37,000, and in the remaining 7 from 4,800 to nearly 10,000. They comprise the Divisional and District head-quarter towns, and a few of the *tāluk* head-quarters.

Taxation.

The incidence of taxation per head of population in the city and Chādarghāt municipalities in 1901 was R. 0-8-2 and R. 0-7-8 respectively, the chief items of receipt being hackney carriage licences, bazars, slaughter-houses, rents, and house tax.

The latter is levied at the rate of 3 per cent. on the annual rent. A water tax has been levied in the city since 1897, and in Chādarghāt since 1896. Among the results of municipal administration may be mentioned the widening of narrow streets and lanes, the construction of sewers and drains, and the supply of pure filtered water to the city from the Mīr Alam tank, and to Chādarghāt from the Husain Sāgar tank.

The Public Works department was first organized in 1868, when a Chief Engineer, with a staff of assistants, was appointed, and a code was compiled for their guidance. The Chief Engineer exercised a general control over the department, and audited the entire expenditure. The State was divided into fourteen districts, each under a district engineer. In 1869 a departmental Minister was appointed to work under the Minister, the Chief Engineer being secretary in the department. In 1875 the department was reorganized into two distinct branches, administrative and executive, the immediate head of the former being the Minister, and that of the latter the departmental Minister, styled the *Sadr-ul-Mahām*, while a secretary was appointed for each branch. The Municipal and Irrigation departments remained separate, and had not shown much progress, but were amalgamated with the Public Works department in 1884–5, the latter being separated from the Buildings and Roads branch in 1887. Subsequently the designation of the *Sadr-ul-Mahām* was changed to that of *Muīn-ul-Mahām*, who became head of both branches of control and executive, and was made an Assistant to the Minister. In 1894, owing to the increase in the volume of work, the office of secretary in the Public Works department was separated from that of Chief Engineer, and business connected with railways and mines, municipalities, and telephones was entrusted to the charge of the former. Since 1901, cases connected with railways and mines have been dealt with by the secretary in the Financial department. Public works.

Other changes have been made in the administration of the department, which at present is organized as follows: At the head is an Assistant Minister, styled the *Muīn-ul-Mahām*. Under him is a secretary, who holds charge of the administrative section, divided into two branches known as the Irrigation and the General branches, the latter including buildings, roads, water-works, municipalities, and telephones. A Superintending Engineer holds executive and partial administrative charge of the Irrigation branch, and a Superintending Engineer is at the head of the General branch. These two Present organization.

officers, the secretary to the municipal committee, and the superintendents of the public gardens and telephone departments are all under the secretary.

Buildings and roads branch.

Work in the Districts is supervised by the District Engineers, who are in charge of the construction and repairs of civil buildings and roads. At present 1,614 miles of roads are maintained by the department at an annual expenditure of about $5\frac{1}{2}$ lakhs, while others are in course of construction.

Works executed.

The more important works executed during the past few years include the African cavalry guard lines, commanding officers' quarters at Sūrāpur, military lines at Naldrug, an armoury and general hospital at Golconda, bandsmen's lines at Chādarghāt, the palace at Surūrnagar, the Malakpet State stables, the *thagī* jail, police barracks, Government House and the Commissioner's court at Hanamkonda, revenue survey offices at Raichūr, Gulbarga, and Hanamkonda, Central jails at Aurangābād, Gulbarga, and Warangal, and jails at Nānder and Medak, a clock-tower and medical storeroom at Hyderābād city, dispensaries at Nānder, Wādi, Bhongīr, Nalgonda, Nizāmābād, Makhtal, Hingoli, and Yādgir, the Race Stand, the Public Works office, and the Afzal Ganj hospital at Hyderābād city. The roads constructed have already been referred to. Important bridges have been made in Gulbarga District and over part of the Husain Sāgar tank.

Drainage and waterworks.

At Hyderābād city the Murkinalla drain has been diverted and improved, the Afzal Sāgar and Shāh Ganj drains have been constructed, and a channel made from the public gardens to the Gosha Mahal *kunta*. Hyderābād (with Chādarghāt), Aurangābād, and Nizāmābād are the only towns at present provided with regular systems of water-supply, executed under the supervision and control of the department. Those at Hyderābād and Aurangābād were constructed, and are maintained, at the cost of the State, while the Nizāmābād supply was paid for by the Rānī of Sirnapalli but is maintained from Local funds.

Telephones.

A telephone department was formed in 1884. It was organized by the Bombay Telephone Company and worked by them for eight months, after which it was taken over by the State. The principal nobles of the State, wealthy private individuals, and all important officials are subscribers to the system. The annual upkeep costs Rs. 15,000, and the fees collected from the non-official class of subscribers amount to Rs. 10,000. The total number of offices and dwelling-houses to which the wires are laid is 154, including 71 State instalments.

The Irrigation and the General branches of the Public Works department were separated in 1888, the former dealing with irrigation works only. In 1896, when it was found that the larger tanks required not only extensive repairs but restoration also, it was considered expedient to form a separate Irrigation department under a Chief Engineer, whose services had been lent to the State by the Government of India. The Irrigation board was abolished, and the posts of Superintending and Divisional Engineers were also dispensed with, the Chief Engineer submitting his proposals, &c., relating to irrigation works to Government through the Public Works secretary. Under the Chief Engineer are seven Irrigation engineers, one for each District, with an adequate subordinate staff and establishment, who are responsible for the maintenance of all irrigation works in their respective Districts. The designation of Chief Engineer was again changed to that of Superintending Engineer towards the close of 1903. Irrigation.

The operations of the Irrigation department have been practically confined to the Telingāna and Carnatic Districts. The Marāthā Districts are now being surveyed, to ascertain suitable sites for extensive storage works, so as to ensure a supply of water in all years, as well as to afford useful employment to labourers in those Districts.

The irrigation works completed during the three years 1901–3 were of three distinct classes: (*a*) original works, including reconstruction of abandoned works; (*b*) restoration of recently damaged works; and (*c*) extensions and improvements. The amount spent on class (*a*) during the three years was 48·7 lakhs, on class (*b*) 60·4 lakhs, and on class (*c*) 89·5 lakhs, the aggregate being 199 lakhs. The increase of revenue derived from these was 1·2 lakhs, 5·8 lakhs, and 3·2 lakhs respectively, the total increase of revenue thus exceeding 10 lakhs, or 5 per cent. on the capital outlay.

The total expenditure on public works rose from an average of 18 lakhs in the decade 1881–90 to 23 lakhs in the next decade, and was $31\frac{1}{2}$ lakhs in 1901–2 and 36·2 lakhs in 1903. Since 1895 the expenditure on each branch has been separately recorded. That of the General branch decreased from $18\frac{3}{4}$ lakhs in 1895 to $14\frac{1}{4}$ in 1901, while the cost of irrigation works rose from 7 lakhs to $16\frac{3}{4}$ lakhs. Expenditure.

The total strength of the State army in 1901 was 24,012 men, classed as regular (6,481) or irregular (17,531). The regular troops consist of three regiments of cavalry (915 strong), two regiments of Imperial Service cavalry (806), three batteries State army.

of artillery (360), and six regiments of Hyderābād infantry (4,400). Small detachments of the infantry regiments are stationed at Aurangābād, Gulbarga, Nizāmābād, and Warangal, to guard the jails at those places. Strong detachments from the cavalry regiments have latterly been posted at Amba (Mominābād) and Hingoli, since their vacation by the Hyderābād Contingent. The irregular troops consist of 2,679 horse and 14,852 foot. Of these, 3,152 infantry and 1,355 cavalry are stationed at various posts to guard the jails, while the cavalry also escort the British and Nizām's posts. A small Volunteer Corps, called 'His Highness the Nizām's Own Mounted Volunteers,' numbers 120. In 1903 the total strength of the army was 24,035, the regulars and irregulars being 6,535 and 17,500 respectively. The expenditure on the army averaged 68.8 lakhs between 1881 and 1890, 69.4 lakhs during the next decade, and was 63.9 lakhs in 1901 and 63.7 lakhs in 1904.

Imperial forces.

The total strength of the British army stationed within the State in 1903 consisted of 2,988 European and 5,549 Native troops. Hyderābād is partly in the Secunderābād division, which was in 1903 directly under the Commander-in-Chief, and partly in the Poona division of the Southern Command. The military stations at present are Bolārum and Secunderābād in the former, and Aurangābād in the latter. The headquarters of the Hyderābād Volunteer Rifles are at Secunderābād, and detachments of the Berār Volunteer Rifles and Great Indian Peninsula Railway Volunteer Rifles are also located within the State. The total strength of these in 1903 was 1,278.

Police and jails.

Prior to the ministry of the late Sir Sālār Jang, there was no organized police in the State, and the arrangements made in the different Divisions depended to a great extent on the revenue officials. In 1866, when Districts were first formed, a regular police force was also raised and placed under the revenue authorities, but the system did not work satisfactorily. In 1869 a special *Sadr-ul-Mahām* or Police Minister was appointed, with full powers over the police. A year later *Sadr Mohtamims* were appointed, one for each Division; but their appointments were abolished in 1884, and an Inspector-General of District Police was appointed, the designation of *Sadr-ul-Mahām* being changed to *Muīn-ul-Mahām* or Assistant Minister, Police department. The District police were placed under the First Tālukdār, and the District Police Superintendent was made his executive deputy. Subsequently a detective branch was organized, under an officer deputed from the Berār force. Besides the city police, which is quite separate from that of the District police, there are three distinct police jurisdictions in the State: the *Sarf-i-khās*, the *Dīwāni* or *Khālsa*, and the *paigāh* and *jāgīr* police.

The supervising staff consists of an Inspector-General, 5 Assistants, 17 *Mohtamims* or Superintendents, 17 Assistant Superintendents, and 119 *Amīns* or inspectors; while the subordinate force comprises foot and mounted police, numbering 11,173 and 413 respectively. In addition to the regular force, the rural police are under the revenue officers or Tālukdārs, and have scarcely any connexion with the District police. They include 12,776 police *pātels*, 2,798 *kotwāls*, and 17,532 *rāmosīs* or watchmen, numbering altogether 33,106. **Present organization.**

The following table gives statistics of number and pay in 1901 and 1903:—

Particulars.	1901.		1903.	
	Number.	Pay.	Number.	Pay.
Dīwāni.		Rs.		Rs.
Supervising staff .	142	2,03,460	139	2,00,580
Subordinate staff .	40,008	18,95,850	38,293	19,41,990
Sarf-i-khās.				
Supervising staff .	17	22,260	20	26,520
Subordinate staff .	4,684	1,99,155	6,265	3,05,013
Total	44,851	23,20,725	44,717	24,74,103

The strength of the regular force is equivalent to one policeman to every 990 persons in the *Dīwāni* and to 609 in the *Sarf-i-khās*, while there is one policeman to 7·1 and 4·3 square miles in those areas.

Recruits are medically examined as to their physical fitness, and their character is verified. The maximum age of recruits is 25, and their minimum height 5 feet 5 inches. The recruit on enlistment undergoes a year's course of training at District head-quarters in law and procedure, drill, gymnastics, signalling, &c. Educated natives are averse to police service, owing to the low scale of pay offered. The detective branch is under a selected officer, who has an assistant and a staff of *amīns*, *jemadārs*, *daffadārs*, and constables working under him. This branch has done excellent service in arresting a large number of notorious dacoits and other criminals. A system of identification by means of finger-prints was introduced in 1898, and has been successful. The District police are armed with muzzle-loaders of an old and inferior type, but the officers are provided with swords and pistols. No special military police force is maintained in the State.

City police. The city police is quite distinct from the District police and is under a Commissioner, known as the *Kotwāl*, who exercises control within the municipal area. The total strength of this force is about 3,000, including 50 mounted men and nearly 100 Arabs; and the cost was 4·4 lakhs in 1901.

Railway police. The railway police is a distinct corps and has no connexion with the District police. In 1871 through traffic was established between Bombay and Madras, necessitating the employment of 117 officers and men. This force has been gradually increased as new lines were opened, and in 1903 consisted of 520 men and officers under a Superintendent, the proportion being one man to every 1·6 miles of railway. A small body of specially selected men are employed as detectives, who travel in all passenger trains, and have been instrumental in bringing professional thieves to justice. There are 8 lock-ups in charge of the railway police, but prisoners are sent to the Secunderābād jail to serve their term.

The following table gives the results of cases dealt with by the *Dīwāni*, *Sarf-i-khās*, and railway police:—

	Average of five years ending 1901.			
	Dīwāni.	*Sarf-i-khās.*	Railway.	Total.
Number of cases reported	7,806	971	247	9,024
Number of cases decided in criminal courts	3,767	441	157	4,365
Number of cases ending in acquittal	1,746	178	9	1,933
Number of cases ending in conviction	2,021	263	148	2,432

Jails. The administration of jails is in charge of the Inspector-General of Police, who is also the Inspector-General of Prisons. Each of the outlying Central jails is in charge of a Superintendent, controlled by the First Tālukdār in his capacity of *Nāzim-i-Mahābis* or Inspector of jails. The Third Tālukdārs or head-quarters *tahsīldārs* supervise District jails. The Central jail at Hyderābād is also in charge of a Superintendent, who is directly subordinate to the Inspector-General of Prisons. Central jails are maintained at Hyderābād, Aurangābād, Gulbarga, Warangal, and Nizāmābād, and District jails at the head-quarters of other Districts. Lock-ups or subsidiary jails are located in some of the *tāluk* offices. The average jail mortality in 1891 was 28·9; but in 1901 it rose to 65·3 per 1,000, owing to the effects of famine on the population and also to cholera, the mortality for the same years at the Central jail at Hyderābād city being only 17·7 and 13·9 respectively. Tents, rugs, and carpets of all descriptions, belts and shoes, table linen and towels, furniture, *tātpattis*, cotton tweeds, checks and shirtings, and police clothing and dress for office peons are made in the jails. Printing work and bookbinding are also done, and the *Jarīda* or *State Gazette*, as well as a large quantity of vernacular litho-printing, is turned out by the Hyderābād Central jail press. The total expenditure in 1901 was 5·2 lakhs, but the jails were then unusually full owing to the bad season. More detailed statistics of the jails in the State are given in Table VII (p. 87) at the end of this article.

Education. History.

Indigenous schools of the ordinary Indian type are found in many places. Reading, writing, and elementary arithmetic are taught, and the teacher is generally paid in kind, his income varying according to the size and importance of the village. The first English public school at Hyderābād city was opened in 1834 by a clergyman of the Church of England, followed shortly after by a Roman Catholic school. An Arabic and Persian school was also founded in the city about the same time by the first Amīr-i-kabīr, a liberal patron of learning, and himself a mathematician of no mean order. State education commenced in 1854, when a school called the Dār-ul-ulūm was founded in the city of Hyderābād. In 1859 orders were issued directing that two schools, one Persian and the other vernacular, should be opened in each *tāluk*, and one at the headquarters of each District. Committees were appointed to supervise these schools, consisting, in the case of *tāluk* schools, of two *pātels* and two *patwāris*, with the *tahsīldār* as president, and for District schools of a *pātel*, a *patwāri*, the *tahsīldār*, and the police inspector, with the Third Tālukdār as president. The last-named officer was *ex-officio* educational inspector of the District, and, as such, had to examine all schools during his tours. Education was thus entirely in the hands of the revenue authorities, and did not receive due attention.

In 1868 education was transferred to the Assistant Minister of what was then called the Miscellaneous department, and all candidates for masterships were required to go through a training at the Dār-ul-ulūm and obtain certificates. Two years later the control of public instruction was handed over to the late Mr. Wilkinson, then Principal of the Engineering College; but this change had no effect outside the city of Hyderābād. Here, however, it led to the splitting up of the Dār-ul-ulūm into five branch schools, and the establishment of an Anglo-vernacular school. In 1871 a Director of Vernacular Education was appointed, who improved the system of District schools; but the actual management remained in the hands of revenue officials as before, entailing much delay in the administration. Under this cumbrous system all circular orders issued from the office of the Director of Public Instruction had to pass through the hands of the entire series of revenue officials before they reached the various schools in the Districts.

Later developments. In 1872 there were sixteen schools in the city and suburbs, in one of which English was taught. The Districts contained 125 vernacular schools. The decade 1871–80 saw a great development in educational matters. In 1875 five deputy-inspectors were appointed for the Districts, relieving the revenue officials of educational work. Two years later the Anglo-vernacular high school in the city was abolished, and its pupils transferred to the Chādarghāt school. An Anglo-vernacular school was also opened for the first time at Aurangābād. In 1878 the payment of fees was made compulsory in the District schools. About 1880 the Chādarghāt high school was affiliated to the Madras University as a second-grade college; and in 1881 it was raised to the rank of a first-grade college. During this decade two important schools were opened to educate the higher classes in the city. The *Madrasa-i-Aliya*, which had been opened as a private school under English teachers for the education of Sir Sālār Jang's sons and relations, became a public school for the education of the higher classes, and as such has since had an uninterrupted career of success. In the year 1879 there were only 19 pupils on the rolls, the cost to the State per head being Rs. 1,643, whereas the school now has 200 pupils, and the cost per head is only Rs. 70 to Rs. 80. The *Madrasa-i-Aizza* was opened under private agency for pupils of the same class, lower fees being charged, and a number of scholarships being granted.

Present constitution. As at present constituted the Educational department is under a Director of Public Instruction, whose proposals are submitted to the Minister through the Secretary in the Judicial, Police, and General departments and through the Assistant Minister for education. No officers are recruited in England, except a few of the staff of the Chādarghāt high school, now called the Nizām College. The work of inspection is carried on by five chief Inspectors. Until about ten years ago all the schools in the State were directly under the department. Gradually, however, schools are being transferred to the local boards, but it is impossible as yet for the State to withdraw altogether from the management of these schools.

University education.

There are three Arts colleges: the Nizām College at Hyderābād (first grade), the Aurangābād College (second grade), both affiliated to the Madras University, and the Dār-ul-ulūm or Oriental College, which sends up candidates for the Punjab Oriental titles examinations. All three are purely State institutions. Although an excellent boarding-house is attached to the Nizām College, the accommodation available is so limited, and the fees so high, that the poorer students who come from outside are not able to take advantage of it. Something is being done to provide hostels for the students at some of the District high schools.

The following table illustrates the progress made in university education:—

Passes in	1881.	1891.	1901.	1903.
Matriculation	3	42	18	13
First Intermediate in Arts or Science	2	3	4	3
Ordinary Bachelors' degrees	1	1	20	8
Higher and special degrees	...	14	47	...

Secondary education.

In 1901 the number of high schools was 16, two new ones having been added during the decade between 1891 and 1900. In all the high schools for boys English is treated as the first language, and the curriculum leads up to the Madras matriculation. The middle schools prepare pupils for the local middle school examination. In 38 English is the first language, while 15 are purely vernacular. Of the high schools, 8 are supported by the State, 7 are aided, and one is unaided, while the middle schools include 38 State, 9 aided, and 6 unaided. At present no secondary schools are under the local boards. In 1901 these schools were attended by 1·5 per cent. of the population of school-going age.

Primary education.

In 1883 there were 148 primary schools, of which 13 were at the capital. The total number of pupils attending these schools was 7,757, representing 0·5 per cent. of the population of school-going age. In 1891 the percentage rose to 2·5. In 1901 the number of primary schools increased to 753, and the number of pupils to 41,876, giving a percentage under instruction of 2·4 to children of school-going age in that year. A system of grading the teachers has recently been introduced; and all the masters in primary schools, who formerly possessed no qualifications as a rule, are being gradually passed through the normal school. Some of the lower primary masters still receive Rs. 7, Rs. 8, or Rs. 9 a month, but a minimum of Rs. 10 is being introduced. Roughly the rate of pay may be said to be from Rs. 10 to Rs. 15 in a lower primary school, and from Rs. 15 to Rs. 25 in an upper primary. The inspectors are allowed to use their discretion in agricultural tracts in dispensing with full-time attendance during the months when the children's services are required in the fields.

Female education. Here, as elsewhere in India, the education of girls has not kept pace with that of boys, and the number of children under instruction is 6·1 per cent. on the school-going age population for boys, and only 0·5 for girls. Progress in this direction is slow, and as far as the Districts are concerned is hardly satisfactory. On the reorganization of the department in 1885, the State contained, outside the capital, only one Korān school for girls, with an attendance of 30. Another school was opened to provide for a head-master who had lost his eyesight, his wife being appointed mistress. There were at this time three English middle schools at the capital, with a total attendance of 224 girls, and 4 English and an equal number of vernacular primary schools, attended by 99 and 323 girls respectively. The number of schools for girls was 71 in 1891 and 77 in 1901; and in the last year the total number of female pupils was 4,467. Most of the girls' schools are directly under the State, but local boards have now taken over some of these schools.

There are three main obstacles in the way of progress. The first is the reluctance of Muhammadans to teach their daughters anything beyond their scriptures; but popular sentiment is slowly giving way, and reading, writing, and arithmetic up to an elementary standard are now taught in most of the schools, besides needlework, and in one school cooking. Early marriage among Hindus is the next difficulty, but this is not of so great importance in view of the very elementary instruction it is proposed to impart. The greatest difficulty, however, is the absence of trained mistresses. The pay offered is too small to attract outsiders, and there is as yet no training school for school-mistresses. No tangible impression can be made until this want is supplied. The most notable feature under the head of female education is the foundation of a high-class *zanāna* school at Hyderābād. This institution has since its foundation succeeded to a certain extent in turning out fairly well-educated members of the gentler sex, whose influence on public opinion is evidenced by an increasing desire on the part of parents of the higher classes to procure a sound education for their daughters, either by engaging the services of competent governesses at home, or sending them to this or some school outside the State. The *zanāna* school, with a roll of 41 girls, has a larger though still somewhat insufficient staff of European and native teachers; English, Arabic, and Persian are taught, besides the usual branches that form the curriculum of an upper middle school for girls. It is expected before long to take rank as a high school. The girls' schools established by the Wesleyan and American Missionary Societies are invariably well managed and do a great amount of good work.

Special schools.

A small engineering school, first opened at Warangal for the purpose of training young men for the subordinate grades of the Public Works department, was transferred to Hyderābād in 1896. A law school with two lecturers was organized in 1899. There is also a medical school at Hyderābād, supported by the State, of which the Residency Surgeon is the principal. It has, however, no connexion with the Educational department. A thriving normal school exists at the capital, through which all teachers of primary schools are being gradually passed, while another for girls at Secunderābād, founded by the Wesleyan Mission, supplies teachers for the girls' schools under that agency and is doing excellent work. The industrial school at Aurangābād was established about 1889, and has done a great deal to revive and improve many industries for which that place was once famous. Another industrial school was opened at Warangal in 1890, and has been transferred to Hyderābād, where it is doing good work. A Sanskrit school, started at Hyderābād in 1899, is aided by the State.

European and Eurasian education.

Provision is made for the education of Europeans and Eurasians in eight schools at the capital, which receive grants from the British Government and work under the Bengal code for European schools. Three of them receive an additional grant from the Hyderābād State. In 1901 these schools contained 650 pupils. Some of the pupils find employment as officers in the Hyderābād regular troops, while the Nizām's Guaranteed State Railway, in its various departments, provides for others.

Muhammadan education.

While the Muhammadans form only 10·4 per cent. of the population of the State, they include 83 per cent. of the students in colleges, 45 per cent. of the pupils in secondary, and 42 per cent. of the pupils in primary schools. These results are due to the position held by Muhammadans in a

State of which the ruler belongs to their religion. It is noticeable that the Hindus are more successful in examinations, proportionately to their numbers, than the Muhammadans.

Education of low castes.

Of the aboriginal tribes, the Gonds and Lambādis form the majority, but none avail themselves of the opportunities for educating their children placed within their reach. The Bhīls, chiefly found in the Aurangābād Division, are beginning to send their children to school. The schools throughout the State are open to children of all castes without distinction; but in practice few of the lower classes avail themselves of the permission, partly owing to the prejudices of the higher castes. In 1901, 23 boys belonging to the aboriginal tribes and 626 outcastes were at school, the greater number of the latter being found in the different mission schools.

According to the Census of 1901 literate persons numbered 29.55 per 1,000 of the total population, but taking males and females separately, the proportions are 54.7 and 3.4 respectively. Persons literate in English were 1.3 per 1,000 of the total population. Of the various religions, the Christians were far ahead of the others in point of literacy, there being 443 literate persons in every 1,000 professing that faith. The Musalmāns came next with 54, while the Hindus and Animists followed with 25 and 1 respectively.

Particulars of the expenditure on education and number of institutions and scholars will be found in Tables VIII and IX (p. 88).

News-papers.

The first systematic attempt to control the Press and the registration of books and newspapers in the State was made in 1886. The total number of newspapers and periodicals published in 1901 was 14, of which 12 were in Urdū, and 2 in Urdū and Marāthī combined. No English papers are issued here, although several published elsewhere have a large circulation in the State, and are mainly devoted to Hyderābād affairs. Seven of the fourteen were newspapers, and the remainder monthly magazines. Politics are discussed in the former, while the latter are devoted to legal, social, and literary topics. The *Mushīr-i-Deccan*, a daily paper, has the largest circulation.

Books.

The total number of books registered in 1901 was 23, which may be classified according to their subject matter as follows: law (6), history (2), religion (4), poetry (3), medical (1), mathematics (1), fiction (2), and miscellaneous (4). Apart from an Urdū translation of the biography of the late Amīr of Kābul, these books are more or less original in character.

The first medical institution opened in the State was the Hyderābād Medical School, founded in 1846, which has done much useful work in training medical officers and subordinates for the Hyderābād medical service, and hospital assistants for Berār. At first instruction was imparted in Urdū, but since 1884 English has been the medium. Till 1885 a board of medical officers from Secunderābād conducted the examinations; but since that year the written part has been supervised by a board of examiners of the Madras Medical College or the Grant Medical College at Bombay, the oral examination being conducted by a medical board from Secunderābād. The course is approximately the same as the L. M. & S. of the Madras University. Medical.

At present the State Medical department is under a Director, who is also the Residency Surgeon, assisted by a competent staff of surgeons at head-quarters. The District staff consists of from 3 to 5 surgeons, 1 to 5 hospital assistants, 4 to 7 compounders, and from 5 to 11 vaccinators, according to the extent and requirements of each District. Most of the surgeons are passed students of the Hyderābād Medical School. There are two lady doctors at Aurangābād; while Gulbarga, Raichūr, and Warangal Districts each have one. At Hyderābād a large staff of medical men is maintained, there being 15 surgeons, 7 hospital assistants, 24 compounders, and 11 vaccinators, besides a number of nurses with diplomas who tend the sick in the hospitals. The total strength for the State is 74 surgeons, 12 lady doctors, 31 hospital assistants, 104 compounders, and 116 vaccinators. Present organization.

Statistics are only available from 1884–5. In that year there were 6 hospitals in the city and suburbs and 48 dispensaries in the Districts. By 1891 the number of dispensaries had increased to 67, and in 1901 it rose to 84. The total number of out-patients treated in all institutions in 1884–5, 1891, and 1901 was 292,515, 384,660, and 636,044 respectively. The 'major' operations performed in the same years were 393, 3,313, and 4,628, while 'minor' operations numbered 3,377, 16,795, and 15,007. In the *zanāna* department for *pardā* females attached to the Afzal Ganj Hospital at Hyderābād city, the number of cases treated in 1901 was about 3,000 and the operations performed 2,000. The whole cost of the department is met from State funds, and the expenditure in 1901 was 5·4 lakhs. Hospitals and dispensaries.

No separate lunatic asylum is maintained, though there is some accommodation for lunatics in the Hyderābād Central Lunatic asylums.

jail. In 1891 this contained 7 criminal and 29 other lunatics, while in 1901 their numbers were 21 and 109 respectively. The whole of the expenditure is borne by the State, the cost in 1891 and 1901 being Rs. 2,411 and Rs. 9,600 respectively. The principal cause of insanity is said to be the use of narcotic drugs and spirits.

Vaccination. Vaccination was commenced in 1884–5, when 48 vaccinators were employed, and the number of successful operations was 44,062, the cost per case being Rs. 1–3. In 1891 there were 76,880 successful cases, while in 1901 the number was only 37,880. The increase in 1891 was due to the larger number of vaccinators employed by the local boards, while in 1901 a large number of vaccinators were deputed on famine and plague duty. The cost of the department in 1891 and 1901 was Rs. 49,160 and Rs. 57,302 respectively; the average per successful case for these years being R. 0–10–3 and Rs. 1–3. Operations are carried out exclusively with calf lymph, which is prepared at the vaccination dépôt in the State. Vaccination is performed according to the European method, and inoculation does not seem to be practised.

Surveys. Hyderābād State was included in the Great Trigonometrical Survey. The subsequent topographical surveys were based on, or extended from, the main series of triangulation. The Darbār co-operated in this important work. It appears probable that Todar Mal's revenue system was introduced in most of the Marāthā Districts of the State early in the seventeenth century by Malik Ambar and Murshid Kuli Khān, and was based on a rough survey of lands. On the formation of regular Districts about 1865–6, the *bīgha* of 3,600 square yards was taken as a standard, and lands were roughly measured. About 1876 it was decided to commence accurate survey operations, and the work was first undertaken in Aurangābād District, and subsequently extended to other *tāluks* and Districts. In this systematic survey the areas were reckoned in English acres. The Aurangābād and Gulbarga Divisions were surveyed and settled by the end of 1894. The Bīdar and Warangal Divisions were also surveyed and settled by the end of 1904 and 1905, the only portions still remaining unsurveyed and unsettled being the District of Adilābād (Sirpur Tāndūr) and certain *tāluks* of Karīmnagar (Elgandal) District.

Bibliography. [Syed Hossain Bilgrami and C. Willmott, *Historical and Descriptive Sketch of the Nizam's Dominions*, 2 vols. (Bombay, 1883–4); *Gazetteer of Aurangabad* (Bombay, 1884); Hastings Fraser, *Memoir and Correspondence of Colonel James Stuart*

Fraser (1885); Meadows Taylor, *Story of My Life*, 2 vols. (1877); J. S. King, *The History of the Bahmani Dynasty* (1900); J. D. B. Gribble, *A History of the Deccan* (1896); Mirza Mehdy Khān, *Hyderabad Census Report*, 1901; A. J. Dunlop, *Administration Report of the Nizam's Dominions for* 1303 *and* 1304–7 *Fasli* (1894 and 1895–8); *Report on the Famine Relief Operations in the Nizam's Dominions in* 1899–1900; *Departmental Administration Reports*.]

TABLE I. DISTRIBUTION OF POPULATION, HYDERĀBĀD STATE, 1901

District or State.	Area in square miles.	Number of towns.	Number of villages.	Total Population. Persons.	Total Population. Males.	Total Population. Females.	Urban Population. Persons.	Urban Population. Males.	Urban Population. Females.	Persons per square mile in rural areas.
Atrāf-i-balda, including Hyderābād city and suburbs	3,399	1	847	869,168	446,258	422,910	448,466	232,295	216,171	125
Medak (Gulshanābād) Division.										
Indūr (Nizāmābād)	4,822	7	1,152	634,588	316,528	318,060	53,806	26,482	27,324	120
Medak (Gulshanābād)	2,005	3	631	366,722	186,272	180,450	20,285	10,460	9,825	173
Mahbūbnagar	6,543	2	1,353	705,725	357,098	348,627	19,616	9,942	9,674	105
Nalgonda	4,143	2	972	699,779	374,577	325,202	11,695	5,955	5,740	166
Total	17,513	14	4,108	2,406,814	1,234,475	1,172,339	105,402	52,839	52,563	131
Warangal Division.										
Warangal	9,729	3	1,488	952,646	496,041	456,605	28,242	15,517	12,725	95
Elgandal (Karīmnagar)	7,203	7	1,516	1,035,582	540,649	494,933	49,372	25,662	23,710	136
Sirpur Tāndūr (Adilābād)	5,029	1	983	272,815	137,572	135,243	6,303	2,976	3,327	53
Total	21,961	11	3,987	2,261,043	1,174,262	1,086,781	83,917	44,155	39,762	99
Gulbarga Division.										
Gulbarga	4,092	7	1,102	742,745	376,876	365,869	69,223	35,557	33,666	165
Osmānābād	4,010	6	860	535,027	270,924	264,103	46,743	23,701	23,042	122
Raichūr	3,604	6	893	509,249	256,332	252,917	58,113	27,558	30,555	126
Lingsugūr	4,879	7	1,266	675,813	338,415	337,398	46,996	23,212	23,784	129
Bīdar	4,168	7	1,457	766,129	385,067	381,062	53,585	26,468	27,117	171
Total	20,753	33	5,578	3,228,963	1,627,614	1,601,349	274,660	136,496	138,164	142
Aurangābād Division.										
Aurangābād	6,172	5	1,825	721,407	361,082	360,325	82,355	41,846	40,509	103
Parbhani	5,091	7	1,495	645,765	323,312	322,453	59,648	30,161	29,487	115
Nānder	3,349	4	1,170	503,684	251,081	252,603	34,375	17,182	17,193	140
Bhīr	4,460	4	1,000	492,258	248,151	244,107	43,286	22,338	20,948	101
Total	19,072	20	5,490	2,363,114	1,183,626	1,179,488	219,664	111,527	108,137	112
Railways	...	...	...	12,040	7,394	4,646	...	...	...	...
Grand total	82,698	79	20,010	11,141,142	5,673,629	5,467,513	1,132,109	577,312	554,797	121

TABLE II

Statistics of Agriculture, Hyderābād State

(In square miles)

	1881-90 (average).	1891-1900 (average).	1901.	1903.
Total area	33,281	40,861	47,096	60,734
Total uncultivated area	12,608	13,375	16,854	28,862
Cultivable, but not cultivated	5,061	5,270	5,997	6,172
Uncultivable	7,547	8,105	10,857	22,690
Total area cultivated	20,673	27,486	30,242	31,872
Irrigated from canals	41	57	46	48
,, ,, wells and tanks	687	1,156	1,579	1,732
,, ,, other sources	37	29	34	36
Total area irrigated	765	1,242	1,659	1,816
Unirrigated area	19,908	26,244	28,583	30,056
Cropped area.				
Rice	1,032	1,180	1,358	1,402
Wheat	761	873	914	941
Jowār	7,189	10,784	12,531	12,530
Bājra	2,911	3,145	2,487	2,556
Other food-grains	1,591	2,041	3,631	3,698
Oilseeds	2,910	3,009	3,294	3,420
Chillies	123	120	149	164
Cotton	1,543	1,761	3,226	3,517
Other fibres	50	53	85	86
Sugar-cane	18	20	29	29
Tobacco	107	110	125	124
Indigo	93	108	94	99
Miscellaneous	2,345	4,282	2,319	3,306
Total	20,673	27,486	30,242	31,872

TABLE III

Average Prices of Food-grains, &c., Hyderābād State

Selected staples.	Selected centres.	Average for ten years ending 1890.	1900.	1901.
Rice	Parbhani	11	10	9
	Osmānābād	8	9	8
	Raichūr	10	10	9
	Hyderābād city	10	8	6
	Medak	10	10	10
	Warangal	11	11	11
Jowār	Parbhani	34	32	26
	Osmānābād	22	21	17
	Raichūr	24	27	18
	Hyderābād city	24	20	10
	Medak	15	15	15
	Warangal	21	30	20
Bājra	Parbhani	26	16	13
	Raichūr	24	26	19
	Hyderābād city	20	18	13
	Warangal	24	29	21
Wheat	Parbhani	20	17	14
	Osmānābād	13	15	11
	Raichūr	10	12	8
	Hyderābād city	12	10	6
	Medak	10	10	10
	Warangal	12	12	10
Salt	Hyderābād city	8	8½	10¼

Note.—The prices are in seers (2 lb.) per Hyderābād rupee, which was in 1907 equivalent to about 13 annas 9 pies in British currency.

Acute famine years, such as 1877-8 and 1899-1900, have been omitted from the averages.

TABLE IV

Trade of Hyderābād State with British Provinces

(In thousands of rupees)

	1890–1.	1900–1.	1902–3.
Imports.			
Cotton piece-goods	1,34,67	59,52	96,65
,, twist and yarn	34,49	35,44	35,72
Silk	12,50	39,94	11,83
Salt	56,77	50,74	43,46
Sugar	15,45	17,43	25,19
Fruits	22,73	20,36	10,83
Nuts	11,17	7,16	6,77
Cattle and sheep	32,83	34,29	8,23
Silver	14,21	3,70	11,78
Brass and copper manufactures	6,04	2,89	5,58
Iron	6,17	5,46	5,71
Wood	7,76	5,65	1,48
All other articles	1,33,01	1,57,08	2,06,29
Total	4,87,80	4,39,66	4,69,52
Exports.			
Grain and pulse	72,86	67,71	25,56
Cotton (raw)	1,28,48	2,29,90	2,01,17
Linseed	52,58	24,78	59,85
Oilseeds	28,56	32,75	12,07
Ground-nuts	11,12	48	36
Castor-seed	24,60	57,79	52,82
Indigo	7,92	2,92	1,90
Oils	17,20	16,53	42,36
Wood	3,61	2,41	2,56
Cotton goods	12,76	7,01	9,85
Hides and skins	25,97	28,78	23,07
Cattle and sheep	17,43	19,97	15,19
All other articles	32,58	38,30	22,55
Total	4,35,67	5,29,33	4,69,31

TABLE V

Principal Sources of Ordinary Revenue, Hyderābād State

(In thousands of rupees)

	Average for ten years ending 1890.	Average for ten years ending 1900.	1901.	1904.
Land revenue	1,89,07	2,06,38	2,24,90	2,43,06
Customs	43,22	48,37	54,67	56,50
Stamps	4,65	8,33	7,91	8,57
Excise	37,62	49,30	49,03	58,32
Forests	1,86	2,54	4,13	5,20
Registration	8	48	41	41
Railways	11,94	21,62	48,03	36,43
Berār surplus	18,05	9,05	...	29,87
Other sources	20,29	36,72	27,60	30,68
Total	3,26,78	3,82,79	4,16,68	4,69,04

TABLE VI

Principal Heads of Expenditure, Hyderābād State

(In thousands of rupees)

	Average for ten years ending 1890.	Average for ten years ending 1900.	1901.	1904.
Charges in respect of collections	53,54	66,54	61,15	56,38
Salaries and expenses of civil departments:—				
(*a*) General administration	14,94	16,67	16,77	13,67
(*b*) Law and justice	10,58	12,53	13,78	11,65
(*c*) Police	24,52	26,12	28,76	27,86
(*d*) Education	3,36	7,00	7,49	7,29
(*e*) Medical	2,60	5,00	6,21	6,72
(*f*) Minor departments	3,65	3,23	4,34	1,93
Total	59,65	70,55	77,35	69,12
Mint	52	53	37	9,78
Pensions, allowances, and religious grants	42,24	43,78	40,70	39,44
Contributions to palace expenditure	41,22	58,79	50,28	50,00
Public works and irrigation	18,17	23,16	31,52	46,07
Military department	68,76	69,44	63,93	63,72
Railways	21,95	31,18	42,51	43,32
Miscellaneous and other charges (including famine)	9,96	38,05	43,22	72,66
Total expenditure	3,16,01	4,02,02	4,11,03	4,50,49

TABLE VII

Statistics of Jails, Hyderābād State

	1881.	1891.	1901.	1903.
Number of Central jails . .	1	1	5	5
Number of District jails . .	16	16	12	12
Number of Subsidiary jails (lock-ups)	100	95	95	95
Average daily jail population—				
(*a*) Male:				
In Central jails . .	743	2,187	4,364	3,882
In other jails . . .	...	1,626	2,230	860
(*b*) Female:				
In Central jails . .	33	98	65	67
In other jails . . .	...	83	55	23
Total	776	3,994	6,714	4,832
Rate of jail mortality per 1,000	...	28·9	65·3	26·9
Expenditure on jail maintenance . . . . . Rs.	...	1,89,831	5,14,920	3,88,284
Cost per prisoner . . Rs.	...	47-8-6	76-11-1	80-5-7
Profits on jail manufactures Rs.	...	15,512	48,172	1,28,313
Earnings per prisoner . Rs.	...	3-14-0	7-2-1	45-1-3

TABLE VIII

Colleges, Schools, and Scholars, Hyderābād State

Class of institutions.	1900-1.			1903-4.		
	Number of institutions.	Scholars.		Number of institutions.	Scholars.	
		Males.	Females.		Males.	Fema
Public.						
Arts colleges	2	39	...	2	55	...
Oriental colleges	1	132	...	1	129	...
Secondary schools—						
Upper (High)	16	4,099	169	15	4,107	24
Lower (Middle)	53	8,550	399	58	9,524	36
Primary schools—						
Upper	133	13,214	1,160	137	13,656	1,13
Lower	620	24,852	2,650	638	25,066	2,79
Training schools	2	246	89	2	367	9
Other special schools	5	428	...	8	612	...
Private.						
Advanced	14	1,373	...	5	...	26
Elementary	1,826	38,181	...	1,801	36,559	...
Total	2,672	91,114	4,467	2,667	90,075	4,90

Note.—Statistics for 1880-1 and 1890-1 are not available.

TABLE IX

Educational Finance, Hyderābād State

	Expenditure on institutions maintained or aided by public funds.					
	State revenue.	District and municipal funds.	Fees.	Other sources.	Total (1901).	Tot (190
	Rs.	Rs.	Rs.	Rs.	Rs.	Rs
Arts and professional colleges	57,353	...	456	...	57,809	53,
Training and special colleges	26,508	6,939	1,963	1,320	36,730	37,
Secondary schools	2,36,221	979	41,467	48,994	3,27,661	3,20,
Primary schools	91,010	87,063	7,955	16,977	2,03,005	2,01,
Girls' schools	15,581	5,098	1,497	14,486	36,662	84,
Total	4,26,673	1,00,079	53,338	81,777	6,61,867	6,95,

TABLE X

Statistics of Hospitals and Vaccination, Hyderābād State

	1884-5.	1891.	1901.	1903.
Hospitals, &c.				
umber of civil hospitals and dispensaries	48	67	84	84
verage daily number of—				
(*a*) In-patients . . .	...	...	12	28
(*b*) Out-patients . . .	801	1,054	1,743	1,796
icome from—				
State funds (the only source) Rs.	2,03,263	4,01,244	5,40,005	6,83,495
xpenditure on—				
(*a*) Establishment . . Rs.	...	3,13,161	4,37,525	4,63,349
(*b*) Medicines, diet, buildings, &c. . . . Rs.	...	88,083	1,02,480	3,46,562
Lunatic Asylums.				
umber of asylums . . .	...	1	1	1
verage daily number of—				
(*a*) Criminal lunatics . .	...	7	21	26
(*b*) Other lunatics . . .	...	29	109	122
xpenditure on—				
(*a*) Establishment . . Rs.	...	120	1,140	1,140
(*b*) Diet, buildings, &c. Rs.	...	2,291	8,460	31,765
Vaccination.				
opulation among whom vaccination was carried on . .	9,845,594	11,537,040	11,141,142	11,141,142
umber of successful operations .	44,062	76,880	37,880	26,591
atio per 1,000 of population .	4·47	6.66	3·42	2·38
otal expenditure on vaccination . . . . . . Rs.	...	49,160	57,302	34,878
ost per successful case . Rs.	1-3-0	0-10-3	1-3-0	1-5-0

MOUNTAINS, LAKES, RIVERS, HISTORIC AREAS, ETC.

Bālāghāt (*Bālā*, 'above,' and *ghāt*, 'a mountain pass'). —Range of hills in the western half of Hyderābād State. It extends from the Biloli *tāluk* in Nānder District in the east, through the southern portion of Parbhani District, past Dhārūr and Pātoda to Ashti in Bhīr District in the west, having a length of 200 miles and a width which varies between 3 and 6 miles. A spur of this range branches off from Ashti, and taking a south-easterly direction traverses the tracts which lie between the Sīna, Mānjra, and Kāgna rivers, comprising the Districts of Bhīr, Osmānābād, and Gulbarga, and terminates in the last-named District. Another spur starts from the south of Parbhani District, also in a south-easterly direction, and passes through the Rājūra *tāluk* of Bīdar District, south of Kaulās in Nizāmābād District. The country enclosed by the range and its two spurs forms a plateau, known locally as the Bālāghāt.

Jālna Hills.—Range of hills in Hyderābād State, running eastward from Daulatābād in Aurangābād District. Close to the border of Berār it is joined by a spur of hills from Jālna in the south, from which the range derives its name. After entering Berār it merges into the Sahyādriparvat or SĀTMĀLA range. The Jālna Hills are about 2,400 feet high, one of the peaks, Daulatābād, rising to 3,022 feet above the level of the sea. The total length of the range is about 120 miles.

Sātmāla.—Range of hills in Bombay, Berār, and the Hyderābād State, which also bears the names of the Ajanta, Chāndor, and Indhyādri hills, and Sahyādriparvat.

Pākhāl Lake.—An extensive lake in Hyderābād State, situated in 17° 57′ N. and 79° 59′ E., in the Pākhāl *tāluk* of Warangal District, and enclosed on the north, south, and east by ranges of low and densely wooded hills. It was formed by throwing a dam across the Pākhāl river, which here cuts its way between two low hills. It is the largest artificial piece of water in the State, the length and breadth being 8,000 and 6,000 yards, while the dam is more than 2,000 yards long, and the water covers an area of nearly 13 square miles. Several channels convey water from the lake to some distance for irrigation. At the centre of the dam are the ruins of a small pavilion known as the *chabūtra* of Shitāb Khān. The lake abounds with fish, otters, and crocodiles, and the surrounding country contains game of all descriptions. The average depth of the water is between 30 and 40 feet.

Godāvarī.—A great river of Southern India, which runs across the Deccan from the Western to the Eastern Ghāts; for sanctity, picturesque scenery, and utility to man, surpassed only by the Ganges and the Indus; total length about 900 miles; estimated area of drainage basin, 112,000 square miles. The source of the river is on the side of a hill behind the village of Trimbak, in Nāsik District, Bombay, only about 50 miles from the shore of the Indian Ocean. At this spot is an artificial reservoir reached by a flight of 690 steps, into which the water trickles drop by drop from the lips of a carven image, shrouded by a canopy of stone. From first to last the general direction of the river is towards the south-east. It passes by Nāsik town, and then separates Ahmadnagar District from the State of Hyderābād, its total course in the Bombay Presidency being about 100 miles. Above Nāsik it flows along a narrow rocky bed, but farther east the banks are lower and more earthy. Fifteen miles below Nāsik it receives, on the right, the Dārna from the hills of Igatpuri, and 17 miles farther down, on the left, the Kādva from Dindori. At the latter confluence, at Nander, the stream is dammed for irrigation. Near Nevāsa it receives on the right bank the combined waters of the Pravara and Mulā, which rise in the hills of Akola, near Harischandragarh.

After passing the old town of PAITHAN on its left bank, the Godāvari now runs for a length of about 176 miles right across the Hyderābād State, receiving on its left bank the Pūrna, which flows in near Kararkher in Parbhani District, and on the right the Mānjra near Kondalwādi in Nānder, while near Dharmsāgar in the Chinnūr *tāluk* of Adilābād District it receives, again on the right, the Māner. Below Sironchā it is joined by the PRĀNHITA, conveying the united waters of the WARDHĀ and Waingangā; and from this point it takes a marked south-easterly bend, and for about 100 miles divides Chānda District and the Bastar Feudatory State of the Central Provinces from the Karīmnagar and Warangal Districts of Hyderābād. Thirty miles below the confluence of the Prānhita, the Godāvari receives the Indrāvati river from Bastar State and lower down the Tāl. The bed of the

Godāvari where it adjoins the Central Provinces is broad and sandy, from one to two miles in width, and broken by rocks at only two points, called the First and Second Barriers, each about 15 miles long. In 1854 it was proposed to remove these barriers, and a third one on the Prānhita, with the object of making a waterway from the cotton-growing Districts of Nāgpur and Wardhā to the sea; but in 1871, after very considerable sums had been expended, the project was finally abandoned as impracticable. One of the dams erected in connexion with this project still stands, with its locks and canal, at Dummagudem in the north of the Godāvari District of Madras. Although the Godāvari only skirts the Central Provinces, it is one of the most important rivers in their drainage system, as it receives through the Wardhā and Wain-gangā the waters of a portion of the Sātpurā plateau and of the whole of the Nāgpur plain.

Some distance below Sironchā the Godāvari leaves the Central Provinces behind, and for a while forms the boundary between the Godāvari District of the Madras Presidency and the Hyderābād State; and in this part of its course it is joined on the left bank by a considerable tributary, the Sabarī. Thence it flows to the sea through the centre of the old Godāvari District, which has recently been divided, mainly by the course of the river, into the two Districts of Godāvari and Kistna. At the beginning of its course along Madras territory, the river flows placidly through a flat and somewhat monotonous country, but shortly afterwards it begins to force its way through the Eastern Ghāts, and a sudden change takes place. The banks become wild and mountainous, the stream contracts, and at length the whole body of the river pours through a narrow and very deep passage known as 'the Gorge,' on either side of which the picturesque wooded slopes of the hills rise almost sheer from the dark water. Once through the hills, the river again opens out and forms a series of broad reaches dotted with low alluvial islands (*lankas*), which are famous for the tobacco they produce. The current here is nowhere rapid. At Rājahmundry, where the river is crossed by the East Coast line of the Madras Railway on a bridge more than 1½ miles in length, it varies from 4 to 11 feet a second. In floods, however, the Godāvari brings down an enormous volume of water, and embankments on both of its banks are necessary to prevent it from inundating the surrounding country.

A few miles below Rājahmundry the river divides into two

main streams, the Gautami Godāvari on the east and the Vasishta Godāvari on the west, which run down to the sea through a wide alluvial delta formed in the course of ages by the masses of silt which the river has here deposited. It is in this delta that the waters of the Godāvari are first utilized on any considerable scale for irrigation. At Dowlaishweram, above the bifurcation, a great 'anicut' or dam has been thrown across the stream, and from this the whole delta has been irrigated.

The Godāvari is navigable for small boats throughout Godāvari District. Vessels get round the anicut by means of the main canals, of which nearly 500 miles are also navigable, and which connect with the navigable canals of the Kistna delta to the south. Above the anicut there are several steamboats belonging to Government; but, as already observed, the attempts to utilize the Upper Godāvari as an important waterway have proved a failure.

The coast of the Godāvari delta was the scene of some of the earliest settlements of Europeans in India, the Dutch, the English, and the French having all established factories there. The channels of the river which led to these have now greatly silted up. The little French settlement of Yanam still remains, but the others—Bandamūrlanka, Injaram, Madapollam, and Pālakollu—now retain none of their former importance.

The peculiar sacredness of the Godāvari is said to have been revealed by Rāma himself to the *rishi* Gautama. The river is sometimes called Godā, and the sacred character especially attaches to the Gautami mouth. According to popular legend, it proceeds from the same source as the Ganges, by an underground passage; and this identity is preserved in the familiar name of Vriddha-Gangā. But every part of its course is holy ground, and to bathe in its waters will wash away the blackest sin. The great bathing festival, called Pushkaram, celebrated in different years on the most sacred rivers of India, is held every twelfth year on the banks of the Godāvari at Rājahmundry. The spots most frequented by pilgrims are—the source at Trimbak; the town of Bhadrāchalam on the left bank, about 100 miles above Rājahmundry, where stands an ancient temple of Rāmachandra, surrounded by twenty-four smaller pagodas; Rājahmundry itself; and the village of Kotipalli, on the left bank of the eastern mouth.

Mānjra.—River of Hyderābād State, rising on the plateau

of Pātoda in Bhīr District. After flowing through or along the Districts of Osmānābād, Bīdar, and Medak, generally in a south-eastern direction, it takes a sudden turn 10 miles east of Kalabgūr in the last-named District and thence flows almost due north, forming the boundary between Nānder and Indūr Districts, till it joins the Godāvari from the right near Kondalwādi, after a course of 387 miles. During its course it receives the Tirnā on the right bank in the Nilanga *tāluk* of Bīdar District, and 18 miles farther down, the Karanja on the same side. In Nānder two smaller streams, the Lendi and the Manār, join it on the left bank. The banks of the Mānjra are nowhere steep, and are earthy. Several ferries are maintained, and its waters are largely used for irrigation. Two new projects, known as the Mānjra and the Mānjra Extension, which are in course of construction, comprise extensive schemes for irrigating lands in Medak District.

Pengangā.—River of Berār, having its source in the hills beyond Deūlghāt, on the western border of Buldāna District, in 20° 31′ N. and 76° 2′ E. After flowing in a south-easterly direction through this District and a portion of Akola, it forms the southern boundary of Berār, joining the Wardhā, which forms the eastern boundary of the province, at Jugād, in the south-eastern corner of Yeotmāl District (19° 52′ N. and 79° 11′ E.). The course of the Pengangā, from its source to the point where it joins the Wardhā, exceeds 200 miles in length; and its principal tributaries are the Pūs, the Arna and Arān, which unite before they flow into it, the Chandrabhāga, the Wāghāri, which displays on its banks a curious laminated formation of Purāna sandstone, and the Vaidarbha, which is the adjectival form of the name of the old kingdom of heroic times. All these tributaries flow into the Pengangā from the north.

Wardhā.—River of the Central Provinces, which rises in the Multai plateau of Betūl District, at 21° 50′ N. and 78° 24′ E., about 70 miles north-west of Nāgpur city, and, flowing south and south-east, separates the Nāgpur, Wardhā, and Chānda Districts of the Central Provinces from Amraoti and Yeotmāl of Berār and Sirpur Tāndūr of Hyderābād State. After a course of 290 miles from its source, the Wardhā meets the Waingangā at Seonī in Chānda District, and the united stream under the name of the PRĀNHITA flows on to join the GODĀVARI. The bed of the Wardhā, from its source to its junction with the Pengangā at Jugād in the south-east corner of Yeotmāl, is deep and rocky, changing from a swift torrent in the monsoon months to a succession of nearly stagnant pools in the summer. For the last hundred miles of its course below Chānda, it flows in a clear channel broken only by a barrier of rocks commencing above the confluence of the Waingangā and extending into the Prānhita. The project entertained in the years 1866–71 for rendering the Godāvari and Wardhā fit for navigation included the excavation of a channel through this expanse of rock, which was known as the Third Barrier. The scheme proved impracticable; and except that timber is sometimes floated down from the Ahiri forests in the monsoon months, no use is now made of the river for navigation. The area drained by the Wardhā includes Wardhā District, with parts of Nāgpur and Chānda in the Central Provinces, and the eastern and southern portion of Berār. The principal tributaries of the Wardhā are the Wunnā and Erai from the east, and the Bembla and Pengangā which drain the southern and eastern portions of the plain of Berār. The banks of the river are in several places picturesquely crowned by small temples and tombs, and numerous ruined forts in the background recall the wild period of Marāthā wars and Pindāri raids. Kundalpur (Dewalwāra) on the Berār bank opposite to Wardhā District is believed to represent the site of a buried city, celebrated in the *Bhagavadgītā* as the metropolis of the kingdom of Vidarbha (Berār). A large religious fair is held there. At Ballālpur near Chānda are the ruins of a palace of the Gond kings, and a curious temple on an islet in the river which for some months in the year is several feet under water. The Wardhā is crossed by the Great Indian Peninsula Railway at Pulgaon.

Prānhita ('helpful to life').—River of the Central Provinces, formed by the united streams of the WARDHĀ and Waingangā, whose junction is at Seonī in Chānda District (19° 36′ N. and 79° 49′ E.). From here the river has a course of 72 miles, until it joins the Godāvari above Sironchā. Throughout its length the Prānhita is the western boundary of Chānda District and of the Central Provinces, which it separates from Hyderābād State. Its bed is broad and sandy, with the exception of a long stretch of rock below the confluence at Seonī.

Kistna (Sanskrit, *Krishna*, 'the black').—A great river of Southern India, which, like the Godāvari and Cauvery, flows almost across the Peninsula from west to east. In traditional sanctity it is surpassed by both these rivers, and in actual length by the Godāvari; but the area of its drainage, including its two great tributaries, the Bhīma and Tungabhadra, is the largest of the three. Its total length is about 800 miles, and the total area of its catchment basin about 97,000 square miles.

The Kistna rises about 40 miles from the Arabian Sea (17° 59′ N. and 73° 38′ E.) in the Western Ghāts just north of the hill station of Mahābaleshwar, and flows southwards, skirting the eastern spurs of the hills, past Karād (Sātāra District), where it receives on the right bank the Koyna from the western side of the Mahābaleshwar hills, and Sāngli, where it receives the waters of the Vārna, also from the west, until it reaches Kurundvād, when the Pānchgangā joins it, again on the right bank. The river then turns eastward and flows through Belgaum District, the States of the Southern Marāthā Agency, and Bijāpur, into the State of Hyderābād, after a course of about 300 miles in the Bombay Presidency. In Bijāpur District it is joined on the right bank by the Ghatprabha and Malprabha from the Western Ghāts. Near the hills the channel is too rocky and the stream too swift for navigation, but its waters are largely used for irrigation in Sātāra District and in the more open country to the south-east. In Belgaum and Bijāpur its banks of black soil or laterite are 20 to 50 feet high, especially on the south side, and the stream forms many islands covered with *babūl* bushes.

On entering the State of Hyderābād (at Echampet in Raichūr District) the Kistna drops from the table-land of the Deccan proper down to the alluvial *doābs* of Shorāpur and Raichūr. The fall is as much as 408 feet in about 3 miles. In time of flood a mighty volume of water rushes with a great roar over a succession of broken ledges of granite, dashing up a lofty column of spray. The first of the *doābs* mentioned above is formed by the confluence of the BHĪMA, which brings down the drainage of Ahmadnagar, Poona, and Sholāpur; the second by the confluence of the TUNGABHADRA, which drains the north of Mysore and the 'Ceded Districts' of Bellary and Kurnool. At the point of junction with the Tungabhadra in the eastern corner of Raichūr District, the Kistna again strikes upon British territory, and forms for a considerable distance the boundary between the eastern portion of Hyderābād and the Kurnool and Guntūr Districts of Madras. Its bed is here for many miles a deep, rocky channel, with a rapid fall, winding in a north-easterly direction through the spurs of the Nallamalai range and other smaller hills. At Wazīrābād in Nalgonda District it receives its last important tributary, the MŪSI, on whose banks stands the city of Hyderābād. The total course of the river within and along the State of Hyderābād is about 400 miles.

On reaching the chain of the Eastern Ghāts, the river turns

sharply south-eastwards and flows for about 100 miles between the Kistna and Guntūr Districts (formerly the Kistna District) of Madras direct to the sea, which it enters by two principal mouths. It is in this last part of its course that the Kistna is for the first time largely utilized for irrigation. From the point where it turns southwards the rate of fall of its channel drops rapidly from an average of $3\frac{1}{2}$ feet a mile to $1\frac{1}{2}$ feet, and eventually, as it nears the sea, to as little as from 7 to 9 inches. The enormous mass of silt it carries—which has been estimated to be sufficient in flood-time to cover daily an area of 5 square miles to a depth of 1 foot—has consequently in the course of ages been deposited in the form of a wide alluvial delta which runs far out into the sea and slopes gradually away from either bank of the river, with an average fall of 18 inches to the mile. At Bezwāda, at the head of this delta, the Kistna runs through a gap 1,300 yards in width in a low range of gneissic hills, and here a great masonry dam has been thrown across the river and turns its waters into a network of irrigation channels which spread throughout the delta. Immediately below the dam the river is also crossed by the East Coast line of the Madras Railway on a girder-bridge of twelve spans of 300 feet. The flood velocity of the Kistna at this point is about $6\frac{1}{2}$ miles an hour, and the flood discharge has been estimated to reach the enormous figure of 761,000 cubic feet a second.

The Kistna is too rapid for navigation above the dam, but between Bezwāda and its mouth sea-going native craft ply upon it for about six months in the year. The main irrigation canals are also navigable, connecting Kistna District with its northern neighbour Godāvari, and, by means of the Buckingham Canal, with the country to the southwards and the City of Madras.

Bhīma (Sanskrit, 'The Terrible,' one of the names of Pārvatī).—A river of Southern India. It rises at the well-known shrine of Bhīmāshankar (19° 4′ N. and 73° 32′ E.) in the Western Ghāts, and flows south-eastwards, with many windings, through or along the boundary of the Bombay Districts of Poona, Sholāpur, and Bijāpur, for about 340 miles, till it enters the State of Hyderābād, where after a farther course of 176 miles it eventually falls into the Kistna, about 16 miles north of Raichūr. The first 40 miles of its course lie in a narrow and rugged valley, but farther east the banks are low and alluvial, though broken here and there by dikes of rock. In the dry season the stream is narrow and sluggish.

At Rānjangaon the Bhīma receives on the right the combined waters of the Mulā and Muthā from Poona, and about 15 miles farther, on the left bank, the Ghod river from the northern side of the Bhīmāshankar hills. Not far from Tembhurni it is joined on the right bank by the Nīra from the Bhor State, and, after passing the holy city of Pandharpur, receives on the right bank the Mān from the Mahādeo hills, and on the left the Sīna, which rises near Ahmadnagar. There are important irrigation works on the Muthā, Nīra, and Sīna. Near Wādi junction (Hyderābād State) the Bhīma is joined on the left by the Kāgna river.

Tungabhadra.—River of Southern India, the chief tributary of the Kistna, which is fed by all the streams of the northern half of Mysore State. It is formed by the union of the twin rivers Tunga and Bhadra, which rise together in the Western Ghāts at Gangāmūla, on the frontier of Kadūr District, Mysore. The Tunga runs north-east to beyond Sringeri, and then takes a sharp turn north-west to Tīrthahalli, whence its course is again north-east past Shimoga town. The Bhadra runs east to the western base of the Bābā Budan range, and then north past Benkipur. The two unite at Kūdali in the north of Shimoga District (14° N. and 75° 43′ E.) The united river forms the boundary between Mysore and Bombay, and then between Bombay and Madras. Turning north-east it forms the boundary between Madras and the State of Hyderābād, and bending east in the north of Bellary District it joins the Kistna, beyond Kurnool, after a total course of about 400 miles. From Shimoga District the Tungabhadra receives the Choradi or Kumadvati and the Varadā on the west, and the Haridrā on the south. From Chitaldroog District it receives the Chinna Hagari and the Vedāvati or Hagari on the south.

The Tungabhadra is bridged for the trunk road at Harihar, where it is also crossed by the railway from Hubli to Bangalore; and again at Hosūru and Rāmpuram in Bellary District, where the lines from Hubli to Bellary and from Madras to Bombay pass over it.

There are thirty-eight small irrigation dams on the Tunga and the Bhadra in Mysore, but the beds of both rivers are for the most part rocky, and consequently unsuitable for navigation. The manner in which the country rises rapidly away from either side of the Tungabhadra has also hitherto prevented it from being greatly utilized for irrigation in either the State of Hyderābād or the Madras Presidency, though in the former State its left bank is dammed for a distance of about 30 miles. The kings of the ancient dynasty of Vijayanagar (1336–1565), the ruins of whose capital still stand on its bank near the little village of Hampi in Bellary District, threw across it, above and below the city, a number of dams made of huge blocks of uncemented stone, of which ten are still used for watering narrow strips of land along the southern edge of the river. A few miles above the point where the Tungabhadra falls into the Kistna a dam also turns part of the water into the Kurnool-Cuddapah Canal. The river is, however, perennial and comes down in frequent heavy freshes, which cannot be utilized by any of these works, and are not required for irrigation in the delta of the Kistna lower down. The Irrigation Commission of 1901–3 accordingly recommended the reinvestigation of a project, which has been several times mooted in different shapes, for constructing a reservoir upon the river in Bellary District. It is calculated that a masonry dam about 145 feet long near Hospet, where the river cuts through some low hills, would hold back the water for a distance of nearly 40 miles, and form a lake with an area of 160 square miles and a capacity four and a half times as great as that of the Assuān reservoir on the Nile. From this a canal would be led to Bellary, tunnelling in its course through some rocky hills, and thence across the Hagari, through the watershed between this river and the Penner, and finally into the bed of the latter river. The canal and its distributaries would command portions of the Bellary, Kurnool, Anantapur, Cuddapah, and Nellore Districts of Madras. Detailed estimates for this great scheme, the cost of which is roughly estimated at 8 crores, are now under preparation.

The origin of the river is thus accounted for in local legend. A demon having seized the earth and carried it into the lower world, Vishnu became incarnate as a boar, and plunging into the ocean brought it up again. Resting after this exertion on the Varāha-parvat or 'boar mountain,' the perspiration trickling off his left tusk became the Tunga, and that from his right tusk the Bhadra.

Mūsi.—River of Hyderābād State, rising in the Anantagiri hills in the Patlūr *tāluk* of Atrāf-i-balda District. It flows almost due east for a distance of 112 miles, when it receives the Aler on the left, near Chittūr, and thence runs in a south-easterly direction until it falls into the Kistna, after a total course of about 150 miles. Several channels have been made at different parts of the course of this river, which act as feeders for arge tanks or supply direct irrigation. The city of Hyderābād stands on its right bank.

Carnatic (*Kannada, Karnāta, Karnātaka-desa*).—Properly, as the name implies, 'the Kanarese country.' The name has, however, been erroneously applied by modern European writers to the Tamil country of Madras, including the Telugu District of Nellore. The boundaries of the true Carnatic, or Karnātaka-desa, are given by Wilks as

'Commencing near the town of Bīdar, 18° 45′ N., about 60 miles north-west from Hyderābād (Deccan). Following the course of the Kanarese language to the south-east, it is found to be limited by a waving line which nearly touches Adoni, winds to the west of Gooty, skirts the town of Anantapur, and passing through Nandidroog, touches the range of the Eastern Ghāts; thence pursuing their southern course to the mountainous pass of Gazzalhati, it continues to follow the abrupt turn caused by the great chasm of the western hills between the towns of Coimbatore, Pollāchi, and Pālghāt; and, sweeping to the north-west, skirts the edges of the precipitous Western Ghāts, nearly as far north as the sources of the Kistna; whence following first an eastern and afterwards a north-eastern course, it terminates in rather an acute angle near Bidar, already described as its northern limit.'

This country has been ruled wholly or in part by many dynasties, of whom the Andhras or Sātavāhanas, the Kadambas, the Pallavas, the Gangas, the Chālukyas, the Rāshtrakūtas, the Cholas, the later Chālukyas, the Hoysalas, and the house of Vijayanagar are the most prominent. The Vijayanagar kings, who came into power about the year 1336, conquered the whole of the peninsula south of the Tungabhadra river. They were completely overthrown by the Muhammadans in 1565, and retired first to Penukonda, and then to Chandragiri, one branch of the family remaining at Anagundi opposite to their old capital. It was these conquests that probably led to the extension of the term 'Carnatic' to the southern plain country; and this latter region came to be called Karnāta Pāyānghāt, or 'lowlands,' to distinguish it from Karnāta Bālāghāt, or the 'hill country.' When the Muhammadan kings of the Deccan ousted the Vijayanagar dynasty, they divided the north of the Vijayanagar country between them into Carnatic Hyderābād (or Golconda) and Carnatic Bijāpur, each being further subdivided into Pāyānghāt and Bālāghāt. At this time, according to Wilks, the northern boundary of Karnāta (Carnatic) was the Tungabhadra.

Speaking of this period and the modern misapplication of

the name, Bishop Caldwell says (*Grammar of the Dravidian Languages*, pp. 34–5):—

'The term *Karnāta* or *Karnātaka* is said to have been a generic term, including both the Telugu and Kanarese peoples and their languages, though it is admitted that it usually denoted the latter alone, and though it is to the latter that the abbreviated form Kannadam has been appropriated. Karnātaka (that which belongs to Karnāta) is regarded as a Sanskrit word by native Pandits; but I agree with Dr. Gundert in preferring to derive it from the Dravidian words *kār*, "black," *nādu* (the adjective form of which in Telugu is *nāti*), "country," that is, "the black country," a term very suitable to designate the "black cotton soil," as it is called, of the plateau of the Southern Deccan. The use of the term is of considerable antiquity, as we find it in the *Varāha-Mihira* at the beginning of the fifth[1] century A.D. Tārānātha also mentions Karnāta. The word Karnāta or Karnātaka, though at first a generic term, became in process of time the appellation of the Kanarese people and of their language alone, to the entire exclusion of the Telugu. Karnātaka has now got into the hands of foreigners, who have given it a new and entirely erroneous application. When the Muhammadans arrived in Southern India, they found that part of it with which they first became acquainted—the country above the Ghāts, including Mysore and part of Telingāna—called the Karnātaka country. In course of time, by a misapplication of terms, they applied the same name Karnātak, or Carnatic, to designate the country below the Ghāts, as well as that which was above. The English have carried the misapplication a step farther, and restricted the name to the country below the Ghāts, which never had any right to it whatever. Hence the Mysore country, which is probably the true Carnatic, is no longer called by that name; and what is now geographically termed "the Carnatic" is exclusively the country below the Ghāts on the Coromandel coast.'

It is this latter country which formed the dominions of the Nawābs of the Carnatic, who played such an important part in the struggle for supremacy between the English and the French in the eighteenth century, and which now forms the greater portion of the present Madras Presidency. This connotation still survives in the designation of Madras regiments as Carnatic infantry. Administratively, however, the term Carnatic (or Karnātak as it is there used) is now restricted to the Bombay portion of the original Karnāta: namely, the Districts of Belgaum, Dhārwār, and Bijāpur, and part of North Kanara, with the Native States of the Southern Marāthā Agency and Kolhāpur.

[1] *Recte* 'sixth.'

Deccan (or *Dakhin*).—This name, a corruption of the Sanskrit *dakshina* = 'southern,' includes, in its widest sense, the whole of India south of the Narbadā river, or, which is nearly the same thing, south of the Vindhya mountains. In its narrower sense it has much the same meaning as Mahārāshtra, or the country where the Marāthī language is spoken, if the below-Ghāt tract be omitted. In this connotation its southern boundary lies along the course of the Kistna river. In a still narrower sense the Deccan is regarded as bounded on the north by the Sātmāla hills. Adopting the broadest meaning, the Deccan on its western side descends seaward by a succession of terraces from the Western Ghāts, which rise in parts to over 4,000 feet in height and terminate abruptly near Cape Comorin, the extreme southern point of the peninsula, at an elevation of 2,000 feet. From here, following the coast-line, the Eastern Ghāts commence in a series of detached groups, which, uniting in about latitude 11° 40′ N., run north-eastward along the Coromandel coast, with an average elevation of 1,500 feet, and join the Vindhyas, which cross the peninsula from west to east, in nearly the same latitude (13° 20′ N.) as their western counterpart. The Vindhyan range thus joins the northern extremities of the two Ghāts and completes the peninsula triangle of the Deccan. The eastern side of the enclosed table-land being much lower than the western, all the principal rivers of the Deccan—the Godāvari, Kistna, and Cauvery—rising in the Western Ghāts, flow eastward, and escape by openings in the Eastern Ghāts into the Bay of Bengal. Between the Ghāts and the sea on either side the land differs in being, on the east, composed in part of alluvial deposits, brought down from the mountains, and sloping gently; while on the west the incline is abrupt, and the coast strip is broken by irregular spurs from the Ghāts, which at places descend into the sea in steep cliffs.

Geology[1]. The Deccan table-land is one of the relics of the old Gondwāna continent which formerly connected India with Africa, and which broke up at about the time that the chalk was forming in Europe. It is one of the few solid blocks of ancient land which have not suffered any of the folding movements so marked in most lands, and which, so far as we know, have never been depressed below the ocean. Except near the present coasts at low levels, not a single marine fossil has been found in the whole Deccan. The 'basement complex' of the Deccan table-land includes the usual assemblage of gneisses

[1] Contributed by Sir T. H. Holland, Director, Geological Survey of India.

and schists, among them the band of schists distinguished by the name of the Dhārwārs, containing the auriferous veins of Mysore which have, since they were opened up in 1881, yielded gold to the value of 19 millions sterling. Lying on the denuded surfaces of these ancient schists and gneisses are enormous thicknesses of unfossiliferous strata which, in default of evidence to the contrary, are regarded as pre-Cambrian in age. These occur as isolated patches in the Cuddapah and Kurnool Districts of Madras; in the Southern Marāthā country; in parts of the Godāvari valley; and in Gwalior, Bundelkhand, and the Vindhyan region of Central India. In small basins, generally preserved at lower levels, we find the coal-bearing deposits formed by the great rivers of the old Gondwāna continent in upper palaeozoic and mesozoic times, while for an area of some 200,000 square miles the older rocks are covered with great masses of basaltic lava, which spread over the country in Upper Cretaceous times and now form the highlands of the Deccan, remaining practically as horizontal as they must have been when they flowed as molten sheets over the country. Here and there, where the Deccan trap has been cut through by weather influences, we get glimpses of the old land-surface which was overwhelmed by lava-flows, while between the flows there were apparently interruptions sufficient to permit of the development of life in the lakes and rivers, of which the records are preserved in the so-called inter-trappean beds of fresh-water limestone, shales, and sandstones. The scenery of the Deccan trap highlands is the result of the subaerial erosion of the horizontal sheets of lava; the first plateaux of the hill-tops, and the horizontal terraces which are traceable for miles along the scarps, are features eminently characteristic of the weathering of basaltic lava-flows. The long grass, the general absence of large trees, and the occurrence of almost purely deciduous species, combine with the outlines of the hills to distinguish the trap areas from all others in the Deccan.

Two peculiar features of the Deccan are worth special mention: one is the occurrence, over most of the trap area, of the peculiar black, argillaceous, and calcareous soil known as *regar*, and, from its suitability for cotton-growing, as 'cotton soil'; the other is the peculiar decomposition product known as laterite, which is essentially a dirty mixture of aluminic and ferric hydrates, formed by a special form of rock alteration confined to moist tropical climates, and often resembling the material known as bauxite, which is worked as a source of aluminium.

History. Little is known in detail of the history of the Deccan before the close of the thirteenth century. Hindu legends tell of its invasion by Rāma, and the main authentic points known are the coming of the first Aryans (*c.* seventh century B.C.), the advance of the Mauryas (250 B.C.), and the Scythic invasion of A.D. 100. Archaeological remains and inscriptions bear witness to a series of dynasties, of which the Andhras or Sātavāhanas, the Cholas, the Chālukyas, the Rāshtrakūtas, and the Yādavas of Deogiri were the most important. The country was known to the author of the *Periplus* in the third century A.D. as Dachina Badcs (Dakshināpata), and to the Chinese pilgrim Fa Hian in the fifth century as Ta Thsin. Continuous history commences with the Muhammadan invasion of 1294–1300, when Alā-ud-dīn, the Khiljī emperor of Delhi, overran Mahārāshtra, Telingāna, and Karnāta. In 1338 the reduction of the Deccan was completed by Muhammad bin Tughlak; but a few years later a general revolt resulted in the establishment of the Muhammadan Bahmani dynasty, and the retrogression of Delhi supremacy beyond the Narbadā. The Bahmani dynasty advanced its eastern frontier at the expense of the Hindu kingdom of Telingāna to Golconda in 1373, to Warangal in 1421, and to the Bay of Bengal in 1472. A few years later (1482) it began to disintegrate, and was broken up into the five rival Muhammadan kingdoms of Bijāpur, Ahmadnagar, Golconda, Bīdar, and Berār. These were counterbalanced in the south, as the Bahmani empire had been, by the great Hindu kingdom of Vijayanagar, which was however destroyed in 1565, at the battle of Tālikotā, by a coalition of the Muhammadan powers. Of these, Bīdar and Berār became extinct before 1630; the other three kingdoms were restored to the Delhi empire by the victories of Akbar, Shāh Jahān, and Aurangzeb. The Deccan was thus for a second time brought under the Delhi rule, but not for long. The Marāthās in 1706 obtained the right of levying tribute over Southern India, and their leading chiefs, who had practically superseded the dynasty of Sivājī, were the Peshwās of Poona. A great Delhi viceroy (the Nīzam-ul-mulk), rallying all the Muhammadans of the South round him, established the Nizāmat of HYDERĀBĀD. The remainder of the imperial possessions in the Deccan was divided among minor princes, who generally acknowledged the supremacy of the Peshwā or the Nizām, according as they were north or south of the Tungabhadra. Mysore, alternately tributary to both, became eventually the prize of Haidar Alī, while in the extreme south the

Travancore State enjoyed, by its isolated position, uninterrupted independence.

Such was the position of affairs early in the eighteenth century. Meanwhile Portugal, Holland, France, and England had effected settlements on the coast; but the two former on so small a scale that they took no important part in the wars of succession between the native princes which occupied the middle of the century. The French and English, however, espoused opposite sides, and their struggles eventually resulted in establishing the supremacy of the latter (1761), which became definitely affirmed, under Lords Wellesley and Hastings, by the establishment of British influence at Hyderābād, the overthrow of Tipū Sultān, and the Marāthā Wars which followed, and the annexation of the Peshwā's dominions in 1818. The dominions of the other important Marāthā chief of the Deccan, the Bhonsla Rājā of Nāgpur, lapsed to the British on the extinction of the dynasty in 1854. The Deccan is to-day included in the Presidency of Madras, part of Bombay and the Central Provinces, together with Hyderābād, Mysore and other Native States.

ATRĀF-I-BALDA DISTRICT

Boundaries, configuration, and hill and river systems.

Atrāf-i balda (= 'Suburbs of the city').—District of Hyderābād State, lying almost in the centre of the State. It is situated between the Districts of Medak and Elgandal on the north, Mahbūbnagar on the south, Nalgonda on the east, Gulbarga on the west, and Bīdar on the north-west. Owing to its villages being interspersed with those of the surrounding districts, its spherical values cannot be accurately given, but the limits are approximately between $16^\circ 30'$ and $18^\circ 20'$ N. and $77^\circ 30'$ and $79^\circ 30'$ E. It is a *Sarf-i-khās* or 'crown' District, and has a total area of 3,399 square miles, including the city of Hyderābād (26 square miles). The area of the 'crown' lands is 2,040 square miles, the rest being *jāgīr*. The country is mostly hilly; and thickly wooded hills, known as the Rājkonda range, stretch from Pīpalpād in the Ambarpet *tāluk* in a south-easterly direction, entering Nalgonda District. The Anantagiri range, which begins in Mahbūbnagar District, enters the Patlūr *tāluk*, and, cutting across the Nizām's State Railway and passing north of it, runs almost parallel to the line from Vikārābād as far as Dhārūr. A large portion of this range is composed of high-level laterite. Isolated granite hills are seen everywhere; and the city of Hyderābād is surrounded by rocky eminences, from 200 to 300 feet in height, among which may be mentioned the Maulā Alī, the Golconda Rock, and the Black Rock at Trimulgherry. The slope of country is from west to east and south-east.

The most important river is the Mūsi, which passes through three *tāluks* of the District. It rises in the Anantagiri hills near Sivareddipet, and flows almost due east, passing between Hyderābād city and its northern suburbs or Chādarghāt into Nalgonda District. The Mānjra just touches two of the villages of the Asafnagar *tāluk* in the north-west of the District. Other smaller streams are the Sākalvāni in the west, a tributary of the Mūsi; the Haldi or Paspaver in the north, a tributary of the Mānjra; and the Deo stream in the Jūkal sub-*tāluk*, which is also a tributary of the Mānjra.

Geology.

The geological formation is the Archaean gneiss. Around Hyderābād, and stretching as far west as Lingampalli, 15 miles from the city, tors and boulders of fantastic shapes are seen everywhere, composed of basalt and granite piled up in picturesque confusion.

Low scrubby jungles give cover to leopards, bears, hyenas, and occasionally tigers, while in the more open plains antelope abound. The Nizām's preserves, extending about 24 miles east of the city, are stocked with them. Partridges, quail, and wild pigeons are very common, and in the tanks and rice-fields wild duck, teal, and snipe are plentiful in the cold season. **Fauna.**

The numerous tanks and streams make the climate damp, and malarial fevers are common in the rainy season. From October to the end of March the District is generally very healthy. **Climate.**

The annual rainfall during the twenty-one years ending 1901 averaged 33 inches. The amounts received in 1892, 1893, and 1894 were much above the normal, being 46, 55, and 50 inches, while in 1899 only 19 inches fell. **Rainfall.**

The District formed part of the territory of the Kākatīyas of Warangal (1150–1325), but has been under Muhammadan rule since the conquest of the Deccan in the fourteenth century. During the reign of Sultān Mahmūd Shāh Bahmani, the governor of the Telingāna districts declared his independence, and in 1512 assumed royal dignity under the title of Sultān Kuli Kutb Shāh. The Kutb Shahis reigned until the conquest of the Deccan by Aurangzeb, who incorporated their kingdom in the empire of Delhi, from which it was again separated on the foundation of the Hyderābād State early in the eighteenth century. **History.**

Among the places of archaeological interest, the following deserve mention. The fort of Golconda, also known as Muhammadnagar, 5 miles west of Hyderābād, was once the capital of the Kutb Shāhi kings. Outside the fort, to the north, are the tombs of these kings, which rank among the most remarkable Musalmān sepulchres in the Deccan. Most of the tombstones are of black polished basalt with beautifully engraved inscriptions. At Maisaram, 10 miles south of Hyderābād, are the remains of some Hindu temples destroyed by Aurangzeb after the fall of Golconda. A mosque built from the materials of a large temple 200 years ago is still standing. The buildings in the city and its suburbs are comparatively modern, and are described in the article on HYDERĀBĀD CITY. **Archaeology.**

The number of villages in the District, including *jāgīrs*, is 847. The population (excluding the city) at the last three **Population.**

enumerations was: (1881) 355,787, (1891) 389,784, and (1901) 420,702. The District is divided into five *tāluks* and one sub-*tāluk*, statistics of which, according to the Census of 1901, are given below:—

Tāluk.	Area in square miles.	Number of Towns.	Number of Villages.	Population.	Population per square mile.	Percentage of variation in population between 1891 and 1901.	Number of persons able to read and write.
Medchal	279	...	61	33,544	120	− 11.8	Not available.
Ambarpet	560	...	124	81,535	145	+ 13.0	
Shāhābād	302	...	65	41,384	137	+ 4.9	
Asafnagar	290	...	64	47,217	162	+ 20.4	
Patlūr	522	...	115	45,006	86	− 2.0	
Jūkal sub-*tāluk*	87	...	22	15,789	181	+ 45.1	
Jagīrs, &c.	1,333	...	396	156,227	117	+ 6.6	
District total	3,373	...	847	420,702	128	+ 7.9	14,745

More than 87 per cent. of the population are Hindus, and about 86 per cent. speak Telugu.

Castes and occupations. The most numerous caste is that of the agriculturist Kāpus, who number 75,774, or more than 18 per cent. of the total. Brāhmans number as many as 39,600; Komatis or trading castes, 13,400; Gollas or shepherds, 32,900; Gaundlas or toddy-drawers, 23,500; and Sālas or weavers, 17,500. Of the lower castes, the Dhers or village menials number 26,000, and the Chamārs or leather-workers 49,800. The population directly engaged in agriculture forms 33 per cent. of the total.

General agricultural conditions. The District is situated in the granitic region, and most of its soil is *chalka* or sandy, derived from the disintegration of granite, with patches of *regar* or black soil interspersed here and there. In the Patlūr and Jūkal *tāluks regar* prevails to a greater extent, and in the former a large area of laterite or ferruginous clay exists, both these soils being very fertile. The *chalka* soil is chiefly suitable for *kharīf* or rainy season cultivation, such as yellow *jowār*, *bājra*, *rāgi*, and maize; while *rabi* crops, such as white *jowār*, cotton, and linseed, are raised on the *regar* and lateritic soils. The red soil or laterite is well suited for garden produce, wherever water is available. The soils in the river valleys and at the foot of the hills are particularly fertile.

Chief agricultural statistics and principal crops. The tenure of lands is mainly *ryotwāri*. Excluding *jagīrs*, 393 square miles were cultivated in 1901, out of a total of 2,040. Forests and land not available for cultivation occupied 1,480 square miles, and cultivable waste and fallows 167 square miles. The staple food-crops are *jowār*, *bājra*, and rice, grown on 123, 48, and 34 square miles, or 32, 12, and 9 per cent. of the net area cropped. Oilseeds, such as sesamum, linseed, and castor, are cultivated in all parts, the aggregate area occupied by them being 81 square miles, while gram covered 24 square miles.

The District possesses no characteristic breed of cattle, and the ponies are of the commonest description. Sheep and goats of the ordinary kind are reared by shepherds. Near Golconda, a stud farm exists for the supply of horses to the State troops. Cattle, &c.

As in other Telingāna Districts, 'wet' cultivation is largely practised. Numerous dams have been constructed in the Mūsi, the channels being used as feeders to large tanks, such as the Husain Sāgar, and also directly for irrigating lands through which they pass. Water is also supplied from 139 large and 310 small tanks or *kuntas*, and from 2,253 wells. The total area irrigated in 1901 was 40 square miles. Irrigation.

In two forest tracts, one in the Patlūr and the other in the Shāhābād *tāluk*, certain kinds of timber are protected, including teak (*Tectona grandis*), ebony, and *nallāmaddi* (*Terminalia tomentosa*). The produce of these forests is, however, of small size. Unprotected forest tracts exist in all parts, consisting of *ghairi* or common wood used as fuel and also for thatching and wattling. Forests.

No minerals of any economic value are found, except *kankar* or nodular limestone, basalt, and granite. Crude carbonate of soda is collected at Chandūr and Kāparti in the Ambarpet *tāluk*, by lixiviating saline earth. In the Patlūr *tāluk* laminated limestone known as Shāhābād stone, red ochre, and ironstone occur, the last being smelted for local use. Minerals.

At Chandūr *sārīs* and handkerchiefs are made, and at Asafnagar brass and copper vessels of a superior kind. The Chamārs cure leather in a primitive way for manufacture into water-buckets and sandals. Arts and manufactures.

The chief exports are *jowār*, rice and other food-grains, cotton, *ghī*, oilseeds, chillies, sheep and cattle, bones, jaggery, tobacco, hides and skins, and *tarvar* bark for tanning. The principal imports are salt, salted fish, opium, spices, gold and silver, copper and brass utensils, refined sugar, iron, sulphur, kerosene oil, raw silk, and silk and cotton cloths of every description. The city of Hyderābād is the chief centre of trade; but weekly fairs are held at several places, such as at Commerce.

Chintalcherū, Krishnareddipet, Kanktūr, Dilāvarganj, Tūpran, and Dhārūr. The principal trading castes are the Komatis and a few Mārwāris.

Railways.

The District is well favoured as regards railways. The Nizām's State Railway crosses it from east to west, with six stations, and the Hyderābād-Godāvari Valley line starting from Hyderābād has one station within its limits. The total length of railways is about 98 miles.

Roads.

There are six roads: namely, from Hyderābād via Shamsābād to Mahbūbnagar, 45 miles; Hyderābād to Nalgonda, 80 miles; Hyderābād via Bībīnagar to Bhongīr, 28 miles; Hyderābād to Medchal, 34 miles; Hyderābād to Patancheru via Lingampalli, 16 miles; and Dhārūr to Kohīr in Bīdar District, 24 miles: making a total of 227 miles. The first, second, and fourth are portions of the military roads leading to Raichūr, Masulipatam, and Nāgpur respectively.

Famine.

The District generally escapes famine, but it suffered severely from drought owing to scanty and unseasonable rain in 1896, 1897, 1899, 1901, and 1902. In the first two years no fodder was obtainable, and large numbers of cattle died.

District subdivisions and staff.

There are three subdivisions: one consisting of the Medchal and Jūkal *tāluks*, under a Second Tālukdār; the second, comprising the Patlūr and Asafnagar *tāluks*, under a Third Tālukdār; and the remaining two *tāluks* of Ambarpet and Shāhābād are managed by the First Tālukdār, who also exercises a general supervision over all his subordinates. Each *tāluk* is under a *tahsīldār*, while the sub-*tāluk* of Jūkal has a *naib-tahsīldār*.

Civil and criminal justice.

The District civil court is presided over by the Judicial Assistant to the First Tālukdār, the latter being also the *Nāzim-i-Dīwāni* or Civil Judge. Cases decided or inquired into by the Assistant are submitted to the First Tālukdār for confirmation or decision. The subordinate civil courts are those of the *tahsīldārs*. The First Tālukdār is the chief magistrate of the District, and his Judicial Assistant is also a joint-magistrate, who exercises powers as such during the absence of the First Tālukdār from head-quarters. The Second and Third Tālukdārs exercise magisterial powers of the second, and the *tahsīldārs* powers of the third class. Serious crime is not heavy.

Land revenue.

Very little is known of the revenue history before the introduction of District administration in 1866; but the management was based on the farming of groups of villages or *tāluks* to revenue contractors for fixed sums, the farmers receiving

1½ annas per rupee for collection. In 1866 the present *tāluks* were formed, except the sub-*tāluk* of Jūkal, which was a *jāgīr* resumed on the death of the *jāgīrdār* in 1895 without heirs. The District has not been surveyed. The average rate of assessment on 'wet' land is Rs. 12 per acre (maximum Rs. 47, minimum Rs. 8), and on 'dry' land Rs. 1-3 (maximum Rs. 4, minimum R. 0-6).

The land revenue and total revenue for a series of years are given below, in thousands of rupees:—

	1881.	1891.	1901.	1904.
Land revenue . .	6,08	7,06	8,02	6,06
Total revenue . .	9,36	11,30	11,34	10,12

The ordinary one anna cess is not in force here; but an old tax known as the *rāsta-patti* or 'road tax' is levied at the rate of 1 per cent. on the land revenue collected, yielding about Rs. 6,800 annually. No local boards have been established; but at the head-quarters of the *tāluks*, as well as at Maulā Alī, Surūrnagar, Golconda, and Maisaram, conservancy establishments are maintained, the cost of which is paid from the *Sarf-i-khās* treasury, the general supervision being under the First Tālukdār's Assistant in the irrigation branch. **Local and municipal government.**

The First Tālukdār is the head of the police, with a *Mohtamim* or Superintendent as his executive deputy. Under the latter are 6 inspectors, 115 subordinate officers, 696 constables, and 25 mounted police. These are distributed among 48 police stations. In addition, 1,179 rural police are under the police *pātels* of the villages. **Police and jails.**

The District has no jail, prisoners being sent to the Central jail at Hyderābād. At the outlying *tahsīl* offices, excluding Asafnagar and Ambarpet, there are small lock-ups.

The District takes a high place in the State as regards the literacy of its population, of whom 3·5 per cent. (6·3 males and 0·6 females) were able to read and write in 1901. There are, however, only 9 schools, of which 8 are primary schools, and one is a middle school. The number of pupils under instruction in 1881, 1891, 1901, and 1903 was 321, 461, 511, and 667 respectively. The total expenditure on education in 1901 amounted to Rs. 4,100, towards which fees contributed Rs. 484. **Education.**

Two dispensaries are maintained, with accommodation for 40 in-patients. The total number of in-patients treated in 1901 was 33, and of out-patients 9,317. The operations performed numbered 280, and the total expenditure was Rs. 6,124. **Medical.**

The number of persons successfully vaccinated in 1901 was only 543, or 1·08 per 1,000 of population.

Medchal.—'Crown' *tāluk* in the north-east of Atrāf-i-balda District, Hyderābād State, also called the *Shimāli* or 'northern' *tāluk*, with an area of 634 square miles. The population in 1901, including *jāgīrs*, was 80,520, compared with 91,113 in 1891. The *tāluk* contains 167 villages, of which 106 are *jāgīr*; and Medchal (population, 3,019) is the head-quarters. The land revenue in 1901 was one lakh. Medchal is well supplied with tanks from which much rice is irrigated. The *jāgīr tāluk* of Alīābād, with 2 villages, a population of 3,201, and an area of about 8 square miles, lies to the east of Medchal.

Ambarpet.—'Crown' *tāluk* in Atrāf-i-balda District, Hyderābād State, also called the *Sharki* or 'eastern' *tāluk*, with an area, including *jāgīrs*, of 750 square miles. The population in 1901 was 108,325, compared with 98,858 in 1891. The *tāluk* contains 180 villages, of which 56 are *jāgīr*; and Ambarpet (population, 2,648) is the head-quarters. The land revenue in 1901 was 1·7 lakhs. Ambarpet contains many tanks near which rice is grown. The *paigāh tāluk* of Upal, with 17 villages, a population of 6,485, and an area of about 66 square miles, is situated to the east of Ambarpet.

Shāhābād Tāluk.—'Crown' *tāluk* in the south of Atrāf-i-balda District, Hyderābād State, also known as the *Junūbi* or 'southern' *tāluk*, with an area, including *jāgīrs*, of 654 square miles. The population in 1901 was 76,905, compared with 73,245 in 1891. The *tāluk* contains 168 villages, of which 103 are *jāgīr*; and Shāhābād (population, 3,955) is the head-quarters. The land revenue in 1901 was 1·1 lakhs. The *paigāh tāluk* of Vikārābād, with 25 villages, a population of 11,270, and an area of about 82 square miles, is situated to the north-west of Shāhābād.

Asafnagar.—'Crown' *tāluk* in Atrāf-i-balda District, Hyderābād State, also known as the *Gharbi* or 'western' *tāluk*, with an area, including *jāgīrs*, of 402 square miles. The population in 1901 was 56,928, compared with 47,264 in 1891. The *tāluk* contains 97 villages, of which 33 are *jāgīr*; and Asafnagar (population, 1,694) is the head-quarters. The land revenue in 1901 was 2 lakhs. The *tāluk* is composed of sandy soils, and is well supplied with tanks. The *paigāh tāluk* of Farīdābād, with 31 villages, a population of 8,446, and an area of about 126 square miles, lies to the west.

Patlūr.—'Crown' *tāluk* in Atrāf-i-balda District, Hyderābād State, lying south of Bīdar District, with an area of 595 square miles including *jāgīrs*. The population in 1901 was 52,833, compared with 53,878 in 1891. It contains 138 villages, of which 23 are *jāgīr*; and Dhārūr (population, 1,949) is the head-quarters. The land revenue in 1901 was 1·6 lakhs.

Jūkal.—'Crown' sub-*tāluk* in Atrāf-i-balda District, Hyderābād State, lying to the south-west of Nizāmābād District, with an area of 87 square miles. The population in 1901 was 15,789, compared with 10,883 in 1891. The sub-*tāluk* contains 22 villages; and Jūkal (population, 3,350) is the head-quarters. The land revenue in 1901 was Rs. 66,000. The soil is mostly *regar* or black cotton soil.

Bolārum.—Formerly a cantonment of the Hyderābād Contingent, and now part of SECUNDERĀBĀD, Hyderābād State.

Chādarghāt.—Northern suburb of the city of Hyderābād, Hyderābād State, separated from it by the Mūsi river. It derives its name from a dam 12 feet high thrown across the Mūsi, over which the water falls like a sheet (*chādar*). This suburb, which contains most of the houses of the Europeans in the service of the Nizām and also of native officials, has sprung up within the last fifty years. In 1850, with the exception of the Residency and its bazars, there was scarcely a building to be found where houses may be now counted by thousands, many of them fine buildings. It forms the principal section of the Chādarghāt branch of the Hyderābād municipality. It contains the Roman Catholic Cathedral and All Saints' schools; the old French gun-foundry erected by M. Raymond, and referred to by Malcolm (1798) as a place in which 'they cast excellent cannon and made serviceable muskets'; Sir W. Rumbold's house (Rumbold's *kothi*), now occupied by the Nizām College; the King *kothi*, where the Nizām's eldest son resides; the Public Works Office; the Hyderābād College; and the fine buildings known as the Saifābād Palace, now used as the offices of the Financial, Public Works, and the Private Secretaries. Adjoining the compound of this palace on the west is the Mint and Stamp Office, an immense building which was completed in 1904. Many other offices and institutions are situated in Chādarghāt. The public gardens lie to the north-west, and adjoining them on the south is the Hyderābād railway station. Below the Husain Sāgar, or tank, an ice factory, a steam saw-mill, and the Hyderābād Spinning and Weaving Mills have been established.

Golconda.—Fortress and ruined city in Atrāf-i-balda District, Hyderābād State, situated in 17° 23′ N. and 78° 24′ E., 5 miles west of Hyderābād city. The fort was originally constructed by the Rājā of Warangal, who ceded it in 1364, together with its dependencies, to Muhammad Shāh Bahmani of Gulbarga. For a time it was known as Muhammadnagar. In 1512 the place passed from the Bahmanis to the Kutb Shāhis, who had their capital here till the foundation of Hyderābād. In 1687 the city was taken by Aurangzeb after a siege of eight months, and the last of the Kutb Shāhis was deported to Daulatābād. The fortress, which is situated on a rocky ridge of granite, is extensive, and contains many enclosures. It is surrounded by a strong crenellated stone wall, over 3 miles in circumference, with 87 bastions at the angles; some of these still contain large pieces of ordnance bearing Persian inscriptions. Inside the walls are ruins of numerous palaces, mosques, and dwellings, scattered everywhere, while the citadel or *bālā hisār* is in good preservation. There are eight gates to the fort, of which four are now in use. The moat which surrounds the fort is choked with rubbish in most places. About half a mile to the north of the fort are the tombs of the Kutb Shāhi kings. These buildings, though constructed of granite, have suffered from the ravages of time and the damage done by the siege guns of Aurangzeb, while the enamelled tiles which once adorned them have been stolen. In shape the tombs are oblong or square, the lower portion being an arcade of pointed arches on a raised terrace, and the whole crowned by a dome. The actual sarcophagus is usually of black basalt or greenstone, beautifully carved. Golconda is now garrisoned by a few Arabs and by the Golconda Brigade, consisting of a battery and one regiment each of cavalry and infantry. The Mūsi river flows south of the fort. In English literature Golconda has given its name to the diamonds which were found at many places within the dominions of the Kutb Shāhi dynasty. There are no diamond mines within the immediate neighbourhood of Golconda itself.

Hyderābād City (*Haidarābād*).—Capital of Hyderābād State, or the Nizām's Dominions, situated in 17° 22′ N. and 78° 27′ E., on the right bank of the Mūsi river, a tributary of the Kistna. It is the fourth largest city in the Indian Empire. The population (including the suburbs, Residency Bazars, and the adjoining cantonment) was: (1881) 367,417, (1891) 415,039, and (1901) 448,466. In the last year, Hindus numbered 243,241, Musalmāns 189,152, and Christians 13,923. There were also 863 Sikhs, 929 Pārsīs, 318 Jains, and 40 others. Hyderābād is on the Nizām's State Railway, distant by rail from Bombay 492 miles, from Madras 533 miles, and from Calcutta

987 miles. The city was founded in 1589 by Muhammad Kuli, the fifth Kutb Shāhi king, who ruled at Golconda, five miles west of Hyderābād. It was first named Bhāgnagar, but the name was afterwards changed to Hyderābād. It continued to prosper until Aurangzeb began to interfere between the king and his discontented minister, Mīr Jumla, in 1665. In 1687 Golconda was stormed and Hyderābād fell into the hands of the Mughals, in whose possession it remained until the first Nizām proclaimed his independence, and made it his capital.

The city. The city is surrounded by a stone wall flanked with bastions, and pierced with thirteen gates and twelve *khirkīs* or posterns. It is built in the form of a parallelogram, 6 miles in circumference and 2¼ square miles in area. The wall was commenced by Mubāriz Khān, the last Mughal *Sūbahdār*, and completed by the first of the Nizāms. The city has extended beyond its former limits on the north and east. Four bridges span the Mūsi. The Purāna Pul, or 'old bridge,' is the westernmost, and the Oliphant Bridge the easternmost, while between these two are the Afzal Bridge and the Champā Gate Bridge.

Kutb Shāhi buildings. The most imposing of the buildings due to the Kutb Shāhi kings is the Chār Minār, or 'four minarets,' erected in 1591, and occupying a central position in the city, with four roads radiating from its base. The minarets, 180 feet high, spring from the abutments of open arches facing the cardinal points. During the occupation of the Mughals, one of the minarets was struck by lightning, and its reconstruction cost Rs. 60,000. M. Bussy, the French general, and his troops occupied the Chār Minār in 1756. The building was thoroughly renovated by Sir Sālār Jang a few years before his death. Close to the Chār Minār are the Chār Kamān, or 'four arches,' built in 1593 over four streets, leading to the four quarters of the city. The Chār-sū-kā-Hauz, or 'cistern of four roads,' is situated to the north of the Chār Minār. The king had a pavilion erected near the cistern, from which he used to witness the manœuvring of his troops. The Dār-ush-shifa (hospital), about 200 yards to the north-west of the Purānī Havelī ('old palace'), built by Sultān Kuli Kutb Shāh, is a large building consisting of a paved quadrangular courtyard, with chambers all round for the accommodation of the sick. A number of native physicians were formerly maintained to minister to the sick and to teach medicine, but the building is now used as a barrack for some of the irregular troops. Opposite the entrance is a fine mosque erected at the same time as the hospital. The Ashūr Khāna, a large building west of Sir Sālār Jang's palace, was erected by Sultān

Muhammad Kuli Kutb Shāh in 1594, at a cost of Rs. 66,000. It is used for the Muharram ceremonies. The Purāna Pul ('old bridge') connects the city with the Kārvān road to Golconda. It consists of 23 arches, and is 600 feet long, 33 broad, and 54 above the river-bed, and was built in 1593. The river is very narrow here, and the banks are steep. The Gosha Mahal palace, erected by Abul Hasan, the last Kutb Shāhi king, stands a mile north of the city, and has a large cistern and pleasure-grounds for the *zanāna*. It was used until lately as a barrack, but is now a military club. The Mecca mosque, situated to the south-west of the Chār Minār, is 225 feet long, 180 broad, and 75 high, and is built entirely of stone, occupying a paved quadrangle 360 feet square. Fifteen arches support the roof, which is surmounted by two large domes, rising 100 feet above it. It can accommodate 10,000 worshippers. Muhammad[1] Kutb Shāh commenced the building, and after his death its construction was continued by Abul Hasan, but Aurangzeb completed it. Nizām Alī Khān and all his successors are interred in the grounds of this mosque. The Jāma Masjid, which is near the Chār Minār, was built in 1596. Ruins of a Turkish bath are to be seen in the courtyard. With the exception of the Mecca Masjid and the Gosha Mahal, all these buildings were constructed by Sultān Muhammad Kuli Kutb Shāh, who is said to have spent three millions sterling on public buildings and irrigation works, while his nobles followed his example. An extensive burial-ground, known as Mīr Momin's Daira, was originally consecrated as the necropolis of the Shiah sect by Mīr Momin, who came to Hyderābād from Karbalā in the reign of Abdullāh Kutb Shāh. It contains his remains, but now both Shiahs and Sunnis are buried here. Sir Sālār Jang's family burial-ground lies to the south of the Daira.

Recent buildings. Among the more recent buildings may be mentioned the Purānī Havelī ('old palace'), an extensive building in the north-eastern quarter of the city, built by the first of the Nizāms, and still occasionally used by the present ruler. The Nizām's Chaumahalla Palace consists of three quadrangles, with handsome buildings on either side, and large cisterns in the centre. The palace is luxuriously and tastefully furnished, and the *zanāna* or ladies' apartments lie beyond the third quadrangle. There are other royal residences at Golconda, Surūrnagar, Maulā Alī, Asafnagar, Lingampalli, and Malakpet; but His Highness

[1] Not to be confounded with his uncle and predecessor, Muhammad Kuli, the founder of Hyderābād city.

at present usually resides in Sirdār Villa at Malakpet near the racecourse. Sālār Jang's palace is situated near the Afzal Gate and consists of two portions: one containing the Bārādari and Lakkar Kot ('wooden palace') lies on the right bank of the Mūsi, and the other is beyond the road leading to the Purānī Havelī. Both are extensive buildings covering a large space of ground. Shams-ul-Umarā's Bārādari, situated in the west of the city, was built by the first Shams-ul-Umarā on an extensive piece of ground. The Falaknumā, a very fine palace, was built by the late Sir Vikār-ul-Umarā on the summit of a hill in the southern suburb of the city, at a cost, it is said, of 35 lakhs. The view of the city and suburbs from this palace is most striking, and no building in Hyderābād equals it in point of architecture or design. It was purchased by the Nizām in 1897. The Jahānnumā Palace and its beautiful gardens, belonging to the late Sir Asmān Jāh, are situated north of the Falaknumā. The palace and the bungalows in the gardens contain a great number of ingenious mechanical toys.

The suburbs. The suburbs may be divided into those beyond the Mūsi river and those adjoining the city. The former comprise Begam Bāzār, Kārvān, Afzal Ganj, Mushīrābād, Khairatābād, Saitābād, and CHĀDARGHĀT, extending for a distance of 3 miles from east to west and an average breadth of 1½ miles from north to south, covering an area of over 5 square miles. The Residency Bazars are situated to the south-east of these suburbs and to the north-east of the city. The other suburbs adjoining the city to the east and south are known as Yākūtpura, Malakpet, and Jahānnumā, and occupy an area of 4 square miles.

The Residency. The Residency is situated on the left bank of the Mūsi, opposite the north-eastern corner of the city. The building is an imposing one, and stands in the midst of a beautiful park-like expanse, with handsomely laid-out gardens. It was commenced in 1800, under the supervision of Mr. Russell of the Madras Engineers, and was completed about 1807. It contains a Darbār Hall on the ground floor, measuring 60 feet by 33 and 50 feet high. The grounds contain bungalows for the First and Second Assistant Residents, while the Residency Surgeon resides in a bungalow outside the walls. On the south side are large ranges of offices. Beyond the north gate are the court of the Superintendent of Residency Bazars, the Residency hospital, and the Residency high school and clock-tower; while the telegraph office is situated to the west of the building. A cemetery close by contains, among other tombs, those of two Residents, Mr. G. A. Bushby and Mr. Roberts, who died respectively in 1856 and 1868; and of Sir W. Rumbold, Bart., a partner in the house of Palmer & Co., who died in 1833.

The Residency is surrounded on all sides by populous bazars, over which the Resident exercises civil and criminal jurisdiction. The population of the bazars in 1901 was 16,904, and they form a great centre of trade, where branch houses and representatives of all the wealthy bankers in India are to be found. West of the Residency hospital is the Local Funds building. On the right of the road leading from the western gate of the Residency is located the Hyderābād branch of the Bank of Bengal, an imposing stone building. The British Post Office is situated in the north-west corner of the limits of the Residency Bazars, and a little to the north lie St. George's Church and schools, adjoining which is the old cemetery.

Tanks. The Husain Sāgar, a large sheet of water, which when full extends over an area of 8 square miles, lies between SECUNDERĀBĀD on the north and Saifābād, a portion of Hyderābād, on the south, and is the source of water-supply for the Residency and suburbs north of the Mūsi river. The dam is 2,500 yards long, and forms the road connecting the northern suburbs with Secunderābād. It was built by Sultān Ibrāhīm Kutb Shāh, in about 1575, at a cost of 2½ lakhs. The Mīr Alam, situated to the south-west of the city, is another magnificent sheet of water, 8 miles in circumference. The dam consists of a series of 21 semicircular retaining walls with their convex side facing the water. Its total length is 1,120 yards, and it was constructed by French engineers in the Nizām's service. Mīr Alam, the Minister, built this, and the Bārādari and other buildings, out of the prize-money which fell to his share after the fall of Seringapatam. The dam alone cost 8 lakhs. The city and suburbs are now amply supplied with water from these two large tanks. Water-works have been constructed, though the systems are not yet complete. This supply has led to a considerable improvement in sanitation; and cholera, which used to be an annual visitant, has not been known in the city for the last few years.

Houses. The houses of well-to-do people in the city are chiefly built of stone and brick, standing within large gardens. Those of the commoner people were formerly built of mud, but are now gradually being replaced by brick structures. The old streets and lanes were narrow, but have of late been widened through the exertions of the municipality. In the northern suburbs, however, most of the houses are of a much superior plan, resembling the bungalows of Europeans, and are situated in suitable compounds. It may be said that practically three-fourths of the old city and suburbs have been rebuilt or renovated since the ministry of the late Sir Sālār Jang, in addition to the buildings erected during the last half-century.

Hyderābād now contains three colleges, several English and vernacular schools, a large Roman Catholic church, and a number of places of worship for other Christian denominations. The public gardens, beautifully laid out, with two large tanks in the centre, and surrounded by a picturesque wall, lie at the foot of the Naubat Pahār. To the south of these gardens is the Hyderābād station of the Nizām's Guaranteed State Railway. Near the Afzal Bridge are the Afzal Ganj Hospital and Mosque; the former has accommodation for 78 in-patients, and a large staff of surgeons and nurses. Most of the State secretariats and other offices are situated in Saifābād and Chādarghāt; but the High Court and the Small Cause and Magistrates' Courts, the Treasury, and the Accountant-General's and certain other offices are located in the city. The system of municipal administration and the arts and manufactures carried on in the city are described in the article on HYDERĀBĀD STATE[1]. Public institutions.

Secunderābād (*Sikandarābād*).—British cantonment in Hyderābād State, situated in 17° 27′ N. and 78° 30′ E., 6 miles north-east of Hyderābād city. The population of Secunderābād in 1901 was 83,550, and the population of Bolārum and Trimulgherry 12,888.

Secunderābād, named after the Nizām Sikandar Jāh, is one of the largest military stations in India. The British troops stationed here were formerly known as the Subsidiary Force, and were paid from the revenues of the districts ceded by the Nizām for this purpose under the treaty of 1800. The Nizām also agreed to maintain a Contingent to act with the Subsidiary Force in case of necessity. This Contingent, for the payment of which Berār was assigned to the British Government by the treaty of 1853, modified by the treaty of 1860, had its headquarters at Bolārum, other stations being Ellichpur in Berār, and five towns in Hyderābād State: namely, Aurangābād, Hingoli, Jālna, Amba (Mominābād), and Raichūr. During the Mutiny of 1857 an unsuccessful attempt was made to tamper

[1] At the end of September, 1908, a terrible disaster occurred at Hyderābād. As the result of some days' continuous rain, the Mūsi river suddenly rose in flood, carrying away several arches of three bridges—the Purāna Pul, Afzal, and Chādarghāt—inundating many quarters of the city on both sides of the river, and causing widespread destruction of life and property.

with the fidelity of the troops at Secunderābād. An attack on the Residency was repulsed, and during the troubled times of 1857–8 much good service was rendered by both the Subsidiary Force and the Hyderābād Contingent. By an agreement entered into in 1902, the Contingent ceased to exist as a separate force, and was incorporated in the Indian Army. The cantonments, except Aurangābād, were vacated, and Bolārum was merged in Secunderābād. The garrison of Secunderābād and Bolārum consisted in 1904 of one regiment of British and two of Native cavalry; one battery of horse and three of field artillery, with ammunition columns; two battalions of British and six regiments of Native infantry; a company of sappers and miners, with a proportion of mule corps and transport bearers. The combined cantonment comprises the areas of Secunderābād, Chilkalguda, Bowanpalli, Begampett, Trimulgherry, North Trimulgherry, and Bolārum.

Up to 1850 the cantonment of Secunderābād consisted of a line of barracks and huts, extending for a distance of three miles from east to west, with the artillery in front and on the left flank, and the infantry on the right. Since that date, however, the cantonment boundaries have been extended so as to include the areas already mentioned, covering 22 square miles, including many interspersed villages. New double-storeyed barracks have been erected for the European troops, and improved quarters for the Native troops.

The country for miles round Secunderābād undulates into hummocks, with outcrops of underlying rock, crossed from east to west by greenstone dikes. East of the cantonment are two large outcrops of granite and a hill of some size, known as Maulā Alī, and near it another called Kadam Rasūl from a legend that it bears an impress of the Prophet's foot. Shady trees line the roads of the cantonment, and here and there are clusters of date and palmyra palms; but otherwise the face of the country is bare, with but little depth of soil on the more elevated spots. Rice is cultivated in the dips and villages, in most of which tanks have been constructed. The water-supply from wells is not abundant; and of late years the Jidimatla tank, which has not been an unqualified success, has been constructed for the purpose of providing an adequate supply of water for the troops and civil population of Secunderābād.

The climate of Secunderābād is generally healthy, though at the latter end of the rainy season, in September, fever is somewhat prevalent. The rainfall varies considerably; during the twenty-five years ending 1903 it averaged 33 inches.

MEDAK GULSHANĀBĀD DIVISION

Medak Gulshanābād Division.—Division of the Hyderābād State, formed in 1905 from the old BĪDAR DIVISION. It includes four Districts, as shown below:—

District.	Area in square miles.	Population, 1901.	Land revenue and cesses, in thousands of rupees.
Nizāmābād (Indūr) .	3,282	467,367	16,11
Medak . . .	3,447	536,027	15,52
Mahbūbnagar . .	5,842	613,771	8,86
Nalgonda . . .	4,913	823,121	15,53
Total	17,484	2,440,286	56,02

The density of population is 1,396 persons per square mile; and the Division contains 11 towns and 2,747 villages. The chief places of commercial importance are the towns of NIZĀMĀBĀD, MEDAK, SADĀSEOPET, SIDDIPET, MAHBŪBNAGAR, NĀRĀYANPET, NALGONDA, and BHONGĪR. Medak, Nalgonda, and Bhongīr are also places of historic interest. The head-quarters of the *Sūbahdār* or Commissioner are at PATANCHERŪ.

Bīdar Division.—Formerly a Division, occupying almost the centre of Hyderābād State, and extending from the Yeotmāl District of Berār in the north as far as the Kistna river in the south. It lay between 16° 5′ and 19° 55′ N. and 77° 9′ and 80° E. The head-quarters of the Commissioner (*Sūbahdār*) were at Patancherū, a village in the Kalabgūr *tāluk* of Medak. The population of the Division increased from 2,455,179 in 1881 to 2,812,720 in 1891, but declined to 2,745,979 in 1901. The total area was 22,567 square miles, and the density of population 122 persons per square mile, compared with 135 for the whole State, of which the Division was the largest in both area and population. Of the total population in 1901, 88·2 per cent. were Hindus and 9·6 per cent. Musalmāns, while Christians numbered 816 (of whom 719 were natives), Jains 1,320, Pārsīs 4, Sikhs 493, and Animists 54,357. The Division included five Districts, as shown in the table on the next page.

In 1905 Bīdar District was transferred to the Gulbarga Division, and Sirpur Tāndūr (now known as Adilābād) to

Warangal, while the Division was increased by the addition of Nalgonda from Warangal, and is now called MEDAK GULSHANĀBĀD. Other changes were made in the areas of the remaining Districts, and the name of Indūr District has been changed to Nizāmābād.

District.	Area in square miles.	Population, 1901.	Land revenue and cesses, 1901, in thousands of rupees.
Bīdar . . .	4,168	766,129	11,64
Indūr . . .	4,822	634,588	19,60
Mahbūbnagar . .	6,543	705,725	10,15
Medak . . .	2,005	366,722	12,88
Sirpur Tāndūr . .	5,029	272,815	2,66
Total	22,567	2,745,979	56,93

Nizāmābād District.—District in the Medak Gulshanābād Division of Hyderābād State, formerly known as INDŪR DISTRICT. It is bounded on the north by Nānder and Adilābād; on the east by Karīmnagar; on the south by Medak; and on the west by Nānder. Its present area, including *jāgīrs*, is about 3,282 square miles. A few minor ranges of hills are found in the east and west. The largest river in the District is the Godāvari, which forms its northern boundary, separating it from Nānder and Adilābād. The Mānjra, the chief tributary of the Godāvari, flows along the western border, separating it from Nānder on the west. Smaller streams are the Phulāng, traversing the Nizāmābād and Armūr *tāluks*, and the Yedlakatta Vāgū, a perennial stream in the Kāmāreddipet *tāluk*.

The most important trees are teak, black-wood, ebony, *nallāmaddi* (*Terminalia tomentosa*), *eppa* (*Hardwickia binata*), *bījāsāl* (*Pterocarpus Marsupium*), *tarvar* (*Cassia auriculata*), custard-apple, mango, and tamarind.

The rocks are related to the Archaean and Deccan trap formations, the former occupying a very large area.

Tigers, leopards, wolves, bears, and wild hog are common, while *sāmbar*, spotted deer, and *nīlgai* are also found.

The climate is dry and healthy from February to the end of May, but damp and malarious during the rains and the cold season, giving rise to ague and various forms of fever. The temperature ranges between 45° in December and 110° in May. The annual rainfall averages about 42 inches.

Details of the population and the area before the changes made in 1905, when the District was constituted, are given under INDŪR DISTRICT, the name by which it was formerly known. It now has a population (1901) of 467,367, and in its present form comprises the five *tāluks* of NIZĀMĀBĀD, BODHAN, ARMŪR, KĀMĀREDDIPET, and YELLĀREDDIPET, besides a *paigāh* estate, three *samasthāns*, and seven large *jāgīrs*. The chief towns are NIZĀMĀBĀD (population, 12,871), the head-quarters of the District, ARMŪR (9,031), BODHAN (6,438), and BALKONDA (5,118). Of the total population, more than 91 per cent. are Hindus, the rest being Musalmāns. More than 78 per cent. of the people speak Telugu. The land revenue demand is about 14·7 lakhs.

Indūr District[1].—District in the Bīdar Division of Hyderābād State, lying between the Districts of Sirpur Tāndūr on the north, Elgandal on the east, Medak on the south, and Bīdar and Nānder on the west, and between 18° 5′ and 19° 30′ N. and 77° 40′ and 79° 0′ E. It has an area of 4,822 square miles, including *jāgīr* and *paigāh* lands, the area of the *khālsa* lands being 3,574 square miles. A range of hills runs through the north between Nānder and Elgandal. There are also minor ranges in the west and east. The largest river is the Godāvari, which enters from the adjoining District of Nānder on the west, and, after traversing the northern portion for about 70 miles, passes into Elgandal District. The Mānjra, the chief tributary of the Godāvari, crosses the District from the south-west and joins the Godāvari near Kandkurti in the Bodhan *tāluk*, after a course of 62 miles. The Pengangā forms the boundary between the Narsāpur *tāluk* in the north and the Pusad *tāluk* of Berār. Smaller rivers are the Siddha in the Narsāpur *tāluk*, the Phulāng in the Indūr and Armūr *tāluks*, and the Sūran which passes through Narsāpur and Nirmal. All these are tributaries of the Godāvari. The Yedlakatta Vāgū is a small perennial stream in Kāmāreddipet. Boundaries, configuration, and hill and river systems.

The rocks belong to the Archaean and the Deccan trap formations, the former occupying the larger area. The Deccan trap occurs principally along the northern frontier. Geology.

The chief trees are teak, black-wood, ebony, *nallāmaddi* (*Terminalia tomentosa*), *eppa* (*Hardwickia binata*), *bījāsāl* (*Pterocarpus Marsupium*), and *tarvar* (*Cassia auriculata*). Botany.

All the *tāluks* except Mudhol are largely overgrown with jungle, giving cover to tigers, leopards, cheetahs, bears, wild dogs, hyenas, wild hog, *sāmbar*, spotted deer, and *nīlgai*. Fauna.

From February to the end of May the climate is dry and healthy, but during the monsoons and the cold season it is Climate, tempera-

[1] This District ceased to exist in 1905. *See* section on Population and the article on NIZĀMĀBĀD DISTRICT, which has taken its place.

ture, and rainfall. damp and malarious, giving rise to fever and ague. The temperature ranges between 40° in December and 110° in May. In the Nirmal *tāluk* the water is bad, and dropsy and malarial fevers are common. The annual rainfall for the twenty years ending 1901 averaged 42 inches.

History. The District was conquered by Alā-ud-dīn Khiljī in 1311. Later it formed part of the Bahmani, and subsequently of the Kutb Shāhi kingdoms; and on the fall of the latter was annexed by Aurangzeb to the Mughal empire, from which it was separated on the foundation of the Hyderābād State, early in the eighteenth century.

Archaeology. Chief among the archaeological and historical remains of the District may be mentioned the fort of Nirmal. The surrounding country is literally dotted with hills, the majority of which still bear signs of former fortifications. The main defences which surround Nirmal are of European design and construction, having been built by French officers in the Nizām's service. South-west of the town of Nizāmābād are the remains of a great fortified temple known as the fort of Indūr, which has now been converted into a Central jail. There are two old and richly carved temples at the village of Yellāreddipet, with an abundance of figure sculpture adorning both. Ten miles south of Nizāmābād, at the small village of Gaursamudram, are the tombs of three Armenians, dating from the latter part of the seventeenth century.

Population. The number of towns and villages in the District is 1,159. The population at each Census during the last twenty years was: (1881) 577,264, (1891) 639,598, and (1901) 634,588. The famine of 1899–1900 accounts for the decline of population in the last decade. The chief towns are NIZĀMĀBĀD (or Indūr), ARMŪR, NIRMAL, BODHAN, MUDHOL, KONDALWĀDI, and BĀLKONDA, the last two being in a *paigāh* and a *jāgīr* respectively. Nizāmābād is the District head-quarters. More than 91 per cent. of the population are Hindus, and nearly all the rest Musalmāns. About 78 per cent. of the population speak Telugu. The table on the next page gives the chief statistics of population in 1901.

In 1905 the *tāluks* of Nirmal and Narsāpur were transferred to the new District of Adilābād, and Mudhol and part of Bānswāda to Nānder. The rest of Bānswāda was divided between Bodhan and Yellāreddipet, while Bīmgal was merged in Armūr. Other changes were made in Yellāreddipet and Kāmāreddipet, and the District in its new shape is known as NIZĀMĀBĀD.

Castes and occupations.

The purely agricultural castes number 175,600, or about 28 per cent. of the population, the most important being Kāpus (83,000), Munnūrs (40,000), and Kolīs (30,000). Next come the Dhangars or shepherds (36,000), and the Baniās or trading castes, consisting mainly of Komatis (13,800) and Vānīs (17,000). There are 11,500 Brāhmans. The weaver castes comprise Sālās (12,000), Julāhās (13,600), and Koshtīs (5,100). The Bestās or *pālki*-bearers number 17,000. There are also 12,000 Lammānis or grain-carriers. Among the low castes are Mālas or Dhers (64,000), and Māngs or Chamārs who are leather-workers (32,000). These last also work as field-labourers. The Kalāls or toddy-drawers number about 12,000. More than 51 per cent. of the population are dependent on the land.

Tāluk.	Area in square miles.	Number of Towns.	Number of Villages.	Population.	Population per square mile.	Percentage of variation in population between 1891 and 1901.	Number of persons able to read and write.
Indūr	415	1	69	52,778	127	+ 1·0	
Nirmal	500	1	100	41,351	83	−16·4	
Armūr	479	1	72	50,717	106	− 2·9	
Bīmgal	311	...	37	29,508	95	+ 2·2	
Kāmāreddipet	338	...	71	43,375	128	+ 2·4	
Yellāreddipet	172	...	70	27,574	160	− 3·6	Not available.
Bānswāda	319	...	65	37,972	119	+ 2·8	
Bodhan	237	1	42	31,668	133	+ 4·1	
Mudhol	282	1	90	42,640	151	−11·1	
Narsāpur	521	...	133	48,489	93	− 0·8	
Jāgīrs, &c.	1,248	2	403	228,516	175	− 2·2	
District total	4,822	7	1,152	634,588	131	− 1·3	13,519

Christian missions.

A Methodist mission was started at Kanteshwar close to Nizāmābād in 1899, which manages two schools and a carpenter's workshop. Native Christians numbered 32 in 1901, of whom 2 were Methodists.

General agricultural conditions.

In the *tāluks* of Narsāpur and Mudhol *regar* or black cotton soil predominates, while *masab*, *kharab*, and *chalka*, which are mostly sandy, gravelly, and light-coloured soils, are found in the rest of the District. 'Wet' cultivation is not practised in these two *tāluks*, while numerous tanks form a marked feature in the others. The soil at the foot of the hills and in valleys is generally very fertile.

Chief agricultural statistics and principal crops.

The tenure of lands is entirely *ryotwāri*. In 1901, out of 3,574 square miles of *khālsa* land, 1,042 were cultivated, 497 were fallows and cultivable waste, 1,388 were forests, and 647 were not available for cultivation The staple food-crop is *jowār*, grown on 58 per cent. of the net area cropped. Next in importance is rice, covering 191 square miles. The other food-grains, such as *kodro*, *lachhna*, and maize, occupy 128 square miles; and cotton 34.

Cattle, &c. The ordinary breeds of cattle, ponies, sheep, and goats are met with throughout the District. The cattle reared in the hilly portions are more hardy than those of the plains, but both are small. The *tāluk* of Nirmal was once noted for its fine cattle, supposed to have been introduced from Sirpur Tāndūr. Two stallions are kept for improving the breed of horses, one at Nizāmābād and the other at Kāmāreddipet.

Irrigation. In 1901, 119 square miles were irrigated. The principal irrigation channels take off from the Phulāng and Sūran rivers and the Yedlakatta stream, and supply some of the chief tanks. Other canals and channels are supplied from irrigation dams; and there are 635 large tanks, 837 *kuntas* or smaller tanks, and 3,112 wells in good working order.

Forests. Indūr has large tracts of forests. Every *tāluk*, except Mudhol, contains some forest lands, and the growth in Nirmal and Bīmgal is dense. Teak, black-wood (*Dalbergia latifolia*), ebony (*Diospyros melanoxylon*), *nallāmaddi* (*Terminalia tomentosa*), *eppa* (*Hardwickia binata*), and *bījāsāl* (*Pterocarpus Marsupium*) grow well in these two *tāluks*, producing timber of good scantling. The timber trees elsewhere are inferior, but supply railway sleepers and poles. Fuel is abundant in all the *tāluks* except Mudhol, where the ryots plant *babūl* and *nīm* trees. 'Reserved' forests cover 795 square miles, and unprotected forests 593.

Minerals. The District possesses good basaltic and granitic building stone. The ironstone found in Bīmgal and Armūr is excellent, and sword-blades made from the Konasamudram (Armūr *tāluk*) steel were once famous for their strength and peculiar damascening.

Arts and manufactures. Coarse cotton cloth of every description is made throughout the District. In Armūr the Khatris weave various kinds of silk *sārīs* and silk cloth, more than half of which, valued at Rs. 35,000 annually, is exported. In Bīmgal and Nirmal palanquins, trays, chairs and tables, toys and native playing-cards, leathern shields, and panels for screens are neatly painted with colours of local manufacture and with embossed patterns. Brass vessels, glass bangles, and stone tumblers and cups are exported from these *tāluks*, and also steel knives and other cutting instruments of good finish. In Nizāmābād town prayer-cloths and *pardas* are printed; and scented hair oils and *agar battis*[1] of a good quality are prepared. A rice-mill has lately been erected, which is capable of husking 11 tons of paddy daily, and employs 33 hands. The Mudhol *tāluk* contains a ginning factory and a cotton-press driven by steam power. The former employs 76 and the latter 46 hands. Leather is tanned in the ordinary way by Chamārs for the manufacture of water-buckets.

Commerce. The principal exports consist of rice, gram, and other food-grains, cotton, oilseeds, oil, chillies, jaggery, tamarinds, cattle, bones and horns, tobacco, leather, *tarvar* bark for tanning, coarse cloth, silk *sārīs*, and brass vessels. The chief imports are cotton, silk and woollen cloth, salt, salted fish, opium, condiments, gold and silver, copper and brass, iron, kerosene oil, refined sugar, and raw silk. Trade is mainly with the adjoining Districts; but cotton, leather, *tarvar* bark, bones, horns, and oilseeds are sent to Bombay and Madras. Nizāmābād is the chief centre of general trade, especially for those parts not served by the railway. Weekly bazars are held at the several *tāluk* head-quarters, from which merchandise is distributed to distant parts of the District. The Komatis are the chief trading caste.

Railways. The Hyderābād-Godāvari Valley Railway traverses the District from the north-west to the south for 80 miles, with ten railway stations within its limits.

Roads. About 142 miles of road are metalled with *morum* or gravel. The old Nāgpur trunk road from Hyderābād to Nāgpur in the Central Provinces crosses the District for 84 miles, and is maintained by the Public Works department. Another road, 39 miles long, runs from Nizāmābād to Bānswāda. There are four railway feeder-roads with an aggregate length of 19 miles, and ordinary country roads connect Nizāmābād with the head-quarters of the *tāluks*. The District is on the whole well supplied with communications.

Famine Owing to its large forest area and numerous wells and tanks, Indūr has been fairly free from famine. In 1819, while there was famine in Gulbarga, Lingsugūr, Bhīr, and Parbhani, only slight distress was experienced here. In the famine of 1833, though the people were not much affected, large numbers of cattle died for want of fodder. The great famine of 1899–1900, which was most seriously felt in the Aurangābād Division and Osmānābād, affected this District also, the rainfall in 1899 being only 16 inches, or less than two-fifths of the

[1] Sticks composed of fragrant herbs, frankincense, and musk, which are burnt for their fragrance at religious ceremonials and sacrifices.

average. But as 1898 had been a good year, the ryots did not suffer acutely, though the loss to the State by remissions was considerable.

District subdivisions and staff. The District is divided into three subdivisions: one, consisting of the *tāluks* of Bodhan and Yellāreddipet, under a Third Tālukdār; the second, comprising the *tāluks* of Kāmāreddipet and Armūr, under a Second Tālukdār; and the third, consisting of the Indūr *tāluk* only, under a Third Tālukdār. Each *tāluk* is under a *tahsīldār*. The First Tālukdār is the head of the District, having a general supervision over the work of all his subordinates.

Civil and criminal justice. The District civil court is presided over by a Civil Judge styled the *Nazim-i-Dīwani*, and the subordinate civil courts are those of the *tahsīldārs*. The First Tālukdār is the chief magistrate, and the District Civil Judge is also a joint-magistrate, exercising powers during the absence of the First Tālukdār from head-quarters. The Second Tālukdār exercises first-class magisterial powers, and the Third Tālukdārs second-class powers, while the *tahsīldārs* have third-class powers. There is little serious crime in ordinary times, but bad seasons lead to cattle-thefts and dacoities.

Land revenue. Little is known of the revenue history of the District. Formerly villages were made over to revenue farmers, who were allowed 10 per cent. for collections. They levied cash payments on 'dry' cultivation and sugar-cane, but for 'wet' crops they obtained a share in kind. In 1866, when the whole State was divided into Districts and *tāluks*, revenue in kind was commuted to cash payments. A survey was completed in 1898, but the periods of settlement vary in the different *tāluks*. Mudhol, Bodhan, Yellāreddipet, Kāmāreddipet, and Bānswāda were settled for fifteen years, Nirmal and Narsāpur for ten, and Indūr, Armūr, and Bīmgal for seven years. The system followed resembles that of the Mysore settlement. The settlement caused an increase in the revenue of 5 per cent., while the survey showed that the area in holdings was greater than that recorded in the old accounts by 216 square miles. The average assessment on 'dry' land is Rs. 1-4 (maximum Rs. 2, minimum one anna), and on 'wet' land including gardens, Rs. 14 (maximum Rs. 24, minimum Rs. 3).

The land revenue and the total revenue of the District in recent years are shown in the table on the next page, in thousands of rupees.

Since 1899 a cess of one anna in the rupee has been levied,

and local boards established. The First Tālukdār is the president of the District board, and the *tahsīldārs* are chairmen of the subordinate *tāluk* boards. At Nizāmābād there is a municipality, and each of the *tāluk* head-quarters has a small conservancy establishment; the District and *tāluk* boards manage the municipalities as well. The local board expenditure in 1901 was Rs. 71,725. The District Engineer has charge of all the roads and buildings constructed or maintained by the Public Works department. The Irrigation Engineer superintends the repair and construction of irrigation works. **Local boards and municipalities.**

	1881.	1891.	1901.	1903.
Land revenue . .	14,60	19,22	18,53	16,01
Total revenue . .	23,68	28,20	24,31	28,89

The First Tālukdār is the head of the police administration, with the Superintendent (*Mohtamim*) as his executive deputy. Under him are 10 inspectors, 115 subordinate officers, 684 constables, and 25 mounted police, distributed among 45 *thānas* and 43 outposts, except the mounted police who are at head-quarters. **Police and jails.**

The fort of Indūr has been converted into a Central jail, and receives convicts sentenced to more than six months' imprisonment from the Districts of Medak, Mahbūbnagar, Bīdar, and Sirpur Tāndūr. In 1901 there were 426 convicts in the Central jail. Female convicts are sent to the Warangal Central jail, as there is no separate accommodation here. *Shatranjīs*, cotton-tweeds, counterpanes, towels, *khāki* cloth, &c., are manufactured in large quantities. Tailors', carpenters', and blacksmiths' workshops are also at work, besides a printing press. All the cloth required for the convicts is manufactured in the jail, and surplus products are sold.

The District occupies a medium place as regards the literacy of its population, of whom 2·1 per cent. (4·1 males and 0·2 females) were able to read and write in 1901. The total number of pupils under instruction in 1881, 1891, 1901, and 1903 was 226, 1,496, 1,994, and 2,476 respectively. In 1903 there were 44 primary schools and one middle school, with 103 girls under instruction. The total expenditure on education in 1901 amounted to Rs. 12,278, of which Rs. 10,864 was met by the State and the remainder by local boards. The sum derived from fees was Rs. 780. **Education.**

The District contained six dispensaries in 1901, with accommodation for 25 in-patients. The cases treated in that **Medical.**

year numbered 30,791, of whom 142 were in-patients, and 612 operations were performed. The total expenditure amounted to Rs. 15,086, of which Rs. 13,694 was paid by the State and the balance was met from Local funds.

The number of persons successfully vaccinated in 1901 was, 1,110, or 1·75 per 1,000 of the population.

Nizamābād Tāluk.—*Tāluk* in Nizāmābād District, Hyderābād State, formerly known as the Indūr *tāluk*, with an area of 550 square miles. The population in 1901, including *jāgīrs*, was 75,483, compared with 74,466 in 1891. The *tāluk* contains 107 villages, of which 38 are *jāgīr*. NIZĀMĀBĀD or Indūr (population, 12,871), the only town, is the head-quarters of the District and *tāluk*. The land revenue in 1901 was 2·5 lakhs. The soils are mostly sandy, and rice is extensively raised by tank-irrigation. The Godāvari flows in the north of the *tāluk*.

Armūr Tāluk.—*Tāluk* in Nizāmābād District, Hyderābād State, with an area of 1,038 square miles. The population in 1901, including *jāgīrs*, was 122,455, compared with 123,285 in 1891. The *tāluk* contains two towns, ARMŪR (population, 9,031), the head-quarters, and BĀLKONDA (5,118), a *jāgīr* town; and 160 villages, of which 51 are *jāgīr*. The land revenue in 1901 was 3·6 lakhs. The statistics include the sub-*tāluk* of Bīmgal, which was merged in Armūr in 1905, and had an area of 491 square miles and a population of 54,290 in 1901. Rice is largely raised by tank-irrigation. The *tāluk* is hilly in the centre, and the Godāvari flows through the north.

Kāmāreddipet.—*Tāluk* in Nizāmābād District, Hyderābād State. In 1901 the area was 413 square miles, and the population, including *jāgīrs*, was 64,933, compared with 63,366 in 1891. It contained 96 villages, of which 25 were *jāgīr*, Kāmāreddipet (population, 2,503) being the head-quarters. The land revenue in 1901 was 2·2 lakhs. In 1905 the *tāluk* was enlarged by the transfer of villages from the Medak and Rāmāyampet *tāluks* of Medak District, and Sirsilla in Karīmnagar (formerly Elgandal). It is hilly in some parts.

Yellāreddipet.—*Tāluk* in Nizāmābād District, Hyderābād State. In 1901 the area was 218 square miles, and the population, including *jāgīrs*, was 35,514, compared with 36,810 in 1891. It contained 89 villages, of which 19 were *jāgīr*, Yellāreddipet (population, 3,065) being the head-quarters. The land revenue in 1901 was 2 lakhs. By the changes made in 1905 this *tāluk* has received a number of villages from the former Bānswāda *tāluk*, and from Medak and Rāmāyampet in

Medak. The Mānjra river forms its western and southern boundary.

Bānswāda.—Formerly a *tāluk* in Indūr (now Nizāmābād) District, Hyderābād State. In 1901 the area was 542 square miles, and the population, including *jāgīrs*, was 80,888, compared with 78,657 in 1891. It contained 141 villages, of which 76 were *jāgīr*. The land revenue in 1901 was 2·4 lakhs. In 1905 the *tāluk* was divided between the Deglūr *tāluk* of Nānder District and Bodhan and Yellāreddipet in Nizāmābād.

Bodhan Tāluk.—*Tāluk* in Nizāmābād District, Hyderābād State, with an area of 317 square miles. The population in 1901, including *jāgīrs*, was 52,862, compared with 50,779 in 1891. The *tāluk* has one town, Bodhan (population, 6,438), the head-quarters; and 65 villages, of which 23 are *jāgīr*. The land revenue in 1901 was 1·7 lakhs. In 1905 the area was increased by the addition of part of the Bānswāda *tāluk*. The Mānjra river forms the western boundary. Kotgīr, a *paigāh tāluk*, having a population of 24,267 and an area of about 120 square miles, lies to the south, with 49 villages and one town, Kondalwādi (population, 6,557). The *jāgīr tāluk* of Gāndhārī, having a population of 10,180, lies to the south-east, with 28 villages and an area of about 85 square miles.

Narsāpur.—Former *tāluk* in Nizāmābād (Indūr) District, Hyderābād State, with an area of 537 square miles. The population in 1901, including *jāgīrs*, was 52,056, compared with 52,443 in 1891. The *tāluk* contained 139 villages, of which 6 are *jāgīr*; and Narsāpur (1,773) was the head-quarters. The land revenue in 1901 was 1·3 lakhs. In 1905 the *tāluk* was divided between Nirmal and a new *tāluk* of Kinwat in Adilābād District.

Armūr Town.—Head-quarters of the *tāluk* of the same name in Nizāmābād District, Hyderābād State, situated in 18° 48′ N. and 78° 16′ E., 16 miles north-east of Nizāmābād town. Population (1901), 9,031. It contains a sub-post office, a police inspector's office, a dispensary, and a school with 127 pupils. Silk cloth and *sārīs* are largely manufactured.

Bālkonda.—*Jāgīr* town in the Armūr *tāluk* of Nizāmābād District, Hyderābād State, situated in 18° 53′ N. and 78° 21′ E., six miles north-east of Armūr town, and 24 miles from Indūr station on the Hyderābād-Godāvari Valley Railway. Population (1901), 5,118. The town is surrounded by an old ruined wall, still having a few gates and posterns. It contains one temple, four mosques, one of the latter being built of stone, several tombs and shrines, and an *idgāh* used for prayers on Musalmān holidays. A fort stands near a large tank in the vicinity of the town, on the Hyderabad-Nagpur road, and small watch-towers are perched on the topmost crags of the hills in the neighbourhood. A post office and a police station are located here, besides the *jāgīr tahsīl* office, and a civil and criminal court.

Bodhan Town.—Head-quarters of the *tāluk* of the same name in Nizāmābād District, Hyderābād State, situated in 18° 40′ N. and 77° 53′ E., 16 miles west of Nizāmābād town. Population (1901), 6,438. It contains a Jāma Masjid, a temple of Narsingaswāmi, a police inspector's office, a sub-post office, and one school with 117 pupils. Three large tanks are situated on the east, north, and south of the town, irrigating 2,000 acres of land.

Kondalwādi.—Head-quarters of the *paigāh tāluk* of Kotgīr in Nizāmābād District, Hyderābād State, situated in 18° 48′ N. and 77° 46′ E., 28 miles north-west of Nizāmābād and 9 miles west of the confluence of the Godāvari and Mānjra rivers. Population (1901), 6,557.

Nizāmābād Town (or Indūr).—Head-quarters of the District and *tāluk* of the same name in Hyderābād State, situated in 18° 40′ N. and 78° 6′ E., on the Hyderābād-Godāvari Valley Railway. Population (1901), 12,871. It contains the offices of the First and Third Tālukdārs, the District and Irrigation Engineers, and the Police Superintendent, the District court, one school with 324 pupils, a Central jail, a dispensary, and a District post office. The water-supply system, originally a gift from the Rānī of Sirnāpalli, is now maintained by the local board. Nizāmābād also has a rice-husking factory, cotton-ginning and pressing factories, and an American mission, all situated in the north-eastern quarter, known as Kanteshwar. The fort on a hill to the south-west of the town was originally a temple built by Raghunāth Das, who made the tank which now forms the source of water-supply.

Boundaries, configuration, and hill and river systems.

Medak District.—District in the Medak Gulshanābād Division of Hyderābād State, lying between 17° 25′ and 18° 19′ N. and 77° 48′ and 78° 31′ E., with a total area of 2,005 square miles, including 856 square miles of *jāgīr* and *paigāh* lands[1]. It is bounded on the north-east and north by Karīmnagar and Nizāmābād; on the east and south by Atrāf-i-balda District; and on the west by Bīdar District and

[1] Except where otherwise stated, the statistics in this article relate to the District as it stood before the changes of 1905 referred to in the section on Population.

paigāh estates. There are numerous low hills. One range extends from Rāmāyampet in the north to the southern portion of Nizāmābād, and then turning to the south again enters the District. Another range extends from the north-western corner to the east. The fort of Medak stands on the summit of one of these hills to the west of the town.

The most important river is the Mānjra, which enters Medak from Bīdar, and passes through its western and north-western *tāluks*, its total length in the District being 60 miles. The Haldi or Paspaver, a tributary of the Mānjra, which enters the District from the north, flows under Medak town; its length is only 10 miles.

The rock formation is the Archaean gneiss. **Geology.**

The trees commonly found are teak, *bījāsāl* (*Pterocarpus Marsupium*), *nallāmaddi* (*Terminalia tomentosa*), *eppa* (*Hardwickia binata*), *mahuā* (*Bassia latifolia*), *nīm* (*Melia Azadirachta*), mango, tamarind, *tarvar* (*Cassia auriculata*), and various species of *Ficus*. **Botany.**

The District contains large tracts of woody and scrubby jungle, where *nīlgai*, spotted deer, *sāmbar*, and wild dogs are found. Partridge, quail, duck, teal, snipe, &c., abound everywhere. **Fauna.**

The climate is very healthy from September to June; but during the rainy season malarial fevers and agues prevail, the *tāluks* of Rāmāyampet, Medak, and Bāghat being especially liable to these ailments, owing to the excessive humidity of the atmosphere. The temperature during the winter falls to 45°, while in May it rises to 100°. The annual rainfall averages 31 inches; but in 1899 the amount received was only 17½ inches, and in 1902 about 13 inches. **Climate, temperature, and rainfall.**

This District formed part of the ancient kingdom of Warangal. In 1309 Alā-ud-dīn's general, Malik Kāfūr, marched with a large army against the Rājā of Warangal, and took Medak on his route. In the fourteenth century Medak formed part of the Bahmani kingdom, and subsequently passed to the Kutb Shāhi dynasty of Golconda. On the fall of Golconda, it was annexed to the Mughal empire, from which it was detached in the early part of the eighteenth century on the foundation of Hyderābād State. **History.**

The District contains many places of archaeological interest. The fort of Medak stands about 300 feet above the surrounding plain. PATANCHERŪ, 16 miles north-west of Hyderābād, contains some old Hindu underground temples, where ancient coins have recently been discovered. Andol and Komatūr have old **Archaeology.**

mosques of note; and Chatkūr, Kalabgur, Kāndi, Nandi, Patancherū, and Venkatāpur have ancient Hindu temples. At Yedupailū, south-east of Medak, where seven tributaries of the Mānjra meet, a large religious fair is held annually.

Population. There are 634 towns and villages in the District. The total population at each Census in the last twenty years was: (1881) 326,720, (1891) 364,735, and (1901) 366,722. The towns are MEDAK and LINGĀMPET in the Medak *tāluk*, SIDDIPET, and SADĀSEOPET. SANGAREDDIPET is the District head-quarters. About 90 per cent. of the population are Hindus, and nearly all the rest Muhammadans. Telugu is the language chiefly spoken. The following table shows the distribution of population in 1901:—

Tāluk.	Area in square miles.	Number of Towns.	Number of Villages.	Population.	Population per square mile.	Percentage of variation in population between 1891 and 1901.	Number of persons able to read and write.
Medak	294	2	70	56,495	192	+ 4·4	Not available.
Rāmāyampet	273	...	79	55,485	203	+ 2·9	
Bāghāt	25	...	15	5,544	222	+ 125·3	
Kalabgūr	234	1	85	56,313	240	− 18·8	
Andol	212	...	77	48,849	230	+ 3·7	
Tekmāl	111	...	45	20,684	186	− 1·1	
Jāgīrs, &c.	856	...	260	123,352	144	+ 3·2	
District total	2,005	3	631	366,722	183	+ 0·5	9,360

In 1905 Tekmāl was merged in Andol, and Rāmāyampet partly in Medak and partly in the Kāmāreddipet *tāluk* of Nizāmābād (Indūr) District. Ibrāhīmpatan was transferred from Mahbūbnagar District and added to Bāghāt, while Siddipet was transferred to this District from Karīmnagar (Elgandal). In its present form the District consists of five *tāluks*: Medak, Siddipet, Bāghāt, Kalabgūr, and Andol, besides the four large estates of Hatnūra, Narsāpur, Nārsingi, and Nawābpet, and other minor *jāgīrs*.

Castes and occupations. The most numerous caste is that of the Kāpus (69,000). Next come the Mādigas or leather-workers (40,300), and the Mālas or Dhers (32,400), both of whom work also as agricultural labourers. There are 37,400 Brāhmans, 32,300 Gollas or shepherds, and 13,600 Komatis, who form the trading and money-lending caste. Nearly 42 per cent. of the population depend directly upon agriculture, and 11 per cent. on general labour and earthwork.

The total number of Christians, according to the last Census, was 373, of whom 327 were natives. A Wesleyan mission at Medak town was started in 1887, and has a staff of 8 Europeans and 45 natives. The adherents are chiefly of the Māla caste. The mission maintains a school and a hospital. The former was opened in 1887 and the latter in 1895, a large *zanāna* ward being added in 1902. Christian missions.

There is hardly any difference in the agricultural condition of the several *tāluks*. The soils on the highlands are mostly sandy and gravelly, while black soil is found in small patches in hollows or depressed areas. General agricultural conditions.

The tenure of lands is chiefly *ryotwāri*. In 1901 the District contained 1,149 square miles of *khālsa* lands, of which 489 were cultivated. Of the remainder, 114 were cultivable waste and fallows, 387 were forests, and 159 were not available for cultivation. The staple food-crops are rice, *bājra*, and *jowār*, the areas under which were 106, 207, and 168 square miles respectively. The rice in this District compares favourably with the finest qualities produced elsewhere. Next in importance are *kodro*, *lachna*, and various pulses. Sugar-cane is grown in all the *tāluks*, covering about one square mile. Chief agricultural statistics and principal crops.

The cattle are of the ordinary kind, and buffaloes are extensively employed in rice and sugar-cane cultivation. No special breed of ponies or horses is indigenous to the District, those found being very inferior. At Rājampet, near Sangareddipet, there is a State stud farm, where several stallions are kept with the object of improving the breed; but ryots are slow in taking advantage of the facilities offered them in this respect. Sheep and goats of the ordinary description are reared. Cattle, &c.

The total area of irrigated land in 1900–1 was 109 square miles, or more than 22 per cent. of the cultivated area. The different sources of irrigation and the areas supplied by each are as follows: Canals and channels, 17 square miles; tanks, 68; and wells, 24. Tank-irrigation is the mainstay of the District, which contains 351 large and 1,658 small tanks. The number of wells is 2,018; and the other sources of irrigation are small anicuts, called *mathris*, of which there are 74. The Malkāpur tank irrigates the lands of 12 villages. Generally two crops of rice are raised with tank and well irrigation. Water is raised from wells in leathern buckets. A large canal taking off from the Mānjra has been constructed at a cost of over 10 lakhs, which is estimated to irrigate 10,000 acres of land, and to yield a revenue of 2 lakhs. It was opened Irrigation.

in 1904. Another project, called the Mānjra Extension, when completed will cost 6½ lakhs and irrigate 7,000 acres, securing a revenue of 2½ lakhs. The District has always been immune from famine, owing to the large number of tanks it contains.

Forests. Medak contains no 'reserved' forests, but there are 387 square miles of unprotected forest.

Minerals. No minerals of any value are found. In the hills of Lingampet nodular ironstone is smelted, and the iron is largely employed in the local manufacture of agricultural implements.

Arts and manufactures. There is no important hand industry in the District. Cotton cloth is printed with fast dyes for use as screens, tablecloths, floor-cloths, &c. Coarse cotton cloth and silk stuffs of superior quality are made, the latter after European patterns, and are largely used for coats, *sārīs*, &c. Brass vessels are made at Lingampet and Rāmāyampet. Sivanagar and Jogipet contain tanneries, whence leather is exported to Hyderābād, Bombay, and Madras. The Chamārs prepare leather for the manufacture of water buckets and sandals for the ryots. The Hyderābād Spinning and Weaving Mill is situated near Mushīrābād, in the Bāghāt *tāluk*, north of the city of Hyderābād.

Commerce. The main exports are rice, both fine and coarse, unrefined sugar, jaggery, *jowār*, tobacco, *mahuā* oil, cotton, gram, other cereals and pulses, brass and copper vessels, cattle, and leather; while the chief imports are salt, opium, salted fish, gold and silver, copper and brass, sulphur, kerosene oil, refined sugar, silk and cotton piece-goods. Rice is sent to Hyderābād and other parts of the State, and leather to Madras and Bombay. Imported articles are brought to Sadāseopet from Shankarpalli, on the Nizām's Guaranteed State Railway; and from Mirzapalli, on the Hyderābād-Godāvari Valley Railway, to Rāmāyampet, and there distributed to Sangareddipet, Jogipet, Lingampet, Medak, &c., whence they find their way to distant parts through weekly bazars. Komatis, Mārwāris, and Baljawārs are the trading castes, and they also lend money.

Railways. The Nizām's Guaranteed State Railway enters Medak from the west at Gullaguda and passes out at Lingampalli in the east, a distance of 22 miles. The Hyderābād-Godāvari Valley Railway runs almost due north and south through Manoharābād, Māsaipet, and Mirzapalli on the eastern border of the District.

Roads. The total length of roads is 183 miles, of which 81 miles are metalled. The metalled roads are in three sections: Sadāseopet to Kūkatpalli, 32 miles; Shankarpalli to Sangareddipet, 14 miles; and part of the old Nāgpur road, 35 miles.

Unmetalled roads lead to the remaining head-quarters of *tāluks*.

District subdivisions and staff.

This District, though a small one, has been divided into three subdivisions. The Medak and Siddipet *tāluks* are under a Third Tālukdār, Andol under the Second Tālukdār of Andol, and Kalabgūr and Bāghāt under another Second Tālukdār. There is also another Third Tālukdār who acts as Assistant to the First Tālukdār, the First Tālukdār or Collector overlooking the revenue and magisterial work of his subordinates. Each *tāluk* is under a *tahsīldār*.

Civil and criminal justice.

The District civil court at Sangareddipet is presided over by the *Nāzim-i-Dīwāni* or Civil Judge, who is also a joint-magistrate in the absence of the First Tālukdār from head-quarters. The First Tālukdār is the chief magistrate. The *tahsīldārs* exercise third-class civil and magisterial powers, and preside over *tāluk* civil courts. The Second and Third Tālukdārs exercise second-class magisterial powers. There is not much serious crime in ordinary years, but dacoities and cattle-thefts increase in number during the dry season when the roads are open.

Land revenue.

Little information is available as to the revenue history of the District. Formerly groups of villages or *tāluks* were farmed out by the State to contractors, who received 10 per cent. for collection. This was followed by the *batai* or share system, under which the State received three-fifths of the produce of lands irrigated from tanks, and an equal share from lands supplied by wells. In 1866 the *ryotwāri* system was introduced, and revenue was collected in cash from individual ryots. Kalabgūr *tāluk* was regularly settled in 1892, Andol in 1898, Rāmāyampet and Medak in 1900, Tekmāl in 1901, and Bāghāt in 1905. Sugar-cane was charged Rs. 200 per acre under the old system, but now water rates are levied for 'wet crops' according to the class of land. Before the commencement of the survey, the records showed an area of 67,400 acres of 'wet' lands and 119,463 acres of 'dry.' The result of the survey was a decrease of 3 per cent. in the 'wet,' and an increase of 103 per cent. in the 'dry' lands, while the settlement raised the revenue by 2 lakhs or 16 per cent. in the five *tāluks* surveyed. The average assessment on 'dry' land is Rs. 2 (maximum Rs. 4, minimum R. 0-4), and on 'wet' land Rs. 13 (maximum Rs. 20, minimum Rs. 6). The rates given for 'wet' lands are for the *ābi* (rainy season) crop, the *tābi* (hot season) crop rates being Rs. 35 maximum, Rs. 10 minimum, and Rs. 20 average.

The land revenue and the total revenue of the District for a series of years are shown below, in thousands of rupees :—

	1881.	1891.	1901.	1903.
Land revenue .	8,50	8,40	12,12	8,96
Total revenue .	11,45	14,13	17,75	13,63

Owing to the changes in area made in 1905, the revenue demand is now about 14·6 lakhs.

Local boards and municipalities. There is a municipality at SANGAREDDIPET, and each of the other *tāluk* head-quarters has a small conservancy establishment. The District board manages both the municipal and local affairs of the head-quarters, and also supervises the work of the outlying *tāluk* boards. Its expenditure in 1900–1 was Rs. 12,600, of which Rs. 497 was laid out on roads. The income was, as usual, derived from a portion of the land cess, levied at one anna in the rupee on the land revenue assessments.

Police and jails. The First Tālukdār is the head of the District police, with the Superintendent (*Mohtamim*) as his executive deputy. The force consists of 67 subordinate officers, 499 constables, and 25 mounted police, under 6 inspectors and one sub-inspector, distributed among 32 police stations. There is a District jail at Sangareddipet, but only short-sentence prisoners are kept there, the rest being sent to the Central jail at Nizāmābād.

Education The District takes a medium position in point of literacy, 2·6 per cent. (4·6 males and 0·35 females) of the population being able to read and write in 1901. The total number of pupils under instruction in 1881, 1891, 1901, and 1903 was 774, 2,293, 1,907, and 2,044 respectively. In 1903 there were 25 primary schools and one middle school, with 159 girls under instruction. The total expenditure on education in 1901 was Rs. 13,100, and the fee receipts amounted to Rs. 731.

Medical. The District contains 4 dispensaries, with accommodation for 11 in-patients. The total number of cases treated at these during 1901 was 200 in-patients and 31,422 out-patients; and the number of operations performed was 920. The total expenditure amounted to Rs. 11,200.

The number of persons successfully vaccinated in 1901 was 540, or only 1·47 per 1,000 of population.

Medak Tāluk.—*Tāluk* in Medak District, Hyderābād State, with an area of 359 square miles. Its population in 1901, including *jāgīrs*, was 65,852, compared with 63,066 in 1891. The *tāluk* contains two towns, MEDAK (population,

8,511), the head-quarters, and LINGAMPET (5,102); and 89 villages, of which 19 are *jāgīr*. The land revenue in 1901 was 3·2 lakhs. The *tāluk* is somewhat hilly, and its soils are mostly sandy. Rice and sugar-cane are largely raised by tank-irrigation. The Hyderābād-Godāvari Valley Railway passes through the eastern portion. The *paigāh tāluks* of Narsāpur, Hatnūra, and Nawābpet lie to the south, with populations of 15,567, 14,183, and 6,179 respectively. The two former consist of 39 villages each, and the latter of 8 villages. Their respective areas are about 130, 128, and 26 square miles. The *jāgīr tāluk* of Nārsingi, with 11 villages and a population of 8,093, also lies to the south, and has an area of about 36 square miles. In 1905 some villages were added to the *tāluk* from Rāmāyampet, while others were transferred from it to Kāmāreddipet and Yellāreddipet in Nizāmābād District.

Siddipet Tāluk.—*Tāluk* in Medak District, Hyderābād State, with an area of 1,199 square miles. The population in 1901 was 150,551, compared with 155,523 in 1891, the decrease being due to cholera. The *tāluk* has one town, SIDDIPET (population, 8,302), the head-quarters; and 233 villages, of which 102 are *jāgīr*. The land revenue in 1901 was 3·6 lakhs. Tanks supply a considerable area of rice cultivation.

Bāghāt.—*Tāluk* in Medak District, Hyderābād State, with an area of 451 square miles. The population in 1901, including *jāgīrs*, was 57,073, compared with 52,819 in 1891. There are 110 villages, of which 52 are *jāgīr*; and Mushīrābād (population, 815) is the head-quarters. The land revenue in 1901 was Rs. 75,000. These statistics include the *tāluk* of Ibrāhīmpatan, transferred from Mahbūbnagar District in 1905, which had an area of 393 square miles in 1901, with a population of 46,604. The *paigāh tāluk* of Shamsābād lies to the west, with two villages, a population of 5,446, and an area of about 9 square miles. The name Bāghāt ('gardens') was given to the original *tāluk*, because most of the 'crown' gardens were included in it. The *tāluk* is watered by the Mūsi river and the Husain Sāgar lake.

Kalabgūr.—*Tāluk* in Medak District, Hyderābād State, with an area of 432 square miles. The population in 1901, including *jāgīrs*, was 78,052, compared with 96,100 in 1891, the decrease being due to emigration and transfer of villages. The *tāluk* contains one town, SADĀSEOPET (population, 6,672); and SANGAREDDIPET (4,809) is the head-quarters of the District and *tāluk*. There are also 144 other villages, of which 60 are *jāgīr*. The land revenue in 1901 was 2·4 lakhs. Kalabgūr is well supplied with tanks, and rice and sugar-cane are largely cultivated. The Nizām's State Railway passes through its southern portion, and the Mānjra river flows through the north.

Andol.—Western *tāluk* of Medak District, Hyderābād State, with an area of 433 square miles. The population in 1901, including *jāgīrs*, was 92,963, compared with 91,208 in 1891. It has 156 villages, of which 34 are *jāgīr*; and Andol (population, 3,030) is the head-quarters. The land revenue in 1901 was 3·5 lakhs. These statistics include the Tekmāl *tāluk*, which was amalgamated with Andol in 1905; the area of the former is 162 square miles and the population 34,425. The western portion is composed of black and lateritic soils, while the eastern and southern portions are sandy.

Rāmāyampet.—Former *tāluk* in Medak District, Hyderābād State, with an area of 403 square miles. The population in 1901, including *jāgīrs*, was 75,364, compared with 73,217 in 1891. The land revenue in 1901 was 2·8 lakhs. In 1905 the *tāluk* was split up, and its villages transferred to the Medak *tāluk* of this District and the Kāmāreddipet *tāluk* of Nizāmābād.

Kāndi.—Village in the Kalabgūr *tāluk* of Medak District, Hyderābād State, situated in 17° 35′ N. and 78° 6′ E., 5 miles south-east of Sangareddipet. Population (1901), 1,573. Upon the open plain close by stand two stones with Telugu or old Kanarese inscriptions, surmounted by the sun and moon.

Lingampet.—Town in the District and *tāluk* of Medak, Hyderābād State, situated in 18° 11′ N. and 78° 5′ E., 20 miles north-west of Medak town. Population (1901), 5,102. Nodular ironstone is smelted for the manufacture of agricultural implements, and brass vessels are also made and exported.

Medak Town.—Head-quarters of the *tāluk* of the same name in Medak District, Hyderābād State, situated in 18° 3′ N. and 78° 26′ E. Population (1901), 8,511. The town is built on the northern and eastern sides of a high hill, which was at one time strongly fortified. The fortifications are said to have been built originally by a Warangal Rājā, but the present fort was constructed about the middle of the sixteenth century. It contains a brass gun 10 feet long, cast at Rotterdam for the Dutch in 1620. A Persian inscription on a slab in the *tāluk* office alludes to the building of a mosque in 1641, on the ruins of a demolished temple. A large mission school, with 180 pupils, and several mission buildings stand north-east of the town.

Patancherū.—Village in the Kalabgūr *tāluk* of Medak

District, Hyderābād State, situated in 17° 32′ N. and 78° 16′ E. Population (1901), 1,886. It was formerly the head-quarters of the *Sūbahdār* (Commissioner) of the Bīdar Division, and is still the head-quarters of the Commissioner of the Medak Gulshanābād Division. Groups of underground Hindu temples are said to exist in the vicinity of the village, buried under the sand. Some old copper coins were recently discovered here. A pillar bearing the zodiacal signs, sculptured in a circle around a lotus or conventional representation of the sun, is an interesting relic. The place contains many buildings and tombs of Musalmān origin.

Sadāseopet.—Town in the Kalabgūr *tāluk* of Medak District, Hyderābād State, situated in 17° 37′ N. and 77° 58′ E., 10 miles west of Sangareddipet. Population (1901), 6,672. It is a large emporium, with a flourishing trade in both exports and imports.

Sangareddipet.—Head-quarters of Medak District and of the Kalabgūr *tāluk*, Hyderābād State, situated in 17° 38′ N. and 78° 5′ E., 34 miles north-west of Hyderābād city, and 14 miles north of Shankarpalli station on the Nizām's State Railway. Population (1901), 4,809. The offices of the First and Third Tālukdārs, the Irrigation Engineer, the Police Superintendent, a District civil court, a District jail and dispensary, and two schools with 201 pupils are located here. Six private schools have 85 pupils. Two miles to the west of the town is the Rājampet State stud farm.

Siddipet Town.—Head-quarters of the *tāluk* of the same name in Medak District, Hyderābād State, situated in 18° 6′ N. and 78° 61′ E. Population (1901), 8,302. Siddipet is a commercial place of some importance, and contains a dispensary, a State school, a mission school, and a post office. An old fort adjoins it to the west. Brass and copper vessels of a superior kind, as well as silk and cotton fabrics, are manufactured here.

Mahbūbnagar District (formerly called Nāgar Karnūl).—District in the Medak Gulshanābād Division, Hyderābād State, lying between 16° 2′ and 17° 14′ N. and 77° 12′ and 79° 10′ E., with a total area of 6,543 square miles, of which 3,586 square miles are *khālsa*, the rest being *jāgīr*[1]. It is separated from the Madras Districts of Kurnool and Guntūr by the Kistna river, which bounds it to the south; on the north lie the Districts of Medak and Atrāf-i-balda; on the east, Nalgonda; on the north-west, Gulbarga; and on the west, Raichūr. Boundaries, configuration, and hill and river systems.

[1] The statistics in this article relate to the District as it stood before the rearrangements made in 1905; see paragraph on Population.

In the south-east corner a range extends from the north to the south of the Amrābād *tāluk*, consisting of flat-topped hills, rising one above the other, the summits forming extensive plateaux. The surface of the District is highest in the north and west, and the general slope is from north-west to south-east.

The two principal rivers, which flow along the westernmost part of the District, are the Kistna and the Bhīma. The Dindi, which rises in the Jedcherla *tāluk*, passes through the Kalvakurti and Amrābād *tāluks*, and falls into the Kistna about 18 miles east of Chandragiri.

Geology. The District is occupied by Archaean gneiss, except along the banks of the Kistna, where the rocks belong to the Cuddapah and Kurnool series[1]. The famous Golconda diamonds were formerly obtained from the Cuddapahs and Kurnools, particularly the basement-beds of the latter.

Botany. The District is well wooded, having a large forest area. The timber trees are *bījāsāl* (*Pterocarpus Marsupium*), *nallāmaddi* (*Terminalia tomentosa*), *eppa* (*Hardwickia binata*), ebony, teak, *babūl* (*Acacia arabica*), mango, and tamarind. The scrubby jungle consists of brushwood, *tarvar* (*Cassia auriculata*), and other plants used for fuel.

Fauna. Antelope and spotted deer are found in the Ibrāhīmpatan, Makhtal, and Nārāyanpet *tāluks*; tigers, leopards, and bears are met with in the wooded hills of the rest of the District. In the Amrābād *tāluk* wild hog, *nīlgai*, *sāmbar*, hyenas, porcupines, several species of monkeys, large red squirrels, and wild dogs are also found. Peafowl, jungle-fowl, red parrots and red *mīnās*, yellow and red bulbuls as large as pigeons, and many other birds are also met with.

Climate and rainfall. Climatically the District may be divided into three portions. The *tāluks* of Nārāyanpet, Makhtal, and Jedcherla are hot and dry, but healthy; Mahbūbnagar, Koilkonda, Ibrāhīmpatan, and Kalvakurti are hot and damp, and are not so healthy; while the remaining *tāluks* of Pargi, Nāgar Karnūl, and Amrābād are damp, unhealthy, and malarious. The annual rainfall for the twenty-one years ending 1901 averaged 34 inches.

History. Little is known of the history of the District. The Rājās of Warangal at one period held sway over it, but after the Muhammadan conquest of the Deccan it came into the possession of the Bahmani kings. On the dissolution of their power, a portion of it was annexed by the Kutb Shāhis, and another portion became part of Bijāpur. In 1686, when Sikandar Adil Shāh

[1] *Memoirs, Geological Survey of India*, vol. viii, parts i and xvii.

was defeated by Aurangzeb, Bijāpur with its dependencies was annexed to the empire of Delhi. In 1706 prince Kām Bakhsh was appointed Sūbahdār of Bijāpur and Hyderābād; and on the foundation of the Hyderābād State early in the eighteenth century the District was included in the Nizām's Dominions.

Archaeology. The fort of Koilkonda was built by Ibrāhīm Kutb Shāh, one of the Golconda kings, and contained substantial buildings which are now in ruins. In the Amrābād *tāluk* is a fort, now in ruins, called the Pratāp Rudra Kot, which could shelter a large garrison. The old ruined city of Chandragupta, 32 miles south of Amrābād on the left bank of the Kistna, was a very populous place during the reign of Pratāp Rudra, Rājā of Warangal. Besides these, there are four old temples, one of which, called the Maheswara temple, is built on a hill with 900 steps from the foot to the summit. In the Nāgar Karnūl *tāluk* is the hill fort of PĀNGAL, a mile and a half long and one mile broad, possessing seven walls with a citadel in the centre.

Population. The number of towns and villages in the District, including *jāgīrs*, is 1,355. The population at each Census in the last twenty years was: (1881) 547,694, (1891) 674,649, and (1901) 705,725. The towns are NĀRĀYANPET and MAHBŪBNAGAR. More than 91 per cent. of its population are Hindus and over 8 per cent. Musalmāns. About 86 per cent. speak Telugu, 6 per cent. Urdū, and nearly 5 per cent. Kanarese. The following table gives the chief statistics of population in 1901:—

Tāluk.	Area in square miles.	Number of: Towns.	Number of: Villages.	Population.	Population per square mile.	Percentage of variation in population between 1891 and 1901.	Number of persons able to read and write.
Mahbūbnagar	250	1	59	45,604	182	+ 3·1	Not available.
Jedcherla	234	...	79	38,961	166	+ 0·8	
Ibrāhīmpatan	194	...	43	27,143	139	− 3·3	
Kalvakurti	436	...	70	41,069	94	+ 4·3	
Amrābād	679	...	37	16,794	24	+ 6·5	
Nāgar Karnūl	532	...	127	67,990	127	+ 5·4	
Makhtal	447	...	107	64,208	143	+ 2·2	
Nārāyanpet	315	1	72	66,579	211	+ 13·9	
Koilkonda	384	...	91	45,572	118	+ 5·9	
Pargi	115	...	49	21,511	187	+ 42·3	
Jāgīrs, &c.	2,957	...	619	270,294	91	+ 5·1	
District total	6,543	2	1,353	705,725	107	+ 4·6	23,688

In 1905 the Ibrāhīmpatan *tāluk* was transferred to Medak District, and 73 villages from Koilkonda, Nārāyanpet, and Makhtal were made over to the adjoining *tāluks* of Gulbarga District.

Koilkonda and Jedcherla were merged in adjoining *tāluks*, and Nārāyanpet in Makhtal. The Pargi and Amrābād sub *tāluks* have been raised to the status of *tāluks*. The District in its present form thus comprises six *tāluks*: Mahbūbnagar, Kalvakurti, Amrābād, Nāgar Karnūl, Makhtal, and Pargi.

Castes and occupations. The most numerous caste is that of the agricultural Kāpus, numbering 130,000, or about 19 per cent. of the total population. Next come the Chamārs or leather-workers, who number 93,000, or 13 per cent. The Brāhmans number 87,600, or over 12 per cent. The Dhangars or shepherds follow with 74,600, or 11 per cent. The Mahārs (village menials) and Komatis (traders) number 44,800 and 21,000, or 6 and 3 per cent. respectively. The Mahārs and Chamārs also work as field labourers. The population directly engaged in agriculture forms 29 per cent. of the total.

Christian missions. There is an American mission at Mahbūbnagar town, which has established a school for low-caste children, the total staff and pupils numbering 163. The number of Christians in the District in 1901 was 359, of whom 350 were natives.

General agricultural conditions. The northern portion of the District is situated on the border of the trap region, the remainder being granitic. The soils of the Pargi *tāluk* and parts of Ibrāhīmpatan, Mahbūbnagar, and Jedcherla are composed of stiff black *regar*. Makhtal, Nārāyanpet, and Nāgar Karnūl, as well as the remaining portions of the above-mentioned *tāluks*, consist of granitic or sandy soils, known as *masab* and *chalka*. The soils of Amrābād are of granitic origin, but contain a large admixture of organic matter. *Jowār*, gram, linseed, and other *rabi* crops are raised on the *regar* lands, while rice, sesamum, castor, and other *kharīf* or rainy season crops are grown on the *chalka* and *masab* soils.

Chief agricultural statistics and principal crops. The tenure of lands is mainly *ryotwāri*. The area cultivated in 1901 amounted to 1,278 square miles, out of a total *khālsa* area of 3,586, while 790 square miles were cultivable waste and fallows, 1,363 were forests, and 155 were not available for cultivation.

The staple food-crops are *jowār* and *bājra*, grown on 48 and 12½ per cent. of the total area cropped. Rice, *lachhna*, *sāvān*, and *kodro* are next in importance, the areas under these being 120, 87, 57, and 32 square miles respectively. Oilseeds are raised on 116 square miles, about three-fourths of this area being under castor.

Cattle, &c. No special breed of cattle is characteristic of the District; but the Amrābād *tāluk* is noted for its swift-trotting bullocks, which though small are very handsome. These are largely bred, and an extensive trade in them is carried on with other parts of the State, and with the Madras Presidency. They resemble the Mysore breed. Ponies are found everywhere, but are of an inferior class. Sheep and goats are largely reared, and are sold at prices varying from Rs. 1–8 to Rs. 3 per head. Extensive pasture lands exist in the *tāluks* of Pargi, Koilkonda, and Amrābād ; the grazing lands in the last of these are said to comprise nearly three-fourths of the total area.

The irrigated area in 1901 was 162 square miles. The principal channels take off from the Nandipalli Vāgū in the Nārāyanpet *tāluk*, from the Turikunda Vāgū in the Mahbūbnagar *tāluk*, and from the Mūsi river in the Ibrāhīmpatan *tāluk*. The first two supply 23 large tanks, and the third was constructed at a cost of 14 lakhs to supply the Ibrāhīmpatan tank, which irrigates the lands of 13 villages. Besides these, there are 505 large tanks, 1,863 *kuntas* or smaller tanks, and 9,615 wells in good repair. Irrigation.

Mahbūbnagar District has several large tracts of forest, especially in the Amrābād, Pargi, and Koilkonda *tāluks*. These contain 'reserved' and protected forests, the trees attaining a good size. The principal timber trees are teak, ebony, *eppa* (*Hardwickia binata*), *bījāsāl* (*Pterocarpus Marsupium*), *nallāmaddi* (*Terminalia tomentosa*), and bamboos, besides mango, tamarind, and *babūl* (*Acacia arabica*). Fuel is abundant. Nāgar Karnūl and Mahbūbnagar also contain smaller areas of forest. The 'reserved' forests cover 800 square miles, and the protected and unprotected forests 400 and 163 square miles respectively. Forests.

The District possesses good building stone. In the Pargi *tāluk* ironstone is smelted to a small extent. In the Nārāyanpet, Nāgar Karnūl, Amrābād, and Mahbūbnagar *tāluks* carbonate of soda and common salt are obtained by lixiviating saline earth. The salt produced is bitter, owing to an admixture of magnesium sulphate. Six miles south of Farahābād, a bright brick-red laminated limestone is found, similar to the Shāhābād stone, but much harder. A hard stone resembling emery, found in Amrābād, is used for making mortars. Minerals.

Coarse cotton cloth of every description is woven in all parts. In the Nārāyanpet *tāluk* silk *sārīs* and *dhotīs*, with gold borders, are made for export to Poona, Sholāpur, Bombay, and Baroda. Ordinary blankets are made by the Dhangars ; and leather is cured in a crude way by the Chāmars for water-buckets. A coarse sort of paper used to be largely made in the Koilkonda and Mahbūbnagar *tāluks*, but the trade has died out owing to the cheapness of imported paper. Arts and manufactures.

Commerce. The chief exports are food-grains, cotton, and castor-seed, the last two being sent to Bombay and the grain to Hyderābād city. The imports consist of cloth and chintzes of sorts, gram, wheat, sugar, salt, opium, kerosene oil, brass and copper vessels, and gold and silver.

Railways. The Great Indian Peninsula Railway passes through the south-western portion of the Makhtal *tāluk*, with one station.

Roads. There are 269 miles of gravelled roads, of which 207 miles are maintained by the Public Works department and 62 by the local boards. Of the former, one traverses the District from Hyderābād to Kurnool in British territory, 112 miles in length. A branch of this, 63 miles long, called the Kistna road, proceeds via Mahbūbnagar to the railway. Two other roads, 21 and 11 miles long, run from Nārāyanpet to the Saidāpur station and from Mahbūbnagar to Nawābpet. The local board roads are: Makhtal to Nārāyanpet, 18 miles; Mahbūbnagar to Koilkonda, 14 miles; and Mahbūbnagar to Nāgar Karnūl, 30 miles.

Famine. In the great famine of 1876–8 thousands of people perished in this District, when *jowār* sold at 3 seers per rupee. The famines of 1897 and 1900, though very severe in other parts of the State, did not seriously affect Mahbūbnagar, and the total amount spent on relief was only Rs. 2,700.

District subdivisions and staff. The District is divided into four subdivisions: one, consisting of the *tāluks* of Makhtal and Mahbūbnagar, is under a Second Tālukdār; the second, comprising the *tāluks* of Nāgar Karnūl and Amrābād, is under another Second Tālukdār; while the third, consisting of the *tāluks* of Kalvakurti and Pargi, is under a Third Tālukdār. Another Third Tālukdār acts as assistant to the First Tālukdār, who exercises a general supervision over the work of all his subordinates. Each *tāluk* is under a *tahsīldār*.

Civil and criminal justice. The District civil court is presided over by a Judge, styled the *Nāzim-i-Dīwāni*, while the *tahsīldārs* hold subordinate civil courts. The First Tālukdār is the chief magistrate of the District, and the *Nāzim-i-Dīwāni* or Civil Judge is also a Joint-Magistrate, who exercises magisterial powers during the absence of the First Tālukdār from head-quarters. The Second and Third Tālukdārs and the *tahsīldārs* exercise magisterial powers of the second and third class. Serious crime is not heavy, except in adverse seasons when dacoities and cattle-thefts increase.

Land revenue. Hardly anything is known about the revenue history of the District. Some of the *tāluks* were resumed from time to time from Arab and Pathān *jemadārs*, who had held them in lieu of payment for troops. The old system of farming *tāluks* was formerly in force, and the revenue farmers received two annas in the rupee for collection. But this system was discontinued in 1866, on the introduction of District administration, when the holdings of the cultivators were roughly measured and a fair revenue was fixed. Though the whole of the District had been surveyed some years previously, only two *tāluks* (Mahbūbnagar and Nārāyanpet) were settled in 1900, and the remaining *tāluks* in 1903. The settlement raised the land revenue by 2·6 lakhs, or 21 per cent. (from 13·2 lakhs to 15·8 lakhs), and the area of the holdings was found to be 981,029 acres, compared with 455,461 acres shown in the old accounts, a difference of 115 per cent. The average assessment on 'dry' land is R. 1 (maximum Rs. 2–2, minimum three annas), and on 'wet' land Rs. 7 (maximum Rs. 18–12, minimum Rs. 3). The 'wet' lands include *bāghāt* or garden lands.

The land revenue and the total revenue of the District in recent years are shown below, in thousands of rupees:—

	1881.	1891.	1901.	1903.
Land revenue . .	8,14	10,77	9,81	11,31
Total revenue . .	17,64	20,93	17,26	19,96

Owing to the changes in area made in 1905, the revenue demand is now about 8·3 lakhs.

Local boards and municipalities. Local boards were established in 1895, a year after the completion of the survey. The District board at Mahbūbnagar town supervises the working of the *tāluk* boards. Municipal establishments are maintained at Mahbūbnagar and Nārāyanpet. The total income derived from the one anna cess in 1901 amounted to Rs. 34,000; and the expenditure on municipal and local works and roads was Rs. 45,000.

Police and jails. The First Tālukdār is the head of the District police, with the Superintendent (*Mohtamim*) as his executive deputy. Under him are 9 inspectors, 128 subordinate officers, 754 constables, and 25 mounted police, distributed among 38 *thānas* and 61 outposts. The District jail at Mahbūbnagar has accommodation for 250 prisoners, but those whose terms exceed six months are transferred to the Central jail at Nizāmābād.

Education. The District occupies a comparatively high position as regards the literacy of its population, of whom 3·3 per cent. (5·9 males and 0·65 females) were able to read and write in 1901. The total number of pupils under instruction in 1881, 1891, 1901, and 1903 was 619, 3,093, 3,292, and 3,208 respectively. In 1903 there were 46 primary and 3 middle schools, with 390 girls under instruction. A small school is maintained at Makhtal for the depressed castes. The total amount spent on education in 1901 was Rs. 15,300, of which Rs. 12,200 was contributed by the State and the rest by the local boards. The fee receipts amounted to Rs. 333.

Medical. In 1901 there were 7 dispensaries, with accommodation for 22 in-patients. The total number of patients treated during the year was 26,912, of whom 116 were in-patients; and the number of operations performed was 606. The expenditure was Rs. 20,000.

To every dispensary a vaccinator is attached, but the number of persons vaccinated during 1901 was only 2,113, or 2·99 per 1,000 of the population.

Mahbūbnagar Tāluk.—*Tāluk* in Mahbūbnagar District, Hyderābād State, with an area of 339 square miles. The population in 1901, including *jāgīrs*, was 54,563, compared with 52,888 in 1891. The *tāluk* contained one town, MAHBŪBNAGAR (population, 7,605), the District and *tāluk* head-quarters; and 78 villages, of which 19 are *jāgīr*. The land revenue in 1901 was Rs. 68,000. In 1905 the *tāluk* was increased by transfers from Jedcherla and Koilkonda *tāluks*. It now contains 132 *khālsa* villages.

Jedcherla.—Former *tāluk* in the north of Mahbūbnagar District, Hyderābād State, with an area of 946 square miles. The population in 1901, including *jāgīrs*, was 96,886, compared with 96,106 in 1891. The land revenue in 1901 was Rs. 80,000. In 1905 the *tāluk* was divided between Mahbūbnagar, Pargi, and Kalvakurti. The *jāgīr tāluk* of Changomal lies to the south, with a population of 12,480 and 22 villages, and an area of about 106 square miles. It has now been transferred to the Pargi *tāluk*.

Kalvakurti.—Eastern *tāluk* of Mahbūbnagar District, Hyderābād State, with an area of 583 square miles. The population in 1901, including *jāgīrs*, was 54,384, compared with 52,132 in 1891. The *tāluk* in 1901 contained 101 villages, of which 31 are *jāgīr*; and Kalvakurti (population, 2,230) is the head-quarters. The land revenue was Rs. 85,000. In 1905 this *tāluk* received some additions from the adjoining *tāluk* of Jedcherla, and now contains 99 *khālsa* villages.

Amrābād.—*Tāluk* in Mahbūbnagar District, Hyderābād State, with an area of 727 square miles. The population in 1901, including *jāgīrs*, was 20,880, compared with 19,601 in 1891. The *tāluk* contained 46 villages, of which 9 are *jāgīr*;

and Amrābād (population, 2,267) is the head-quarters. The land revenue in 1901 was Rs. 25,000. The *tāluk*, which is situated on a plateau, contains a large forest area, and the surrounding country is very hilly. In 1905 the limits of this *tāluk* were increased; it now contains 67 *khālsa* villages.

Nāgar Karnūl.—South-eastern *tāluk* of Mahbūbnagar District, Hyderābād State, with an area of 621 square miles. The population in 1901, including *jāgīrs*, was 77,095, compared with 73,155 in 1891. The *tāluk* contained 146 villages, of which 19 are *jāgīr*. In 1905 some villages from this *tāluk* were transferred to Amrābād, and the number of *khālsa* villages in it is now 112. Nāgar Karnūl (population, 2,428) is the head-quarters. The land revenue in 1901 was 2·5 lakhs. The Wanparti and Gopālpet *samasthāns* are situated to the south-west, with populations of 62,293 and 16,301, and 124 and 35 villages, respectively; their areas are about 599 and 169 square miles. Farther south lies the *samasthān* of Jatpol with 89 villages, a population of 31,613, and an area of about 429 square miles.

Makhtal.—*Tāluk* in Mahbūbnagar District, Hyderābād State, with an area of 511 square miles. The population in 1901, including *jāgīrs*, was 69,560, compared with 68,031 in 1891. The *tāluk* contained 120 villages, of which 13 are *jāgīr*; and Makhtal (population, 4,476) is the head-quarters. The land revenue in 1901 amounted to 1·8 lakhs. In 1905 the *tāluk* was enlarged by the addition of some villages from Nārāyanpet, but lost 31 villages to Yādgīr in Gulbarga District. The town of Nārāyanpet is now included in this *tāluk*, which forms the borderland between the Carnatic and the Telingāna country.

Nārāyanpet Tāluk.—Former *tāluk* in Mahbūbnagar District, Hyderābād State, with an area of 345 square miles. The population in 1901, including *jāgīrs*, was 68,164, compared with 59,967 in 1891. It contained one town, NĀRĀYANPET (population, 12,011) the head-quarters; and 78 villages, of which 6 were *jāgīr*. The land revenue in 1901 was 1·3 lakhs. In 1905 the *tāluk* was broken up, and its villages were transferred to the Makhtal *tāluk* and the Yādgīr *tāluk* in Gulbargā District.

Koilkonda.—Former *tāluk* in Mahbūbnagar District, Hyderābād State, with an area of 546 square miles. The population in 1901, including *jāgīrs*, was 58,031, compared with 54,802 in 1891. The land revenue in 1901 was Rs. 64,000. In 1905 the *tāluk* was divided between Kodangal in Gulbarga District, and Pargi and Mahbūbnagar in Mahbūbnagar.

Pargi.—*Tāluk* in Mahbūbnagar District, Hyderābād State, with an area of 220 square miles. The population in 1901, including *jāgīrs*, was 31,425, compared with 22,008 in 1891. It contained 71 villages, of which 22 are *jāgīr*. Pargi (population, 2,361) is the head-quarters. The land revenue in 1901 was Rs. 48,000. In 1905 this *tāluk* was enlarged by the addition of villages from the Koilkonda and Jedcherla *tāluks*, and now contains 114 *khālsa* villages.

Mahbūbnagar Town.—Head-quarters of the District and *tāluk* of the same name, Hyderābād State, situated in 16° 44′ N. and 77° 59′ E. Population (1901), 7,605. It contains the offices of the First Tālukdār, the District and Irrigation Engineers, the Police Superintendent, as well as the District civil court, a mission school and other schools, a District jail, a post office, and a dispensary. It was formerly called Pālmūr.

Nārāyanpet Town.—Town in the Makhtal *tāluk* of Mahbūbnagar District, Hyderābād State, situated in 16° 45′ N. and 77° 30′ E., 36 miles west of Mahbūbnagar town. Population (1901), 12,011. It is noted for the manufacture of superior silk and cotton *sārīs*, and slippers of coloured leather, which are largely exported. It is the head-quarters of the Second Tālukdār, and has a Munsif's court, a post office, a dispensary, a boys' and a girls' school with 319 and 36 pupils respectively, and the police inspector's office. It is a flourishing commercial centre, connected with Saidāpur station on the Great Indian Peninsula Railway by a feeder-road 21 miles long.

Pāngal.—Hill-fort in the Nāgar Karnūl *tāluk* of Mahbūbnagar District, Hyderābād State, situated in 16° 15′ N. and 78° 8′ E., south of Pāngal village, 1,800 feet above sea-level. Population of fort and village (1901), 1,227. The fort is a mile and a half long by a mile broad, having seven walls, a citadel (*bālā hisār*) in the centre, and seven towers. Two illegible inscriptions are engraved on a couple of slabs outside the fort. A battle was fought here in 1417, between the Rājās of Warangal and Vijayanagar and Fīroz Shāh Bahmani, when the latter was defeated. Sultān Muhammad Kuli Kutb Shāh gained a decisive victory at this place over the Vijayanagar Rājā in 1513. According to a Telugu inscription on the *bālā hisār*, the king's mother, with the *kiladār*, Khairāt Khān, lived in the fort in 1604. Nawāb Nizām Alī Khān of Hyderābād also resided in one of the fort buildings from 1786 to 1789.

Boundaries, configuration, and hill

Nalgonda District.—District in the Medak Gulshanābād Division, Hyderābād State, lying between 16° 20′ and 17° 47′ N. and 78° 45′ and 79° 55′ E., with an area of 4,143 square miles, including *jāgīrs*[1]. The Hyderābād Districts of Warangal, Karīmnagar, Mahbūbnagar, and Atrāf-i-balda bound it on the east, north, and west. On the south it is separated from the Guntūr District of the Madras Presidency by the Kistna river. and river systems.

A range of hills runs through the *tāluks* of Nalgonda and Devarkonda, and enters the Amrābād *tāluk* in the south of Mahbūbnagar District. Another range of low hills starts in the south-west of the District and extends from the vicinity of the Dandi river in a north-eastern direction as far as Warangal District. A third range, known as the Nalla Pahād, after reaching the Dandi and the Peddavāgu, bifurcates, one spur extending north, the other joining the second range. A fourth range, in the north-west of the District, runs from the west of Pāsnūr in a north-westerly direction as far as Surikonda, and then taking a sudden turn towards the east extends for 12 miles and turns again due north, passing between Nārāyanpur and Ibrāhīmpatan, curving again towards Vemalkonda. This range lies almost wholly in the District, its total length being about 60 miles. Besides these there are nearly a hundred isolated hills, some of which are situated in one or other of the ranges mentioned. The general slope of the District is from west and north-west towards the south-east.

The most important river is the Kistna, which forms the southern boundary. It first touches the District at Yellaisharam in the Devarkonda *tāluk* and has fifteen fords, one in Devarkonda and fourteen in Devalpalli *tāluk*, served by boats or coracles. Its length in the District is 53 miles. The Mūsi, a tributary of the Kistna, enters the District from the north-west, and flows due east for a distance of 40 miles; but after its junction with the Aler river, it flows in a south-easterly direction till it falls into the Kistna near Wazīrābād, after a course in the District of 95 miles. The other rivers are the Peddavāgu and the Dandi in the Devarkonda *tāluk*. The Hallia river, which rises in the hills west of Nārāyanpur in the Nalgonda *tāluk*, flows in a south-easterly direction for about 45 miles, when it is joined by the Kongal river near the village of Kongal, and continuing in the same direction falls into the Kistna. Its total length is 82 miles.

Geology. The District is occupied by Archaean gneiss, except along the banks of the Kistna, where the rocks belong to Cuddapah and Kurnool series[2]. The famous Golconda diamonds were

[1] The dimensions relate to the District as it stood up to 1905. The changes then made are described below under Population.

[2] W. King, *Memoirs, Geological Survey of India*, vol. viii, pt. i.

formerly obtained from the Cuddapahs and Kurnools, particularly the basement beds of the latter.

Botany. The jungles and hilly portions of the District contain the common trees met with elsewhere, such as teak, ebony, *eppa* (*Hardwickia binata*), *nallāmaddi* (*Terminalia tomentosa*), *sandra* (*Acacia Catechu*), *babūl* (*Acacia arabica*), mango, tamarind, *tarvar* (*Cassia auriculata*), and various species of *Ficus*.

Fauna. In the jungly portions of Devarkonda and Devalpalli and parts of Bhongīr and Suriapet, tigers, leopards, cheetahs, bears, hyenas, and wolves, as well as *sāmbar*, spotted deer, antelope, and hares, are found. Among birds, peafowl, partridges, quail, rock pigeon, and jungle-fowl are abundant.

Climate, temperature, and rainfall. The District is malarious from August to October, and healthy from November to the end of May. It is very hot during April and May, the temperature rising to 110°. In August and September the moist heat is very oppressive. The average rainfall for the twenty-one years ending 1901 was 26 inches.

History. The District was part of the dominions of the Warangal Rājās, one of whose governors built Pāngal, 2 miles north-east of the town of Nalgonda, and made it his head-quarters, afterwards removing to Nalgonda. That place was conquered during the reign of Ahmad Shāh Wali, the Bahmani king. After the dissolution of the Bahmani power, the District became part of the Kutb Shāhi kingdom of Golconda, and though it had been reoccupied for a time by the Rājā of Warangal, it was eventually retaken by Sultān Kuli Kutb Shāh. After the fall of Golconda, the District was annexed with the other Deccan *Sūbahs* by Aurangzeb; but it was separated from the Delhi empire on the foundation of the Hyderābād State in the beginning of the eighteenth century.

Archaeology. There are several places of archaeological interest in the District, the chief among them being the forts of NALGONDA, Devarkonda, Orlakonda in the Suriapet *tāluk*, and BHONGĪR. The fort of Devarkonda is surrounded by seven hills, and was at one time considered a formidable stronghold, but is now in ruins. The temples at Pāngal in the Nalgonda *tāluk*, at Nāgalpād in Devalpalli, and at Pālalmari in Suriapet are fine specimens of Hindu religious architecture.

Population. The number of towns and villages in the District, including *jāgīrs*, is 974. The population at the three enumerations was: (1881) 494,190, (1891) 624,617, and (1901) 699,799. The towns are NALGONDA and BHONGĪR. About 95 per cent. of the population are Hindus, and as many as 91 per cent.

speak Telugu. The following table shows the distribution of population in 1901:—

Tāluk.	Area in square miles.	Number of Towns.	Number of Villages.	Population.	Population per square mile.	Percentage of variation in population between 1891 and 1901.	Number of persons able to read and write.
Nalgonda . .	762	1	190	131,836	173	− 5·1	Not available.
Suriapet . .	644	...	182	166,586	258	+ 18·4	
Devalpalli. .	749	...	150	76,904	103	− 9·9	
Devarkonda .	662	...	152	85,370	129	+ 16·8	
Bhongīr . .	454	1	92	73,031	161	+ 34·6	
Jāgīrs, &c. .	872	...	206	166,052	190	+ 10·9	
District total	4,143	2	972	699,779	168	+ 12·0	13,038

In 1905 Cherial and Kodār were transferred to this District from Warangal, the latter sub-*tāluk* being made a *tāluk* and its name changed to Pochamcherla. The District in its present form thus consists of the following seven *tāluks*: Nalgonda, Cherial, Suriapet, Pochamcherla, Mirialguda (Devalpalli), Devarkonda, and Bhongīr.

Castes and occupations. The most numerous caste is that of the agricultural Kāpus, who number 125,500, or 18 per cent. of the population, the most important classes among them being the Kunbīs (82,800) and Mutrāsis (33,100). Next come the Mādigas or leather-workers (95,500), the Dhangars or shepherds (71,700), the Mahārs or village menials (57,200), the Brāhmans (31,400), the Sālas or weavers (28,900), the Komatis or trading caste (26,600), and the Ausalas or smiths (22,300). The Mādigas and Mahārs work as agricultural labourers, and most of the Dhangars are engaged in agriculture as well as grazing. The population directly engaged in agriculture forms more than 36 per cent. of the total.

Christian missions. There is an American mission at Nalgonda, having a church, a mission school, and a hospital, with a competent staff of native Christian teachers for the school, and a lady doctor in charge of the hospital. The mission has two branches, one at Devarkonda and the other at Mirialguda. In 1901 the District contained 1,212 native Christians, of whom 429 were Roman Catholics, 225 Methodists, and 235 Baptists. The converts are mostly from the lower castes.

General agricultural conditions. The entire District is situated in the granitic region, hence most of its soils are derived from the decomposition of granite and are generally sandy, such as *chalka* and *masab*. In the Devalpalli *tāluk* the soil near the Kistna is alluvial, and also consists to a large extent of *regar* or black cotton soil. Both these varieties are utilized for raising *rabi* crops. *Regar* is found in the other *tāluks* to a smaller extent, but with an admixture of sand. The *kharīf* crops raised on the *chalka* and *masab* soils are *jowār*, *bājra*, cotton, *kulthi*, and castor-seed.

Chief agricultural statistics and principal crops.

The tenure of lands is mainly *ryotwāri*. *Khālsa* and 'crown' lands covered a total area of 3,271 square miles in 1901, of which 1,525 were cultivated, 874 cultivable waste and fallows, 574 forests, and 298 were not available for cultivation. *Jowār* and *bājra* form the staple food-crops, being grown on 17 and 22 per cent. of the net area cropped. Rice is next in importance, the area under it being 138 square miles. Cotton is produced on 11½ square miles, and castor-seed on 386 square miles.

Improvements in agricultural practice.

The District has not yet been settled, but the revenue survey has been completed. The total cultivated area increased from 1,187 square miles in 1891 to 1,525 in 1901, or by 41 per cent. No steps have been taken to improve the cultivation by importing new varieties of seed or introducing better agricultural implements.

Cattle, &c.

A special breed of cattle is found in the Devarkonda *tāluk*, generally black or red in colour, very sturdy and well suited for agricultural work. The animals are supposed to be descended from the Mysore breed, and are well-known beyond the frontier, a large number being acquired by purchasers from British territory. The white cattle bred in the Suriapet and Devalpalli *tāluks* are handsome animals. In other parts the cattle are of the ordinary strain. Goats are largely bred in the Devarkonda, Devalpalli, and Suriapet *tāluks*, as the great extent of jungle and hill tracts provides plenty of grazing, while in the Nalgonda and Bhongīr *tāluks* sheep are more commonly kept. The ponies are of a very inferior class.

Irrigation.

The area irrigated in 1901 was 229 square miles, supplied by 352 large tanks, 1,110 *kuntas* or small tanks, 12,456 wells, and 208 other sources. The principal channels are those from the Mūsi, Aler, and Peddavāgū rivers, and from other minor streams, which supply some of the chief tanks, as well as provide direct irrigation.

Forests.

There are small forest areas in all the *tāluks*, amounting to a total of 574 square miles, of which 190 square miles are 'protected.' In the hilly jungles bordering on the Kistna river, in the Devalpalli and Devarkonda *tāluks*, large tracts are covered with *eppa* (*Hardwickia binata*) and *sandra* (*Acacia*

Catechu). No forest is 'reserved,' but 17 species of timber trees have been reserved wherever found. The revenue obtained from the sale of fuel, charcoal, and forest produce in 1901 was Rs. 2,750.

Minerals. In the Devalpalli *tāluk* laminated limestone resembling the Shāhābād stone is found, which is used for building purposes and also burnt for making lime. Slate is also found in the same *tāluk*. Gold was discovered at Chitrial in the same *tāluk*, and worked for a time, but the yield was so small that the mine was given up. At Nandkonda and the neighbouring villages on the left bank of the Kistna diamonds are said to be found.

Arts and manufactures. At Charlapalli and Pāngal in the Nalgonda *tāluk* silk cloth scarves and *sārīs* of various patterns and colours are made, which are very durable and are largely used by the better classes. The Sālas or weavers also manufacture ordinary coarse cotton cloth and *sārīs* for the use of the ryots. Light earthen vessels, such as goblets and drinking cups of a fine quality, are made at Bhongīr, and are exported to Hyderābād and adjoining Districts. To the east of the town of Nalgonda there is a tannery where leather of a superior quality is prepared; the number of hands employed in 1901 was 30.

Commerce. The chief exports consist of castor-seed, cotton, *tarvar* bark, hides and skins, both raw and prepared, bones and horns, rice, *jowār*, and *bājra*; while the imports are salt, opium, gold and silver, copper and brass, iron, refined sugar, kerosene oil, raw silk, yarn, and silken, woollen, and cotton fabrics. The chief centres of trade are the towns of Nalgonda and Bhongīr. Articles for export from the northern portions of the District find their way to Bhongīr and Aler stations on the Nizām's Guaranteed State Railway, and those from the southern portions are sent direct by the old Masulipatam road to Hyderābād. The number of carts that pass through the town of Nalgonda varies between 200 per diem in the slack season to 700 in busy times.

Railways. The Nizām's Guaranteed State Railway traverses the Bhongīr *tāluk* from west-south-west to east-north-east for a distance of 21 miles, with five stations in the District.

Roads. The principal road is that from Hyderābād to Masulipatam, which was constructed by the Madras Sappers and Miners in 1832 for military purposes. Its length in the District as far as Gumpal in the Suriapet *tāluk* is 71 miles. The road from Hyderābād to Madras branches off at the sixty-seventh mile, near Nakrekal, and terminates at Wazīrābād near the Kistna, its length in the District being 40 miles. This road was also made about the same time as the former, and by the same agency. About 21 miles of the Hyderābād-Warangal road lie in the District. Other roads are railway feeders, such as the Nalgonda-Bhongīr road, 44 miles; the Khammamett station feeder-road, 18 miles; Nalgonda to Devarkonda, 36 miles; to Tipparti, 12 miles; and to Nakrekal, 14 miles. The last three were made during the famine of 1877-8.

Famine. In 1790 a great famine affected the District, and grain was sold at one seer per rupee. Another famine in 1877 caused severe distress among the poor; grain was sold at 4 seers per rupee, and the District lost more than 34,000 head of cattle. The famine of 1899-1900 was not so severe as that of 1877, but its effects lasted for nearly two years.

District subdivisions and staff. The District is divided into three subdivisions; one consisting of the *tāluks* of Bhongīr and Cherial, under a Second Tālukdār; the second consisting of the *tāluks* of Mirialguda (Devalpalli) and Devarkonda, under a Third Tālukdār; and the third consisting of the *tāluks* of Nalgonda, Suriapet, and Pochamcherla (Kodār), under the head-quarters Third Tālukdār. The First Tālukdār exercises a general supervision over the work of all his subordinates. Each *tāluk* is under a *tahsīldār*.

Civil and criminal justice. The District civil court is presided over by the First Tālukdār with a *Madadgār* or Judicial Assistant for both civil and criminal work, there being no *Nāzim-i-Dīwāni*. There are altogether ten subordinate civil courts, three presided over by the Second and Third Tālukdārs, and seven by the *tahsīldārs*. The First Tālukdār is the chief magistrate of the District and his Assistant is also a joint-magistrate, who exercises powers in the absence of the First Tālukdār from head-quarters. The Second and Third Tālukdārs and the *tahsīldārs* have magisterial powers of the second and third class. Serious crime is not heavy, dacoities, theft, and house-breaking being the common offences in ordinary years.

Land revenue. Little is known of the early history of land revenue. Up to 1821 an *anchanadār* (estimator) was appointed to every ten villages, who estimated the standing crops and submitted his estimates to the *āmils*. On 'wet' lands irrigated by tanks, and 'dry' lands, the State and the ryot had equal shares; but on 'wet' lands supplied by channels and wells the ryot's share was three-fifths and three-fourths respectively. In 1821 *zila-dārs* (revenue managers) were appointed, who entered into an agreement for a period of ten years with *pātels* or village headmen to pay annually a sum equal to the average receipts of the previous ten years. In 1835 groups of villages were made over to *zamīndārs* on the *sarbasta* or contract system, which continued to the time of Messrs. Dighton and Azam Alī Khān, the revenue managers or *ziladārs* in 1840. Five years later this was changed in certain *tāluks* and the revenue was collected departmentally, partly in kind and partly in cash. The *sarbasta* or contract system was completely abolished on the formation of regular Districts in 1866, when rates of assessment were fixed per *bīgha* (¾ acre). The revenue survey of the whole District has not yet been completed. The *tāluks* of Nalgonda and Devalpalli have very recently been settled, the increase in their revenue being nearly Rs. 46,200, or more than 16 per cent. The average assessment on 'dry' land is Rs. 1-14 (maximum Rs. 2-12, minimum Rs. 1-4), and on 'wet' land Rs. 15 (maximum Rs. 18, minimum Rs. 11).

The land revenue and total revenue in recent years are given below, in thousands of rupees:—

	1881.	1891.	1901.	1903.
Land revenue	8,20	10,93	11,97	12,38
Total revenue	12,99	16,83	22,49	22,22

Owing to the changes in area effected in 1905, the revenue demand is now about 14·6 lakhs.

Local boards and municipalities. In 1902, after the settlement of the two *tāluks* of Nalgonda and Devalpalli, a cess of one anna in the rupee was levied for local purposes, and boards were formed for every *tāluk* except Nalgonda, with the *tahsīldārs* as chairmen. A District board was also constituted, with the First Tālukdār as president. Prior to the formation of these boards and the levying of the one anna cess, the municipal expenditure of the town of Nalgonda and of all the head-quarters of *tāluks* was met from State funds, amounting to Rs. 2,844 in 1901. The District board supervises the work of the municipality of Nalgonda.

Police and jails. The First Tālukdār is the head of the police, with a Superintendent (*Mohtamim*) as his executive deputy. Under him are 6 inspectors, 92 subordinate officers, 589 constables, and 25 mounted police. These are distributed among 29 *thānas* or police stations and 39 outposts. The rural police number 666, besides 1,098 *setsindīs* or village watchmen. Short-term prisoners are kept in the District jail at Nalgonda, those with terms exceeding six months being sent to the Central jail at Warangal. Since the recent changes, they have been transferred to the Central jail at Nizāmābād.

Education. The District occupies a low position as regards the literacy of its population, of whom only 1·9 per cent. (3·2 males and 0·3 females) were able to read and write in 1901. The total number of pupils under instruction in 1881, 1891, 1901, and 1903 was 242, 1,097, 1,316, and 1,472 respectively. In 1903 there were 29 primary and 2 middle schools, with 84 girls under instruction. The total expenditure in 1901 was Rs. 8,800, all of which was paid by the State. Of this, Rs. 8,336 was spent on State schools and Rs. 468 granted to the aided schools. The fee receipts for the State schools amounted to Rs. 603, and for the aided schools to Rs. 430.

Medical. There were 3 dispensaries in the District in 1901, with accommodation for 12 in-patients. The total number of out-patients treated was 24,739 and of in-patients 157, and 551 operations were performed. The expenditure amounted to Rs. 10,074. The number of persons successfully vaccinated was 1,811, or 2·6 per 1,000 of the population.

Nalgonda Tāluk.—*Tāluk* in Nalgonda District, Hyderābād State, with an area of 874 square miles. The population in 1901, including *jāgīrs*, was 151,133, compared with 159,225 in 1891, the decrease being due to transfer of certain villages. The *tāluk* contains one town, NALGONDA (population, 5,889), the District and *tāluk* head-quarters; and 216 villages, of which 26 are *jāgīr*. The land revenue in 1901 was 3·5 lakhs. The soils are sandy, and irrigation by tanks and channels is extensively resorted to for rice cultivation.

Cherial.—*Tāluk* in Nalgonda District, Hyderābād State, with an area of 647 square miles. The population in 1901, including *jāgīrs*, was 104,142, compared with 89,868 in 1891. The *tāluk* contained 128 villages, of which 27 are *jāgīr*; and Cherial (population, 2,731) was the head-quarters. The land revenue in 1901 was 1·7 lakhs. Rice is extensively raised by tank-irrigation. In 1905 a number of villages were added to Cherial from the Vardannāpet *tāluk* of Warangal District, which was abolished, and Cherial was transferred to Nalgonda District. The present head-quarters are at Jangaon (population, 1,696), a station on the Nizām's State Railway.

Suriapet.—*Tāluk* in Nalgonda District, Hyderābād State, with an area of 687 square miles. The population in 1901, including *jāgīrs*, was 175,436, compared with 148,103 in 1891. The *tāluk* contained 192 villages, of which 10 are *jāgīr*; and Suriapet (population, 4,418) is the head-quarters. The land revenue in 1901 was 3·1 lakhs. Rice is extensively raised by irrigation from tanks, wells, and channels. In 1905, 15 villages from Suriapet were transferred to the new *tāluk* of Pochamcherla.

Pochamcherla.—*Tāluk* in Nalgonda District, Hyderābād State. It was formed in 1905 from the Kodār sub-*tāluk* of Warangal District, and 15 and 35 villages taken from the Suriapet and Mirialguda *tāluks* of this District. Pochamcherla (population, 1,899) is the head-quarters; and the *tāluk* consists of 100 *khālsa* villages, its land revenue being 2·77 lakhs. Rice is extensively cultivated by tank-irrigation.

Mirialguda.—Southern *tāluk* of Nalgonda District, Hyderābād State, separated from the Guntūr District of Madras by the Kistna river. Till 1905 it was also called Devalpalli. The population in 1901, including *jāgīrs*, was 78,545, and the area 768 square miles. In 1891 the population was 87,130, the decrease being due to the transfer of villages. The *tāluk* contained 154 villages, of which 4 are *jāgīr*; and Mirialguda (population, 3,660) is the head-quarters. The land revenue in 1901 was 2·4 lakhs. Rice is extensively irrigated from tanks, channels, and wells. The new *tāluk* of Pochamcherla, constituted in 1905, received 35 villages from Mirialguda.

Devarkonda.—South-western *tāluk* of Nalgonda District, Hyderābād State, separated from the Guntūr District of Madras by the Kistna river. The population in 1901, including *jāgīrs*, was 100,059, and the area 760 square miles. In 1891 the population was 85,613. The *tāluk* contains 175 villages, of which 23 are *jāgīr*; and Devarkoṇḍa (population, 3,186) is the head-quarters. The land revenue in 1901 was 1·7 lakhs. The *tāluk* is very hilly in the west. Rice is largely cultivated, being irrigated from tanks and wells.

Bhongīr Tāluk.—North-western *tāluk* of Nalgonda District, Hyderābād State, with an area of 1,054 square miles. The population in 1901, including *jāgīrs*, was 194,606, compared with 144,546 in 1891. The *tāluk* contains one town, BHONGĪR (population, 5,806), the head-quarters; and 235 villages, of which 143 are *jāgīr*. The Nizām's State Railway passes through the *tāluk* from west-south-west to east-north-east. The land revenue in 1901 was 1·4 lakhs. Rice, castor-seed, plantains, and betel-leaf are extensively grown, and irrigated from wells, tanks, and channels.

Bhongīr Town.—Head-quarters of the *tāluk* of the same name in Nalgonda District, Hyderābād State, situated in 17° 31′ N. and 78° 53′ E. Population (1901), 5,806. The town is situated at the foot of a fortified rock, 2,000 feet above sea-level. In 1709 a freebooter, Pāp Rai, raised a large body of followers and committed depredations in the Deccan by plundering Warangal and Bhongīr, but was eventually captured and executed. Bhongīr is an important centre of trade and is celebrated for its pottery. It contains the offices of the Second Tālukdār, the engineer, and the *tahsīldār*, and also a post office, a dispensary, and a vernacular school. The fort is built on an isolated rock, the eastern and southern sides of which are quite unscalable; from the *bālā hisār* or citadel on the top a good view over the surrounding country may be obtained for long distances.

Nalgonda Town.—Head-quarters of the District and *tāluk* of the same name, Hyderābād State, situated in 17° 3′ N. and 79° 16′ E., between two hills. Population (1901), 5,889. On the northorn hill stands Shāh Latīf's tomb, and on the southern is a strong fortress surrounded with masonry wall. The town was formerly named Nīlgiri by its Rājput rulers, but its present name was given after its conquest by Alā-ud-dīn Bahman Shāh. Nalgonda contains a spacious *sarai* built by Mīr Alam, a Hindu temple, a travellers' bungalow, and a busy market called Osmānganj, the usual offices, a post office, a dispensary, a District jail, a middle school with 256 boys, and a girls' school. A British post office is situated at Nakrekal, 12 miles from Nalgonda. There is also a tannery, 2 miles distant from the town.

WARANGAL DIVISION

Warangal Division.—Division of the Hyderābād State, forming the eastern portions of the Nizām's Dominions, and extending from the Pengangā in the north to the Kistna in the south. It is bounded on the north by Berār and the Central Provinces; on the east by the Pranhitā and Godāvari rivers, and by the Godāvari District of Madras; on the south by the Kistna river and the Kistna District of Madras; and on the west by the Districts of Nizāmābād, Medak, Atrāf-i-balda, and Mahbūbnagar. The head-quarters of the Commissioner are at HANAMKONDA, once a suburb of the old city of Warangal. Up to 1905 the Division consisted of three Districts—ELGANDAL, NALGONDA, and WARANGAL—the population of which increased from 2,109,475 in 1881 to 2,572,347 in 1891 and 2,688,007 in 1901. During the last decade the increase was greater than in any other Division. The total area was 21,075 square miles, and the density 128 persons per square mile, compared with 135 for the whole State, of which the Division was the second largest in both area and population. In 1901 Hindus and Musalmāns formed respectively 95 and 4·5 per cent. of the population, while the other religions comprised Christians (2,934, of whom 2,881 were natives), Sikhs (332), Pārsīs (34), Jains (13), and Animists (1,339). Owing to changes made in 1905, this Division now comprises the Districts shown in the subjoined table, which gives their area, population, and land revenue in their present form:—

Districts.	Area in square miles.	Population, 1901.	Land revenue and cesses, 1901, in thousands of rupees.
Warangal . . .	8,305	745,757	17,13
Karīmnagar (Elgandal) .	5,369	861,833	23,98
Adilābād (Sirpur Tāndūr)	7,403	477,848	6,72
Total	21,077	2,085,438	47,83

The Division contains 11 towns, or about one-seventh of the total number in the State, but none with a population of 20,000; and 3,809 villages. The chief places of commercial importance are HANAMKONDA, KARĪMNAGAR, and EDLĀBĀD. YELLANDLAPĀD is the centre of the coal-mining area.

Boundaries, configuration, and hill and river systems.

Warangal District (formerly called Khammamett).—District of the Warangal Division in the south-east of Hyderābād State, lying between 16° 38′ and 18° 36′ N. and 78° 50′ and 81° 33′ E., with a total area of 9,729 square miles, of which about 6,319 are *khālsa* lands, the rest being *jāgīr*[1]. It is bounded by the Central Provinces District of Chānda and the Madras Districts of Godāvari and Kistna on the east and south-east; and by the Hyderābād Districts of Nalgonda, Atrāf-i-balda, Medak, and Karīmnagar on the south, west, and north.

A range of low hills runs from Pākhāl and Singareni to Ashwaraopet in the south-east, bounding the lower Godāvari valley. The Kandikal Gutta range extends from the south-east to Chinnūr in Adilābād District. Ten miles north-west of Warangal are the Chandragiri hills, and 14 miles west of it the well-known iron hills of Hasanparti. The country around the town of Hanamkonda is about 1,700 feet above sea-level, but the average elevation of the District is only 870 feet. The whole country is dotted with isolated hills.

The two principal rivers are the Godāvari and the Kistna. The former touches the District north of Mangapet in the Pākhāl *tāluk*, and, flowing in a south-easterly direction along its eastern boundary, leaves it at the south-east of Pāloncha, whence it enters the Godāvari District of Madras, after a course of 113 miles in Warangal. The Kistna passes along the southern boundary of the Khammamett *tāluk* for a short distance only. The other rivers are the Muner, the Pāler, the Kinārsāni, and the Wīra, besides some minor streams. The Muner flows from the Pākhāl Lake, and, joining the Wīra, falls into the Kistna after a course of 96 miles. The Pāler, rising in the Vardannāpet *tāluk*, flows almost parallel to the Muner, and also falls into the Kistna, 7 miles south of Jaggayyapeta. The Kinārsāni, after traversing the Pākhāl, Yellandlapād, and Pāloncha *tāluks* for a distance of 55 miles, falls into the Godāvari near Bhadrāchalam. The Wīra is a tributary of the Muner and joins it near Jalpalli. The minor streams are the Pākhāl, Kalter, and Laknāvaram.

The Pākhāl Lake in the Pākhāl *tāluk* has been formed by throwing a dam, 2,000 yards long, across the Pākhāl river, between two low headlands. The lake is 8,000 yards long by 6,000 broad, and when full covers an area of 13 square miles.

Geology.

The geological formations are the Archaean gneiss and schists, the Cuddapahs and Kurnools, the Sullavais (perhaps

[1] These figures refer to the District before the reorganization of 1905. See paragraph on Population.

identical with the Kurnools), the Gondwānas (including Tālcher, Barākar, Kamptee, Kota-Māleri, and Chikiāla beds), and alluvium. The Archaean occupies principally the south-west, and the remaining beds the north-east of the District[1]. The Barākar is the most important group from an economic point of view, on account of its thick seams of coal, which are actively worked in the Singareni coal-fields[2]. The famous Golconda diamonds were formerly obtained from the Cuddapahs and Kurnools, principally from the basement beds of the latter. The Chikiala sandstones and the Archaean schists contain rich iron ores.

Botany. The forest flora of the District consists chiefly of teak, satin-wood, *eppa* (*Hardwickia binata*), *nallāmaddi* (*Terminalia tomentosa*), *sandra* (*Acacia Catechu*), bamboo, and *tarvar* (*Cassia auriculata*).

Fauna. In the extensive forests large game is abundant, such as tigers, leopards, cheetahs, bears, wolves, hyenas, wild hog, *sāmbar*, spotted deer, *nīlgai*, bison, 'jungle sheep' (*Cervulus muntjac*), and antelope. The Pākhāl forests are preserved for His Highness the Nizām. Wild duck, teal, snipe, blue and green pigeons, partridges, quail, and wild geese are abundant. Wild elephants were found at one period in the Samatmanyam jungle in the Parkāl *tāluk*, but there is now only a single female.

Climate, temperature, and rainfall. The climate of Warangal, Cherial, and Vardannāpet is dry and healthy; but the remaining *tāluks* are damp and malarious from June to January, when fevers and lung diseases prevail. From February till the beginning of the rains the climate is generally good. It is excessively hot in summer, the temperature rising to 112° in the month of May. The annual rainfall during the twenty-one years ending 1901 averaged 29 inches. The heaviest fall, 49 inches, was registered in 1893.

History. The District originally formed a portion of the ancient kingdom of the Andhra kings, who subdued the whole of the Deccan. For nearly two hundred years, from the middle of the twelfth century, it formed part of the territories of the Kākatīyas or Ganpatis of Warangal. Proda Rājā is said to have captured the Chālukya king, Taila III, and to have warred successfully against other kings. His son Rudra I extended his possessions, while Rājā Ganpati claims to have defeated the king of Kalinga and to have had the kings of Southern Gujarāt and Bengal as his vassals, ruling as far south

[1] W. King, *Memoirs, Geological Survey of India*, vol. viii, pt. i, and vol. xvii, pt. iii.

[2] W. Saise, *Records, Geological Survey of India*, vol. xxvii, pt. ii.

as the Nellore District of Madras. Ganpati was succeeded by his wife or daughter Rudramā Devī, about 1257, who is mentioned as the ruler of the country by Marco Polo. The Muhammadans invaded and partially subdued the country in 1303, but had to retire. In 1310 Warangal was again besieged by Malik Kāfūr, Alā-ud-dīn's general; and Rudra Deva II, the Hindu ruler, submitted. In 1321 Ulugh Khān, afterwards Muhammad bin Tughlak, was made ruler of the Deccan, and after an unsuccessful attempt captured Warangal with the aid of fresh troops and sent Rudrā Deva as a prisoner to Delhi. The last Kākatīya was Vīrabhadra, who succeeded about 1325, and is said to have retired to Kondavīd, after which the family is heard of no more. After the collapse of the Saiyid dynasty at Delhi, Alā-ud-dīn Hasan, the first Bahmani king (1347), compelled the Hindu Rājā of Warangal to pay him the tribute which had hitherto been paid to Delhi. In 1422 Warangal was finally captured by the Bahmani troops, and on the break-up of that kingdom it fell to the Kutb Shāhis of Golconda.

Archaeology. Among the archaeological remains in the District may be mentioned the thousand-pillared temple of HANAMKONDA, built in 1162 in the Chālukyan style by the last Hindu dynasty. It consists of three spacious detached halls with a portico supported by about 300 pillars. Opposite the portico is a star-shaped *mandapa* supported on 200 pillars. Three of the pillars have inscriptions in Old Telugu and Sanskrit. In the neighbourhood are several Jain figures cut in the rocks, close to the ruined town of Hanmantgiri. The fort of WARANGAL was commenced by Ganpati Rājā and completed by his widow. The eastern and western gates, as well as various pillars, are covered with inscriptions in Old Telugu and Sanskrit. In the Parkāl *tāluk*, Rāmappa's temple, 40 feet square and 40 feet high, is built of black basalt and exquisitely carved. The ancient fort of Khammamett is said to have been built 900 years ago, and was captured by Sultān Kuli Kutb Shāh of Golconda in 1516. It contains several guns of a much later period. The fort of Zafargarh, the ancient Valabgonda, in the Vardannāpet *tāluk*, has two stone walls and seven bastions, containing 16 guns.

Population. The number of towns and villages in the District, including *jāgīrs*, is 1,491. Its population at each Census in the last twenty years was: (1881) 675,746, (1891) 853,129, and (1901) 952,646. The towns are YELLANDLAPĀD, HANAMKONDA, the District head-quarters, and HASANPARTI. The population of Yellandlapād consists chiefly of miners working in the Singareni coal-mines. More than 94 per cent. of the population are

Hindus, and about 86 per cent. speak Telugu. The following table gives the chief statistics of population in 1901 :—

Tāluk.	Area in square miles.	Number of Towns.	Number of Villages.	Population.	Population per square mile.	Percentage of variation in population between 1891 and 1901.	Number of persons able to read and write.
Mahbūbābād	536	...	130	90,336	168	+ 23·1	Not available.
Pākhāl	1,270	...	192	38,501	30	+ 6·3	
Yellandlapād	488	1	51	42,811	88	+ 17·3	
Pāloncha	331	...	41	12,652	38	− 4·4	
Khammamett	850	...	182	146,083	172	+ 0·2	
Madhra	730	...	159	89,616	123	+ 11·9	
Cherial	417	..	101	84,301	202	+ 15·9	
Vardannāpet	536	...	112	92,772	173	+ 20·5	
Parkāl	604	...	112	81,026	134	+ 13·7	
Warangal	557	2	140	124,115	229	+ 12·7	
Jāgīrs, &c.	3,410	...	268	150,433	44	+ 11·7	
District total	9,729	3	1,488	952,646	98	+ 11.6	26,736

In 1905 Vardannāpet was divided between Warangal and Cherial; Cherial and the Kodār sub-*tāluk* were transferred to Nalgonda District, and Parkāl to Karīmnagar (formerly Elgandal). Pākhāl has been divided into two portions, the northern forming the new *tāluk* of Tārvai. Madhra will henceforth be known as Kallūr, after its head-quarters. The District in its present form comprises 8 *tāluks*—Warangal, Pākhāl, Tārvai, Khammamett, Yellandlapād, Mahbūbābād, Kallūr, and Pāloncha—besides the Pāloncha *samasthān* and other large *jāgīrs*. The area of the present District is 8,305 square miles, and the population (according to the Census of 1901) 745,757.

Castes and occupations.

The most numerous caste is that of the cultivating Kāpus, numbering 151,700, or about 16 per cent. of the total population, the most important divisions among them being the Mutrāsi (31,000) and Motāti Kāpus (22,000). Next in point of numbers come the Dhangars or shepherds (106,000), the Mādigas or leather-workers (99,900), the Brāhmans (79,600), the Mālas or village menials (58,100), the Gaundlās or toddy-drawers (57,500), the Koyas, a forest tribe (46,400), the Lambādas or grain-carriers (41,000), the Sālas or weaver caste (39,700), the Komatis or trading caste (35,600), and the Chākalas or washermen (31,000). The Mādigas and Mālas also work as field-labourers. The total population directly engaged in agriculture is 367,000, or more than 38 per cent. of the total.

Christian missions.

Three missions have been established in the District: one by the American Baptists at Hanamkonda, another by the Church of England at Khammamett, and the third by the Methodists at Yellandlapād. The total number of native Christians returned at the Census of 1901 was 1,457, of whom 629 were of the Church of England, 236 Methodists, and 511 Roman Catholics, the Baptists numbering only 81.

General agricultural conditions.

The soils consist of *masab*, *kharab*, *chalka*, and *regar* or black cotton soil. In the Mahbūbābād, Khammamett, Kallūr (Madhra), Yellandlapād, Pāloncha, and Pakhāl *tāluks*, *regar* predominates, in which *rabi* crops are extensively grown; while the *chalka* lands are more common in the Warangal, Parkāl, Cherial, and Vardannāpet *tāluks*, with a sprinkling of *regar*. 'Wet' cultivation is supplied by tanks, wells, and channels.

Chief agricultural statistics and principal crops.

The tenure of lands is *ryotwāri*. In 1901 the *khālsa* lands had an area of 6,319 square miles, of which 2,427 were cultivated, while 644 square miles were cultivable waste and fallows, 2,370 forests, and 878 square miles were not available for cultivation. The staple food-crops are *jowār*, rice, *bājra*, and maize, the areas under these being 854, 247, 250, and 212 square miles respectively. Cotton is grown to a small extent in all *tāluks*, the total area under it being only 32 square miles. Other crops are oilseeds (219 square miles) and pulses (92 square miles). In 1903-4 the total cultivated area was 2,555 square miles.

Cattle, &c.

There are two special breeds of cattle in the District. The Khammamett and Madhra breeds much resemble the Mysore cattle, being of a superior kind and of large size. The Telingāna cattle are found chiefly in the Parkāl and Pākhāl *tāluks*; they are small and hardy, and white in colour, only the tip of the tail being black. They are chiefly bred and used by the Banjārās, and roam in large droves through the forest tracts and waste lands, where plenty of pasture is found. The Khammamett and Madhra cattle fetch as much as Rs. 200 to Rs. 250 per pair. A breed of sheep in Madhra, of a reddish colour and large size, is very different from the ordinary black sheep of the country. The ponies are of no particular excellence.

Irrigation

The irrigated area in 1903-4 was 326 square miles, supplied by 1,433 large tanks, 3,826 *kuntas* or smaller tanks, 10,797 wells, and 89 channels. There are several large tanks in the District, the chief being the Pākhāl, Laknāvaram, Rāmappa, Ghanpur, Katāchpūr, Atmākūr, Dharmasāgar, and Yelgargū tanks; but some of these are in disrepair.

Forests.

Warangal District contains extensive forests, the area 'reserved' being 2,370 square miles, while 2,000 square miles are not protected. The forests contain teak (*Tectona grandis*), ebony (*Diospyros melanoxylon*), *shīsham* (*Dalbergia Sissoo*), satin-wood (*Chloroxylon Swietenea*), sandal-wood (*Santalum album*), *bhandārā* (*Adina cardifolia*), *tirman* (*Anogeissus latifolia*), *eppa* (*Hardwickia binata*), *chinnangi* (*Lagerstroemia parviflora*), *kodsha* (*Cleistanthus collinus*), *bījāsāl* (*Pterocarpus Marsupium*), *mokāb* (*Schrebera swietenioides*), *somi* (*Soymida febrifuga*), *nallāmaddi* (*Terminalia tomentosa*), *sandra* (*Acacia Catechu*), and bamboo. The revenue derived from the sale of timber in 1901 was Rs. 68,775, and from other forest products Rs. 46,165, making a total of 1·1 lakhs.

Among the more important minerals of the District may be mentioned coal, garnets, iron ore or haematite, steatite, and building stones. The coal-mines, situated near SINGARENI in the Yellandlapād sub-*tāluk*, are worked by the Hyderābād (Deccan) Mining Company, giving employment to 6,360 miners. The output in 1904 was 419,546 tons, a large proportion of which was sent to Bombay and Madras. The royalty paid to the State is 12 annas per ton. The coal is worked on the stall and pillar system, and the mines are supplied with machinery of the latest type. Talc is found in the Kallūr (Madhra) and Khammamett *tāluks*, and laminated limestone in Khammamett, while corundum and garnets occur in Pāloncha. Minerals.

The District is noted for some of its manufactures. Hanamkonda is celebrated for its silk and other cloths, such as cotton tweeds and coloured shirtings largely used for coats and shirts; and also for its carpets. In Mathwādā, Karīmābād, and Warangal cotton, silk, and woollen carpets of excellent make are turned out, in which a large trade is done with Europe. In Parkāl also carpets and *shatranjīs* of very superior quality are made, the price of the cotton ones ranging from Rs. 1–4 to Rs. 4–8 per square yard, and that of silk *shatranjīs* from Rs. 60 to Rs. 150 per square yard. *Tasar* silk is largely spun from cocoons. The Koyawārs rear the worms, and when the cocoons are ready they are boiled and the silk so obtained is sold to the weavers. *Sārīs*, *cholīs*, turbans, handkerchiefs, and other products of *tasar* silk are made at Parkāl, Jokalva, Hasanparti, and other places. Besides these, ordinary coarse cotton cloth and *dhotīs* and *sārīs* are manufactured everywhere for local use. Hides and skins are salted and sent to Madras by Labbais. There are four cotton-ginning factories and four oil-mills in the District, employing altogether 132 hands. The total weight of cotton Arts and manufactures.

cleaned in 1901 was 714 tons, and the weight of oil expressed 131 tons.

Commerce and trade. The main exports consist of rice, wheat, *jowār* and other food-grains and pulses, cotton, tobacco, sesamum, castor-seed, carpets, *shatranjīs*, silk and cotton cloths, *sārīs* and *dhotīs*, hides and skins, and *san*-hemp. The chief imports are salt, refined sugar, betel-nuts, spices, opium, gold and silver, copper and brass, kerosene oil, and matches. Trade is mainly with the adjoining Districts; but cotton is sent to Aurangābād, Hyderabad, Gulbarga, and also to Madras and Bombay, and the hides are sent mostly to Madras. The most important centre of trade is Mathwāda near Warangal, and next to it the village of Khammamett. The castes engaged in trade are principally Komatis, Mārwāris, Memons from Bombay, and Labbais from Madras. The Komatis also do a large banking business.

Railways The Nizām's Guaranteed State Railway traverses the District from Jangaon in the west, through Kāzīpett and Warangal, to Yerrupālayam in the east, a distance of 146 miles, with 17 stations within the District, besides the mineral line, 16 miles long, from Dornakal to Yellandlapād, making a total of 162 miles

Roads. There are 212 miles of gravelled roads, all maintained by the Public Works Department. Hanamkonda, the head-quarters of the District, is connected with all the *tāluk* head-quarters by means of roads. Since the construction of the railway the traffic on some of these has diminished, but most of them serve as feeders.

Famine. The effects of the famines of 1862, 1866, 1877–8, and 1900 were felt in this District, though far removed from the area of actual distress. In 1900, Rs. 5,000 was sanctioned for affording relief to the poor. Owing to its extensive forests and numerous tanks and wells, Warangal has been fairly free from serious famine.

District subdivisions and staff. The District is divided into three subdivisions, each under a Second Tālukdār. The first consists of the Mahbūbābād, Tārvai, and Pāloncha *tāluks*; the second consists of the Khammamett, Kalūr (Madhra), and Yellandlapād *tāluks*; and the third of Warangal and Pākhāl. Each *tāluk* is under a *tahsīldār*, except the sub-*tāluk* of Yellandlapād, which has a *naib-tahsīldār*. The First Tālukdār exercises a general supervision over the work of his subordinates.

Civil and criminal justice. The District civil court is presided over by a civil judge, styled the *Adālat Madadgār* or Judicial Assistant. There is also a Munsif's court at Hanamkonda, and eleven subordinate courts, the former presided over by the Munsif and the latter by the *tahsīldārs* and *naib-tahsīldār*. The First Tālukdār is the chief magistrate and the civil judge is a joint-magistrate, exercising powers during the absence of the First Tālukdār from head-quarters. The Second and Third Tālukdārs exercise second-class, and the *tahsīldārs* third-class magisterial powers. Serious crime is not heavy in ordinary times. As Hanamkonda is the head-quarters of the Division, the *Sūbahdār* and the Divisional Judge also hold their courts here.

Little is known of the revenue history. Prior to the formation of regular Districts in 1866, villages were farmed out at fixed sums, and the revenue was collected in cash. The survey of Warangal was completed in 1904, when the *tāluks* were settled for fifteen years. It was found that the area included in holdings was 814 square miles more than that shown in the old accounts, or a total of 1,913 square miles, while the land revenue was raised from 20·6 to 26·1 lakhs, or by about 27 per cent. The average assessment on 'dry' land is Rs. 1-11-2 (maximum Rs. 3, minimum R. 0-9), and on 'wet' land Rs. 11-8-7 (maximum Rs. 20, minimum Rs. 7-8). Land revenue.

The land revenue and the total revenue for a series of years are shown below, in thousands of rupees:—

	1881.	1891.	1901.	1903.
Land revenue .	10,97	17,23	21,86	18,16
Total revenue .	13,99	21,77	28,33	23,71

Owing to the changes of area effected in 1905, the revenue demand is now about 16·1 lakhs.

In 1899 a one anna cess was levied and local boards were established. There is a District board at Hanamkonda, which supervises the working of the *tāluk* boards. The First Tālukdār is the president of the District board and the *tahsīldārs* are chairmen of the *tāluk* boards. At Hanamkonda there is a municipality; and each of the *tāluk* head-quarters has a small conservancy establishment, the District and *tāluk* boards managing the municipalities as well. The total expenditure in 1901 on local works and roads amounted to Rs. 42,600. Local boards and municipalities.

The First Tālukdār is the head of the police administration, with the *Mohtamim* (Superintendent) as his executive deputy. Under him are 10 inspectors and 124 subordinate officers, 728 constables, and 25 mounted police, distributed among Police and jails.

36 *thānas* and 45 outposts. The Central jail lies between Hanamkonda and Mathwādā, and has accommodation for 707 male and 20 female prisoners. Convicts from Karīmnagar and Nalgonda Districts, whose sentences exceed six months, are received here. In 1901 there were 1,207 male and 13 female convicts in the Central jail. Carpets and *shatranjīs* of a superior quality are manufactured, besides furniture, cotton tweeds, counterpanes, towels, and other cloths for prison and police use. The jail products are also sold to the local traders.

Education. Warangal takes a medium place as regards the literacy of its population, of whom 2·8 per cent. (5·2 males and 0·23 females) were able to read and write in 1901. The total number of pupils under instruction in 1881, 1891, 1901, and 1903 was 429, 2,891, 4,247, and 4,258 respectively. In 1903 there were 74 primary, 3 middle schools, one high school, and one industrial school, with 360 girls under instruction. The total amount spent on education in 1901 was Rs. 35,700, of which the State paid Rs. 24,700 and the local board Rs. 11,000, including Rs. 1,824 granted to aided schools. The fees realized at the State and board schools were Rs. 1,568 and Rs. 555 respectively. The amount realized by the aided schools as fees and subscriptions in 1901 was Rs. 1,359.

Medical. A large dispensary is maintained at Hanamkonda, and there are 8 others in the *tāluks*, with accommodation for 77 in-patients, besides two *yunāni* dispensaries. In 1901 the total number of cases treated was 50,862, of whom 217 were in-patients; and the number of operations performed was 1,675. The total expenditure was Rs. 16,700, of which the local board contributed Rs. 6,000.

The number of persons successfully vaccinated in 1901 was 1,600, representing 1·67 per 1,000 of population.

Mahbūbābād (or Mānkota).—*Tāluk* in Warangal District, Hyderābād State, with an area of 778 square miles. The population in 1901, including *jāgīrs*, was 98,552, compared with 80,071 in 1891. Some villages were transferred from the Warangal *tāluk* in 1905. The *tāluk* now contains 158 villages, of which 28 are *jāgīr*; and Mahbūbābād (population, 2,769) is the head-quarters. The land revenue in 1901 was 2·3 lakhs. Rice is largely grown and irrigated from tanks. The Nizām's Guaranteed State Railway passes through the *tāluk* from north-west to east. There are 3,817 Koyas (a jungle tribe).

Tārvai.—*Tāluk* in Warangal District, Hyderābād State, formed in 1905 from the northern villages of the former Pākhāl *tāluk*. The number of *khālsa* villages is 155, of which Tārvai (population, 97) is the head-quarters. The land revenue is only Rs. 27,800. The *tāluk* is very thinly populated and has a large area of forest.

Pākhāl Tāluk.—*Tāluk* in Warangal District, Hyderābād State, with an area of 1,320 square miles. The population in 1901, including *jāgīrs*, was 39,030, compared with 36,719 in 1891. It is very thinly populated, owing to large forests and a malarious climate. The *tāluk* contained 195 villages, of which 3 are *jāgīr*, Narsampet (population, 1,803) being the head-quarters. The land revenue in 1901 was 1·2 lakhs. In 1905 some villages were added from the Warangal *tāluk*, and the northern portion became a separate *tāluk* called Tārvai. The Pākhāl Lake, 13 square miles in area, is situated 8 miles east of Narsampet. The Muner river flows out from this lake. Rice is largely grown near tanks. The aboriginal tribes of Gonds and Koyas numbered 4,696 and 4,826 respectively in 1901.

Yellandlapād Sub-tāluk.—Sub-*tāluk* in Warangal District, Hyderābād State, with an area of 618 square miles. The population in 1901, including *jāgīrs*, was 45,340, compared with 38,649 in 1901. This sub-*tāluk* was formed in 1892 from the Khammamett, Madhra, and Mahbūbābād *tāluks*. It contains one large mining town, Yellandlapād (population, 12,377), the head-quarters; and 61 villages, of which 10 are *jāgīr*. The coal-mine of Singareni is situated close to the town. The land revenue in 1901 was Rs. 42,000.

Pāloncha Tāluk.—Easternmost *tāluk* of Warangal District, Hyderābād State, with an area of 1,297 square miles. The population in 1901, including *jāgīrs*, was 31,329, compared with 32,757 in 1891. The *tāluk* contains 89 villages, of which 48 are *jāgīr*; and Borgampād (population, 3,200) is the head-quarters. This is a very thinly populated *tāluk*, containing a large forest tract, and is very malarious. The land revenue in 1901 was only Rs. 16,000. The Godāvari river forms its eastern boundary, separating it from the Godāvari District of Madras on the east. The aboriginal tribes of Gonds and Koyas number 4,480 and 10,055 respectively. Situated to the east is the *samasthān* of Pāloncha, with a population of 38,742, 62 villages, and an area of about 800 square miles.

Khammamett.—Southern *tāluk* of Warangal District, Hyderābād State, with an area of 990 square miles. The population in 1901, including *jāgīrs*, was 154,540, compared with 154,159 in 1891. The *tāluk* contains 195 villages, of which 13 are *jāgīr*; and Khammamett (population, 3,001) is the head-quarters. The land revenue in 1901 was 4·6 lakhs. Rice is largely grown and irrigated from tanks and wells. The Nizām's Guaranteed State Railway runs through the *tāluk* from north to south.

Kallūr (formerly called Madhra).—Southern *tāluk* of Warangal District, Hyderābād State, north of the Kistna District of Madras, with an area of 966 square miles. The population in 1901, including *jāgīrs*, was 103,829, compared with 92,738 in 1891. The *tāluk* contains 184 villages, of which 25 are *jāgīr*; and Kallūr (population, 2,741) is the head-quarters. The land revenue in 1901 was 2·5 lakhs. The Nizām's Guaranteed State Railway passes through the *tāluk* from north-west to south-east. Rice is largely cultivated near tanks. The diamond mines of Partyal are situated in this *tāluk*.

Warangal Tāluk.—*Tāluk* in Warangal District, Hyderābād State, with an area of 773 square miles. The population in 1901, including *jāgīrs*, was 142,751, compared with 126,604 in 1891. The *tāluk* contained two towns, HANAMKONDA (population, 10,487), the Division, District, and *tāluk* head-quarters, and HASANPARTI (5,378); and 161 villages, of which 21 are *jāgīr*. The commercial town of Mathwādā, which is a suburb of Hanamkonda, is 4 miles east of the latter, and the fort of WARANGAL is about 4 miles south-east of Hanamkonda. The land revenue in 1901 was 3·3 lakhs. In 1905 the *tāluk* was considerably altered by the transfer of villages to Mahbūbābād and Pākhāl, and by the addition of part of the former *tāluk* of Vardannāpet. Rice is largely raised by tank-irrigation. The Nizām's Guaranteed State Railway passes through the *tāluk*.

Hanamkonda.—Head-quarters of the Warangal Division and District, Hyderābād State, situated in 18° 1′ N. and 79° 34′ E., near the stations of Kāzīpet and Warangal on the Nizām's State Railway. Population (1901), 10,487. According to local tradition, it was the capital of the surrounding country before the foundation of Warangal. The *Pratāp Charitrā*, a Telugu work, says that a Chālukya king reigned at Nandagiri (Nānder), on whose death the kingdom was divided between his two sons, one ruling at Hanamkonda and the other at Kandahār. Ballahundu, king of Cuttack, having killed Somadeo, the king of Kandahār, Siriyal Devī, wife of the latter, fled to Hanamkonda, and gave birth to a posthumous son, Mādhava Varma, who succeeded to the throne as the first king of the Kākatīya line. This event is placed about A.D. 314, but the Kākatīyas are not referred to in authentic records before the middle of the twelfth century (*see* WARANGAL DISTRICT).

Hanamkonda contains some very interesting buildings, of which the 'thousand-pillared' temple is specially noteworthy. It was built in 1162 in the Chālukyan style by the last Hindu dynasty, and consists of three spacious detached halls with a portico supported by nearly 300 pillars. Opposite the portico is a star-shaped *mandapa* supported on 200 pillars, three of which bear Old Telugu and Sanskrit inscriptions. Near the temple is a fine well. Around Hanamkonda several Jain figures are cut in the rocks, close to the ruined town of Hanmantgiri. There are two large tanks on each side of the town. The modern town of Hanamkonda extends from near Kāzīpet on the west to Mathwādā on the east. It contains the offices of the *Sūbahdār*, the Divisional and District civil courts, the District and Irrigation Engineer's offices, the survey office, several schools, a Central jail, the Tālukdār's offices, a large dispensary and two *yunāni* dispensaries, an American Mission school and hospital, and a District post office.

Hasanparti.—Town in the District and *tāluk* of Warangal, Hyderābād State, situated in 18° 5′ N. and 79° 31′ E. Population (1901), 5,378. The special feature of the place is that it contains about a hundred houses of weavers, who are engaged in making silk *sārīs* and other silk cloths, and also in manufacturing silk from *tasar* gathered by the Dandra tribe. It contains a State school where Urdū and Telugu are taught, and also a police station. In the neighbourhood iron ore is found, from which iron and steel are manufactured in small quantities, and used by the ryots for implements of husbandry. A temple of Venkateshwar Swāmi is situated in the town, and a religious fair is held annually.

Warangal Village.—Ancient town in Warangal District, Hyderābād State, situated in 17° 58′ N. and 79° 37′ E., on the Nizām's State Railway, 86 miles north-east of Hyderābād city. Population (1901), 4,741. The place was founded in the twelfth century by Proda Rājā of the Kākatīya dynasty; but some identify it with Worakalli, the capital of the Adeva Rājās of Teluva Andhra or Telingāna in the eighth century. Warangal or Varanakal is believed to be the Korun Kula of Ptolemy, while another name is Akshalingar, evidently the Yeksilanagar or Yeksilapatan mentioned by Raghunāth Bhāskar in his *Aravachan Kosh.* Ganpati, the grandson of Prodā Rājā, began the stone wall of Warangal, which was completed by his widow or daughter, Rudramā Devī, who also surrounded it with an outer mud wall, about the middle of the thirteenth century. The place is about 1,050 feet above the level of the sea, and lies on the watershed separating the basins of the Godāvari and Kistna in the lower part of their course. The surrounding country consists of large undulating plains of reddish sandy loam and black soil, broken here and there by piles of huge granite boulders and basaltic dikes. The extent of the fort and town may be gathered from the fact that the 'dry' cultivated lands within the outer wall yield a revenue of Rs. 5,000. The city was of considerable size in the days of its prosperity, including the present sites of Hanamkonda, Mathwādā, Karīmābād, and Warangal proper, while Mathwadā alone consists of a group of five villages: Mathwādā, Rāmannāpet, Girmājīpet, Bālānagar, and Govindāpur.

Yellandlapād Town.—Formerly a small hamlet, but now a town with a large mining population, and the head-quarters of the sub-*tāluk* of Yellandlapād, in Warangal District, Hyderābād State, situated in 17° 31′ N. and 80° 16′ E. Population (1901), 12,377. The coal-mining industry is responsible for the growth of the town, the Singareni coal-fields lying in the neighbourhood. A special magistrate has been appointed for the trying of cases. The mines are served by a mineral line which connects them with Dornakal on the Nizām's State Railway. The production of coal at Singareni increased rapidly from 3,259 tons in 1887 (the first year of working) to 144,668 in 1891 and 421,218 in 1901. In 1904 the total output was 419,546. The mines employ 6,360 hands. Yellandlapād contains, besides the *tahsīl* office, a sub-post office and a police sub-inspector's office.

Karīmnagar District.—District in the Warangal Division of the Hyderābād State, formerly known as ELGANDAL. It is bounded on the north by Adilābād; on the east by the Bastar State of the Central Provinces; on the south by Warangal; and on the west by Medak and Nizāmābād. In consequence of the changes made in 1905, its area has been reduced to 5,369 square miles, including *jāgīrs*. A range of hills extends in a north-easterly direction between Gurrapalli and Jagtial, terminating at Vemalkurti near the Godāvari. A second range, running parallel to the former, stretches from Sunigram to Mallangūr. A third range starts in the south-western corner of the District from the valley of the Māner river, runs in a north-easterly direction, and, after intersecting the Sunigram range, passes beyond Rāmgīr and terminates near the Godāvari. The principal river is the Godāvari, which flows through the northern portion, forming the northern and eastern boundary, and partially separating the District from Adilābād in the north and from Bastar in the east. The next important river is the Māner, a tributary of the Godāvari, which traverses the District from west to east as far as Kārlagunta, and thence flows due north, till it falls into the Godāvari in the Mahādeopur *tāluk*. The Peddavāgu and Chelluvāgu are minor tributaries of the Godāvari.

The geological formations are the Archaean gneiss, and the Cuddapah, Sullavai, and Gondwāna series. Gneiss occupies most of the District, the remaining formations occurring in the east.

The flora of the District includes teak, mango, custard-apple, tamarind, ebony, black-wood, satin-wood, *tarvar* (*Cassia auriculata*), *babūl* (*Acacia arabica*), *nallāmaddi* (*Terminalia tomentosa*), and *eppa* (*Hardwickia binata*).

Karīmnagar is covered with a large extent of jungle and forest, which give cover to tigers, leopards, bears, hyenas, wolves, wild hog, and wild dogs, while in the plains *sāmbar*, spotted deer, and *nīlgai* are met with everywhere.

With the exception of Mahādeopur and parts of Sirsilla and Jagtial, the District is healthy. The temperature at Karīmnagar and Jamikunta in May rises to 110°, and in the remaining *tāluks* it ranges between 100° and 105°. In December it falls to 60°. The annual rainfall averages about 33 inches.

The population of the area of the present District in 1901 was 861,833. It comprises seven *tāluks*: KARĪMNAGAR, JAMIKUNTA, SULTĀNĀBĀD, JAGTIAL, SIRSILLA, MAHĀDEOPUR, and PARKĀL. The chief towns are JAGTIAL, MANTHANI, KORATLA, KARĪMNAGAR, and VEMALWĀDĀ. About 96 per cent. of the population are Hindus; 90 per cent. speak Telugu, and 6 per cent. Urdū.

The land revenue demand of the District as at present constituted is about 22·6 lakhs.

Elgandal District[1].—Former District in the Warangal Division of the Hyderābād State, lying between Adilābād and Nizāmābād on the north and north-west, Medak on the west, and Warangal on the south, while on the east the rivers Prānhita and Godāvari separated it from Chānda District and Bastar State of the Central Provinces. It had an area of 7,203 square miles, including *jāgīr* lands, and lay between 17° 14′ and 19° 15′ N. and 78° 30′ and 80° 25′ E. The area of the State and *Sarf-i-khās* or 'crown' lands was 5,898 square miles. Changes made in 1905 will be referred to below.

Boundaries, configuration, and hill and river systems.

[1] Elgandal ceased to exist in its present form in 1905. The new District called Karīmnagar is briefly described in the paragraph on Population. *See also* KARĪMNAGAR DISTRICT.

A range of hills, commencing at Gurrapalli, runs in a north-easterly direction as far as Jagtial, whence it proceeds to Vemalkurti near the Godāvari. A second range, known as the Sunigram range, proceeds from Sunigram and Mallangūr parallel to the former range, at a distance of about 32 miles. The villages of Kuncherla, Minola, and Marmulagutta on this range are between 2,200 and 2,300 feet above the sea. A third range starts in the south-west corner of the District from the valley of the Māner river, and runs in a north-easterly direction. Intersecting the Sunigram range, it passes beyond Rāmgīr, where it is about 1,600 feet above the sea. This range ends near the Godāvari.

The most important river in Elgandal is the Godāvari, which enters the north-west corner of the District and flows for a distance of 176 miles within its limits, dividing it from Chānda and Bastar in the Central Provinces. Another important river is the Māner, which traverses the District from west to east as far as Kārlagunta, whence it flows due north till it falls into the Godāvari in the Mahādeopur *tāluk*. Its length in the District is about 145 miles. The Pranhitā, another tributary of the Godāvari, joins it in the Chinnūr *tāluk*. The Peddavāgu, 50 miles long, and the Chelluvāgu, 12 miles long, are also tributaries of the Godāvari, which they join on the southern or right bank.

Geology. The geological formations are the Archaean gneiss, the Cuddapah, Sullavai, and Gondwāna series, the latter including the Tālcher, Barākar, Kamptee, Kota-Māleri, and Chikiāla formations. The Archaean series occupies most of the District, the remaining formations occurring at its eastern end[1].

Botany. Among the trees of the District may be mentioned teak, mango, ebony, custard-apple, tamarind, black-wood, *tarvar* (*Cassia auriculata*), *babūl* (*Acacia arabica*), *eppa* (*Hardwickia binata*), and *nallāmaddi* (*Terminalia tomentosa*).

Fauna. All kinds of large game abound, including tigers, leopards, bears, wolves, hyenas, *sāmbar*, spotted deer, &c., while pea-fowl, jungle-fowl, partridges, and quail are also found. In the vicinity of tanks and rivers water-fowl, duck, teal, &c., are abundant.

Climate, temperature, and rainfall. The portions of the District near the Godāvari are malarious, but the remaining *tāluks* are healthy. The temperature in Karīmnagar and Jamikunta rises in May to 110°, while in the rest of the *tāluks* the maximum varies between 100° and 105°. During December it falls to 60°. The annual rainfall for the

[1] W. King, *Memoirs, Geological Survey of India*, vol. xviii, part iii.

twenty-one years ending 1901 averaged 33 inches, but considerrable fluctuations are recorded. Thus in 1881 and 1900 only 15 inches, or less than half the average, was received.

Nothing is known of the early history of the District; but it certainly formed part of the Warangal territory, and after the conquest of Telingāna by the Musalmāns, and the fall of Warangal, it was included successively in the Bahmani and the Kutb Shāhi kingdoms. Upon the conquest of Golconda, it was annexed to the empire of Delhi by Aurangzeb, but was again separated from it on the foundation of the Hyderābād State, early in the eighteenth century, by Asaf Jāh. History.

Places of archaeological interest comprise a number of forts, temples, and mosques. The fort at Elgandal is an ancient structure, and contains a mosque built by Zafar-ud-daula about 1754, with a minaret which oscillates when shaken. In the Jamikunta *tāluk* are the two forts of Bājgūr and Malangūr, said to have been built respectively 700 and 1,000 years ago; and the two temples of Gurshāl and Katkūr, the former built about 1229, during the reign of Rājā Pratāp Rudra of Warangal. Though now in ruins, its exquisite stone carving is still in a good state of preservation. A pillar outside the temple has an inscription in Oriyā. The fort of JAGTIAL was built for Zafar-ud-daula, in 1747, by French engineers. In the same *tāluk* is an old temple at Dharampuri on the right bank of the Godāvari. The old fort of Anantagiri in the Sirsilla *tāluk*, now in ruins, is built on a hill. Two mosques in the Mahādeopur *tāluk*, one at Kālesar and the other at Sonipet, were built by Aurangzeb, as was the mosque at Rājgopālpet in the Siddipet *tāluk*. Pratāpgiri fort, in the Mahādeopur *tāluk*, is said to have been built by Rājā Pratāp Rudra. Archaeology.

The number of towns and villages in the District is 1,523. The population at the last three enumerations was: (1881) 939,539, (1891) 1,094,601, and (1901) 1,035,582. The decrease during the last decade was due to cholera and distress during the famine of 1900. The important towns are JAGTIAL, KORATLA, MANTHANI, KARĪMNAGAR, the District head-quarters, and VEMALWĀDĀ. About 96 per cent. of the population are Hindus. Telugu is spoken by 90 per cent. and Urdū by 6 per cent. The table on the next page exhibits the chief statistics of population in 1901. Population.

In 1905 the Parkāl *tāluk* was added to the District from Warangal, while Chinnūr and Lakhsetipet were transferred to Adilābād (Sirpur Tāndūr), and Siddipet to Medak. In its present form the District, henceforth to be known as KARĪM-

NAGAR, comprises the seven *tāluks* of Karīmnagar, Sultānābād, Mahādeopur, Jamikunta, Parkāl, Sirsilla, and Jagtial.

Tāluk.	Area in square miles.	Number of		Population.	Population per square mile.	Percentage of variation in population between 1891 and 1901.	Number of persons able to read and write.
		Towns.	Villages.				
Karīmnagar .	869	1	160	122,874	141	− 18.8	Not available.
Lakhsetipet .	462	...	114	46,254	100	− 3.4	
Chinnūr .	710	1	99	47,072	66	+ 7.0	
Sultānābād .	205	...	105	88,436	431	+ 0.7	
Mahādeopur .	759	1	124	55,655	73	+ 4.6	
Jamikunta .	590	...	149	117,894	199	− 9.6	
Siddipet .	670	1	131	88,850	133	− 3.2	
Sirsilla .	874	...	154	103,372	118	− 7.9	
Jagtial .	759	2	197	156,942	207	− 2.0	
Jāgīrs, &c. .	1,305	1	283	208,233	159	− 3.6	
District total	7,203	7	1,516	1,035,582	144	− 5.4	18,324

Castes and occupations. The purely agricultural castes number 164,000, or about 16 per cent. of the total, the most important being Kunbīs (89,000), Mītaiwārs (28,000), and Velmas (21,000). The Brāhmans muster strong, being 221,000, or over 21 per cent. The Dhangars or shepherds number 89,000, excluding Hatkars (64,400) and Kurmas (21,800). The Sālas, or weaver caste, number 80,400; the Mālas, or village menials, 67,300; the Komatis, or traders, 39,600; and the Ausalas, or smith caste, 30,000. More than 35 per cent. of the population are directly engaged in agriculture.

Christian missions. A Wesleyan mission was started in 1884 at Karīmnagar, with a European missionary and a staff of native catechists, and has branches at Kottapali and Mānākondūr. The mission supports several schools and a dispensary. The Wesleyan Mission at Siddipet, established in 1886, maintains nine schools. The Census of 1901 showed the Christian population as 214, of whom 212 were natives.

General agricultural conditions. The soils consist of *chalka*, *masab*, and *regar*. The *regar* is utilized for *rabi* crops, the *masab* partly for garden crops and partly for *rabi*, while the *kharīf* crops are raised on *chalka* lands, which occupy about three-fifths of the entire cultivated area. The existence of numerous tanks is a marked feature. The alluvial soil of the river valleys is very fertile.

Chief agricultural statistics and principal crops. The tenure of lands is mainly *ryotwāri*. *Khālsa* and 'crown' lands occupy 5,898 square miles, of which 1,244 were cultivated in 1901, 778 square miles were cultivable waste and fallows, 3,018 were forest, and 858 were not available for cultivation. The staple food-crop is *jowār*, grown on 570 square miles, or 45 per cent. of the net area cropped. Next to it is rice with 169 square miles. The areas occupied by gram, cotton, pulses, and oilseeds were 11, 58, 225, and 197 square miles respectively.

No breed of cattle is characteristic of the District; those found are small, but are well suited for light ploughing in the *chalka* lands. Ponies of very inferior class are bred. The sheep and goats are of the ordinary kind. Cattle, &c.

The irrigated lands cover an area of 183 square miles. The principal sources of irrigation are 5,694 tanks, large and small, and 16,693 masonry and 6,323 unbricked wells, all in good repair. A staff of irrigation engineers is engaged in preparing estimates for the tanks in disrepair, which number over 1,750. Irrigation.

The District contains large tracts of forest, especially in the *tāluks* of Chinnūr, Mahādeopur, Lakhsetipet, and in parts of Jagtial and Sirsilla, all under the Forest department. The total area of forests is 3,018 square miles, of which 816 square miles are 'reserved,' and 2,202 square miles protected and unprotected forests. The trees include teak, ebony, rosewood, satin-wood, *somi* (*Soymida febrifuga*), *tirman* (*Anogeissus latifolia*), *sandra* (*Acacia Catechu*), *kodsha* (*Cleistanthus collinus*), *eppa* (*Hardwickia binata*), *nallāmaddi* (*Terminalia tomentosa*), and *chinnangi* (*Lagerstroemia parviflora*), all of which produce good timber. Forests.

Ironstone of very good quality is found almost everywhere, and is smelted by a primitive process for making ploughshares and other implements of husbandry. The Konasamudram and Ibrāhīmpatan steel is famous for the fine watered sword-blades that were formerly made from it. Steatite and talc are found in the vicinity of the iron mines throughout the District. Minerals.

Silk *sārīs* and scarfs are made in the Siddipet and Jagtial *tāluks* and exported to Hyderābād. Coarse cotton cloth of every description is made in all parts and is extensively used by the people. The Sālas or Khatris, who number over 80,000, are engaged in weaving silk and cotton cloth. Coarse paper is manufactured at Koratla in the Jagtial *tāluk*, and used by the *patwāris* for their village account books. In Chinnūr, silk cloth is made from *tasar* cocoons, which is strong and durable. Silver filigree work of superior quality is turned out by the goldsmiths of Karīmnagar and Mānakondūr. Fine brass vessels are also made. There is a tannery at Karīmnagar, established in 1869; it employs 30 workmen and turns Arts and manufactures.

out leather to the value of Rs. 73,000 annually, which is exported to Madras.

Commerce. The chief exports consist of rice, *jowār*, sesamum, mustard, castor-seed, tobacco, silk cloth, cotton, chillies, sheep, hides and leather, bones and horns, and brass vessels, which are sent to Warangal and Hyderābād. The principal imports are cotton and woollen cloth of European manufacture, glass-ware, refined sugar, jaggery, gold and silver, salt, opium, kerosene oil, and brass and copper sheets. The chief centres of trade are SIDDIPET, Peddapalli, Kamanpur, JAGTIAL, Ghambiraopet, and KARĪMNAGAR. The Komatis are the principal trading caste.

Roads. No railway passes through the District. There are 220 miles of road, of which 168 are gravelled, the rest being merely fair-weather roads. The principal route is the Karīmnagar-Kāzipet road. The other roads connect the District and *tāluk* head-quarters with one another.

Famine. Elgandal has generally been immune from famine, owing to its numerous tanks and wells and large forest tracts. In 1897, though the rainfall was about 28 inches, it fell at such inopportune periods and in such small quantities that the majority of the crops failed. Relief works were opened to alleviate the distress. The effects of the famine had not passed away when cholera supervened, and carried off a large number of people, as is evidenced by the decline of population at the Census of 1901. The great famine of 1900 did not affect this District very seriously.

District subdivisions and staff. The District, as now constituted, is divided into four subdivisions for administrative purposes. The first consists of the *tāluks* of JAMIKUNTA and PARKĀL; the second of SULTĀNĀBĀD and MAHĀDEOPUR; the third of JAGTIAL and SIRSILLA; and the fourth of KARĪMNAGAR. Each of the first two is under a Second Tālukdār, and each of the other two under a Third Tālukdār. The First Tālukdār exercises a general supervision over all his subordinates. Each *tāluk* is under a *tahsīldār*.

Civil and criminal justice. The First Tālukdār is the chief magistrate, as well as the Civil Judge of the District, with a Judicial Assistant. The *tahsīldārs* preside in the subordinate civil courts. The Judicial Assistant is a joint-magistrate. The Second and Third Tālukdārs and the *tahsīldārs* exercise magisterial powers of the second and third classes within their respective jurisdictions.

Land revenue. Up to 1866, villages and *tāluks* were leased out to revenue farmers, and in some instances collections were made from individual ryots, but the State due was received in kind on a summary estimate. After the formation of the District the *ryotwāri* system was adopted, and the lands were roughly measured, the assessment being fixed on the average of the previous ten years. The District has not yet been completely surveyed, and the old rates are still in force. The average assessment on 'dry' land is R. 1 (maximum Rs. 5, minimum R. 0-2), and on 'wet' land Rs. 12 (maximum Rs. 36, minimum Rs. 4).

The land revenue and total revenue for a series of years are shown below, in thousands of rupees:—

	1881.	1891.	1901.	1903.
Land revenue .	13,79	22,60	24,39	18,28
Total revenue .	24,13	31,41	36,80	28,86

Owing to the changes in area made in 1905, the revenue demand is now about 22·6 lakhs.

The one anna cess has been levied since 1903. *Tāluk* boards have been established at all *tāluk* head-quarters, except Karīmnagar, where there is a District board, which supervises the work of the *tāluk* boards as well as that of the Karīmnagar and other municipalities. Small municipal establishments are maintained at all the *tāluk* head-quarters. Local boards and munici-palities.

The First Tālukdār is the head of the police administration of the District, with a Superintendent (*Mohtamim*) as his executive deputy. Under the latter are 10 inspectors, 75 subordinate officers, 608 constables, and 25 mounted police, distributed among 36 *thānas* and 35 outposts. The District jail is at Karīmnagar, but prisoners whose terms exceed six months are sent to the Central jail at Warangal. Police and jails.

The District occupies a low position as regards the literacy of its population, of whom only 1·8 per cent. (3·3 males and 0·08 females) were able to read and write in 1901. The total number of pupils under instruction in State schools in 1881, 1891, 1901, and 1903 was 527, 2,948, 2,732, and 2,870 respectively. In 1903 there were 40 primary and 2 middle schools, with 27 girls under instruction in that year. The total expenditure on education in 1901 was Rs. 18,600, of which Rs. 1,836 was allotted to aided schools. The fee receipts amounted to Rs. 1,012 in the State schools and Rs. 227 in the aided schools. Education.

There were five dispensaries in the District in 1901, with accommodation for 19 in-patients. The total number of outpatients treated was 39,514 and of in-patients 113, and the number of operations performed was 649. The expenditure Medical.

amounted to Rs. 15,400. The number of persons vaccinated in the same year was 3,597, or 3·47 per 1,000 of the population.

Karīmnagar Tāluk.—*Tāluk* in Karīmnagar District, Hyderābād State, with an area of 1,012 square miles. The population in 1901, including *jāgīrs*, was 138,591, compared with 170,676 in 1891, the decrease being due to famine and cholera. The *tāluk* contains one town, KARĪMNAGAR (population, 5,752), the District and *tāluk* head-quarters; and 186 villages, of which 26 are *jāgīr*. The land revenue in 1901 was 4·3 lakhs. Rice is largely raised by irrigation from tanks and wells. The Māner river flows through the *tāluk* from west to east.

Sultānābād.—*Tāluk* in Karīmnagar District, Hyderābād State, with an area of 287 square miles. The population in 1901, including *jāgīrs*, was 131,624, compared with 130,548 in 1891. The number of villages is 146, of which 41 are *jāgīr*; and Sultānābād (population, 1,339) is the head-quarters. The land revenue in 1901 was 1·9 lakhs. Rice is largely raised by tank-irrigation.

Mahādeopur.—*Tāluk* in Karīmnagar District, Hyderābād State, with an area of 801 square miles. It is separated from the Central Provinces District of Chānda on the east by the Godāvari river, which forms its northern and eastern boundary. The population in 1901, including *jāgīrs*, was 58,261, compared with 55,690 in 1891. The *tāluk* contains one town, MANTHANI (population, 6,680), the head-quarters; and 131 villages, of which 7 are *jāgīr*. The land revenue in 1901 was Rs. 90,000. The soil is alluvial in the north and east, and sandy elsewhere. A large area is under forest, which makes the climate malarious.

Jamikunta.—*Tāluk* in Karīmnagar District, Hyderābād State, with an area of 626 square miles, including *jāgīrs*. The population in 1901 was 121,518, compared with 134,309 in 1891, the decrease being due to famine and cholera. The *tāluk* contains 158 villages, of which 9 are *jāgīr*; and Jamikunta (population, 2,687) is the head-quarters. The land revenue in 1901 was 4 lakhs. The *tāluk* is hilly towards the west, while isolated hills are seen everywhere. There is hardly any forest. Rice is largely cultivated, being irrigated from tanks.

Parkāl.—*Tāluk* in Karīmnagar District, Hyderābād State, with an area of 654 square miles. The population in 1901, including *jāgīrs*, was 84,228, compared with 74,048 in 1891. The *tāluk* contains 117 villages, of which 5 are *jāgīr*; and Ambāl (population, 1,849) is the head-quarters. The land revenue in 1901 was 3·1 lakhs. Rice is extensively raised by tank-irrigation.

Sirsilla.—*Tāluk* in Karīmnagar District, Hyderābād State, with an area of 1,018 square miles. The population in 1901, including *jāgīrs*, was 123,722, compared with 134,337 in 1891, the decrease being due to famine and cholera. The *tāluk* contains one *jāgīr* town, VEMALWĀDĀ (population, 5,372), and 178 villages, of which 24 are *jāgīr*; while Sirsilla (3,400) is the head-quarters. The land revenue in 1901 was 3·9 lakhs. Rice is largely grown by means of tank and well irrigation. The Māner river crosses the south of the *tāluk*. The soil is mostly sandy, and well suited for *kharīf* crops, which are largely grown. In 1905 a few villages were transferred from this *tāluk* to Kāmāreddipet in Nizāmābād District.

Jagtial Tāluk.—*Tāluk* of Karīmnagar District, Hyderābād State, with an area of 971 square miles. The population in 1901, including *jāgīrs*, was 203,889, compared with 208,040 in 1891, the decrease being due to famine and cholera. The *tāluk* contains two towns, JAGTIAL (population, 11,181), the head-quarters, and KORATLA (5,524); and 251 villages, of which 54 are *jāgīr*. The land revenue in 1901 was 3·9 lakhs. Rice is extensively raised by means of tank-irrigation. The *tāluk* is crossed by a low range of hills in the south.

Jagtial Town.—Head-quarters of the *tāluk* of the same name in Karīmnagar District, Hyderābād State, situated in 18° 48′ N. and 78° 55′ E. Population (1901), 11,181. To the north of the town is a celebrated old fort, constructed in 1747 by Zafar-ud-daula. The town contains a dispensary and a State school, and is the head-quarters of a Second Tālukdār. Silk *sārīs* and scarfs are woven by the Sālas.

Karīmnagar Town.—Head-quarters of the District and *tāluk* of Karīmnagar, Hyderābād State, situated in 18° 26′ N. and 79° 8′ E., on the Māner river, 6 miles east of Elgandal. Population (1901), 5,572. Besides the District and *tāluk* offices, it contains the District civil court, two dispensaries, one of which provides *yunāni* treatment, a post office, local board and municipal offices, several State schools, a mission school, a female mission hospital, a District jail, and a tannery. The town is noted for its fine filigree work.

Koratla.—Town in the Jagtial *tāluk* of Karīmnagar District, Hyderābād State, situated in 18° 49′ N. and 78° 43′ E. Population (1901), 5,524. Paper of a coarse texture is made, which is largely used by the *patwāris* for their account-books.

Manthani.—Head-quarters of the Mahādeopur *tāluk*,

Karīmnagar District, Hyderābād State, situated in 18° 39′ N. and 79° 40′ E., about one mile south of the Godāvari river. Population (1901), 6,680. The town contains a dispensary, a school, and a post office.

Vemalwādā.—*Jāgīr* town in the Sirsilla *tāluk* of Karīmnagar District, Hyderābād State, situated in 18° 28′ N. and 78° 53′ E., 8 miles north of Sirsilla. Population (1901), 5,372. It contains a temple on the south of a large tank, in the enclosure of which is the tomb of a Musalmān saint regarded as sacred by Hindus and Musalmāns alike.

Adilābād District.—District in the north of the Warangal Division of the Hyderābād State, formerly known as the subdistrict of SIRPUR TĀNDŪR, before the changes made in 1905. It is bounded on the north and north-east by Berār and the Chānda District of the Central Provinces; on the east by Chānda; on the south by Karīmnagar and Nizāmābād Districts; and on the south-west by Nānder and the Bāsim District of Berār. The Pengangā separates it from Berār on the west and north, and the Wardhā and Prānhita from Chānda on the north-east and east. It has an area of 7,403 square miles.

The Sahyādriparvat or Sātmāla range traverses the District from the north-west to the south-east, for about 175 miles. Hills of minor importance lie in the east.

The most important river, which drains its southern portion, is the Godāvari, separating it on the south from Nizāmābād and partly from Karīmnagar. The next in importance is the Pengangā, which runs along the western and northern borders until it falls into the Wardhā. The other rivers are the Wardhā and the Prānhita, which run along the north-eastern and eastern borders of the District. Minor streams are the Peddavāgu, the Kāpnāvarli, and the Amlūn, the first an affluent of the Wardhā, and the two latter of the Pengangā.

The geological formations include the Archaean gneiss, the Cuddapah, Sullavai, and Gondwāna series, and the Deccan trap.

The District is covered to a large extent by forests, in which teak, ebony, *bilgu* (*Chloroxylon Swietenia*), *jittigi* (*Dalbergia latifolia*), mango, tamarind, and *bījāsāl* (*Pterocarpus Marsupium*) grow to a great height.

The hills abound in large game, such as tigers, leopards, bears, hyenas, wolves, and wild dogs. In jungles on the plains, *nīlgai*, *sāmbar*, and spotted deer are met with in large numbers.

The District is the most unhealthy in the State, owing to the large extent of forests. The temperature rises in May to 105°

and falls in December to 56°. The annual rainfall averages about 41 inches.

The population, according to the Census of 1901, is 477,848. In its present form the District comprises eight *tāluks*: ADILĀBĀD (or Edlābād), Sirpur, Rājūra, Nirmal, Kinwat, Chinnūr, Lakhsetipet, and Jangaon. The towns are ADILĀBĀD, the District head-quarters, NIRMAL, and CHINNŪR. About 80 per cent. of the population are Hindus, more than 10 per cent. being Gonds; and about 6 per cent. are Musalmāns. The land revenue demand is about 6·5 lakhs. For further details *see* SIRPUR TĀNDŪR.

The District is divided into three subdivisions for administrative purposes: one consisting of the Adilābād (or Edlābād), Sirpur, and Rājūra *tāluks*, under a Second Tālukdār, while the second, comprising Lakhsetipet, Chinnūr, and Jangaon, and the third, consisting of Nirmal and Kinwat, are each under a Third Tālukdār.

The First Tālukdār is the chief magistrate as well as the Civil Judge of the District, having a Judicial Assistant, called the *Adālat Madadgār*, who is also a joint-magistrate, exercising powers during the absence of the First Tālukdār from head-quarters. The Second and Third Tālukdārs and the *tahsīldārs* exercise second and third-class magisterial powers. The Second and Third Tālukdārs have no civil jurisdiction, but the *tahsīldārs* preside over the *tahsīl* civil courts.

Local boards have recently been established in the District.

Sirpur Tāndūr[1] (also known as the *Amaldāri*).—Formerly a sub-district in the Bīdar Division of Hyderābād State, lying between 19° 0′ and 19° 56′ N. and 77° 53′ and 80° 0′ E., with an area of 5,029 square miles, of which 4,842 square miles are *khālsa*, the rest being *jāgīr*. It is bounded on the north and east by the Yeotmāl District of Berār and the Chānda District of the Central Provinces; on the south by the Karīmnagar and Nizāmābād Districts of Hyderābād; and on the west by the Nānder District and the Yeotmāl District of Berār. The Pengangā river separates it from Berār on the north, and the Wardhā and Prānhita divide it from Chānda on the east. **Boundaries, configuration, and hill and river systems.**

The Sahyādriparvat or Sātmāla range traverses the sub-district from the north-west to the south-east for about 175 miles. Other hills in the east are of minor importance.

The Pengangā is the most important river. It runs along

[1] The sub-district no longer exists; see paragraph on Population below, and article on ADILĀBĀD DISTRICT, which has taken the place of Sirpur Tāndūr.

the western and northern borders of the sub-district, until it falls into the Wardhā, north of the Rājūra *tāluk*. The Wardhā flows along the eastern border of the Rājūra *tāluk*. The other streams are the Peddavāgu, an affluent of the Wardhā, 100 miles long; and the Kāpnāvarli and Amlūn, tributaries of the Pengangā, the latter rising in the Sahyādriparvat range.

Geology. The geological formations are the Archaean gneiss; the Cuddapah, Sullavai, and Gondwāna series, the latter including Tālcher, Barākar, Kamptee, Kota-Māleri, and Chikiala beds; and the Deccan trap[1].

Botany. The sub-district is clothed with scrubby jungle and brushwood, besides having a very large extent of forests, which contain teak, ebony, sandal-wood, rosewood, *dhaurā* (*Anogeissus latifolia*), *bilgu* (*Chloroxylon Swietenia*), tamarind, mango, *nīm*, and *kuchla* (*Nux vomica*).

Fauna. The hills abound in wild animals, such as tigers, leopards, bears, hyenas, wolves, wild dogs, *nīlgai*, and spotted deer. Wild duck, partridges, jungle-fowl, and peafowl are to be found everywhere.

Climate, temperature, and rainfall. The climate is most unhealthy; but the *tāluk* of Edlābād is not so malarious as Rājūra and Sirpur, and the villages on the plain are healthier than those situated in the hilly portions of the sub-district. The temperature ranges from 60° in December to 105° in May. The annual rainfall for the twenty-one years ending 1901 averaged 41 inches. In September, 1891, the Pengangā rose in high flood, and devastated most of the villages situated on its banks. The flood continued for three days, and people had to take refuge in trees and on high grounds. A large number of cattle were drowned. In 1903 a slight shock of earthquake was felt.

History. Very little is known of the history of the sub-district prior to its becoming part of Hyderābād State. It is said that at one period the *tāluk* of Rājūra belonged to a Gond Rājā, and subsequently passed to the Bhonslas.

Archaeology. An old fort on a hill near Māhūr in the Edlābād *tāluk* contains a masonry palace, a mosque, and two large domed buildings. At the foot of a hill, west of Māhūr, is the Pāndo Lena, a cave consisting of two halls, one of which contains a temple. An old temple on the Māhūr hill, 180 feet square and 54 feet high, gives shelter to 400 *gosains* and their *mahant*. *Jāgīrs* have been granted for the expenses of this temple. The Mānikgarh fort is said to have been built by a Gond Rājā.

The number of towns and villages in the sub-district is 984.

[1] W. King, *Memoirs, Geological Survey of India*, vol. xviii, pt. iii.

The population at each Census was: (1881) 214,674, (1891) 231,754, and (1901) 272,815. It is divided into the three *tāluks* of Edlābād, Rājūra, and Sirpur, which are all very sparsely populated. ADILĀBĀD (Edlābād) is the only town. More than 76 per cent. of the population are Hindus, 11 per cent. Animists (Gonds), and only 5 per cent. Musalmāns. About 44 per cent. of the people speak Telugu and 28 per cent. Marāthī. The following table shows the distribution of population in 1901:— Population.

Tāluk.	Area in square miles.	Number of Towns.	Number of Villages.	Population.	Population per square mile.	Percentage of variation in population between 1891 and 1901.	Number of persons able to read and write.
Edlābād	2,168	1	390	104,891	48	+ 13·1	Not available.
Rājūra	545	...	99	20,649	38	– 3·5	
Sirpur	2,129	...	386	120,500	56	+ 27·1	
Jāgīrs, &c.	187	...	108	26,775	143	+ 12·9	
Sub-district total	5,029	1	983	272,815	54	+ 17·7	2,323

In 1905 the sub-district was constituted an independent District, under the name of ADILĀBĀD. It gained two *tāluks*, Nirmal and Narsāpur, from Nizāmābad (Indūr) District, and two, Chinnūr and Lakhsetipet, from Karīmnagar (Elgandal). The northern portions of Nīrmal and Narsāpur, with part of Edlābād, have been formed into a new *tāluk*, Kinwat, the remaining portion of Narsāpur being merged in Nirmal. A new *tāluk*, Jangaon, has been formed midway between Sirpur and Lakhsetipet, consisting of villages from these two.

The Kāpus or Kunbīs are the most numerous agricultural caste, numbering 46,400, or 17 per cent. of the total population. Other agricultural castes are the Munnūrs (5,300), Kolis (4,200), and Banjārās (3,700). The labouring castes are the Dhangars or shepherds (15,300), Mahārs or village menials (8,000), Māngs or leather-workers (8,000), Andhs or carriers (7,900), and Panchāls or smiths (7,500). The last two are strongly represented in this District. Of the trading castes, there are 4,691 Komatis, 2,177 Vānīs, and 1,213 Mārwāris. Brāhmans number only 3,300. The population directly engaged in agriculture is 156,200, or 57 per cent. of the total. There were only 3 native Christians in 1901. Castes and occupations.

The sub-district is situated partly in the trap and partly in the granitic region, the chief soils being *regar* or black cotton, and *kharab* or sandy. *Regar* predominates in the Rājūra *tāluk*, General agricultural conditions.

and sandy and reddish soils in Sirpur, the Edlābād *tāluk* being midway between. Hence rice and *kharīf* crops are grown in Sirpur, the former being irrigated from tanks and wells, while in Rājūra *rabi* crops predominate, and in the Edlābād *tāluk* *kharīf* and *rabi* are almost equally balanced. The soil at the foot of the hills and on the borders of the rivers is very fertile, producing wheat, cotton, and gram.

Chief agricultural statistics and principal crops. The tenure of lands is mainly *ryotwāri*. The *khālsa* lands covered 4,842 square miles in 1901, of which 552 were cultivated, 1,633 were cultivable waste and fallows, 2,213 were forests, and 444 were not available for cultivation. The staple food-crop is *jowār*, grown on about half of the net area cropped. Rice and wheat occupied 4 and 3 square miles; and oilseeds, fibres, and cotton were grown on 54, 29, and 25 square miles respectively.

Improvements in agricultural practice. The sub-district has not been surveyed, and is very thinly populated, containing extensive tracts of protected and unprotected forests and scrub jungle, and cultivation is in a very backward condition. No steps have been taken to improve agricultural methods, but the cultivated area has increased during the past twenty years by about 8 per cent.

Cattle, &c. The cattle bred locally are strong, and the buffaloes of the Māhūr *pargana* in the Edlābād *tāluk* are noted as first-class milkers. There is also a small-sized breed of bullocks, which are very fast trotters. Bullocks of superior quality fetch Rs. 200 a pair, and the ordinary cattle sell at from Rs. 75 to Rs. 100 a pair. Ponies, sheep, and goats are of the common kind.

Irrigation. The irrigated area amounts to only 6½ square miles, which is supplied by 223 tanks, large and small, 99 wells, and 17 channels, all in good repair. The largest area under 'wet' cultivation is in the Sirpur *tāluk*. Quite recently a dam and three large tanks have been constructed in the Edlābād *tāluk*, at a total cost of nearly Rs. 50,000, securing a revenue of Rs. 7,500.

Forests. The sub-district has a very large extent of forests. The protected area covers 2,213 square miles, and the unprotected 2,000 square miles. It is proposed to utilize part of the cultivable waste for planting forests. The principal timber trees are teak, *tunki* or ebony (*Diospyros melanoxylon*), *bilgu* (*Chloroxylon Swietenia*), *jittigi* (*Dalbergia latifolia*) *bījāsāl* (*Pterocarpus Marsupium*), *dhaurā* (*Anogeissus latifolia*), and rosewood. The revenue from the sale of timber in 1901 was Rs. 25,200.

Talc, limestone, and laminated limestone of a quality superior to the Shāhābād stone, and *chalpā*, a red mineral, are found in the Edlābād *tāluk*. On the Rājulgutta hill in the Sirpur *tāluk* soapstone and iron occur. Coal is found near Sāsti and Poona villages in the Rājūra *tāluk*, and experimental excavations were made in 1874–5; but satisfactory results were not obtained, and the work was abandoned. There are three coal-mines near Sāsti village. Sulphur also exists, but is not worked. **Minerals.**

There are no important hand industries. The weavers make coarse cotton cloth, such as *dhotīs* and *sārīs*, for local use. The Rangāris or dyers print cloth for screens and quilts. Ordinary agricultural implements are made by blacksmiths. Leathern water-bottles (*chhāgals*) are made in Sirpur. **Arts and manufactures.**

The chief exports are cotton, linseed, gingelly, and some grain and cattle. The main imports consist of rice, salt, kerosene oil, opium, cloth, spices, gold and silver, brass and copper. Komatis, Mārwāris, and Kachchis are the principal traders. **Commerce.**

No railway or metalled road has been made in the sub-district. The old Nāgpur road between Mannūr and Sāngri, 38 miles long, is unmetalled. From Ẹdlābād to Rājūra and Sirpur there is only a cart track. **Roads.**

No information is available regarding famines in this area. During 1900, when famine was raging in the Aurangābād Division, the ryots here were well off; but the influx of people from the adjoining Hyderābād and British famine-stricken Districts caused some distress, and a poorhouse was opened at Edlābād for 800 destitute persons. It cost the State only Rs. 2,982. **Famine.**

The sub-district was divided into two subdivisions—one, consisting of the *tāluk* of Edlābād, under the Amaldār, corresponding to a First Tālukdār, while the second comprised the *tāluks* of Sirpur and Rājūra, under a Third Tālukdār. There is a *tahsīldār* in each of the *tāluks*. **District subdivisions and staff.**

The Amaldār was the chief magistrate as well as Civil Judge of the sub-district. The Third Tālukdār and three *tahsīldārs* exercise magisterial powers of the second and third class. These officers also preside over the subdivisional and *tahsīl* civil courts. The Amaldār heard appeals from all the courts subordinate to him. There is little serious crime. **Civil and criminal justice.**

Prior to the formation of Districts in 1866, the revenue of the *tāluks* of Edlābād and Sirpur was farmed out, but in 1866 these *tāluks* were included in Indūr District. Rājūra was a *jāgīr tāluk* granted for the payment of troops. In 1867 the **Land revenue.**

first two *tāluks* were transferred to Elgandal District, but were made over to Indūr in 1869. In 1872 the *jāgīr tāluk* of Rājūra was resumed, and with the other two *tāluks* was formed into an Amaldāri or sub-district. The sub-district has not been surveyed. The average assessment on 'dry' land is Rs. 6 per acre (maximum Rs. 8-1, minimum R. 0-2), and on 'wet' land Rs. 15 (maximum Rs. 25, minimum Rs. 6).

The land revenue and the total revenue for a series of years are shown below, in thousands of rupees:—

	1881.	1891.	1901.	1903.
Land revenue . .	2,11	2,33	2,62	2,62
Total revenue . .	3,03	3,04	4,66	3,53

Owing to the changes in area made in 1905, the revenue demand of Adilābād District is now about 6·5 lakhs.

There is no local board in the sub-district. The income from the road cess and ferries is spent on works of public utility. A small conservancy establishment is maintained at the head-quarters of the sub-district and of the other two *tāluks*. The total income is Rs. 3,663, of which Rs. 2,482 is obtained from road cess and Rs. 1,181 from ferries.

Police and jails.

The Amaldār is the head of the police, with the Superintendent (*Mohtamim*) as his executive deputy. Under the latter are 4 inspectors, 43 subordinate officers, 155 constables, and 25 Sikh mounted police. These are distributed at 18 police stations. There is a jail at Edlābād, where prisoners are kept whose term does not exceed six months, those with longer terms being sent to the Central jail at Nizāmābād. The jail has accommodation for 50 prisoners.

Education.

The sub-district takes a very inferior place as regards the literacy of its population, of whom less than one per cent. (1·6 males and 0·17 females) could read and write in 1901. The total number of pupils under instruction in the sub-district in 1891, 1901, and 1903 was 360, 342, and 394 respectively. In 1903 there were four primary schools. The whole of the cost, amounting to Rs. 2,290 per annum, is borne by the Educational department. In 1901 fees brought in Rs. 218.

Medical.

There are two dispensaries, at which the number of cases treated in 1901 was 5,785, and the number of operations performed was 167. The expenditure was Rs. 6,616. The number of persons vaccinated in the same year was 397, or 1·45 per 1,000 of population.

Adilābād Tāluk (or Edlābād).—*Tāluk* in Adilābād District, Hyderābād State, with an area of 2,220 square miles. The population in 1901, including *jāgīrs*, was 112,314, compared with 99,332 in 1891. The *tāluk* contains one town, ADILĀBĀD (population, 6,303), the head-quarters of the District and *tāluk*; and 420 villages, of which 30 are *jāgīr*. The land revenue in 1901 was 1·4 lakhs. In 1905 part of the *tāluk* was transferred to the new *tāluk* of Kinwat. Adilābād is very sparsely populated, containing extensive uncultivated wastes.

Rājūra.—*Tāluk* in Adilābād District, Hyderābād State, with an area of 595 square miles. The population in 1901, including *jāgīrs*, was 24,807, compared with 25,677 in 1891, the decrease being due to emigration to more favoured parts of Sirpur and Adilābād. The *tāluk* contains 128 villages, of which 29 are *jāgīr*; and Rājūra (population, 2,213) is the head-quarters. The land revenue in 1901 was Rs. 38,200. Rājūra is very thinly populated, containing extensive areas of cultivable waste and forest.

Sirpur Tāluk.—*Tāluk* in Adilābād District, Hyderābād State, with an area of 2,214 square miles. The population in 1901, including *jāgīrs*, was 135,694, compared with 106,745 in 1891. The *tāluk* contains 435 villages, of which 49 are *jāgīr*; and Sirpur (population, 3,134) is the head-quarters. The land revenue in 1901 was Rs. 81,800. In 1905 part of this *tāluk* was transferred to form the new *tāluk* of Jangaon. It is very sparsely populated, and contains a large extent of cultivable waste and forests.

Jangaon.—*Tāluk* in Adilābād District, Hyderābād State, situated midway between the Sirpur and Lakhsetipet *tāluks*, and consisting of villages recently taken from those two *tāluks*. The head-quarters are at Jangaon (population, 2,052).

Chinnūr Tāluk.—*Tāluk* in Adilābād District, Hyderābād State, with an area of 790 square miles, including a large forest tract. It is separated from the Central Provinces District of Chānda on the east by the Prānhita river. The population in 1901, including *jāgīrs*, was 56,591, compared with 52,889 in 1891. The *tāluk* contains one town, CHINNŪR (population, 6,561), the head-quarters; and 110 villages, of which 11 are *jāgīr*. The land revenue in 1901 was Rs. 64,000. The Godāvari river forms its southern and the Prānhita its eastern boundary, the soil in the vicinity of these rivers being alluvial. Rice is largely raised with the help of tank-irrigation.

Lakhsetipet.—*Tāluk* in Adilābād District, Hyderābād

State, with an area of 499 square miles. The population in 1901, including *jāgīrs*, was 50,835, compared with 52,589 in 1891, the decrease being due to famine and cholera. The *tāluk* contains 123 villages, of which 9 are *jāgīr*; and Lakhsetipet (population, 1,438), on the left bank of the Godāvari, is the head-quarters. The land revenue in 1901 was Rs. 69,000. Extensive rice cultivation is carried on by irrigation from tanks and wells.

Nirmal Tāluk.—*Tāluk* in Adilābād District, Hyderābād State, with an area of 548 square miles. The population in 1901, including *jāgīrs*, was 45,551, compared with 54,455 in 1891, the decrease being due to the famine of 1900. The *tāluk* contains one town, NIRMAL (population, 7,751), the head-quarters; and 115 villages, of which 15 are *jāgīr*. The land revenue in 1901 was 1·2 lakhs. Rice is extensively grown by tank-irrigation. The Godāvari forms the southern boundary of the *tāluk*, which is hilly in the north. In 1905 the *tāluk* was altered by the transfer of some villages to Kinwat, and the addition of part of Narsāpur. The *paigāh tāluk* of Yelgadap, containing 48 villages, lies to the east, with a population of 13,375, and an area of about 119 square miles.

Kinwat.—*Tāluk* in Adilābād District, Hyderābād State, constituted in 1905 out of the northern villages of the former Narsāpur and Nirmal *tāluks*. The head-quarters are at Kinwat (population, 1,514).

Adilābād Town (or Edlābād).—Head-quarters of the District and *tāluk* of the same name in Hyderābād State, situated in 19° 4′ N. and 78° 33′ E. Population (1901), 6,303. Besides the offices of the First Tālukdār, the police Superintendent, the customs inspector, and the forest *dāroga*, a dispensary, a post office, and a school are situated here. Adilābād contains a Hindu temple, where an annual fair is held. It also has a busy grain market.

Chinnūr Town.—Head-quarters of the *taluk* of the same name in Adilābād District, Hyderābād State, situated in 18° 51′ N. and 79° 48′ E., 10 miles north of the Godāvari river. Population (1901), 6,561. Chinnūr contains the *tāluk* and police inspector's offices, a post office, and a dispensary. Strong and very durable cloth is woven from *tasar* silk.

Nirmal Town.—Fortified town and head-quarters of the *tāluk* of the same name in Adilābād District, Hyderābād State, situated in 19° 6′ N. and 78° 21′ E. Population (1901), 7,751. In 1752 the Rājā of Nirmal attacked the Nizām Salābat Jang, who was marching from Aurangābād to Golconda in company with Bussy. In the battle the Rājā was slain and his forces were dispersed. The offices of the *tahsīldār*, police inspector, Assistant Conservator of Forests, and the Public Works supervisor are located here, besides a dispensary, a sub-post office, and a school. The town is prettily situated in country broken up by granite boulder hills, most of which in the neighbourhood of the town are crowned with forts. The largest of these stands in the centre of the town and includes the ruins of the old palace. The main fortifications were built by French officers in the Nizām's service, and are still in good preservation, and contain a number of guns. Three towers appear to have been made for boring ordnance.

AURANGĀBĀD DIVISION

Aurangābād Division.—North-Western Division of the State of Hyderābād, lying between 18° 28′ and 20° 40′ N. and 74° 40′ and 78° 6′ E. The head-quarters of the *Sūbahdār* (Commissioner) are at Aurangābād city. The total population of the Division increased from 2,610,247 in 1881 to 2,909,561 in 1891, but decreased to 2,363,114 in 1901, owing to the drought and famine in the two preceding years. The total area is 19,071 square miles; and the density is 124 persons per square mile, compared with 135 for the whole State, this Division being the third largest in area and the fourth in population. In 1901 Hindus formed 89 per cent. of the population, and Musalmāns 10 per cent., while Christians numbered 6,846 (of whom 2,613 were natives), Jains 12,477, Pārsīs 256, Sikhs 2,563, and Animists 9,380.

The number of towns in the Division is 20, or about one-fourth of the total number in Hyderābad State, and there are 5,490 villages. The largest towns are AURANGĀBĀD CITY (population, 36,837 with cantonment) and JĀLNA (20,270 with cantonment). The chief places of commercial importance are Aurangābād, Jālna, KĀDIRĀBĀD, NĀNDER, BHĪR, AMBA, and PARLI. Aurangābād is notable as having been the head-quarters of Aurangzeb when he was viceroy of the Deccan. His tomb is at KHULDĀBĀD (Rauza), whither his body was conveyed after his death at Ahmadnagar in 1707. Khuldābād also contains the tombs of Malik Ambar, the famous minister of the Nizām Shāhi kings of Ahmadnagar, and of Abul Hasan (Tāna Shāh), the last of the Kutb Shāhi dynasty, who was made prisoner by Aurangzeb in 1687.

The territorial changes made in 1905 materially affected two Districts in this Division, Parbhani and Nānder. The table on the next page shows the revised area, population, and land revenue of the four Districts now comprising the Division.

Boundaries, configuration, and hill and river systems.

Aurangābād District.—District in the extreme north-west of the Hyderābād State, lying between 19° 18′ and 20° 40′ N. and 74° 40′ and 76° 40′ E., with an area of 6,172 square miles. It is bounded on the north, west, and south by the Khāndesh, Nāsik, and Ahmadnagar Districts of Bombay, and by the

Bhīr District of Hyderābād; and on the east by the Buldāna District of Berār and the Parbhani District of Hyderābād.

Aurangābād may be divided into the Bālāghāt or 'uplands' to the north, and the Pāyānghāt or 'lowlands' to the south, the latter terminating in the valley of the Godāvari. The northern hills are a continuation of the Bālāghāt of Berār, and are named Sātāra, Ajanta, Kannad, &c., after villages in their proximity. The Mahādeo range, a continuation of the Sātāras, is 2,772 feet above the sea. All the hills in the District have a terrace-like appearance with flattened summits. One range, about 2,400 feet high, extends from Khānāpur to Jālna, passing through Aurangābād and Daulatābād, being 3,022 feet high near the latter. The Sarpanāth hill in the Baiamahāl range is 3,517 feet above the sea. The Gaotālā hills, also known as the Ajanta and Sātmālā, form the northern limits of the plateau, running east and west for 70 miles.

District.	Area in square miles.	Population, 1901.	Land revenue and cesses, 1901, in thousands of rupees.
Aurangābād	6,172	721,407	24,16
Parbhani	5,433	696,765	23,42
Nānder	3,612	550,148	15,84
Bhīr	4,460	492,258	15,37
Total	19,677	2,460,578	78,79

The most important river is the Godāvari, which forms the southern boundary for about 127 miles, separating the District from Ahmadnagar and Bhīr. Its principal tributaries are the Sina rising in the Kannad hills, the Dhenda rising near Daulatābād, and the Dudna flowing from the hills east of Aurangābād. The general slope of the country is towards the south and south-east.

The District is situated within the Deccan trap area. In the valley of the Godāvari and some of its tributaries the trap is overlaid by gravels and clay beds of upper pliocene or pleistocene age, containing fossil bones of extinct mammalia. The famous caves of AJANTA and ELLORA have been carved out of the basalt beds of the Deccan trap. Geology.

Jungles of the larger vegetation clothe the slopes of the hills surrounding the Bālāghāt and the ravines of streams issuing from the highlands. The gorges of the Ajanta and Goatālā *ghāts* are well wooded. Botany.

The animals found in the District include antelope, wild hog, bears, wild dogs, wolves, and occasionally tigers and leopards. Fauna.

Climate and temperature. The climate is generally healthy, but during the rains and part of the cold season it is malarious. The Bālāghāt is dry and healthy, its mean temperature for the whole year being 80°. The pleasantest spot in the District is Rauza or Khuldābād, on the hills south-east of the caves of Ellora, where the temperature in the height of the hot season does not exceed 82°.

Rainfall. The rainfall during the twenty-one years ending 1901 averaged 25 inches. The District suffered severely from scanty rainfall (12 inches) and famine during 1899–1900.

History. The District is of great importance in the early history of the Deccan. Long before the Christian era PAITHAN was probably an important place. From Ptolemy's account of India it appears that Paithan was the capital of Pulumāyi II, the Andhra king (A.D. 138–170), whose rule extended across the peninsula. With the decay of the Andhra power in the third century a period commences of which nothing is known, but the country must have fallen under the sway of the Chālukyas three hundred years later, and was ruled by them for a long period. In the seventh century Hiuen Tsiang visited the caves of Ajanta, Pulikesin II being king at the time. About 760 the Chālukyas were conquered by the Rāshtrakūtas, one of whose rulers, Krishna I, constructed the wonderful rock-cut temple of Kailās at Ellora. In 973 the Rāshtrakūtas were overthrown and Chālukya power was restored, but not to its former glories. Among the feudatories of the Chālukyas were the Yādavas, or perhaps more correctly the Seunas. A long list of chiefs has been collected, commencing from the early part of the ninth century; but the first independent ruler was Bhillama I, who established himself about 1187 in the country between Daulatābād and Nāsik, with his capital at the former place, then known as Deogiri. He died fighting the Hoysala ruler of Mysore in 1191; but his grandson Singhana extended the kingdom from Khāndesh on the north to Mysore on the south, so that it practically included the whole of the Western Chālukyan dominions. Singhana also invaded Gujarāt, and claims to have conquered practically the whole of India. In 1294, however, Alā-ud-dīn invaded the Deccan and defeated Rāmchandra, the last of the independent Yādavas, close to his capital, securing an enormous booty and the promise of tribute. Owing to default in the payment of the latter, Malik Kāfūr was dispatched to invade the Deccan again in 1307, and Rāmchandra yielded without a struggle. The default of his son and successor led to further expeditions, and in 1318 Harpāl, the last ruler, was flayed alive; and the Yādava power was finally extinguished. From 1347 the District formed part of the Bahmani kingdom, and in 1499 it was included in Ahmadnagar. In 1600 the Mughals under prince Dāniyāl captured Ahmadnagar after the murder of Chānd Bībī. Malik Ambar, the Ahmadnagar minister, fought several battles with the Mughals, and in 1610 founded Kharki, the present Aurangābād, which he made his capital. After his death in 1626, Ahmadnagar and Aurangābād were annexed to the Mughal empire, but the District was separated from it on the foundation of the Hyderābād State in the beginning of the eighteenth century.

Archaeology.

The most important cave-temples in India are found in the neigbourhood of ELLORA, AURANGĀBĀD, and AJANTA, belonging to the Buddhist, Jain, and Brāhmanical styles of architecture. Those at Ajanta number 29 and contain exquisite paintings, while 11 miles west of Ajanta are the two Ghatotkach caves. North of the city of Aurangābād are twelve Buddhist caves. The Ellora series contain some of the largest and most elaborately carved caves, dating from the second century B.C. to the eighth century A.D. The great fort at DAULATĀBĀD is a remarkable building. Aurangābād, Daulatābād, and JĀLNA contain numerous Muhammadan buildings, but none of great importance. The village of KHULDĀBĀD is marked by the tombs of several historical persons, including the emperor Aurangzeb and Asaf Jāh, the founder of the Hyderābād State.

Population.

The number of towns and villages is 1,831. The population at each Census in the last twenty years was as follows:—(1881) 730,380, (1891) 828,975, and (1901) 726,407. The great famine of 1899–1900 is responsible for the decrease of population in the last decade. The District is divided into the ten *tāluks* of AURANGĀBĀD, AMBARH, JĀLNA, KANNAD, BHOKARDAN, PAITHAN, GANGĀPUR, VAIJĀPUR, SILLOD, and KHULDĀBĀD, the last two being *Sarf-i-khās* or 'crown' *tāluks*. The towns are AURANGĀBĀD, JĀLNA, KĀDIRĀBĀD, PAITHAN, and VAIJĀPUR. Nearly 85 per cent. of the population are Hindus and more than 12 per cent. Musalmāns. About 79 per cent. of the people speak Marāthī. The table on the next page shows the distribution of population in 1901.

In 1905 a few small transfers were made, by which the area and population of individual *tāluks* have been changed.

Castes and occupations.

The agricultural castes include the Marāthā Kunbīs, 257,000, and also Sindes, 15,900; Banjārās, 8,900; Kolīs, 7,000; and Marāthā Holkars, 5,800. The Mālis or gardeners number 18,600. The Mahārs (village menials) and Māngs (leather-workers) number 66,800 and 21,500; Dhangars or shepherds,

31,000; Brāhmans, 28,000. Vānīs, 4,600, and Mārwāris, 7,800, are the principal trading castes. About 46 per cent. of the population depend on agriculture.

Tāluk.	Area in square miles.	Number of Towns.	Number of Villages.	Population.	Population per square mile.	Percentage of variation in population between 1891 and 1901.	Number of persons able to read and write.
Aurangābād	563	1	204	99,007	175	− 8.0	
Sillod	216	...	46	26,966	125	−16.0	Not available.
Bhokardan	425	...	142	37,311	88	−30.0	
Jalna	618	2	167	86,750	140	−13.0	
Ambarh	866	...	218	97,271	112	−13.0	
Paithan	380	1	130	52,552	138	− 0.1	
Gangāpur	453	...	175	46,959	103	−14.0	
Vaijāpur	519	1	113	43,757	84	+ 2.0	
Kannad	541	...	168	59,190	109	+ 7.2	
Khuldābād	97	...	29	10,115	104	−11.3	
Jāgīrs, &c.	1,494	1	433	161,529	108	+ 9.6	
District total	6,172	6	1,825	721,407	116	+12.9	23,171

Christians. The District contained 2,673 Christians in 1901, of whom 2,512 were natives.

General agricultural conditions. The soils are of three kinds: the *regar* or black cotton soil, the *masab* or reddish, and the *milwa*, a mixture of the other two. *Regar* is derived from trap, and the sandy or reddish soil from granitic rock. The *regar* forms more than 55 per cent. of the total cultivable area, and is very fertile, as also is the soil found at the foot of the hills.

Chief agricultural statistics and principal crops. The area of *khālsa* land in 1901 amounted to 4,678 square miles, of which 3,727 were cultivated, 82 were cultivable waste and fallows, 392 forests, and 477 were not available for cultivation. The cultivated area in 1903 was 3,732 square miles. *Jowār*, *bājra*, and wheat are the chief food-crops, covering an area of 991, 535, and 258 square miles respectively. Pulses and rice are next in importance, with areas of 497 and 19 square miles. Cotton and oilseeds are largely grown, occupying 384 and 409 square miles respectively. Sugar-cane is grown on about 9 square miles.

Cattle, &c. The cattle are of the ordinary Deccani breed, being small, hardy, and active, and well adapted for agricultural operations. The valley of the Godāvari was once famous for its breed of horses, noted for their hardiness and powers of endurance, and said to be the offspring of Arab sires; but the stock is now inferior. The State maintains Arab stallions at Aurangābād and Ambarh for improving the breed. The sheep are of the usual black breed. There are two varieties of goats: the Gujarāt short-legged breed, with erect ears, which are good milkers; and the shaggy long-legged breed, with drooping ears.

Irrigation.

The irrigated area in 1901 was 134 square miles, entirely supplied from wells, of which 19,778 are in working order. There are a few small tanks, but they are used only for drinking purposes.

Forests.

The forest area is small, consisting of only 123 square miles of 'reserved,' and 69 and 200 square miles of protected and unprotected forests. Teak (*Tectona grandis*) is the predominant species among the timber trees, while the *sādora* (*Terminalia tomentosa*), *dhāmora* (*Anogeissus latifolia*), and *mālanjar* (*Hardwickia binata*) are fairly plentiful. A considerable portion of the forests contains only brushwood and small trees used for fuel, which is given free of charge to the cultivators.

Minerals.

Very few minerals of economic value are met with; those found are jaspers, agate, carnelian, chalcedony, heliotrope, and rock crystals, both white and amethystine. *Kankar* or nodular limestone, basalt, and granite occur all over the country, and are utilized for building purposes.

Arts and manufactures.

AURANGĀBĀD CITY is noted for its silver ware and embroidery, as well as for silver and gold lace and cloth (*kamkhwāb*), and other silk cloths known as *himrū* and *mashrū*, which are largely produced. Valuable silk and cotton *sārīs* and other silk fabrics are made at PAITHAN and JĀLNA. Paper of several descriptions is manufactured at Kāghazīpura, near Daulatābād. Saltpetre is produced in small quantities from saline earth gathered near villages and old walls. In 1889 a cotton-spinning and weaving mill was erected in Aurangābād city, which employs 700 hands. Since the opening of the Hyderābād-Godāvari Valley Railway in 1900 several ginning factories have been started. In the Jālna *tāluk* alone there are 9 cotton-ginning factories and 5 cotton-presses, besides two ginning factories at Aurangābād and Kannad, and one oil-press at Aurangābād. The total number of hands employed in the cotton-presses and ginning factories in 1901 was 1,016.

Commerce.

The chief exports consist of cotton, food-grains, oilseeds, dyes, live-stock, silk stuff, cloth, hides, tobacco, jaggery (raw sugar), *ghī*, paper, silver ware, copper and brass vessels; the principal imports are food-grains, chiefly rice, salt, opium, cloth, English piece-goods, yarn, sugar, kerosene oil, fruit, raw silk, spices, copper and brass vessels, iron, gold and silver, jewels, paper, hardware, and sulphur. The principal trade centres are Aurangābād city, Jālna (*Pett* Kādirābād) and Paithan. The Vānīs, Bohrās, Bhātias, and Memons from Bombay are the chief traders. Internal trade is carried on by means of weekly markets, held at eighty places in different parts of the District.

Railways. The Hyderābād-Godāvari Valley Railway traverses Aurangābād from west to east, for 110 miles, with eleven railway stations within the District.

Roads. The total length of main roads is 392 miles, of which 154 are metalled. The District is also well supplied with numerous fair-weather roads leading to the head-quarters of *tāluks*, their length being 454 miles, making a total of 846 miles of metalled and fair-weather roads and cart tracks. There are several *ghāts* or mountain passes, the chief being those of Ajanta, Upli near Daulatābād, and Ellora.

Famine. From the second quarter of the nineteenth century up to 1872, there were six years of distress and famine in the District, attended by much loss of cattle. In 1876 the rains failed almost completely, the fall in the previous year also having been deficient. In 1878 the *kharīf* crop was damaged by excessive rain, and the *rabi* crops suffered from rats. In 1897 the number of persons relieved was 267,318, costing Rs. 68,000. The ryots had not recovered from the effects of the distress of 1897 when the great famine of 1899–1900 took place. Owing to the scanty rainfall of 1899 and 1900 (12 and 19 inches), both the *kharīf* and *rabi* crops of these two years failed, and severe distress was felt in all parts. While the famine was raging, cholera supervened and carried off thousands. The District lost 76,000 agricultural and 74,000 non-agricultural cattle, or 38 and 37 per cent. respectively of the total. The total number of units relieved was 19 millions, and the highest attendance in famine camps in one day was about 58,000, the total cost to the State amounting to 17·4 lakhs.

District subdivisions and staff. There are three subdivisions, the first consisting of the *tāluks* of Jālna, Sillod, Ambarh, and Bhokardan; the second, of Vaijāpur, Gangāpur, Paithan, and Kannad; and the third, of Aurangābād and Khuldābād. The first two subdivisions are each under a Second Tālukdār and the third under a Third Tālukdār, each of the ten *tāluks* being under a *tahsīldār*.

Civil and criminal justice. The First Tālukdār is the chief magistrate, and the *Nāzim-i-Dīwāni* or District Civil Judge is also a joint-magistrate, who exercises magisterial powers in the absence of the First Tālukdār from head-quarters. There are three Munsifs' courts—at

Aurangābād, Jālna, and Gangāpur. The Second and Third Tālukdārs exercise second-class, and the *tahsīldārs* third-class criminal powers. The *Nāzim-i-Sūbah*, or the Judge of the Division, one of the puisne judges of the High Court, holds his court at Aurangābād. Serious crime is not heavy in ordinary years, but has shown a tendency to increase in seasons of scarcity. The Bhīls gave much trouble during and immediately after the famine of 1900.

Land revenue.

Authentic records of the revenue history of the district exist from the time of Malik Ambar early in the seventeenth century, who had the whole country surveyed, and fixed the revenue according to the productiveness of the soil in each tract. Prior to 1866, the villages were farmed out, the revenue contractors being allowed 10 per cent. for collection; but on the introduction of administration by Districts in 1866, Tālukdārs and *tahsīldārs* were regularly appointed, and the *ryotwāri* system with cash payments was introduced. The revenue survey was started in 1876 and completed in 1882, the assessments being fixed for thirty years. The survey showed that the area of holdings was larger by 18 per cent. than that shown in the accounts. The average assessment on 'dry' land is Rs. 1-14 (maximum, Rs. 2-6; minimum, R. 1), and on 'wet' land Rs. 5 (maximum, Rs. 6; minimum, Rs. 4).

The land revenue and the total revenue for a series of years are shown below, in thousands of rupees:—

	1881.	1891.	1901.	1903.
Land revenue . . .	16,70	20,91	22,61	22,63
Total revenue . . .	18,17	23,15	38,70	25,25

Local and municipal government.

Both Aurangābād city and the adjoining cantonment are administered as municipalities. The District board, in addition to its own work, manages the city municipality, and also supervises the working of the *tāluk* boards, and is presided over by the First Tālukdār. The cantonment municipality is managed by the cantonment authorities. For each of the *tāluks*, except Aurangābād, there is a *tāluk* board and a small municipal establishment. The principal source of income is the one anna cess on the land revenue, which yielded 1·5 lakhs in 1901, while the total expenditure was 1·8 lakhs, including local works as well as municipal expenditure.

Police and jails.

The First Tālukdār is the head of the District police, with a Superintendent (*Mohtamim*) as his executive deputy. Under the latter are 12 inspectors, a frontier assistant, 79 subordinate officers, 738 constables, and 34 mounted police. These are distributed among 37 police stations and 42 outposts (*thānas* and *chaukīs*), and also guard the District and *tāluk* treasuries. Rural police are appointed at the rate of one man to every fifty houses in the villages, and are under the police *pātel* and subordinate to the *jemadār* of the nearest police station.

There is a Central jail at Aurangābād, with accommodation for 2,000 prisoners. It receives convicts sentenced to more than six months' imprisonment from Bhīr, Parbhani, and Nānder. Carpets, rugs, cotton-tweeds and other kinds of cloth, as well as boots, harness, and belts, are made in the jail.

Education. Aurangābād District takes a comparatively high position as regards the literacy of its population, of whom 3·2 per cent. (6 males and 0·3 females) could read and write in 1901. The total number of pupils under instruction in 1881, 1891, 1901, and 1903 was 1,087, 3,926, 5,648, and 5,054 respectively, including 214 girls in the last year. In 1903 there were 92 primary and 4 middle schools, one high and one industrial or art school, and one college. Of these institutions 11 were private and the remainder State. The total expenditure on education in 1901 was Rs. 44,100, of which Rs. 27,300 was contributed by the State and Rs. 16,800 by Local boards. The fee receipts amounted to Rs. 3,100.

Medical. In 1901 the District contained six dispensaries, including one *yunāni* institution, having accommodation for 37 in-patients. The number of out-patients treated was 45,827, and of in-patients 242. The operations performed numbered 1,503. The expenditure amounted to Rs. 22,400, of which Rs. 3,800 was contributed from Local funds.

The number of persons vaccinated in 1901 was only 2,873, or about 4 per 1,000 of the population.

[J. Fardunjī, *Notes on the Aurangābād Agriculturist.*]

Aurangābād Taluk.—Central *tāluk* of Aurangābād District, Hyderābād State, with an area of 786 square miles. The population in 1901, including *jāgīrs*, was 121,121, compared with 131,582 in 1891, the decrease being due to the famines of 1897 and 1899–1900. The *tāluk* contains one town, AURANGĀBĀD CITY (population, 36,837), the head-quarters of the Division, District, and *tāluk*; and 270 villages, of which 66 are *jāgīr*. The land revenue in 1901 was 2·6 lakhs. The *tāluk* is hilly in the north, and is composed of black cotton soil. The *paigāh tāluk* of Lādsāngvi, with 7 villages and a population of 2,230, lies to the north-east of this *tāluk*, and has an area of about 19 square miles.

Sillod.—'Crown' *tāluk* in the north of Aurangābād District, Hyderābād State, with an area of 249 square miles. The population in 1901, including *jāgīrs*, was 29,916, compared with 35,521 in 1891, the decrease being due to the famines of 1897 and 1899–1900. The *tāluk* contains 54 villages, of which 8 are *jāgīr*; and Seona (population, 3,412) is the head-quarters. The land revenue in 1901 was 1·1 lakhs. The country is hilly in the north, and is composed of black cotton soil.

Bhokardan.—North-eastern *tāluk* of Aurangābād District, Hyderābād State, with an area of 938 square miles. The population in 1901, including *jāgīrs*, was 81,276, compared with 115,657 in 1891, the decrease being due to the famines of 1897 and 1899–1900. The *tāluk* contains 307 villages, of which 165 are *jāgīr*; and Bhokardan (population, 2,082) is the head-quarters. The land revenue in 1901 was 1·7 lakhs. The country is composed of black cotton soil.

Jālna Tāluk.—Eastern *tāluk* of Aurangābād District, Hyderābād State, with an area of 801 square miles. The population in 1901, including *jāgīrs*, was 113,400, compared with 129,832 in 1891, the decrease being due to the famines of 1897 and 1899–1900. The *tāluk* contains two towns, JĀLNA (population, 20,270), the head-quarters, and KĀDIRĀBĀD (11,159), a large commercial centre; and 219 villages, of which 52 are *jāgīr*. The land revenue in 1901 was 2·5 lakhs. The country is composed of black cotton soil, and is hilly towards the north and east.

Ambarh.—South-eastern *tāluk* of Aurangābād District, Hyderābād State, with an area of 972 square miles. The population in 1901, including *jāgīrs*, was 116,188, compared with 132,801 in 1891, the decrease being due to the famines of 1897 and 1899–1900. It contains 242 villages, of which 24 are *jāgīr*; and Ambarh (population, 3,563) is the head-quarters. The land revenue in 1901 was 4·2 lakhs. The Godāvari river flows through the south of the *tāluk*, which is composed of *regar* or black cotton soil. In 1905 eight villages were transferred from Ambarh to Pāthri in Parbhani District, and six villages were transferred from Pāthri to this *tāluk* in exchange.

Paithan Tāluk.—Southern *tāluk* of Aurangābād District, Hyderābād State, with an area of 453 square miles. The population in 1901, including *jāgīrs*, was 57,021, compared with 57,133 in 1891, the decrease being due to the famines of 1897 and 1899–1900. The *tāluk* contains one town,

Paithan (population, 8,638), the head-quarters; and 142 villages, of which 12 are *jāgīr*. The land revenue in 1901 was 2·1 lakhs. The Godāvari river forms the southern boundary, and the *tāluk* is composed of black cotton soil.

Gangāpur.—South-western *tāluk* of Aurangābād District, Hyderābād State, with an area of 518 square miles. The population in 1901, including *jāgīrs*, was 51,413, compared with 59,638 in 1891, the decrease being due to the famines of 1897 and 1899–1900. The *tāluk* has 190 villages, of which 15 are *jāgīr*; and Gangāpur (population, 3,122) is the head-quarters. The land revenue in 1901 was 3·2 lakhs. *Regar* is the predominant soil.

Vaijāpur Tāluk.—Westernmost *tāluk* of Aurangābād District, Hyderābād State, with an area of 558 square miles. The population in 1901, including *jāgīrs*, was 45,429, compared with 44,561 in 1891. The *tāluk* contains one town, Vāijāpur (population, 5,451), the head-quarters; and 120 villages, of which 7 are *jāgīr*. The land revenue in 1901 was 2·8 lakhs. The Godāvari river enters the District at the village of Phultāmba.

Kannad.—North-western *tāluk* of Aurangābād District, Hyderābād State, with an area of 769 square miles. The population in 1901, including *jāgīrs*, was 88,901, compared with 82,887 in 1891. The *tāluk* contains 236 villages, of which 68 are *jāgīr*; and Kannad (population, 3,609) is the head-quarters. The land revenue in 1901 was 1·9 lakhs. From the Gaotāla hill, 7 miles north of Kannad, the Gaotāla *ghāt* descends into Khāndesh. The Contingent troops, sent in pursuit of the Bhīls in 1830, were encamped on this hill for six months.

Khuldābād Tāluk (or Rauza).—'Crown' *tāluk* in the north-west of Aurangābād District, Hyderābād State, with an area of 129 square miles. The population in 1901, including *jāgīrs*, was 14,512, compared with 16,353 in 1891, the decrease being due to the famines of 1897 and 1899–1900. The *tāluk* contains 38 villages, of which 9 are *jāgīr*; and Khuldābād (population, 2,845) is the head-quarters. The land revenue in 1901 was Rs. 43,300. The country is hilly towards the east and north.

Ajanta Village.—Village in the Bhokardan *tāluk* of Aurangābād District, Hyderābād State, and a *jāgīr* of the late Sir Sālār Jang's family, situated in 20° 32′ N. and 75° 46′ E. Population (1901), 2,274. The place, which is situated on the summit of the *ghāt* or pass to which it gives its name, has stone fortifications constructed by the first Nizām in 1727. It is celebrated for the series of Buddhist caves in the Inhyādri Hills, 4 miles north-west, which first became known to the British in 1819. The defile in which the caves are situated is wooded, lonely, and rugged, the caves being excavated in a wall of almost perpendicular rock, about 250 feet high, sweeping round in a hollow semicircle with the Wāghara stream below and a wooded rocky promontory jutting out of its opposite bank. The caves extend about a third of a mile from east to west, in the concave scarp composed of amygdaloid trap, at an elevation of 35 to 110 feet above the bed of the torrent. The ravine, a little higher up, ends abruptly in a waterfall of seven leaps (*sāt kund*), from 70 to over 100 feet in height. From the difficulty of access, the Ajanta caves were but little visited until in 1843 Mr. Fergusson's paper on the rock-cut temples of India created a general interest in these remarkable works of art.

Twenty-four monasteries (*vihāras*) and five temples (*chaityas*) have been hewn out of the solid rock, many of them supported by lofty pillars, richly ornamented with sculpture and covered with highly finished paintings. The following brief description is condensed chiefly from notes by Dr. Burgess. The five *chaityas*, or cave-temples for public worship, are usually about twice as long as they are wide, the largest being 94½ feet by 41¼. The back or inner end of the *chaityas* is almost circular; the roofs are lofty and vaulted, some ribbed with wood, others with stone cut in imitations of wooden ribs. A colonnade hewn out of the solid rock runs round each, dividing the nave from the aisles. The columns in the most ancient caves are plain octagonal pillars without bases or capitals, with richly ornamented shafts. Within the circular end of the cave stands the *daghoba* (relic-holder), a solid mass of rock, either plain or richly sculptured, consisting of a cylindrical base supporting a cupola (*garbha*), which in turn is surmounted by a square capital or 'tee' (*toran*). The twenty-four *vihāras*, or Buddhist monasteries containing cells, are usually square in form, supported by rows of pillars, either running round them and separating the great central hall from the aisles, or disposed in four equidistant lines. In the larger caves, a veranda cut out of the rock, with cells at either end, shades the entrance; the great hall occupies the middle space, with a small chamber behind and a shrine containing a figure of Buddha enthroned. The walls on all the three sides are excavated into cells, the dwelling-places (*grihas*) of the Buddhist monks. The simplest form of the *vihāra* or monastery is a veranda hewn out of the face of the precipice, with cells opening from the back into the rock. Very few of the caves seem to have been completely finished; but nearly all of them appear to have been painted on the walls, ceilings, and pillars inside and out. Even the sculptures have all been richly coloured. Twenty-five inscriptions—seventeen painted ones in the interior, eight rock inscriptions engraved outside—commemorate the names of pious founders in Sanskrit and Prākrit.

One monastery has its whole façade richly carved; but, as a rule, such ornamentation is confined in the monasteries (*viharas*) to the doorways and windows. More lavish decoration was bestowed upon the temples (*chaityas*); the most ancient have sculptured façades, while in the more modern ones the walls, columns, entablatures, and *daghoba* are covered with carving. The sculptures show little knowledge of art, and consist chiefly of Buddhas, or Buddhist teachers, in every variety of posture, instructing their disciples.

'The paintings,' writes Dr. Burgess, 'have much higher pretensions, and have been considered superior to the style of Europe in the age when they were probably executed. The human figure is represented in every possible variety of position, displaying some slight knowledge of anatomy; and attempts at foreshortening have been made with surprising success. The hands are generally well and gracefully drawn, and rude efforts at perspective are to be met with. Besides paintings of Buddha and his disciples and devotees, there are representations of streets, processions, battles, interiors of houses with the inmates pursuing their daily occupations, domestic scenes of love and marriage and death, groups of women performing religious austerities; there are hunts, men on horseback spearing the wild buffalo; animals, from the huge elephant to the diminutive quail; exhibitions of cobras, ships, fish, &c. The small number of domestic utensils depicted is somewhat remarkable,—the common earthen waterpot and *lota*, a drinking cup, and one or two other dishes, a tray, an elegantly shaped sort of jug having an oval body and long thin neck with lip and handle, together with a stone and roller for grinding condiments, being all that are observable. The same lack of weapons of war, either offensive or defensive, is also to be noticed. Swords, straight and crooked, long and short, spears of various kinds, clubs, bows and arrows, a weapon resembling a bayonet reversed, a missile like a quoit with cross-bars in the centre, and shields of different form, exhaust the list. There is also a thing which bears a strong resemblance to a Greek helmet, and three horses are to be seen yoked abreast, but whether they were originally attached to a war-chariot cannot now be determined. The paintings have been in the most brilliant colours—the light and shade are very good; they must have been executed upon a thick layer of stucco. In many places, the colour has penetrated to a considerable depth.'

Of the date of these paintings it is difficult to form a very definite estimate, nor are they all of the same age. The scenes represented are generally from the legendary history of Buddha and the Jātakas, the visit of Asita to the infant Buddha, the temptation of Buddha by Māra and his forces, Buddhist miracles, the Jātaka of king Sībi, legends of the Nāgās, hunting scenes, battle-pieces, the carrying off of the relics of Ceylon, etc.

The cave-temples and monasteries of Ajanta furnish a continuous narrative of Buddhist art during 800 years, from shortly after the reign of Asoka to shortly before the extinction of the faith in India. The oldest of them are assigned to about 200 B.C.; the most modern cannot be placed before the year A.D. 600. For many centuries they enable us to study the progress of Buddhist art, and of Buddhistic conceptions, uninfluenced by Hinduism. The chief interest of the latest *chaitya*, about A.D. 600, is to show how nearly Buddhism had approximated to Brāhmanism, before the convulsions amid which it disappeared. The liberality of the Indian Government had enabled Major Gill to take up his residence in Ajanta, and to prepare a magnificent series of facsimiles from the frescoes. These unfortunately perished in the fire at the Crystal Palace in 1860, but reductions of two of the more important of them, and of eight detached fragments, exist in Mrs. Spier's *Life in Ancient India*. More recently the matchless art series of Ajanta has been made available to the Western world by Mr. Griffiths.

[John Griffiths, *Indian Antiquary*, vol. ii, p. 150; vol. iii, p. 25; J. Fergusson, *History of Indian Architecture* (ed. 1876); J. Burgess, *Bauddha Rock Temples of Ajanta* (1879), and *Cave-Temples of Western India* (1881); J. Griffiths, *The Paintings in the Buddhist Cave-Temples of Ajanta* (1896–7).

Antūr.—Ancient fort in the Kannad *tāluk* of Aurangābād District, Hyderābād State, situated in 20° 27′ N. and 75° 15′ E., on the summit of a spur of the hills extending into Khāndesh. It was built in the fifteenth century by a Marāthā chief, and fell to the Ahmadnagar kingdom, but was annexed by Aurangzeb, who denuded it of its artillery towards the close of the seventeenth century. Two miles south of the fort is a square pillar, bearing a Persian inscription stating that it was erected in 1588, during the reign of Murtaza Nizām Shāh of Ahmadnagar.

Assaye.—Village in the Bhokardan *tāluk* of Aurangābād District, Hyderābād State, situated in 20° 15′ N. and 75° 54′ E. Population (1901), 302. It is famous for the battle fought in 1803, when Sir Arthur Wellesley with only 4,500 men defeated the Marāthās, who numbered 50,000. The battle-field is best visited from Sillod, which is 11 miles north-west of the village.

Aurangābād City.—Head-quarters of the Division, District, and *tāluk* of the same name in Hyderābād State, situated in 19° 53′ N. and 75° 20′ E., on the Hyderābād-Godāvari Valley Railway, near the eastern bank of the Kaum river. In point of historical interest and size it is the second city in the State, and its population at the last three enumerations was as follows: (1881) 30,219, (1891) 33,887, and (1901) 36,837, including cantonments. In 1610 Malik Ambar, minister of the Nizām Shāhi kings of Ahmadnagar, founded the city near the village of Kharki, and called it Fatehnagar. The Mughals and the Nizām Shāhi troops under Malik Ambar were constantly at war during the early part of the seventeenth century. After the death of Malik Ambar in 1626, the power of the Ahmadnagar rulers declined, and in 1637 their territories were incorporated in the Deccan *Sūbah* of the Mughal empire. Aurangzeb was appointed viceroy of the Deccan in 1635, and again in 1653, and during his residence at Kharki changed its name to Aurangābād. It was from here that he directed his earlier campaigns against the Marāthās and the Bijāpur and Golconda kingdoms. In 1658 he dethroned and imprisoned his father, Shāh Jahān. A few years later he undertook the subjugation of the Muhammadan kingdoms of the Deccan, and commenced his wars with the Marāthās, in which he was almost continuously engaged until his death, at Ahmadnagar, in 1707. Bijāpur fell in 1686, and Golconda, the Kutb Shāhi capital, in 1687, these victories being followed by the annexation of the two kingdoms. During the confusion and internal dissension which followed the death of Aurangzeb, Asaf Jāh, the first Nizām, came to Aurangābād, and, having declared his independence, subsequently made Hyderābād his capital.

The city is bounded on the north and south by the Sichel and Sātāra ranges. During the reign of Aurangzeb its population is said to have been not less than 200,000, and the ruins still existing bear testimony to its former populousness. The modern city is situated to the east of Old Aurangābād, while the cantonment lies to the west, across the Kaum river. The garrison consists of two regiments of Native infantry, and one of Native cavalry, four squadrons strong, under the command of British officers.

In 1853 Aurangābād was the scene of a sharp conflict between the Hyderābād Contingent and a body of Arabs, who were defeated. In the eventful year 1857 some of the Contingent showed a spirit of disaffection, and an attack was meditated upon the cantonment. The authorities at Hyderābād had been apprised of this, and a force from Poona was ordered to march to Aurangābād. When the Poona force arrived under General Woodburn, the disaffected cavalry were summoned to a dismounted parade. On the names of the ringleaders being called out, a *jemadār* ordered his men to load their carbines. A scene of wild confusion ensued, and some of the troops profiting by it mounted their horses and fled, and, though pursued by the 14th Dragoons from Poona, they escaped. Two-thirds of the regiment remained loyal; a court martial was held and twenty-one of the condemned were shot, while three were blown away from guns.

At Aurangābād the *Sūbahdār* (Commissioner), the *Nizām-i-Sūbah* (Divisional Judge), the First Tālukdār, and other officers hold their courts. The public buildings include a large Central jail, a college, an industrial school, and several smaller schools. The city is an important centre of trade; and silk, gold and silver cloth, and lace of a superior quality are manufactured and largely exported. A spinning and weaving cotton-mill gives employment to 700 persons, besides an oil-press. The city has suffered severely from plague and from the famines of 1897 and 1900; and, but for the opening of the Hyderābād-Godāvari Valley Railway, the country around would have been depopulated. The increase of population in 1901 is due to the immigration of famine-stricken people from the neighbouring villages. A system of water-supply was introduced by Malik Ambar, and completed by Aurangzeb; and, though it has largely fallen into decay, it still yields sufficient water to supply the needs of the people. A new system of water-works was opened in 1892, to supply filtered water to the cantonment.

Many places of interest are situated in the city and its suburbs, among which may be mentioned the *makbara* or tomb of Aurangzeb's wife, the Jāma Masjid built by Malik Ambar, the ancient palace of the Nizām near Borapal, and the Kila Ark or citadel, which was Aurangzeb's palace. About 2 miles north of the city are the Aurangābād caves, 12 in number. These are of Buddhist origin, and are among the latest known, while they present especially interesting features.

[*Archaeological Survey Reports of Western India*, vol. iii.]

Daulatābād (or Deogiri).—Hill-fort in the District and *tāluk* of Aurangābād, Hyderābād State, situated in 19° 57′ N. and 75° 13′ E. Population (1901), 1,357. The place is celebrated as the capital of the Seunas, more commonly known by their assumed name of Yādavas, who rose from the position of feudatories of the Chālukyas to that of independent princes. Bhillama I, who threw off allegiance about 1187, is said by Hemādri to have founded Deogiri. His grandson, Singhana, acquired practically the whole of the Western Chālukyan kingdom. Ala-ud-dīn Khiljī captured the fort in 1294, and this event marks the first invasion of the Deccan by the Muhammadans. The fort was restored to the Rājā on his agreeing to pay tribute, but later expeditions were undertaken on account of default. Deogiri was occupied by Malik Kāfūr in 1307 and 1310; and in 1318 the last Rājā, Harpāl, was flayed alive. Deogiri then became an important base for operations in Southern India, and Muhammad bin Tughlak conceived the idea of making it his capital. In 1339 he undertook to transport the whole population of Delhi to this place, and changed its name to Daulatābād. From here he directed his campaigns against the Rājās of Warangal. Troubles having broken out in Northern India, the king left his new capital to suppress them. During his absence the Muhammadan governors of the newly acquired provinces revolted; and in the confusion which ensued Zafar Khān, the governor of Gulbarga, succeeded in capturing Daulatābād, which remained in the possession of the Bahmanis until 1526, when it was taken by the Nizām Shāhis, to be again wrested from them by the emperor Akbar. After the fall of Ahmadnagar the Nizām Shāhi capital was transferred to Kharki, the present Aurangābād, which had been founded by Malik Ambar, the Nizām Shāhi minister; and Daulatābād was retaken and remained in their possession until its capture in 1633 by Shāh Jahān's general. It remained part of the Mughal empire until after Aurangzeb's death, when it came into the possession of Asaf Jāh, the first Nizām of Hyderābād.

The fortress is built upon a conical rock, scarped from a height of 150 feet from the base. The hill upon which it stands rises almost perpendicularly from the plain to a height of about 600 feet. The outer wall is $2\frac{3}{4}$ miles in circumference, with three lines of fortifications between it and the base of the upper fort. The outer wall formerly enclosed the ancient city of Deogiri, but a village is now all that remains.

Besides the fortifications, the chief buildings are the Chānd Minār and Chīni Mahal. The Chānd Minār, which is 210 feet high and 70 feet in circumference at the base, was erected by Alā-ud-dīn Bahmani to commemorate his conquest of the fort. The basement is 15 feet high, containing twenty-four chambers, and the whole pillar was originally covered with glazed Persian tiles of much beauty. It is considered one of the most striking pieces of Muhammadan architecture in Southern India. To the south of this is a small mosque, with a Persian inscription giving the date of its erection as 849 Hijri (1445). The Chīni Mahal (or 'China palace'), which was once a building of great beauty, is 40 feet to the right of the eighth gate of the fort; it was here that Abul Hasan or Tāna Shāh, the last of the Kutb Shāhi kings, was imprisoned by Aurangzeb in 1687. The fort has altogether eight gates; and several pieces of ordnance are still to be seen on the bastions. Daulatābād is noted for its black and white grapes, but of late years the produce has deteriorated considerably for want of care and proper pruning.

Ellora (*Verūl*).—Village in the District and *tāluk* of Aurangābād, Hyderābād State, situated in 20° 21′ N. and 75° 10′ E., about 15 miles north-west of Aurangābād city. Population (1901), 1,095. Near the village is a handsome temple of red stone erected by Ahalyā Bai, the Rānī of Indore (1767–95), which is considered a good specimen of modern Hindu architecture (Burgess). Ellora is famous for its rock-temples and caves, which extend along the face of a hill for a mile and a quarter, and are divided into three distinct series—Buddhist, Brāhmanical, and Jain—and are arranged chronologically. They are excavated in the scarp of a large plateau, and run nearly north and south for about a mile and a quarter, the scarp at each end of this interval throwing out a horn towards the west. The Buddhist caves, twelve in number, are situated at the south end; the Indra Sabha or Jain group, consisting of five caves, lies at the other extremity of the series; the Brāhmanical caves, which number seventeen, are between the other two series. In age the caves vary from about the fifth to the ninth or tenth century, and important inscriptions have been found in them. Among the most interesting objects at Ellora is the Kailās temple, one of the most wonderful and interesting specimens of architectural art in India.

'Unlike any of the preceding cave-temples,' says Dr. Burgess, 'Kailās is a great monolithic temple, isolated from surrounding rock, and carved outside as well as in. It stands in a great court averaging 154 feet wide by 276 feet long at the level of the base, entirely cut out of the solid rock, and with a scarp 107 feet high at the back. In front of this court a curtain has been left, carved on the outside with the monstrous forms of Siva and Vishnu and their congeners, and with rooms inside it. It is pierced in the centre by an entrance passage, with rooms on each side. Passing this, the visitor is met by a large sculpture of Lakshmi over the lotuses, with her attendant elephant. There are some letters and a date on the leaves of the lotus on which she sits, but illegible, and probably belonging to the fifteenth century. On the bases of the pilasters on each side have been inscriptions in characters of the eighth century. As we enter, to right and left is the front portion of the court, which is a few feet lower than the rest, and at the north and south ends of which stand two gigantic elephants—that on the south much mutilated. Turning again to the east and ascending a few steps, we enter the great court occupied by the temple, whose base measures 164 feet from east to west, by 109 feet where widest from north to south. In front of it, and connected by a bridge, is a *mandapa* for the Nandi, and on each side of this *mandapa* stands a pillar or *dvajdand* 'ensign staff'—45 feet high, or with what remains of a *trisula* of Siva on the top, a total height of about 49 feet.'

This temple was built by Krishna I, the Rāshtrakūta king of Malkhed (760–83).

[*Archaeological Survey Reports of Western India*, vol. v.]

Jālna Town.—Head-quarters of the *tāluk* of the same name in Aurangābād District, Hyderābād State, situated in 19° 51′ N. and 75° 54′ E., on the right bank of the Kundlika, opposite the town of Kādirābād. Population (1901), 20,270, of whom 13,851 were Hindus, 5,812 Musalmāns, and 317 Christians. According to local traditions, Jālna was founded in the time of Rāma. During Sītā's residence it was styled Jānkapur, but the name was changed to Jālna by a rich Musalmān weaver. Abul Fazl, Akbar's minister, resided here for a time, and Aurangzeb is said to have visited the place occasionally during his viceroyalty. The only public buildings of any note are a mosque and a handsome stone *sarai*, erected according to the inscriptions on them in 1568, and a Turkish bath. The town also contains a number of less important mosques and shrines, besides three Hindu temples, the principal one being that of Anandi Swāmi, which is of considerable size. The fort of Jālna, which was built in 1725, is now in ruins. Its gardens produce large quantities of fruit, which is exported to Bombay and elsewhere. The cantonment of Jālna, till recently a station of the Hyderābād Contingent, lies to the east of the town; it was built in 1827, but has been abandoned since 1903. There are several places of Christian worship, with a couple of schools attached.

Kādirābād.—Walled town in the Jālna *tāluk* of Aurangābād District, Hyderābād State, situated in 19° 51′ N. and 75° 55′ E., on the left bank of the Kundlika, opposite the town of Jālna. Population (1901), 11,159. It is an important centre of the grain and cotton trade, and contains a weekly bazar for grain and cattle. There are three ginning and two pressing mills, employing 470 hands. Post and customs offices are located here.

Khuldābād Village (or Rauza).—Village in the Khuldābād *tāluk* of Aurangābād District, Hyderābād State, situated in 20° 1′ N. and 75° 12′ E., 2,732 feet above sea-level and 500 feet above the plains, 14 miles north-west of Aurangābād city. Population (1901), 2,845. Khuldābād contains the tombs of Aurangzeb and of his son Azam Shāh; of Asaf Jāh, the founder of the Hyderābād State; of Nāsir Jang, Nizām Shāhi king of Ahmadnagar; of Malik Ambar, the Nizām Shāhi minister; of Tāna Shāh, the last of the Kutb Shāhi kings; and of several Musalmān saints. The former name of the place was Rauza, which was changed to Khuldābād in consequence of the title of *Khuld Makān* conferred on Aurangzeb after his death. The extensive ruins of the ancient Hindu city of Buddravanti are situated on an adjoining table-land. In addition to the *tāluk* office, Khuldābād contains a post office, a school, a police *amīn's* office, and a police station. It is largely resorted to as a sanitarium.

Paithan Town.—Head-quarters of the *tāluk* of the same name in Aurangābād District, Hyderābād State, situated in 19° 28′ N. and 75° 24′ E., on the north bank of the Godāvari. Population (1901), 8,638. Paithan, the Pratisthān of the ancients, is one of the oldest cities in the Deccan, and is associated with many historic events. Asoka sent missionaries to the Petenikas, who were probably the inhabitants of the country round this place, while inscriptions of the second century B.C., in the caves at Pitalkhara near Chālisgaon, refer to the king and merchants of Pratisthān. According to Ptolemy this was the capital of Pulumāyi II, the Andhra king (138–70), and the author of the *Periplus* describes it as a great centre of trade. Paithan is said to have been the birthplace and capital of Sālivāhana, with whom is connected the era that bears this name; but it is probable that Sālivāhana is a corruption of Sātavāhana, the title of the Andhra kings. Almost all traces of the ancient city have disappeared. The modern town contains numerous Hindu temples with exquisite wood-carvings. The sect of Mānbhau was founded at Paithan about the middle of the fourteenth century. The tenets of this sect prescribe the exclusive worship of Krishna, the disregard of all caste rules, and a life of mendicancy. Some of the present followers of the creed follow ordinary pursuits, while those who adhere to the stricter rule wander about as beggars, clothed in black. Silk and cotton *sārīs* and other silk fabrics are made at Paithan, which is a trade centre of some importance.

Vaijāpur Town.—Head-quarters of the *tāluk* of the same name in Aurangābād District, Hyderābād State, situated in 19° 56′ N. and 74° 43′ E. Population (1901), 5,451. It is said to have been named after its founder, Rānī Vaiju Bai. Vaijāpur contains the sepulchre of the Muhammadan saint, Saiyid Rukn-ud-dīn, and the grave of *naughāzi* or the 'nine martyrs,' wrongly termed *nau-gazi* ('nine yards'). It contains a post office, a school, a dispensary, and the police inspector's office, and is a large grain mart.

Boundaries, configuration, and hill and river systems.

Parbhani District.—District in the Aurangābād Division of Hyderābād State, lying between 18° 58′ and 20° 2′ N. and 76° 4′ and 77° 42′ E., with an area of 5,091 square miles, including 995 square miles of *jāgīr* and *paigāh* lands. It is bounded on the north by the Buldāna and Bāsim Districts of Berār; on the east and south by Nānder; on the south-west by Bhīr; and on the west by Aurangābād. A small area was transferred to the District from Nānder in 1905.

The chief hill ranges are the Sahyādriparvat and the Bālāghāt; the former runs through the north of the District, and the latter traverses a portion of the Pālam *tāluk* in the south. The *tāluks* of Jintūr, Hingoli, and Kalamnūri are partly situated on the plateau south of the Sahyādriparvat, while the other *tāluks* lie in the plains. The plateau slopes towards the south, and terminates in the valley of the Dudna.

The most important rivers are the Godāvari, the Pengangā, the Pūrna, and the Dudna. The Godāvari enters from the west, and, after traversing the southern *tāluks* for 112 miles, passes into Nānder District. The Pengangā flows along the northern border of the District, separating it from the Bāsim District of Berār. The Dudna flows across the District for about 50 miles from west to east, and joins the Pūrna. The latter river, which enters Parbhani from the south-west corner of Berār, flows first in a south-easterly direction for about 35 miles, and then due south, and falls into the Godāvari. Its length in this District is about 100 miles. A number of minor streams—the Kikia (13 miles), Kharki (13), Kastūra (38), Paingalgira (24), Indrāyani (13), Dhāmor (6), Ashna (12), Kiadho (48), and Kapra (12)—also water the District.

The geological formation is the Deccan trap. In the valley of the Godāvari and some of its tributaries the trap is overlaid by gravels and clay beds of upper pliocene or pleistocene age, containing fossil bones of extinct mammalia. Geology.

The trees found in the forest areas consist of *babūl* (*Acacia arabica*), *khair* (*Acacia Catechu*), *nīm*, mango, tamarind, *eppa* (*Hardwickia binata*), and *mahuā* (*Bassia latifolia*). Botany.

In the jungles of the Jintūr, Hingoli, and Kalamnūri *tāluks*, tigers, leopards, wolves, hyenas, bears, and wild hog are found, while in all the *tāluks sāmbar* and spotted deer are not uncommon. Partridge, quail, and peafowl are also to be found. Fauna.

The climate is dry and healthy from February to the end of May, but feverish during the monsoon and part of the cold season. The plateau is much healthier than the plains, not being so damp during the rainy season. The temperature ranges from 60° in December to 105° in May in the plains, and to 98° on the plateau. The rainfall during the twenty-one years ending 1901 averaged 34 inches. The amount received in 1899 (12 inches) was abnormally small, and resulted in the famine of 1900. Climate, temperature, and rainfall.

The District, which formed part of the Yādava kingdom of Deogiri (the modern Daulatābād), was conquered by Alā-ud-dīn Khiljī in the beginning of the fourteenth century, and has since remained under Muhammadan rule. After the death of Muhammad bin Tughlak in 1351, it fell successively to the Bahmani and Nizām Shāhi kingdoms. On the conquest of the Deccan by Akbar and his successor it was again united to Delhi, but was finally separated in the beginning of the eighteenth century, on the foundation of the Hyderābād State. History.

The District contains four structures of note. The temple of Nāgnāth at Aundah in the Kalamnūri *tāluk* is said to have been a seven-storeyed building which was demolished by Aurangzeb. At present it is 100 feet long, 80 feet broad, and 60 feet high, with a quadrangular court 7,200 square feet in area. It is adorned with hundreds of exquisitely carved figures of men, horses, elephants, bulls, and monkeys, and is locally believed to have been built by a Pāndava Rājā at a fabulous cost. The Jain temple of Pārasnāth near Jintūr has a very narrow, dark passage leading to a domed building, in the centre of which is a carved figure 12 feet high. A plainly Archaeology.

built temple near Bāmu in the Jintūr *tāluk* stands at the junction of the Saraswatī and Pūrna rivers. The shrine of Ramazān Shāh, situated on the summit of a hill near Khari in the Hingoli *tāluk*, is enclosed by a strong wall 30 feet high and 1,200 feet square. The saint is said to have been converted to Islām, and his shrine is visited by both Hindus and Musalmāns. Besides these, a large number of Hemādpanti temples are found throughout the District.

Population. The number of towns and villages, including those in *jāgīrs*, is 1,502. The population at the last three enumerations was: (1881) 685,099, (1891) 805,335, and (1901), 645,765. The famine of 1900 is the cause of the heavy decrease in the last decade. The District is divided into seven *tāluks*, PARBHANI, PĀTHRI, JINTŪR, HINGOLI, KALAMNŪRI, BASMAT, and PĀLAM (a 'crown' *tāluk*), besides the two large *jāgīr tāluks* of Partūr and Gangākher. The towns are HINGOLI, PARBHANI, BASMAT, MĀNWAT, PĀTHRI, SONEPET, and GANGĀKHER. About 90 per cent. of the population are Hindus, and 88 per cent. speak Marāthī. The following table shows the distribution of population in 1901:—

Tāluk.	Area in square miles.	Number of Towns.	Number of Villages.	Population.	Population per square mile.	Percentage of variation in population between 1891 and 1901.	Number of persons able to read and write.
Parbhani	518	1	165	93,325	180	− 1	Not available.
Jintūr	798	...	260	77,906	97	− 29·0	
Hingoli	633	1	190	78,138	123	− 21·4	
Kalamnūri	492	...	175	52,437	106	− 30·5	
Basmat	523	1	194	66,272	126	− 32·2	
Pālam	427	...	121	65,490	153	− 12·2	
Pāthri	705	2	151	109,837	155	− 1·8	
Jāgīrs, &c.	995	2	239	102,360	103	− 23·1	
District total	5,091	7	1,495	645,765	125	− 19·8	16,147

In 1905 the northern villages of the Nānder *tāluk*, Nānder District, were added to Kalamnūri, and a few villages in Pāthri were transferred in exchange for some in the Ambarh *tāluk* of Aurangābād District.

Castes and occupations. The most numerous caste is that of the cultivating Kunbīs, who number 260,800, or more than 40 per cent. of the total population. Mahārs or village menials number 67,400, Dhangars or shepherds 47,900, Baniās or trading castes 33,700, Māngs or leather-workers 24,000, and Brāhmans 20,500. The Mahārs and Māngs also work as agricultural labourers. Persons directly supported by agriculture number 342,000, or 53 per cent. of the total.

There is no Christian mission in the District, but the number of native Christians returned in 1901 was 70.

General agricultural conditions.

The soils of the *tāluks* of Parbhani, Pāthri, Basmat, and Pālam are mostly composed of the fertile *regar* or black cotton soil, with some *masab*; but in the remaining *tāluks masab* and *kharab* soils predominate. *Rabi* crops, such as white *jowār*, wheat, gram, *tuar*, *lākh*, and peas, are extensively grown on the *regar* and *masab*; and yellow *jowar*, *bājra*, cotton, indigo, sesamum, *sāvān*, and oilseeds and pulses are raised on the *kharab* and *masab* soils during the rains. The *kharab* soils also bear garden crops, but they require heavy manuring. The soil at the foot of the hills and in the valleys of rivers is very fertile, producing *rabi* and garden crops.

Chief agricultural statistics and principal crops.

The tenure of lands throughout the District is *ryotwāri*. Out of 4,096 square miles of *khālsa* and *Sarf-i-khās* lands, 3,547 square miles were cultivated in 1901, 54 were cultivable waste and fallows, 255 were forest, and 240 were not available for cultivation. The staple food-crop is *jowār*, grown on 1,797 square miles, or 50 per cent. of the area cropped. Next in importance are wheat (229 square miles), *bājra* (206), and rice (57). Cotton is grown throughout the District, covering 809 square miles, or about 23 per cent. of the net area cropped. Sugar-cane occupies only 3 square miles.

Cattle, &c.

No special breed of cattle is characteristic of the District, but those found are hardy and strong, and well suited for ploughing the prevailing heavy soils. Sheep and goats of the ordinary kind are reared by the Dhangars and some well-to-do ryots. Ordinary Marāthā ponies fetch about Rs. 50, but animals of a better sort command as much as Rs. 100 or Rs. 150 each. The State maintains nine Arab stallions in six of the *tāluks*, for the purpose of improving the local breed, at an annual cost of Rs. 2,400.

Irrigation.

The total irrigated area, which was 74 square miles in 1904, is supplied by wells numbering 10,471. There are no irrigation tanks, but 15 other sources supply water.

Forests.

The area under forest is 255 square miles, of which 55 are 'reserved' and the remainder open. Jintūr, Kalamnūri, Hingoli, and Pālam are the only *tāluks* containing forest.

Minerals.

No minerals of economic value are found in the District. Black basalt and granite are available everywhere, and are used for building and road-metalling.

There is no important hand industry. Ordinary coarse

Arts and manufactures. cotton cloth is woven for local use. The District contains 13 ginning factories and 5 cotton-presses, employing 255 hands. The total quantity of cotton ginned in 1901 was 417 tons.

Commerce. The principal exports consist of *jowār* and other food-grains, cotton, oilseeds, indigo, chillies, cattle and sheep, jaggery, tobacco, hides, bones and horns, *tarvar* bark for tanning, and *mahuā* flowers. The chief imports are salt, salted fish, opium, spices, gold and silver, copper and brass sheets and vessels, sulphur, refined sugar, kerosene oil, iron, raw and manufactured silk, cotton and woollen cloth.

The chief centres of trade are Mānwat, Hingoli, Parbhani, Sonpet, Gangākher, and Mantha, where a large business is done in local produce. Weekly bazars are also held at the *tāluk* head-quarters and other villages. The trading and money-lending castes are the Vānīs, Komatis, Mārwāris, Kachchis, and Bhātias.

Railways and roads. The Hyderābād-Godāvari Valley Railway traverses the District from east to west for a distance of 63 miles, and has 9 stations within its limits. The total length of roads is 341 miles, of which only 18 are metalled. About 26 miles were constructed during the famine of 1900. The principal roads are from Hingoli to Kāvergaon, metalled (18 miles), to Jaipur (28 miles), to Parbhani (44 miles), from Jintūr to Parbhani (24 miles), to Sailū (22 miles), from Basmat to Lāsina (12 miles), and from Parbhani to Gangākher (20 miles). Besides these, about 163 miles of fair-weather tracks lead to the head-quarters of the *tāluks* and other important places.

Famine. The District suffered most severely during the famines of 1819 and 1854–5. It was again affected to a certain extent in 1876–8, but distress was most severe in 1899–1900. The rainfall in 1899 was less than 12 inches, and both the *kharīf* and *rabi* crops failed. The *kharīf* crop gave only 6 per cent., and the *rabi*, which mostly consists of *jowār*, the staple food of the people, was only about 4 per cent. of the normal. The number of units relieved exceeded 14 millions, and the highest attendance in one day was 90,222. While famine was raging in the District, cholera supervened, and carried off thousands; and the Census of 1901 revealed the enormous decrease of 159,570, or 20 per cent., compared with 1891. The people lost about 39 per cent. of their cattle, and the total cost of the famine to the State was more than 14 lakhs.

District subdivisions and staff. The District is divided into three subdivisions: one comprising the *tāluks* of Hingoli, Kalamnūri, and Basmat, under the Second Tālukdār; the second comprising the *tāluks* of

Parbhani, Pāthri, and Jintūr, under the Third Tālukdār; and the third consisting of Pālam only, which is under the First Tālukdār, who exercises a general supervision over the work of all his subordinates. Each *tāluk* is under a *tahsīldār*.

Civil and criminal justice.

The *Nāzim-i-Dīwāni* or Civil Judge presides over the District civil court, and there are two subordinate Munsifs' courts. The First Tālukdār is the chief magistrate of the District, and the District Civil Judge is a joint-magistrate, exercising powers in the absence of the First Tālukdār from head-quarters. The Second and Third Tālukdārs and the seven *tahsīldārs* have magisterial powers of the second and third class. The two Munsifs exercise third-class magisterial powers in the absence of the *tahsīldārs* from their head-quarters. Serious crime is rare in ordinary years; but in adverse seasons dacoities and cattle and grain thefts increase in proportion to the severity of the distress.

Land revenue.

All that is known of the early revenue history of the District is that Malik Ambar's system was in force from the beginning of the seventeenth century. His settlement, which was a modification of Todar Mal's method, was based upon the actual area and the productiveness of the soil. *Tāluks* and villages were subsequently farmed out by the State to revenue contractors, who were allowed 10 per cent. for collections. After the introduction of District administration in 1866, this system was abolished, and cash payments with a *ryotwāri* settlement were introduced. In 1885 the *tāluks* of Pāthri, Kalamnūri, and Hingoli, and in the following two years the remaining four *tāluks*, were settled for fifteen years, the rates fixed approximating to those in the adjoining Districts of Bāsim in Berār, Aurangābād, and Bhīr. The enhancement of revenue resulting from this assessment was Rs. 99,210, or 5¼ per cent. The average rate on 'dry' land is Rs. 1-5 (maximum Rs. 1-14, minimum Rs. 1-1), and on 'wet' land Rs. 3-4 (maximum Rs. 5-6, minimum Rs. 1-2).

The land revenue and the total revenue for a series of years are shown below, in thousands of rupees:—

	1881.	1891.	1901.	1903.
Land revenue . .	14,64	17,78	20,67	19,84
Total revenue . .	19,35	25,47	33,16	34,45

Owing to the changes of area made in 1905, the land revenue demand is now about 22·1 lakhs.

Since 1888 a cess of one anna in the rupee on land revenue

Local and municipal govern- ment.

has been levied for local purposes, and local boards formed for every *tāluk* except Parbhani, under the chairmanship of the *tahsīldārs*. A District board was constituted at the head-quarters, with the First Tālukdār as president. Of the total cess, which yielded 1·3 lakhs in 1901, one-fourth is set apart for local and municipal works. At Parbhani town there is a municipality, and each of the *tāluk* head-quarters has a small conservancy establishment, the District and *tāluk* boards managing the municipalities as well. The local board expenditure in 1901 was Rs. 60,200.

Police and jails.

The First Tālukdār is the head of the police administration, with a Superintendent of police (*Mohtamim*) as his executive deputy. He has under him 8 inspectors, 92 subordinate officers, 548 constables, and 25 mounted police, distributed in 30 police stations. There is a District jail at Parbhani, where short-term prisoners are kept, while those whose sentences exceed six months are sent to the Central jail at Aurangābād.

Education.

The District takes a medium position as regards the literacy of its population, of whom 2·5 per cent. (4·9 males and 0·1 females) could read and write in 1901. The total number of pupils under instruction in 1881, 1891, 1901, and 1903 was 267, 2,042, 3,341, and 3,437 respectively. In 1903 there were 56 primary and 3 middle schools, with 41 girls under instruction. The total expenditure on education in 1901 was Rs. 20,300, of which the State contributed Rs. 11,300. About 44 per cent. of the total was devoted to primary schools. The fee receipts in 1901 amounted to Rs. 1,952.

Medical

In 1901 there were four dispensaries, with accommodation for 15 in-patients, besides a *yunāni* dispensary maintained from Local funds. The total number of cases treated at these was 33,432, of whom 121 were in-patients. The number of operations performed was 663, and the total expenditure amounted to Rs. 12,900. The number of successful cases of vaccination in 1901 was 1,695, or 2·62 per 1,000 of the population.

Parbhani Tāluk.—Central *tāluk* of Parbhani District, Hyderābād State, with an area of 560 square miles. The population in 1901, including *jāgīrs*, was 94,774, compared with 107,136 in 1891, the decrease being due to the famine of 1900. The *tāluk* has one town, PARBHANI (population, 9,958), the head-quarters of the District and *tāluk*; and 175 villages, of which 10 are *jāgīr*. The land revenue in 1901 was 3·4 lakhs. The Godāvari river flows in the south of the *tāluk*. The soils are chiefly alluvial or *regar*.

Jintūr.—Northern *tāluk* of Parbhani District, Hyderābād State, with an area of 952 square miles. The population in 1901, including *jāgīrs*, was 87,797, compared with 123,546 in 1891, the decrease being due to the famine of 1900. The *tāluk* contains 297 villages, of which 37 are *jāgīr*; and Jintūr (population, 3,688) is the head-quarters. The land revenue in 1901 was 3·2 lakhs. The *tāluk* lies between the rivers Pūrna (north) and Dudna (south). The soils are mainly alluvial and *regar*.

Hingoli Tāluk.—North-eastern *tāluk* of Parbhani District, Hyderābād State, with an area of 713 square miles. The population in 1901, including *jāgīrs*, was 85,071, compared with 108,153 in 1891, the decrease being due to the famine of 1900. The *tāluk* contains one town, HINGOLI (population, 17,256), the head-quarters; and 209 villages, of which 19 are *jāgīr*. The land revenue in 1901 was 1·9 lakhs. The Pengangā river separates it on the north and north-east from the Bāsim District of Berār. The soils are mainly *regar* and alluvial.

Kalamnūri.—North-eastern *tāluk* of Parbhani District, Hyderābād State, with an area of 538 square miles. The population in 1901, including *jāgīrs*, was 58,835, compared with 84,685 in 1891, the decrease being due to the famine of 1900. The *tāluk* had till recently 186 villages, of which 11 were *jāgīr*; and Kalamnūri (population, 4,267) is the head-quarters. The land revenue in 1901 was 1·9 lakhs. In 1905 a few villages were added from Nānder District. The Pengangā flows on the north-eastern border, separating the *tāluk* from the Bāsim District of Berār.

Basmat Tāluk.—Eastern *tāluk* of Parbhani District, Hyderābād State, with an area of 610 square miles. The population in 1901, including *jāgīrs*, was 79,569, compared with 117,344 in 1891, the decrease being due to the famine of 1900. The *tāluk* contains one town, BASMAT (population, 8,445), the head-quarters; and 215 villages, of which 21 are *jāgīr*. The land revenue in 1901 was 3·2 lakhs. The country is composed mainly of black cotton soil.

Pālam.—'Crown' *tāluk* in the south of Parbhani District, Hyderābād State, with an area of 560 square miles. The population in 1901, including *jāgīrs*, was 92,182, compared with 104,904 in 1891, the decrease being due to the famine of 1900. The *tāluk* contains two towns, GANGĀKHER (population, 5,007) and SONEPET (5,759), both being *jāgīr* towns; and 153 villages, of which 32 are *jāgīr*. Pālam (3,306) is the head-quarters. The land revenue in 1901 was 3·2 lakhs. The Godāvari river forms the northern boundary.

Pāthri Tāluk.—Western *tāluk* of Parbhani District, Hyderābād State, with an area of 784 square miles. The population in 1901, including *jāgīrs*, was 119,324, compared with 123,553 in 1891, the decline being due to the famine of 1900. The *tāluk* contains two towns, PĀTHRI (population, 5,828), the head-quarters, and MĀNWAT (7,395); and 170 villages, of which 19 are *jāgīr*. In 1905 this *tāluk* received 8 villages from the Ambarh *tāluk* of Aurangābād District, and gave 6 villages to that *tāluk* in exchange. The land revenue in 1901 was 3·8 lakhs. The Godāvari river separates it from Bhīr District on the south. The soils are chiefly alluvial and *regar*. North is the *jāgīr tāluk* of Partūr; population (1901), 28,213. It comprises 90 villages; and Partūr (4,043), the head-quarters, is a station on the Hyderābād-Godāvari Valley Railway. It has an area of about 374 square miles, and contains a ginning factory, a State post office and a British sub-post office, a school, and a dispensary, the last two being maintained by the *jāgīr* authorities.

Basmat Town.—Head-quarters of the *tāluk* of the same name in Parbhani District, Hyderābād State, situated in 19° 20′ N. and 77° 10′ E. Population (1901), 8,445. Besides the *tahsīl* and police inspector's offices, it contains three schools and a post office. Basmat is a busy centre of the grain trade.

Gangākher.—Head-quarters of a *jāgīr* in Parbhani District, Hyderābād State, situated in 18° 58′ N. and 76° 45′ E., on the south bank of the Godāvari, 14 miles north-east of Pingli on the Hyderābād-Godāvari Valley Railway. Population (1901), 5,007. It contains two schools, a State post office, a British sub-post office, and the police inspector's and sub-registrar's offices. The *ghāt*, or steps leading to the river, is built of masonry; and during the rains and part of the cold season a ferry plies across the river.

Hingoli Town.—Head-quarters of the *tāluk* of the same name in Parbhani District, Hyderābād State, situated in 19° 43′ N. and 77° 9′ E. Population (1901), 17,256, of whom 11,395 were Hindus, 5,289 Musalmāns, and 52 Christians. It contains three schools with 230 pupils, of which one is a middle school and one a girls' school. It is also the head-quarters of the Second Tālukdār, and contains a State post office and a British sub-post office, a Munsif's court, a dispensary, two ginning factories, and a cotton-press. It was a cantonment of the Hyderābād Contingent up to 1903. Since the removal of the Contingent, some of the Nizām's troops have been stationed here. Hingoli is a great cotton mart, and is famous as one of the first places in the Deccan at which operations for the suppression of *thagī* were commenced about 1833. Fourteen miles south-west of Hingoli is the village of Aundah, containing the ruins of an immense temple destroyed by Aurangzeb. The carvings in the basement are of a very elaborate description, resembling those on the temple of Kailās at Ellora.

Mānwat.—Town in the Pāthri *tāluk* of Parbhani District, Hyderābād State, situated in 19° 18′ N. and 76° 30′ E., five miles south of the Hyderābād-Godāvari Valley Railway. Population (1901), 7,395. It is a busy centre of the grain trade, and contains a State post office, a British sub-post office, and four schools.

Parbhani Town.—Head-quarters of the District and *tāluk* of the same name, Hyderābād State, situated in 19° 16′ N. and 76° 47′ E. Population (1901), 9,958. Besides the District and *tāluk* offices, it contains the civil court, a Munsif's court, a British sub-post office and a State post office, a dispensary, the Police Superintendent's office, and four schools, of which one is a middle school. Parbhani is a station on the Hyderābād-Godāvari Valley Railway, and is a flourishing centre of the grain and cotton trade. There are three cotton-pressing and ginning factories.

Pāthri Town.—Head-quarters of the *tāluk* of the same name in Parbhani District, Hyderābād State, situated in 19° 15′ N. and 76° 27′ E. Population (1901), 5,828. The town contains a *tahsīl* and police inspector's office, a post office, and two schools.

Sonepet.—Head-quarters of Mahārājā Sir Kishen Prasād Bahādur's *jāgīr tāluk*, Parbhani District, Hyderābād State, situated in 19° 2′ N. and 76° 29′ E., on the Wān river. Population (1901), 5,759. The town suffered much from the inundation of the Wān in 1891 and the famine of 1900. It contains a State post office, a police station, and two private schools with 200 pupils. Silk *sāris* and fine cotton and silk fabrics are made and exported far and wide, and about one-third of the population subsist by weaving. The town is walled and is an important centre of trade.

Nānder District.—District in the Aurangābād Division, in the north of the State of Hyderābād, lying between 18° 28′ and 19° 31′ N. and 77° 4′ and 78° 6′ E., with an area of 3,349 square

Boundaries, configuration, and hill

and river systems. miles[1]. It is separated from the Berār District of Bāsim by the Pengangā, and is bounded on the east by Nizāmābād, on the south by Bīdar, and on the north and west by Parbhani.

A range of hills, known as the Bhāg or Thānāvari, runs through the District from north-west to south-east between Parbhani and Nizāmābād. There are minor ranges in the Nānder, Kandahār, Osmānnagar, and Bhaisa *tāluks*.

The most important river is the Godāvari, which enters from the west, and, flowing past Nānder in the centre of the District in an easterly direction, passes out into Nizāmābād. The Mānjra, its largest tributary, joins the Godāvari on the right at Mānjra Sangam (confluence), 5 miles east of Kondalwādi. The Pengangā forms the northern boundary of the District, flowing in an easterly direction. Other rivers are the Ashna, a tributary of the Godāvari, flowing east and falling into it on the left bank, about 2 miles from Nānder town; the Siddha in the Nānder and Bhaisa *tāluks*, also a tributary of the Godāvari; the Lendi in Deglūr, and the Manār in Deglūr and Kandahār.

Geology. The geological formations are the Archaean gneiss and the Deccan trap, occupying respectively the east and west of the District.

Botany. The District contains teak, *mahuā* (*Bassia latifolia*), *khair* (*Acacia Catechu*), tamarind, mango, *eppa* (*Hardwickia binata*), *nīm*, and various species of *Ficus*.

Fauna. The only *tāluk* in which any large game is regularly found is Hadgaon, where tigers, leopards, bears, wild dogs, hyenas, wolves, wild hog, *sāmbar*, barking-deer, and spotted deer are met with; also partridges, quail, peafowl, green pigeons, and duck.

Climate, temperature, and rainfall. With the exception of the Biloli *tāluk*, which is comparatively damp, the District is dry and healthy. In Nānder and Kandahār the temperature in May rises to 112°, while Hadgaon, Osmānnagar, and Deglūr are cooler, the temperature being about 100° in May. In December it falls to 60°. The average rainfall for the twenty-one years ending 1901 was 36 inches.

History. The District formed part of the Chālukyan and Yādava kingdoms, and Nānder is supposed to be the old Nanagiri fort of the early Kākatīyas. In the beginning of the fourteenth century it was conquered by Alā-ud-dīn Khiljī. It formed part of the Bahmani and subsequently of the Kutb Shāhi kingdom. The tract was annexed to the Mughal empire after the conquest of the Deccan by Aurangzeb, but was separated from it on the

[1] These limits relate to the area of the District before the changes made in 1905; see paragraph on Population.

foundation of the Hyderābād State in the beginning of the eighteenth century.

There are several tombs of Musalmān saints at Kandahār and Nānder, and the fort at the latter place is old. Nānder also contains the *Gurūdwāra* of the Deccan Sikhs, where Gurū Govind is buried. Two old mosques at Nānder were built, one by Malik Ambar and the other during the reign of the Kutb Shāhis. The fort of Kandahār is popularly supposed to have been erected in the fourth century by Somadeva, a Rājā of Kandahār; and it may perhaps be connected with Krishna III, the Rāshtrakūta king of Malkhed, who is styled lord of Kandhārapura. It is surrounded by a ditch and a strong stone wall. DEGLŪR contains an old temple of Ganda Mahārāj, and BHAISA another built after the Hemādpanti style. Archaeology.

The number of towns and villages in the District is 1,174, including *paigāh* and *jāgīrs*. The population at the last three enumerations was: (1881) 636,023, (1891) 632,522, and (1901) 503,684. The famine of 1889–1900 accounts for the decrease of population in the last decade. The towns are NĀNDER, the head-quarters, BHAISA, DEGLŪR, and MUKHER. About 89 per cent. of the population are Hindus and 10 per cent. Musalmāns. More than 70 per cent. speak Marāthī and 14 per cent. Telugu. The following table shows the distribution of population in 1901:— Population.

Tāluk.	Area in square miles.	Number of Towns.	Number of Villages.	Population.	Population per square mile.	Percentage of variation in population between 1891 and 1901.	Number of persons able to read and write.
Osmānnagar	258	...	86	30,577	118	— 22.1	Not available.
Hadgaon	419	...	141	43,602	104	— 41.8	
Bhaisa	217	1	77	39,100	180	— 18.3	
Biloli	198	...	85	33,870	171	— 2.3	
Deglūr	267	1	103	49,324	238	— 2.5	
Kandahār	553	1	153	78,546	142	— 24.0	
Nānder	632	1	250	92,479	146	— 22.2	
Jāgīrs, &c.	805	...	275	136,186	162	— 19.0	
District total	3,349	4	1,170	503,684	150	— 2.04	11,001

In 1905 the Mudhol *tāluk*, and a few villages from Bānswāda, were transferred from Nizāmābād to this District, while Bhaisa was absorbed in Mudhol, and Osmānnagar was divided between Biloli and Kandahār. The northern villages of the Nānder *tāluk* were made over to Kalamnūri in Parbhani District, and other portions were added to Hadgaon and Mudhol. The

District in its present form thus comprises six *tāluks*—Hadgaon, Mudhol, Biloli, Deglūr, Kandahār, and Nānder—besides a large *paigāh* estate and a *jāgīr*.

Castes and occupations.

The purely agricultural castes number 171,600, or about 34 per cent., the most important among them being Marāthā Kunbīs or Kāpus (129,700) and Kolīs (15,500). Next come the trading castes, numbering 48,600, of whom 34,900 are Vānis and 11,600 Komatis. Lower castes include Dhangars or shepherds (45,000), Mahārs or village menials (36,700), and Māngs or leather-workers (33,000). The last two castes work as field-labourers also. There are only 10,200 Brāhmans in the District. More than 65 per cent. of the population are directly dependent on the land. The District contained only 9 Christians in 1901, of whom one was a native.

General agricultural conditions.

With the exception of the soils of the Kandahār *tāluk*, the entire District is composed of black cotton soil or *regar*. Portions of the Kandahār, Nānder, and Bhaisa *tāluks* are slightly hilly, but other parts are flat, with very gentle undulations. *Rabi* crops are extensively raised, consisting of *jowār*, gram, peas, wheat, and oilseeds; while the *kharif* crops include yellow and Berār *jowār*, *bājra*, linseed, cotton, maize, and other food-grains.

Chief agricultural statistics and principal crops.

The tenure is mainly *ryotwāri*. In 1901 *khālsa* lands measured 2,544 square miles, of which 1,967 were cultivated, 202 were cultivable waste and fallows, 310 were forests, and 65 were not available for cultivation. The staple food-crop is *jowār*, grown on 52 per cent. of the net area cropped. Next in importance is cotton (449 square miles); the other food-grains, such as *bājra*, *tuar*, and pulses, cover 190 square miles, oilseeds 99, and wheat 82 square miles.

Cattle, &c.

Although no special breed of cattle is found, those reared in the District are sturdy and well suited for ploughing the heavy *regar* Sheep of the ordinary kind are bred. The milch goats are of a good type, and fetch as much as Rs. 8 per head. Before the closing of the Malegaon horse and cattle fair in Bīdar District, owing to plague (1896), *pātels*, *pātwāris*, and well-to-do ryots used to rear numbers of ponies. The State has provided Arab stallions in all the *tāluks* for the improvement of the breed of horses.

Irrigation.

The principal source of irrigation is wells, which number 5,764. In addition, 169 tanks, large and small, and 163 other sources, such as anicuts and channels, are used. All these are in good working order, and irrigate 46 square miles.

Forests.

The forest area is very limited, only 110 square miles being 'reserved,' and 200 square miles unprotected. The forests contain teak (*Tectona grandis*), *mahuā* (*Bassia latifolia*), ebony (*Diospyros melanoxylon*), *khair* (*Acacia Catechu*), *eppa* (*Hardwickia binata*), and tamarind. Bhaisa, Hadgaon, and Nānder are the only *tāluks* in which any forest areas exist.

Good basalt and granite are found in the vicinity of Nānder, and limestone in the Deglūr, Bhaisa, and Kandahār *tāluks*. Minerals.

Nānder town is famous for its fine muslins, which compare with those of Dacca. The muslin, though produced in small quantities now, is exported. It is much prized at Hyderābād, fetching high prices, especially the kind used for turbans, and the handkerchiefs and *sāris* adorned with gold and silver thread like Benares work. Ordinary cotton cloth is also woven and is used by the poorer classes. In the Deglūr and Bhaisa *tāluks* coarse cloth is printed for screens and tablecloths. There is a small factory at Nānder for gold and silver thread. Coarse paper is made at Mujāhidpet, and copper and brass vessels are turned out at Mukher. There were three cotton-presses and three ginning factories in the District in 1901, employing 450 hands. An impetus has been given to this industry since the opening of the Hyderābād-Godāvari Valley Railway in 1900, and four more factories are in course of construction. Arts and manufactures.

The chief exports consist of cotton, linseed, oils, *ghī*, *jowār*, cloth and muslin, indigo, and food-grains. The principal imports are cotton and woollen goods, raw silk, gold and silver, rice, refined sugar, kerosene oil, opium, copper and brass sheets and vessels. The greater portion of the trade is with the adjoining Districts; but cotton, linseed, and indigo are sent to Bombay, and *ghī*, oils, and grain to Hyderābād. Internal trade is mostly in the hands of the Vānīs, Komatis, and Momins, but Bhātias and Kachchis from Bombay are engaged in export trade. The opening of the Hyderābād-Godāvari Valley Railway in 1900 has diverted the chief channels of trade, which formerly passed through Hyderābād and Akola. Commerce.

The Hyderābād-Godāvari Valley Railway traverses the District from east to west for 40 miles, with six stations. Railways.

The District contains 141 miles of fair-weather roads. One starts from Nānder, and passing through Osmānnagar and Kandahār reaches Deglūr (50 miles). The others are from Deglūr to Bīdar (12 miles), Nānder to Hingoli (12 miles), to Mālakoli (25 miles), to Deglūr (12 miles), and to Nirmal (30 miles). On the Godāvari and Mānjra rivers, large coracles and rafts are kept to transport people from one bank to the other. Roads.

Famine. No reliable records exist of early famines. In 1819 a great scarcity is said to have occurred in this and the neighbouring Districts, known as *Gājarkāl*. In 1897 there was scarcity, and people had not recovered from its effects when the great famine of 1899–1900 occurred. All the wells and streams dried up, and there was not a drop of water in the Godāvari. The rainfall in 1899 was only 15 inches, less than half the normal quantity. The *kharīf* and *rabi* crops were one-fourth and one-sixteenth of the normal. Notwithstanding an expenditure exceeding 2¼ lakhs, thousands died, and the Census of 1901 showed a decrease of 128,845 persons, while about [illegible] per cent. of the cattle were lost.

District subdivisions and staff. The District is divided into three subdivisions, one comprising the *tāluks* of Nander and Kandahār, the second Deglūr and Biloli, and the third Mudhol and Hadgaon. Each of the last two is under a Second Tālukdār, while the first is under a Third Tālukdār, the First Tālukdār having a general supervision over the work of all his subordinates. Each *tāluk* is under a *tahsīldār*, but the Nānder *tāluk* has a *naib* (deputy) *tahsīldār* as well.

Civil and criminal justice. The District civil court is presided over by a Civil Judge, styled the *Nāzim-i-Dīwāni*, while three subordinate civil courts are under Munsifs. The First Tālukdār is the chief magistrate, and the District Civil Judge is also a joint-magistrate, who exercises magisterial powers during the absence of the First Tālukdār from head-quarters. The two Second Tālukdārs, as a special case, exercise first-class powers and the Third Tālukdār second-class powers within their respective subdivisions, while the *tahsīldārs* have third-class powers. In ordinary times serious crime is not heavy, but adverse seasons cause an increase in dacoities and cattle-thefts.

Land revenue. Prior to the introduction of District administration assessments were made on holdings, and revenue was collected either in cash or kind. In 1866 payment in kind was commuted to cash payments, and the *ryotwāri* system was introduced. In 1880 a rough survey was made, and in 1889 the District was regularly settled for a period of fifteen years, the rates being similar to those in Aurangābād and Bhīr Districts and in Berār. The settlement increased the revenue by 39·7 per cent., while the survey showed that the areas of holdings had been understated by 46 per cent. The average assessment on 'dry' land is Rs. 1–13–6 (maximum Rs. 3, minimum R. 0–3), and on 'wet' land Rs. 9 (maximum Rs. 10, minimum Rs. 6). In double-cropped lands the assessment for the second crop is half that for the first. The rates given above for 'wet' lands are for the *ābi* crop, but for the *tābi* crop the maximum is Rs. 20 and the minimum Rs. 15.

The land revenue and the total revenue for a series of years are shown below, in thousands of rupees:—

	1881.	1891.	1901.	1903.
Land revenue . .	13,68	13,37	13,47	13,42
Total revenue . .	15,80	15,03	15,86	16,08

Owing to the changes of area made in 1905, the land revenue demand now is about 15 lakhs.

In 1899 a cess of one anna in the rupee was levied on the land revenue, and local boards were constituted. Of the total cess one-fourth, or Rs. 20,600, is set apart for municipal and local works. The First Tālukdār is the president of the District board, and the *tahsīldārs* are the chairmen of the *tāluk* boards, except where there is a Second Tālukdār, who takes the chair at the head-quarters of his subdivision. There is a municipality at Nānder, and each of the head-quarters of the *tāluks* has a small conservancy establishment, the District and *tāluk* boards managing the municipalities as well. The local board expenditure in 1901 was Rs. 16,000. Local boards and munici-palities.

The First Tālukdār is the head of the police, with the Superintendent (*Mohtamim*) as his executive deputy. Under him are 8 inspectors, 74 subordinate officers, 483 constables, and 25 mounted police, distributed in 29 *thānas* and 36 outposts. There is a District jail at Nānder, and small lock-ups are maintained in the outlying *tahsīl* offices. Short-term prisoners only are kept in the District jail, those whose sentences exceed six months being sent to the Central jail at Aurangābād. Police and jails.

In 1901 the proportion of persons able to read and write was 1·2 per cent. (4·2 males and 0·03 females), so that the District takes a medium place in the State as regards the literacy of its population. The total number of pupils under instruction in 1881, 1891, 1901, and 1903 was 665, 951, 2,346, and 2,905 respectively. In 1903 there were 68 primary and 3 middle schools, with 155 girls under instruction. The total amount spent on education in 1901 was Rs. 16,000, of which Rs. 10,300 was contributed by the State, and the remainder by the boards. The total receipts from fees amounted to Rs. 810. Education.

The District contains two hospitals, with accommodation Medical.

for 6 in-patients. The total number of out-patients treated during 1901 was 20,160, and of in-patients 73, while 348 operations were performed. The total expenditure was Rs. 6,516, which was met by the State. The number of persons successfully vaccinated in 1901 was 860, or 1·71 per 1,000 of population.

Hadgaon.—Northern *tāluk* of Nānder District, Hyderābād State, with an area of 476 square miles. It is separated from the Bāsim District of Berār by the Pengangā river. The population in 1901, including *jāgīrs*, was 50,433, compared with 86,590 in 1891, the decrease being the result of the famine of 1900. Till recently it had 161 villages, of which 20 were *jāgīr*; and Hadgaon (population, 1,712) is the head-quarters. The land revenue in 1901 was 2 lakhs. The soils consist chiefly of *regar* and alluvium. In 1905 a number of villages were transferred to this *tāluk* from Nānder.

Mudhol Tāluk.—*Tāluk* in Nānder District, Hyderābād State, with an area of 335 square miles. In 1901 the population, including *jāgīrs*, was 57,024, compared with 64,124 in 1891, the decrease being due to the famine of 1900. Till recently it had 115 villages, of which 25 are *jāgīr*; and one town, MUDHOL (population, 6,040), the head-quarters. The land revenue in 1901 was 1·7 lakhs. The soil is mostly *regar*. Up to 1905 the *tāluk* formed part of Indūr (Nizāmābād) District; and on its transfer to Nānder District it was enlarged by the addition of the Bhaisa *tāluk* and part of Nānder.

Biloli.—South-eastern *tāluk* of Nānder District, Hyderābād State, with an area of 269 square miles. The population in 1901, including *jāgīrs*, was 54,925, compared with 56,170 in 1901, the decrease being due to the famine of 1900. The *tāluk* till recently contained 118 villages, of which 33 are *jāgīr*; and Biloli (population, 2,926) is the head-quarters. The Godāvari river flows north of it and the Mānjra to the east, the latter separating it from Nizāmābād District. The land revenue in 1901 was 1·6 lakhs. It is composed of alluvial and *regar* soils. In 1905 Biloli was enlarged by the addition of some villages from Osmānnagar.

Deglūr Tāluk.—Southern *tāluk* of Nānder District, Hyderābād State, with an area of 397 square miles. The population in 1901, including *jāgīrs*, was 77,834, compared with 79,793 in 1891, the decrease being due to the famine of 1900. The *tāluk* contained till recently one town, DEGLŪR (population, 6,917), the head-quarters; and 159 villages, of which 56 are *jāgīr*. The land revenue in 1901 was 2 lakhs. The Mānjra river forms the eastern and the Lendi the southern boundary. The soils are alluvial and *regar*, and partly sandy. The *paigāh tāluk* of Kharka, with a population of 27,612 and 67 villages, lies to the west, and has an area of about 265 square miles. In 1905 Deglūr was enlarged by the addition of part of the Bānswāda *tāluk* of Indūr (Nizāmābād) and some villages from Udgīr in Bīdar District.

Kandahār.—Western *tāluk* of Nānder District, Hyderābād State, with an area of 680 square miles. The population in 1901, including *jāgīrs*, was 97,728, compared with 128,525 in 1891, the decrease being due to the famine of 1900. Kandahār contained till recently one town, MUKHER (population, 6,148), the head-quarters; and 190 villages, of which 37 are *jāgīr*. The land revenue in 1901 was 2·5 lakhs. *Regar* forms its predominant soil. In 1905 the *tāluk* was enlarged by the addition of some villages from Osmānnagar.

Nānder Tāluk.—Western *tāluk* of Nānder District, Hyderābād State, with an area of 695 square miles. The population in 1901, including *jāgīrs*, was 102,015, compared with 131,040 in 1891, the decrease being due to the famine of 1900. Till recently the *tāluk* contained one town, NĀNDER (population, 14,184), the head-quarters of the District and *tāluk*; and 276 villages, of which 26 are *jāgīr*. The Godāvari flows south of Nānder from west to east. The land revenue in 1901 was 2·9 lakhs. The soils are chiefly alluvial and *regar*. In 1905 portions of this *tāluk* were transferred to Kalamnūri, Hadgaon, and Mudhol.

Osmānnagar.—A *tāluk* formerly in Nānder District, Hyderābād State, with an area of 290 square miles. The population in 1901, including *jāgīrs*, was 37,667, compared with 48,355 in 1891, the decrease being due to the famine of 1900. The land revenue in 1901 was 1·2 lakhs. In 1905 the *tāluk* was broken up, part being transferred to Biloli and part to Kandahār.

Bhaisa Tāluk.—A former *tāluk* in the east of Nānder District, Hyderābād State, incorporated in MUDHOL in 1905.

Bhaisa Town.—Former head-quarters of the *tāluk* of the same name, and now a town in the Mudhol *tāluk* of Nānder District, Hyderābād State, situated in 19° 7′ N. and 77° 58′ E., on the north bank of the Siddha river. Population (1901), 7,126. It contains the offices of the Second and Third Tālukdārs and of a police inspector, a Munsif's court, a post office, a dispensary, two schools, and a ginning factory.

A weekly bazar is held, at which a large business is done in cattle, grain, and cotton. In the town are situated an old Jāma Masjid and the shrines of three Musalmān saints.

Deglūr Town.—Head-quarters of the *tāluk* of the same name in Nānder District, Hyderābād State, situated in 18° 33′ N. and 77° 35′ E. Population (1901), 6,917. It contains the Second Tālukdār's and police inspector's offices, a post office, a police station, a school, and a dispensary. A weekly market is held, at which large quantities of grain are sold. The tomb of Shah Zia-ud-dīn Rifai is visited by many pilgrims at the annual *urs*, and an old temple stands near a tank.

Mudhol Town.—Head-quarters of the *tāluk* of the same name in Nānder District, Hyderābād State, situated in 18° 59′ N. and 77° 55′ E., 28 miles north-west-by-north of Nizāmābād. Population (1901), 6,040. Besides the *tahsīl* office, the town contains a post office, a police inspector's office, and a school with 120 pupils.

Mukher.—Head-quarters of the Kandahār *tāluk*, Nānder District, Hyderābād State, situated in 18° 42′ N. and 77° 22′ E. Population (1901), 6,148. It is a centre of the cotton trade and contains a ginning factory; brass and copper vessels are largely manufactured. Besides the *tāhsīl* office, it contains a Munsif's court, a police inspector's office, a dispensary, a post office, a school, and an old Hindu temple.

Nānder Town.—Head-quarters of the District and *tāluk* of the same name, Hyderābād State, situated in 19° 9′ N. and 77° 20′ E., on the left or north bank of the Godāvari, 174 miles from Hyderābād and 147 from Aurangābād. Population (1901), 14,184, of whom 653 are Sikhs. Nānder was the capital of Telingāna in the time of Shāh Jahān. The town contains the offices of the First Tālukdār, a *tahsīl* office and Sadr Munsif and Munsif's courts, police offices, two dispensaries, one of which is for treatment after the *yunāni* system, five schools, a State post office, and a British sub-post office. A weekly bazar is held, where a large business is done in cattle, grain, and cotton. Nānder is noted for its fine muslin and gold-bordered scarfs, used as turbans and *sāris*. In fineness the muslin resembles that of Dacca. On the banks of the Godāvari and adjoining the town is an old fort, now used as a jail, which is said to have been built by the Rājā of Kalam. There are several Hindu temples and two old mosques, besides a *sarai* built by Mīr Alam and the shrines of several Musalmān saints. Gurū Govind was murdered here by an Afghān in the reign of Shāh Alam Bahādur, and his shrine or *Gurūdwāra* is visited by Sikhs from all parts of India. Nānder station on the Hyderābād-Godāvari Valley Railway is situated about a mile north of the town.

Bhīr District (*Bīr*).—District in the Aurangābād Division, Hyderābād State, lying between 18° 28′ and 19° 27′ N. and 74° 54′ and 76° 57′ E., with a total area of 4,460 square miles. It is bounded on the west and north by the Bombay District of Ahmadnagar and Aurangābād; on the north-east by Parbhani; on the east by Nānder and Bīdar; and on the south by Osmānābād. The area of the *khālsa* and *Sarf-i-khās* ('crown') lands is 3,926 square miles, the rest being *jāgīr*. **Boundaries, configuration, and hill and river systems.**

The District is divided into two portions: the Bālāghāt or high lands forming the south and east, and the Pāyānghāt or low lands. The *tāluks* of Kaij, Amba, Bhīr, and Pātoda lie partly on the Bālāghāt, while the remaining *tāluks* are all situated in the low lands. A low spur of the Western Ghāts traverses the district from Ahmadnagar to Amba.

The largest river is the Godāvari, which forms the northern boundary, separating Bhīr from Aurangābād. Other streams which cross the District are the Mānjra, the Sindphana and its tributary the Bendsūra, and the Vijarta. The first two rise in the Pātoda *tāluk*, and are tributaries of the Godāvari.

The District is situated within the Deccan trap area. In the valleys of the Godāvari and some of its tributaries the trap is overlaid by gravels and clay beds of upper pliocene or pleistocene age, containing fossil bones of extinct mammalia. **Geology.**

Owing to the small extent of jungles large game is rare, though tigers are occasionally met with in some of the wooded hills. Antelope, hyenas, wild hog, wolves, bears, and leopards are common. **Fauna.**

The climate is generally healthy and temperate. Pātoda, on the Bālāghāt, is the highest part and is cool even in the hot season. The climate of Bhīr, Māzalgaon, and Gevrai, in the lowlands, is warm and humid. **Climate.**

The annual rainfall averages 30 inches. The amount received in 1899 (15 inches) and 1900 (20 inches) was exceedingly deficient, and resulted in the great famine of 1900. **Rainfall.**

According to tradition, Bhīr was called Durgāvati during the time of the Pāndavas and Kurūs, and its name was subsequently changed to Balni; but Champāvati, Vikramāditya's sister, after capturing it, called it Champāvatinagar. Nothing definite is known of its history; but it must have been included successively in the kingdoms of the Andhras, the Chālukyas, **History.**

the Rāshtrakūtas, and the Yādavas of Deogiri, from whom it passed to the Muhammadan kings of Delhi. About 1326 Muhammad bin Tughlak changed the name of Champāvatinagar to Bhīr. After the death of Muhammad bin Tughlak, the town fell successively to the Bahmani, the Nizām Shāhi, and the Adil Shāhi kingdoms. The Mughals eventually captured Bhīr in 1635, and annexed the country to Delhi; but it was again separated on the foundation of the Hyderābād State early in the eighteenth century.

Archaeology. The chief places of archaeological interest are the forts and buildings at BHĪR. At Dhārūr there is a fort built by the Ahmadnagar kings, and a mosque built in the Hindu style of architecture by one of Muhammad bin Tughlak's generals. AMBA contains a temple dedicated to Jogai. The temple of Baijnāth at Parli is a celebrated place of Hindu pilgrimage.

Population. The number of towns and villages, including *jāgīrs*, is 1,004. The population at each Census was: (1881) 558,345, (1891) 642,722, and (1901) 492,258, the decrease during the last decade being due to the famine of 1899-1900. The towns are BHĪR, AMBA, PARLI, and MĀZALGAON. More than 90 per cent. of the population are Hindus, and 87 per cent. speak Marāthī. The following table shows the chief statistics of population in 1901:—

Tāluk.	Area in square miles.	Number of Towns.	Number of Villages.	Population.	Population per square mile.	Percentage of variation in population between 1891 and 1901.	Number of persons able to read and write.
Bhīr	801	1	155	71,608	89	− 27.3	Not available.
Gevrai	456	...	119	50,672	111	− 28.1	
Māzalgaon	622	1	172	96,929	156	− 7.9	
Amba	667	2	114	72,017	108	− 25.0	
Kaij	445	...	104	46,560	104	− 34.4	
Ashti	594	...	122	51,999	88	− 22.7	
Pātoda	341	...	71	29,116	85	− 28.7	
Jāgīrs, &c.	534	...	143	73,357	137	− 24.9	
Total	4,460	4	1,000	492,258	110	− 23.4	14,852

In 1905 the Kaij *tāluk* was amalgamated with Amba, the latter name being retained.

Castes and occupations. The most numerous caste is the Marāthā Kunbī, numbering 196,000, or more than 39 per cent. of the total population. Other important agricultural castes are the Banjārās (36,400) and Kolīs (2,600). Next in point of numbers are the Mahārs or village menials (41,300), the Dhangars or shepherds (26,000), the Māngs and Chamārs or leather-workers (25,400), the Brāhmans (21,600), and the Mālīs or gardeners (12,700). Of the trading castes, Vānīs number 6,960 and Mārwāris 6,100. The population directly supported by agriculture is 265,200, or 54 per cent. of the total. Christians numbered 91 in 1901, of whom 75 were natives.

General agricultural conditions.

The entire District is situated in the trap region, and its soils are mostly the fertile *regar* or black cotton soil, especially in the *tāluks* of Bhīr, Gevrai, Māzalgaon, and Kaij; in the remaining *tāluks masab* and *kharab* soils are interspersed with *regar*. The *rabi* or cold-season crops, such as cotton, white *jowār*, gram, gingelly, and wheat, are grown on *regar*; the *kharīf* or rainy season crops, such as *bājra* and cotton, are sown on the *masab*, and yellow *jowār*, *bājra*, pulses, and oilseeds on the *kharab* or *chalka* lands. Cotton and linseed are produced very largely in the District.

Chief agricultural statistics and principal crops.

The tenure of lands is mainly *ryotwāri*. In 1901 the *khālsa* area and 'crown' lands occupied 3,926 square miles, of which 2,430 were cultivated, 614 were cultivable waste and fallows, and 882 were not available for cultivation. By 1903 the cultivated area had risen to 3,044 square miles. The staple food-crops are *jowār* and *bājra*, grown on 23 and 14 per cent. of the net area cropped. Wheat and rice are next in importance, the area under these being 53 and 98 square miles. Cotton, which is grown in all the *tāluks*, occupied as much as 318 square miles, and oilseeds 118 square miles.

Improvements in agricultural practice.

Since the last settlement, in 1883, all the available land has been taken up, and no extension of the holdings is possible, though the last famine caused a great decrease in the cultivated area, owing to the mortality among the agricultural classes. The ryots have shown no inclination to introduce new varieties of seed or improved agricultural implements.

Cattle, &c.

No particular breed of cattle is characteristic of the District; but the bullocks are strong animals, suitable for ploughing the heavy *regar*. Sheep and goats are of the ordinary kind. Ponies of very fair breed are obtainable for from Rs. 50 to Rs. 75; horses and ponies from Arab sires are of a better class, and fetch from Rs. 100 to Rs. 400 per head. At all the *tāluk* head-quarters stallions are maintained for the purpose of improving the local breed of horses, and the ryots have not been slow to avail themselves of the advantages thus held out.

Irrigation.

The irrigated area is only 86 square miles, supplied by 8,537 wells in good repair. Rivers are utilized to a very small extent, as their beds are too low to allow of water being largely used for irrigation. Three miles west of Bhīr is a large well, called the *Khazāna baoli*, a wonderful work of engineering, which was constructed about 1582 by the *jāgīrdār* of Bhīr. It irrigates 529 acres by means of channels.

Minerals. No minerals of any economic value are found in the District. Granite, basalt, and nodular limestone occur everywhere and are used for building.

Arts and manufactures. Hand industries are of little importance. *Chhāgals*, or leathern water-bottles, and sword-sticks of superior quality are made. Coarse cloth and *sārīs*, of both cotton and silk, are manufactured; but, owing to the cheapness of imported articles, the manufacture is declining. Ordinary black blankets are made by the Dhangars and sold for Rs. 2 or Rs. 3 each. There are two ginning mills, one at Parli in the Amba *tāluk* and the other at Varoni in Māzalgaon. In 1901 the former employed 50 hands, but work in the latter was stopped owing to the famine of 1900.

Commerce. The principal exports are *jowār*, wheat, other cereals and pulses, cotton, linseed, sheep, bones, and jaggery. The chief imports are salt, opium, sugar, gold and silver, copper and brass, iron, kerosene oil, silk, cotton, and woollen cloth.

The most important centres of trade are BHĪR, MĀZALGAON, PARLI, and GEVRAI, where a large business is done in cotton and food-grains. Articles imported from Jālna and Bārsi are distributed from these centres to distant parts of the District, where they are sold at weekly markets.

Roads. There are no railways in the District. The total length of roads is 280 miles. The principal roads are: Bhīr to Bārsi, 24 miles; Amba to Parli, 15 miles; and the Ahmadnagar-Jāmkhed road, 27 miles. Only the last is metalled. Besides these, there are fair-weather roads from Bhīr to Satāra (28), to Ashti (26), to Māzalgaon (50), to Gevrai (27), and the Amba road (47 miles), all of which were made during the famine of 1900.

Famine. In 1899 the rainfall was less than half the average (15 inches), and the District was one of the most seriously affected in the famine area. Both the *kharīf* and *rabi* crops failed, and at one time about one-seventh of the total population were on relief. At this time cholera made its appearance, and the Census of 1901 showed a decrease in the population of 150,464 persons. The cultivators lost 32 per cent. of their cattle, and the total cost of the famine to the State exceeded 12 lakhs.

District subdivisions and staff. The District is divided into three subdivisions: one comprising the *tāluks* of Amba and Māzalgaon, under a Second Tālukdār; and another comprising the *tāluks* of Gevrai,

Pātoda, and Ashti, under a Third Tālukdār; while the *tāluk* of Bhīr is under the direct control of the First Tālukdār, who also exercises general supervision over the work of his subordinates. Each *tāluk* is under a *tahsīldār*.

Civil and criminal justice.

The *Nāzim-i-Dīwāni* or Civil Judge is also a joint-magistrate, and exercises powers as such in the absence of the First Tālukdār from head-quarters. There are three subordinate civil courts, each under a Munsif. The First Tālukdār is the chief magistrate, while the Second and Third Tālukdārs and the *tahsīldārs* exercise second and third-class magisterial powers. There is very little serious crime in the District.

Land revenue.

It appears that in early times revenue was assessed by holdings. This system continued to the time of Malik Ambar, who measured the land and fixed the state dues at one-third the produce, which was subsequently commuted to cash payments. He dealt directly with the ryots and gave them a proprietary right in the land they tilled. In 1866 Districts were formed and the revenue was revised. In 1883 Bhīr District was formally settled. The survey then carried out showed an excess of 178,815 acres, or 11 per cent. over the area returned in the accounts, while the revenue was enhanced by 1·5 lakhs, or 13 per cent. The average assessment on 'dry' land is Rs. 1–8 (maximum Rs. 1–14, minimum R. 1), and on 'wet' land Rs. 5 (maximum Rs. 6, minimum Rs. 4).

The land revenue and the total revenue for a series of years are shown below, in thousands of rupees:—

	1881.	1891.	1901.	1903.
Land revenue . .	11,31	12,84	13,38	13,42
Total revenue . .	11,67	13,36	14,44	14,17

Local and municipal government.

In 1888 the one anna cess was first levied to meet local requirements, five-twelfths being set apart for municipal and local works. *Tāluk* boards were formed at each *tāluk* head-quarters with the *tahsīldārs* as chairmen, except at Bhīr, where a District board was established under the presidency of the First Tālukdār, which supervises the working of the *tāluk* boards and also of the municipality of Bhīr.

Police and jails.

The First Tālukdār is the head of the police, with the Superintendent (*Mohtamim*) as his executive deputy. Under him are 8 inspectors, 69 subordinate officers, 510 constables, and 25 mounted police, distributed in 20 police stations and 15 outposts. There is a jail at Bhīr town with accommodation for 200 prisoners, but convicts with sentences exceeding six months are sent to the Central jail at Aurangābād. A lock-up is maintained at each *tahsīl* office.

Education. In 1901 the proportion of persons able to read and write was 3 per cent. (5·9 males and 0·05 females). The number of pupils under instruction in 1881, 1891, 1901, and 1903 was 436, 2,000, 3,247, and 3,383 respectively. In 1903 there were 3 middle and 54 primary schools, with 44 girls under instruction. The first State school was opened in 1866, and Local fund schools date from 1888. The total expenditure on education in 1901 was Rs. 23,500, of which Rs. 10,600 was contributed by the State and the remainder by local boards. The receipts from fees amounted to Rs. 2,211.

Medical. The District contains one hospital and two dispensaries, with accommodation for 11 in-patients. The total number of cases treated in 1901 was 17,663, of whom 90 were in-patients, and 512 operations were performed. The expenditure amounted to Rs. 11,000, of which Rs. 1,272 was paid from Local funds and the remainder by the State. The total number of persons successfully vaccinated in 1901 was 2,083, or 4·3 per 1,000 of population.

Bhīr Tāluk.—Central *tāluk* of Bhīr District, Hyderābād State, with an area of 870 square miles. The population in 1901, including *jāgīrs*, was 88,160, compared with 121,262 in 1891, the decrease being due to the famines of 1897 and 1899–1900. The *tāluk* contains one town, BHĪR (population, 17,671), the head-quarters of the District and *tāluk*; and 172 villages, of which 17 are *jāgīr*. The land revenue in 1901 was 2·4 lakhs. The *tāluk* is situated partly on the plateau and partly on the plain, and is composed of black cotton soil.

Gevrai.—Northern *tāluk* of Bhīr District, Hyderābād State, with an area of 506 square miles. The population in 1901, including *jāgīrs*, was 58,361, compared with 81,119 in 1891, the decrease being due to the famines of 1897 and 1899–1900. The *tāluk* has 135 villages, of which 16 are *jāgīr*; and Gevrai (population, 3,965) is the head-quarters. The land revenue in 1901 was 2·3 lakhs. The Godāvari in the north separates the *tāluk* from Aurangābād District.

Māzalgaon Tāluk.—North-eastern *tāluk* of Bhīr District, Hyderābād State, with an area of 775 square miles. The population in 1901, including *jāgīrs*, was 122,135, compared with 132,658 in 1891, the decrease being due to the famines of 1897 and 1899–1900. The *tāluk* contains one town, MĀZALGAON (population, 5,698), the head-quarters; and 223 villages, of which 51 are *jāgīr*. The land revenue in 1901 was 3 lakhs. The country is very fertile, being composed of black cotton soil. The Godāvari flows through the northern portion.

Amba Tāluk.—South-eastern *tāluk* of Bhīr District, Hyderābād State, with an area of 1,342 square miles. The population in 1901, including *jāgīrs*, was 139,399, compared with 195,539 in 1891, the decrease being due to the famines of 1897 and 1899–1900. These figures include the former *tāluk* of Kaij, which was amalgamated with Amba in 1905, and had a population of 50,543 and an area of 485 square miles in 1901. The *tāluk* contains two towns, AMBA (population, 12,628), the head-quarters, adjoining the cantonment of Mominābād, and PĀRLI (7,289); and 369 villages of which 51 are *jāgīr*. The land revenue in 1901 was 3·8 lakhs. Amba is hilly in the north, and the Mānjra river separates it on the south from Osmānābād District.

Ashti.—South-western *tāluk* of Bhīr District, Hyderābād State, with an area of 614 square miles. The population in 1901, including *jāgīrs*, was 54,181, compared with 70,059 in 1891, the decrease being due to the famines of 1897 and 1899–1900. The *tāluk* contains 127 villages, of which five are *jāgīr*; and Ashti (population, 4,019) is the head-quarters. The land revenue in 1901 was 1·9 lakhs. The *tāluk* adjoins the Ahmadnagar District of Bombay.

Pātoda.—'Crown' *tāluk* in the south-west of Bhīr District, Hyderābād State, with an area of 353 square miles. The population in 1901, including *jāgīrs*, was 30,022, compared with 42,085 in 1891, the decrease being due to the famines of 1897 and 1899–1900. The *tāluk* contains 74 villages, of which 3 are *jāgīr*; and Pātoda (population, 3,179) is the headquarters. The land revenue in 1901 was 1·1 lakhs. The Mānjra river rises in the hills west of Pātoda. The *tāluk* is situated on a fertile plateau, and is hilly toward the north and west.

Amba Town (or Mominābād).—Head-quarters of the Amba *tāluk* in Bhīr District, Hyderābād State, situated in 18° 41′ N. and 76° 24′ E. Population (1901), 12,628, of whom 8,584 were Hindus, 3,477 Musalmāns, and 25 Christians. The town consists of two portions, separated by the Jivanti river. That part which lies south-west of the river is called Mominābād, and up to 1903 was a cantonment. The Pancham Jainas of Amba are said to be the descendants of a feudatory of the Chālukyas, and are now represented by the Pancham Lingāyats. In one of the bastions of the town is an old temple, built during the reign of Singhana, the Yādava king of Deogiri, and containing an inscription dated in 1240. A number of ruined cave-temples, both Brāhmanical and Jain, are situated in the vicinity. The most important is the temple of Jogai, on the bank of the Jivanti, which consists of a small pavilion in the middle of a courtyard, and a great hall 90 feet by 45, cut in the rock, and supported by four rows of pillars. The town contains a post office and three schools, and is the head-quarters of the Second Tālukdār. It is a flourishing trade centre.

[*Archaeological Survey Reports, Western India*, vol. iii, p. 49.]

Bhīr Town.—Head-quarters of Bhīr District, Hyderābād State, situated in 18° 59′ N. and 75° 46′ E., on the Bendsūra river. Population (1901), 17,671, of whom 12,307 were Hindus, 4,993 Musalmāns, and 68 Christians. Prior to the Muhammadan invasion it belonged to the Chālukyas and subsequently to the Yādavas of Deogiri; but it was taken by Muhammad bin Tughlak, and became the head-quarters of one of his Deccan provinces. Muhammad bin Tughlak's tooth is buried in a tomb near the town. Early in Shāh Jahān's reign several battles were fought near this place between the imperial troops and those of Bijāpur and Ahmadnagar. Bhīr is noted for several kinds of leathern work, especially water-bottles called *chhāgals*, and also for sword-sticks.

Māzalgaon Town.—Head-quarters of the *tāluk* of the same name in Bhīr District, Hyderābād State, situated in 19° 9′ N. and 76° 13′ E., on the left bank of the Sindphana, a tributary of the Godāvari. Population (1901), 5,698. It is a rising town, the principal trade being in grain, while indigo was once largely dealt in.

Parli.—Town in the Amba *tāluk* of Bhīr District, Hyderābād State, situated in 18° 51′ N. and 76° 33′ E., 14 miles north-east of Amba, at the foot of the spur of hills passing through the *tāluk*. Population (1901), 7,289. The temple of Baijnāth, built on a hill to the west of the town, is an important place of pilgrimage. Parli is a centre of the cotton trade, and contains a ginning-mill employing 50 hands.

GULBARGA DIVISION

Gulbarga Division.—Division in the south-western corner of Hyderābād State, also known as the Southern Division. It lies between 15° 11′ and 18° 40′ N. and 75° 16′ and 77° 51′ E., and is bounded on the west and south by the Bombay and Madras Presidencies respectively. The head-quarters of the *Sūbahdār* or Commissioner are at GULBARGA CITY. The total population of the Division rose from 1,946,737 in 1881 to 2,430,999 in 1891, and 2,462,834 in 1901. The area in the latest year was 16,585 square miles, and the density of population 149 persons per square mile, as compared with 135 for the whole State. In 1901 Hindus formed 88 per cent. and Musalmāns 11 per cent. of the total population, while other religions included Jains (6,163), Christians (1,059, of whom 903 were natives), Pārsīs (152), Sikhs (64), and Animists (209).

In 1901 the Division included the four Districts of Gulbarga, Lingsugūr, Osmānābād, and Raichūr. Considerable changes have been made under the reconstitution of 1905. Lingsugūr District has been divided between Gulbarga and Raichūr, and the Yādgīr *tāluk* has been transferred from Raichūr to Gulbarga. Bīdar District has been added to the Division, which is now constituted as follows:—

District.	Area in square miles.	Population, 1901.	Land revenue and cesses, 1901, in thousands of rupees.
Gulbarga . . .	6,004	1,041,067	18,36
Osmānābād . .	4,010	535,027	12,51
Raichūr . . .	6,879	932,090	19,18
Bīdar . . .	4,168	766,129	11,63
Total	21,061	3,274,313	61,68

The Division contains 32 towns, or about two-fifths of the total number in the State, and 5,652 villages. The largest towns are GULBARGA CITY (population, 29,228) and RAICHŪR (22,165). The chief places of commercial importance are Gulbarga, Raichūr, OSMĀNĀBĀD, LĀTŪR, LINGSUGŪR, TULJĀPUR, BĪDAR, and HOMNĀBĀD. Gulbarga, Raichūr, Bīdar, KALYANI, UDGĪR, PARENDA, MUDGAL, Sūrāpur, Kohir, and

ANEGUNDI are famous for their historical or archaeological associations.

Boundaries, configuration, and hill and river systems.

Gulbarga District[1].—District in the Gulbarga Division, Hyderābād State, adjoining Osmānābād and Bīdar on the north; Atrāt-i-balda and Mahbūbnagar on the east; Mahbūbnagar, Raichūr, and Lingsugūr on the south; and part of Osmānābād and the District of Bijāpur and the Akalkot State of Bombay on the west. It lies between 16° 40′ and 17° 44′ N. and 76° 22′ and 78° 20′ E., and had a total area of 4,092 square miles in 1901, including *paigāh* and *jāgīrs*; while the area of the *khālsa* and *Sarf-i-khās* lands was 2,428 square miles.

A range of hills enters the north of the District from Osmānābād on the west, and continues in a south-easterly direction for about 60 miles through the Mahāgaon and Chincholi *tāluks*, which are hilly. The remaining *tāluks* are almost flat, the slope of the country being from north to south and south-east.

The principal river is the Bhīma, a tributary of the Kistna, which rises near Poona in British territory, and, entering the District near Afzalpur in the west, traverses the *tāluks* of Gulbarga and Andola for a distance of 150 miles. The other rivers are the Kāgnā, and its tributaries the Benithora, Mullāmāri, and Kāmāluti. The Kāgnā is itself a tributary of the Bhīma, as is also the Awarja.

Geology.

The geological formations are the Archaean gneiss eastward, the Bhīma series about the centre, and the Deccan trap in the north and west. The region has been fully described by Mr. R. B. Foote (*Memoirs, Geological Survey of India*, vol. xii, pt. i).

Botany.

Generally speaking, the District is devoid of forests, except in the hilly portions of the Mahāgaon and Chincholi *tāluks*, which contain teak (*Tectona grandis*), *eppa* (*Hardwickia binata*), *tirman* (*Anogeissus latifolia*), *sandra* (*Acacia Catechu*), *babūl* (*Acacia arabica*), *tarvar* (*Cassia auriculata*) *bījāsāl* (*Pterocarpus Marsupium*), *mallāmaddi* (*Terminalia tomentosa*), *nīm*, tamarind, mango, and several species of fig.

Fauna.

In the hills and jungles in the northern portion of the District tigers, leopards, bears, *nīlgai*, and wild hog are found; and in the plains, hares and antelope.

Climate.

The climate differs materially in the several geological divisions. The Carnatic or trappean portion is hot and dry during the summer, whereas the Telingāna or granitic portion, which

[1] For the alterations made in 1905 see section on Population. Except where otherwise stated, the article describes the District as it stood before these were effected.

has wooded hills and tanks, is damp, and not so hot in the dry season. Fever prevails from July to October, and during recent years plague has been prevalent in some *tāluks*.

The rainfall is very capricious, causing occasional droughts. Its average amount for the twenty-one years ending 1901 was 29 inches. The great famine of 1900 was the result of the abnormally scanty rainfall (14·7 inches) of 1899. **Rainfall.**

Prior to the Muhammadan conquest the District was included in the territory of the Kākatīyas of Warangal. In the early part of the fourteenth century Ulūgh Khān, afterwards Muhammad bin Tughlak, annexed it to the kingdom of Delhi, since which time it has continued under Muhammadan rule. After the death of Muhammad bin Tughlak it fell to the Bahmani kingdom, and, after the break-up of that power, to Bijāpur. On the conquest of the Deccan by Aurangzeb it was again included in the empire of Delhi, but was separated from it on the establishment of the Hyderābād State by Asaf Jāh. **History.**

The fort of Gulbarga, originally built by Rājā Gulchand, and afterwards strengthened by Alā-ud-dīn Bahmani, is a remarkable building, containing 15 towers and 26 guns, one of which is 25 feet long. A large mosque, 216 by 176 feet, in the fort, is constructed on the model of the mosque of Cordova in Spain, and is the only one of its kind in India. In the eastern quarter of the city are the tombs of the Bahmani kings, huge square buildings surmounted by domes. Near the tomb of Khwāja Banda Nawāz are a mosque, a *sarai*, and a college, all built by Aurangzeb in 1687. The forts of Fīrozābād, on the Bhīma river, and of Chincholi and Chitāpur are worthy of note, especially the last, where the Portuguese from Goa constructed a curious church, which has now been renovated. **Archaeology.**

The number of towns and villages, including *paigāh* and *jāgīrs*, is 1,109. The population at the last three enumerations was: (1881) 523,838, (1891) 649,258, and (1901) 742,745. The towns now are GULBARGA, ALAND, SŪRĀPUR, KOSGI, YĀDGĪR, SERAM, SHĀHĀBĀD, and KODANGAL. About 81 per cent. of the population in 1901 were Hindus and 15 per cent. Musalmāns. Though the District is in the Carnatic division, Kanarese is spoken by only 53 per cent. of the population, Telugu being the language of 25, Urdū of 14, and Marāthī of 6 per cent. The table on the next page exhibits the details of area, towns, villages, and population, according to the Census of 1901. **Population.**

In 1905 the Gurmatkāl and Mahāgaon *tāluks* were divided

between Seram, Kodangal, Gulbarga, and Yādgīr, the last being transferred from Raichūr District. Shāhpur and Sūrāpur have also been added from the recently abolished Lingsugūr District, besides 73 villages from Mahbūbnagar District, included in the Kodangal and Yādgīr *tāluks*. In its present form, the District consists of eight *tāluks*—GULBARGA, ANDOLA, CHINCHOLI, KODANGAL, SERAM, YĀDGĪR, SHĀHPUR, and SŪRĀPUR; five *paigāh ilākās*, Aland, Fīrozābād, Afzalpur, Kālgi, and Chītāpur; and two *jāgīrs*, Tāndūr and Kosgi. The area of *paigāh* and *jāgīrs* is approximately 976 square miles, and the population 253,349.

Tāluk.	Area in square miles.	Number of Towns.	Number of Villages.	Population.	Population per square mile.	Percentage of variation in population between 1891 and 1901.	Number of persons able to read and write.
Gulbarga	524	1	108	75,512	144	− 11.0	Not available.
Mahāgaon	307	...	81	43,090	140	− 3.6	
Chincholi	277	...	69	37,671	136	+ 16.0	
Kodangal	141	1	60	31,182	221	− 8.7	
Seram	267	1	72	50,043	187	+ 52.2	
Gurmatkāl	304	...	86	51,424	169	+ 8.5	
Andola	608	...	117	73,854	121	+ 24.1	
Jāgīrs, &c.	1,664	4	509	379,969	228	+ 11.1	
District total	4,092	7	1,102	742,745	181	+ 14.4	14,880

Castes and occupations. The most numerous agricultural caste is that of the Kunbīs (231,000), of whom 81,000 are Lingāyat or Banjārā Kāpus and 77,500 Kolīs. Next in point of numbers are the Mahārs or village menials (67,600), the Māngs or leather-workers (39,100), the Vānīs or trading caste (30,000), and the Brāhmans (18,000). The Mahārs and Māngs also work as field-labourers. The number directly engaged in agriculture in 1901 was 432,814, or 58 per cent. of the total population.

Christian missions. An American Methodist mission was established at Gulbarga in 1883, with a branch at Karni. A school connected with it has 200 pupils. The District contained 187 native Christians in 1901, of whom 113 were Roman Catholics and 62 Protestants.

General agricultural conditions. Gulbarga falls into two natural divisions, the Carnatic and the Telingāna. In the former *regar* or black cotton soil predominates, which is interspersed with *masab* or *chalka*; in the latter *masab* and *kharab* or sandy soils predominate, though *regar* is not wanting. In the Carnatic portion *rabi* crops, such as white *jowār*, wheat, gram, cotton, and linseed, are extensively grown, while in the latter yellow *jowār*, *bājra*, castor-seed, rice, linseed, and hemp are the common *kharīf* crops. In the two Telingāna *tāluks* of Kodangal and Gurmatkāl rice is largely raised with tank-irrigation. The soils of Chincholi and Mahāgaon are lateritic, and rank next to the *regar* in fertility.

Chief agricultural statistics and principal crops.

The tenure of lands is mainly *ryotwāri*. In 1901, out of an area of 2,428 square miles of *khālsa*, 'crown' lands, and *ināms*, 1,955 were cultivated, 43 being irrigated; 138 square miles were cultivable waste and fallows, 126 were occupied by forests, and 209 were not available for cultivation. The staple food-crop is *jowār*, covering 64 per cent. of the net area cropped. *Bājra*, rice, and wheat come next in importance, the area under each being 206, 32, and 22 square miles. Cotton and oilseeds were grown on 50 and 103 square miles.

On the completion of the settlement of the District in 1893, the whole of the available lands were taken up by the ryots, hence no extension of holdings has been possible. The cultivators have shown no disposition to adopt improved agricultural implements or new varieties of seed.

Cattle, &c.

There is no particular breed of cattle, but those ordinarily reared are strong and suitable for ploughing the stiff *regar* and heavy loamy soils. Sheep and goats are of the ordinary type. Ponies are to be had everywhere for from Rs. 25 to Rs. 30, but those of the Andola *tāluk* command as much as Rs. 100. Two Arab stallions are kept by the State at Gulbarga and Kodangal for the purpose of improving the breed of horses.

Irrigation.

The total area of irrigated land in 1900–1 was 43 square miles, or about 2·2 per cent. of the cultivated area. The different sources of irrigation and the areas under each are as follows: canals and channels 4·5 square miles, and tanks and wells 38·5. Kodangal and Gurmatkāl are the only *tāluks* where tank-irrigation is carried on. There are altogether 107 large and 119 small tanks, 5,255 wells, and 196 other sources of irrigation, such as anicuts and channels, all in good repair.

Forests.

In the Chincholi *tāluk* 51 square miles of land were formed into a 'reserved' forest in 1896, which contains teak and other valuable timber. The *tāluks* of Seram, Kodangal, Gurmatkāl, and Mahāgaon also contain some scrubby jungle and open forests. The total area of protected and unprotected forests is 126 square miles.

Minerals.

The most important mineral found and worked extensively in the District is laminated limestone, which occurs at Shāhābād on the Great Indian Peninsula Railway, Chītāpur on the

Nizām's Guaranteed State Railway, and also in the Gulbarga and Seram *tāluks*. The stone is known as 'Shāhābād stone,' from the name of the place where it was first quarried, and is largely employed in roofing and flooring.

Arts and manufactures. Among hand industries are the weaving of cotton and silk *sārīs* and cloth of gold, ordinary cotton cloth, and cotton tweeds. In the Andola and Chincholi *tāluks* the shepherds make blankets of very superior quality valued at from Rs. 10 to Rs. 50, which are durable and waterproof. A large spinning and weaving mill, 2 miles west of Gulbarga, began working in 1886, with a capital of 12 lakhs. It contains 21,036 spindles and 224 looms, and gives occupation to 970 persons. There is one ginning factory in the Seram *tāluk*.

Commerce. The exports consist of *jowār*, *bājra*, and other cereals and pulses, hides, cotton, jaggery, oilseeds, tobacco, and *tarvar* bark used in tanning. The chief imports are salt, salted fish, opium, spices, gold and silver, refined sugar, sulphur, yarn, raw silk, iron, brass, cotton and woollen stuffs, matches, kerosene oil, and hardware. The city of Gulbarga is the chief centre of trade, to which everything is brought by the Great Indian Peninsula Railway, and thence distributed to all parts of the District. The other centres are Tāndūr and Sulhpet. The trading castes are Lingāyat Vānīs and Komatis, besides Momins, Mārwāris, and Bhātias. The Bhātias, who come from Bombay, are engaged in the export of grain and oilseeds.

Railways. The Great Indian Peninsula Railway line enters the District at Dudneh in the west and leaves it near Wādi junction, with a length of 50 miles. The Nizām's Guaranteed State Railway, starting from Wādi junction, runs north-east and east for 115 miles.

Roads. The total length of roads is only 79 miles. These run from Gulbarga to Homnābād (37½ miles), Tāndūr station to Kosgi (26 miles), Nāwandgi station to Dichkanpalli (11½ miles), and the Malkhaid road (4 miles).

Famine. Altogether eight famines were recorded during the last century, in 1804, 1819, 1833, 1854, 1873, 1877-8, 1897, and 1899-1900. The famine of 1804 was partly due to struggles with the Marāthās, and partly to excessive rain, which prevented sowings; and that of 1873 was caused by the influx of people from the adjoining famine-stricken districts; all the others were the result of local drought and the failure of crops. The rainfall in 1899 was less than half the average, causing the failure of both the *kharīf* and *rabi* crops, which resulted in the famine of 1900. The distress was intense, and relief measures were carried out at a cost to the State of $3\frac{3}{4}$ lakhs. The loss of cattle was computed at 28 per cent.

District subdivisions and staff.

The District is divided into three subdivisions: the first comprising the *tāluks* of Seram, Kodangal, and Yādgīr, under a Second Tālukdār; the second comprising the *tāluks* of Chincholi and Gulbarga, under a Third Tālukdār; and the third comprising the *tāluks* of Andola, Shāhpur, and Sūrāpur, under the head-quarters Second Tālukdār. There is a *tahsīldār* in each *tāluk*.

Civil and criminal justice.

The District civil court is under a Judge called the *Nāzim-i-Dīwāni*, and each *tahsīldār* sits as a subordinate civil court. The First Tālukdār is the chief magistrate of the District, and the *Nāzim-i-Dīwāni* is a joint-magistrate, who exercises magisterial powers during the absence of the First Tālukdār from head-quarters. The Second and Third Tālukdārs and the *tahsīldārs* exercise second and third-class magisterial powers. As Gulbarga city is the head-quarters of the Division, the *Sūbahdār* and the *Nāzim-i-Sūbah* or Divisional Civil and Criminal Judge also hold their courts there. Serious crime in ordinary years is light, but cattle-thefts and dacoities increase in adverse seasons.

Land revenue.

The District was formed in 1873, and then consisted of only six *tāluks*; but on the breaking up of Sūrāpur District in 1883 the Andola *tāluk* was transferred to Gulbarga. Prior to 1866, *tāluks* were made over to revenue farmers who received 10 per cent. on the collections; but in 1866 regular officials were appointed for revenue and judicial work. The first regular settlement was completed in 1893 and the assessment was fixed for fifteen years, resulting in an increase of Rs. 1,76,970, or nearly 18 per cent. The average assessment on 'dry' land is Rs. 1-2 (maximum Rs. 2-2, minimum R. 1), and on 'wet' land Rs. 11 (maximum Rs. 14, minimum Rs. 5).

The land revenue and the total revenue of the District are shown below, in thousands of rupees:—

	1881.	1891.	1901.	1903.
Land revenue . .	7,49	11,32	11,77	11,27
Total revenue . .	13,92	21,82	23,84	25,67

Owing to the changes in area effected in 1905, the land revenue demand is now about 17·4 lakhs.

Local and municipal government.

The levy of a local cess of one anna in the rupee on land revenue was commenced from 1890, five-twelfths of the total being set apart for roads and public purposes. Boards were constituted for every *tāluk*, except Gulbarga, where a District board was formed, which supervises the working of the *tāluk* boards and municipalities of Gulbarga and all *tāluk* head-quarters. The total income in 1901 was Rs. 66,300, and the expenditure Rs. 48,600.

Police and jails. The First Tālukdār is the head of the District police, the *Mohtamim* or Superintendent being his executive deputy. Under him are an assistant, 9 inspectors, 96 subordinate officers, 600 constables, and 30 mounted police, distributed among 34 *thānas*. The Central jail at Gulbarga is capable of accommodating 1,000 prisoners. Convicts with sentences exceeding six months from Osmānābād, Raichūr, and Lingsugūr are sent here. The six outlying *tāluk* offices have lock-ups for temporary confinement. The prisoners in the Central jail are taught various industries; and carpets, *shatranjīs*, counterpanes, towels of sorts, cotton tweeds and other cloths, tents, and furniture of all descriptions are made, most of which are sold locally.

Education. Gulbarga District takes a low place as regards the literacy of its population, of whom only 2 per cent. (3·8 males and 0·11 females) could read and write in 1901. The first State school was opened in 1866, and local board schools were established in 1890. The total number of pupils under instruction in 1881, 1891, 1901, and 1903 was 323, 2,130, 3,600, and 3,317 respectively. In 1903 there were 43 primary schools, one middle, and one high school, 273 girls being under instruction in that year. The total amount expended on education in 1901 was Rs. 26,750, of which 52 per cent. was devoted to primary schools.

Medical. The District possesses one hospital and four dispensaries, with accommodation for 24 in-patients. In 1901 the total number of cases treated in all these institutions was 34,438, of whom 204 were in-patients. The number of operations performed was 652. The total expenditure was Rs. 15,580, of which Rs. 12,555 was contributed by the State and Rs. 3,025 from the local cess. Besides these, there is a *yunāni* dispensary in Gulbarga city, at which the total number of patients treated in 1901 was 24,295. The expenditure was Rs. 2,088, met wholly from the local cess.

The number of persons successfully vaccinated in 1900–1 was 1,766, or 2·37 per 1,000 of the population. Compared with previous years, the proportion has risen.

Gulbarga Tāluk.—Central *tāluk* of Gulbarga District, Hyderābād State. In 1901 the area was 674 square miles, and the population 103,051; including *jāgīrs*. The population in 1891 had been 115,699, the decrease being due to plague. The *tāluk* contains GULBARGA CITY (population, 29,228), the head-quarters of the Division, District, and *tāluk*; and 145 villages, of which 37 are *jāgīr*. The land revenue in 1901 was 2·8 lakhs. In 1905 the Mahāgaon *tāluk* was merged in Gulbarga. The Great Indian Peninsula Railway passes through the *tāluk*, which is composed of black cotton soil. The two *paigāh ilākās* of Afzalpur and Kālgi, with populations of 34,909 and 30,610, and 47 and 43 villages respectively, lie to the west and east of Gulbarga. Their areas are about 151 and 136 square miles.

Mahāgaon.—Former *tāluk* in the north of Gulbarga District, Hyderābād State. The population, including *jāgīrs*, was 61,179 in 1901, and the area 379 square miles, the population having decreased from 63,438 in 1891. It contained 104 villages, of which 23 were *jāgīr*; and Mahāgaon (population, 3,155) was the head-quarters. The land revenue in 1901 was 1·4 lakhs. In 1905 the *tāluk* was merged in the Gulbarga *tāluk*. The *paigāh tāluk* of Aland is situated to the north-west, with 74 villages and a population of 84,795. It contains one town, ALAND (population, 10,130), the head-quarters, and has an area of about 245 square miles.

Chincholi.—North-eastern *tāluk* of Gulbarga District, Hyderābād State, with an area of 413 square miles. The population in 1901 was 58,860, compared with 50,737 in 1891. Chincholi (population, 4,008) is the head-quarters; and the *tāluk* contains 110 villages, of which 41 are *jāgīr*. The land revenue in 1901 was 1·5 lakhs. Chincholi is hilly, and composed of lateritic and black cotton soils. In the rearrangement of 1905 the *tāluk* received a few villages from Kodangal.

Kodangal Tāluk.—Eastern *tāluk* of Gulbarga District, Hyderābād State, with an area of 211 square miles and population in 1901 of 62,091, including *jāgīrs*, compared with 67,983 in 1891. It had three towns, KODANGAL (population, 5,099), the head-quarters, TĀNDŪR (5,930), and KOSGI (8,228); and 95 villages, of which 35 are *jāgīr*. The land revenue in 1901 was 1·1 lakhs. In 1905 the *tāluk* was enlarged by the addition of 59 villages from Gurmatkāl and 15 from Koilkonda in Mahbūbnagar, while it lost 21 villages to Chincholi. Rice is largely grown with tank-irrigation. The two *jāgīr tāluks*, Tāndūr and Kosgi, with 62 and 11 villages, and 23,725 and 15,344 inhabitants respectively, lie to the north and south-east. Tāndūr and Kosgi are their head-quarter towns, and their areas are 202 and 25 square miles respectively.

Seram Tāluk.—Eastern *tāluk* of Gulbarga District, Hyderābād State. The population in 1901, including *jāgīrs*, was 82,349, compared with 54,106 in 1891; the area was 404 square miles. Up to 1905 the *tāluk* contained one town, SERAM (population, 5,503), the head-quarters; and 117 villages, of which 45 were *jāgīr*. The land revenue in 1901 was 1·8 lakhs. In 1905, 21 villages from Gurmatkāl were added to Seram. Rice is grown in the *tāluk* with tank-irrigation. The *paigāh tāluk* of Chītāpur, with a population of 28,930 and 38 villages, lies to the east of this *tāluk*, and has an area of about 121 square miles.

Yādgīr Tāluk.—*Tāluk* in Gulbarga District, Hyderābād State. Till 1905 the *taluk* was attached to Raichūr District. The population in 1901, including *jāgīrs*, was 42,996 and the area 355 square miles. In 1891 the population was 62,264, the decrease being due to the transfer of certain villages to the adjoining *tāluks* and Districts. The *tāluk* contains one town, YĀDGĪR (population, 6,271), the head-quarters; and 64 villages, of which 14 are *jāgīr*. The Bhīma river flows along the western border. The land revenue in 1901 was Rs. 86,000. In 1905 the *tāluk* was enlarged by the addition of some villages from Gurmatkāl and from Mahbūbnagar District.

Gurmatkāl.—Former *tāluk* in the south-east of Gulbarga District, Hyderābād State. In 1901 it had an area of 320 square miles and a population of 52,480, compared with 48,348 in 1891. The 91 villages it contained were divided in 1905 between the Seram, Yādgīr, and Kodangal *tāluks*. The land revenue in 1901 was a lakh.

Shāhpur.—*Tāluk* in Gulbarga District, Hyderābād State, with an area of 585 square miles, including *jāgīrs*. The population in 1901 was 104,274, compared with 93,210 in 1891. It contains one town, SĀGAR (population, 5,445), and 150 villages, of which 40 are *jāgīr*; Shāhpur (3,251) is the head-quarters. The Bhīma river flows along the south-east border. The land revenue in 1901 was 1·7 lakhs. The soil is chiefly of the black cotton description.

Sūrāpur Tāluk.—*Tāluk* in Gulbarga District, Hyderābād State. The area in 1901, including *jāgīrs*, was 664 square miles, and the population 105,702, compared with 101,185 in 1891. It contains one town, SŪRĀPUR (population, 8,271), the head-quarters; and 181 villages, of which 48 are *jāgīr*. The Kistna river forms the southern boundary. The land revenue in 1901 was 1·7 lakhs.

Andola.—Southern *tāluk* of Gulbarga District, Hyderābād State, with an area of 740 square miles. The population in 1901, including *jāgīrs*, was 84,731, compared with 68,279 in 1891. Andola contains 147 villages, of which 30 are *jāgīr*, Jevargi (population, 2,194) being the head-quarters. The land revenue in 1901 was 2·1 lakhs. The *paigāh tāluk* of Fīrozābād lies to the north, with a population of 35,035, and contains 29 villages and one town, SHĀHĀBĀD (population, 5,105), the head-quarters. The area is about 96 square miles.

Aland.—Head-quarters of the *paigāh tāluk* of the same name in Gulbarga District, Hyderābād State, situated in 17° 34′ N. and 76° 35′ E., 20 miles north-west of Gulbarga city. Population (1901), 10,130. Aland is a commercial centre of some importance.

Gulbarga City.—Ancient city and head-quarters of the Gulbarga Division and District, Hyderābād State, situated in 17° 21′ N. and 76° 51′ E. The population in 1901 was 29,228, compared with 28,200 in 1891 and 22,834 in 1881. Gulbarga was formerly a Hindu city of some importance, and before the Musalmān conquest formed part of the dominions of the Rājā of WARANGAL. Warangal, Gulbarga, and Bīdar were successively captured by Muhammad bin Tughlak early in the fourteenth century. About 1345 the Deccan governors rebelled against Muhammad bin Tughlak; and in the confusion that followed Zafar Khān assumed royal dignity and, proclaiming his independence, took possession of the Deccan provinces, including Daulatābād, Gulbarga, and Bīdar, and establishing his capital at Gulbarga commenced to reign in 1347 under the title of Alā-ud-dīn Hasan Shāh Gangū Bahmani, or according to some historians Alā-ud-dīn Bahman Shāh. Gulbarga remained the capital of the Bahmani kings from this date until the reign of Ahmad Shāh Wali, who removed his capital to Bīdar. Gulbarga then rapidly lost its importance. In 1504 it was occupied by the Bijāpur troops; and, though recovered by Amīr Barīd in 1514, it was shortly after again taken by the Bijāpur troops, and remained in the possession of the Adil Shāhi kings until the Mughal invasion of the Deccan, when Mīr Jumla besieged and took it in 1657. From this period Gulbarga formed part of the Deccan possession of the Delhi rulers, till the surrender of Hyderābād to the first of the Nizāms. The old palaces and mosques which were erected by the Bahmani kings were suffered to fall into ruins and decay after the removal of the capital to Bīdar.

The city is situated on an undulating plain, presenting a

somewhat dreary expanse of black soil. It was made the head-quarters of a Division about 1874, when a new era of prosperity commenced. It now contains the residence of the *Sūbahdār*, several large buildings for State offices and officials, a Central jail, a public garden, a large tank, an extensive market-place, schools, post office and other public offices, a cotton-spinning and weaving mill, and a Christian mission with a school attached to it. The south-eastern line of the Great Indian Peninsula Railway has a station 2 miles from the city. Gulbarga is a large centre of trade, and has of late years become a prosperous place and a rival of Sholāpur. In the eastern quarter of the city are the tombs of the Bahmani kings. They are huge square buildings surmounted by domes, and are roughly but strongly built. Not far away is the shrine of Khwāja Banda Nawāz, a celebrated Musalmān saint, who came here during the reign of Fīroz Shāh Bahmani in 1413. To the north-west is the old fort of Gulbarga, the outer walls and gateways of which, together with most of the old buildings in it, are in a dilapidated condition. The *bālā hisār* or citadel is in a better state of preservation. One of the most remarkable buildings in this part of India is the unfinished mosque in the old fort, built in the reign of Fīroz Shāh and modelled after the great mosque of Cordova in Spain, measuring 216 feet east and west, and 176 feet north and south, and covering an area of 38,016 square feet. Its great peculiarity is that the whole area is covered in.

Kodangal Town.—Head-quarters of the *tāluk* of the same name in Gulbarga District, Hyderābād State, situated in 17° 7′ N. and 77° 38′ E., 12 miles south of Tāndūr station on the Nizām's State Railway. Population (1901), 5,099. Besides the *tahsīl* office, the office of the police inspector, a *tāluk* post office, and a vernacular upper primary school with 232 pupils are located here. Kodangal has a mosque said to be 300 years old.

Kosgi.—Head-quarters of the estate of the same name belonging to Sir Sālār Jang's family, in Gulbarga District, Hyderābād State, situated in 16° 59′ N. and 77° 43′ E. Population (1901), 8,228. The town contains a dispensary, a police station, a school with 50 pupils, all maintained by the estate, and three private schools with 140 pupils. Silk and cotton *sārīs* are extensively made, there being 1,500 looms at work.

Sāgar.—*Jāgīr* town in the Shāhpur *tāluk* of Gulbarga District, Hyderābād State, situated in 16° 37′ N. and 76° 48′ E., 6 miles south of Shāhpur town. Population (1901), 5,445.

Two large tanks and the shrine of Sūfi Sarmast, a Musalmān saint, lie close to the town.

Seram Town.—Head-quarters of the *tāluk* of the same name in Gulbarga District, Hyderābād State, situated in 17° 11′ N. and 77° 18′ E., on the Nizām's State Railway. Population (1901), 5,503. Seram contains many old temples and mosques, notable among them being the old Jāma Masjid, constructed in the pillar and lintel style, and the temple of Panchalinga, the pillars of which are richly carved, while the ceilings are well decorated. It has a ginning factory also.

Shāhābād.—Town in the *paigāh tāluk* of Fīrozābād, Gulbarga District, Hyderābād State, situated in 17° 8′ N. and 76° 56′ E. Population (1901), 5,105. Laminated limestone, known as 'Shāhābād stone,' is largely quarried in the vicinity, and takes its name from the town. It is an important station on the Great Indian Peninsula Railway. An elegant masonry enclosure in the centre of the town is supposed to be the wall of a royal palace, and encloses a large mosque and a well. The town contains two post offices, British and Nizām's, a police station, a dispensary, and three primary schools.

Sūrāpur Town.—Head-quarters of the *tāluk* of the same name in Gulbarga District, Hyderābād State, situated in 16° 31′ N. and 76° 46′ E. Population (1901), 8,271. The town belonged to the Rājās of Sūrāpur, the last of whom revolted during the Mutiny of 1857, and the *samasthān* was made over to the Hyderābād State as a gift after the restoration of order. It contains a Munsif's court, a dispensary, an English middle school, a girls' school, a post office, a branch British post office, and the 'New Darbār,' a large building built by Colonel Meadows Taylor during his residence here.

Tāndūr.—Head-quarters of the *jāgīr tāluk* of the same name in the Kodangal *tāluk* of Gulbarga District, Hyderābād State, situated in 17° 15′ N. and 77° 34′ E., on the Nizām's State Railway. Population (1901), 5,930. The Kāgnā river flows one mile south of the town.

Yādgīr Town.—Head-quarters of the *tāluk* of the same name in Gulbarga District, Hyderābād State, situated in 16° 46′ N. and 77° 9′ E., on the Great Indian Peninsula Railway. The fort of Yādgīr was built on a hill by a Yādava king. An inscription on the Nizām Burj gives an account of Nizām Alī Khān's visit to the governor of the place. In the town are a Jāma Masjid and another mosque with an inscription. Yādgīr also contains a post office, a middle school with 237 pupils, and a police inspector's office.

Boundaries, configuration, and hill and river systems.

Lingsugūr District[1].—Frontier District in the Gulbarga Division of Hyderābād State, situated in the south-west corner adjoining the Bombay Districts of Bijāpur and Dhārwār, which bound it to the west; Gulbarga and Raichūr, which border it to the north and east; and the Madras District of Bellary, from which it is separated by the Tungabhadra river to the east and south. It lies between 15° 3′ and 16° 20′ N. and 75° 48′ and 77° 2′ E., and has a total area of 4,879 square miles; but the area of State and 'crown' lands is only 2,968 square miles, the rest being comprised in the two large *jāgīrs* of the Sālār Jang family and other smaller *jāgirs* and the two *samasthāns* of Gurgunta and Anegundi.

A range of hills 14 miles long, known as the Yamnigadh range, begins at Daryāpur village in the Gangāwati *tāluk* and ends in the same *tāluk* at Bamsugūr. In the Shāhpur *tāluk* is a small range called the Muhammadāpur hills, 5 miles long, and Shāhpur town is built on part of this. A third range takes its name from Sūrāpur and is 8 miles in length.

The most important river is the Kistna, which flows from west to east through the District for a length of 94 miles. It enters the District in the Lingsugūr *tāluk*, and receives the Bhīma at a point 16 miles north of the town of Raichūr near the boundary of Raichūr District. The next important river is the Tungabhadra, which enters the south of the Gangāwati *tāluk* and flows along the borders of that and the Sindhnūr *tāluk* for a distance of 44 miles, when it enters Raichūr. The Bhīma enters Lingsugūr near Raoza in the Shāhpur *tāluk* in the north, and falls into the Kistna after a course of 42 miles in the District. The other rivers are the Maski and the Sindhnūr nullahs, both tributaries of the Tungabhadra. The Devāpur nullah flows through the Sūrāpur *tāluk* for 24 miles and falls into the Kistna.

Geology.

The chief geological formations are the Archaean, including various forms of gneiss and groups of crystalline schists known as the Dhārwār series; the Kalādgi rocks, occupying a few spurs and outliers near the western frontiers, extensions of the main area situated in Dhārwār and Belgaum; and the Bhīma series, north, west, and south-west of Sāgar, forming a narrow strip between the gneiss and the Deccan trap which constitutes the frontier beyond them. Complete accounts have been published by R. B. Foote in *Memoirs, Geological Survey of India*, vol. xii, part i, and in *Records*, vols. xv, part iv; xix, part ii;

[1] In 1905 the District of Lingsugūr was abolished, the Shāhpur and Sūrāpur *tāluks* being transferred to Gulbarga and the other four to Raichūr.

xxi, part ii; xxii, part i. The Hatti gold-mine is situated in the auriferous Dhārwār schists.

Botany. The flora of the District is scanty and is characteristic of the dry zone. The predominant trees are *babūl* (*Acacia arabica*), *nīm*, mango, and several species of fig.

Fauna. In the hills of Gangāwati, Shāhpur, and Surāpur, leopards, hunting cheetahs, hyenas, and bears are found; and black-faced monkeys are abundant in the Lingsugūr and Gangāwati *tāluks*. Game-birds are represented by peafowl, partridges, and quail, while duck, teal, and water-fowl are met with in the vicinity of tanks and rivers.

Climate, temperature, and rainfall. From September to May and June the climate is dry and healthy, but during the monsoons the *tāluks* of Gangāwati and Sūrāpur are very malarious. The Sindhnūr, Kushtagi, and Shāhpur *tāluks* are the healthiest. Though the temperature in May rises to 112° in the day, the nights are cool. In December it falls to 56°. The annual rainfall averages about 21 inches.

History. The District formed part of the Vijayanagar kingdom in the fourteenth century. After the foundation of the Bahmani dynasty it became part of that kingdom, but was taken and retaken by the rulers of the two States, until it fell to the Adil Shāhi rulers of Bijāpur. Upon the conquest of Bijāpur by Aurangzeb it was annexed to the empire of Delhi, but was separated from it when the Hyderābād State was founded by Asaf Jāh, early in the eighteenth century. It was 'assigned' to the British Government under the treaty of 1853, but was restored to the Nizām in 1860.

Archaeology. The forts of ANEGUNDI, MUDGAL, Jaldrug, KOPPAL, and Shāhpur are interesting from an historical as well as an archaeological point of view. Ittugi, 60 miles south-west of Lingsugūr, contains a fine old temple, which dates from A.D. 1112–3. In the village of Gūgi are a Jāma Masjid and the tomb of a local saint, named Pīr Chandā Husain. The villages of Kallūr and Kukanūr also contain ancient temples.

Population. The number of towns and villages in the District, including large and small *jāgīrs*, is 1,273. The population at the last three enumerations was: (1881) 480,715, (1891) 620,014, and (1901) 675,813. It is divided into six *tāluks* as shown below, and also contains the two large *jāgīrs* of Koppal and Yelbarga, and the two *samasthāns* of Anegundi and Gurgunta. The towns are KOPPAL, SŪRĀPUR, MUDGAL, GANGĀWATI, SĀGAR, SINDHNUR, and LINGSUGŪR. About 90 per cent. of the population are Hindus; while 87 per cent. speak Kanarese and 7 per cent.

Urdū. The following table gives the chief statistics of population in 1901:—

Tāluk.	Area in square miles.	Number of: Towns.	Number of: Villages.	Population.	Population per square mile.	Percentage of variation in population between 1891 and 1901.	Number of persons able to read and write.
Lingsugūr	499	1	95	47,487	95	+ 19·8	Not available.
Sūrāpur	550	1	133	87,675	159	+ 4·4	
Shāhpur	490	1	110	81,884	167	+ 13·0	
Sindhnūr	476	1	65	40,788	86	+ 31·4	
Gangawati	[illegible]	1	[illegible]	[illegible]	[illegible]	+ [illegible]	
Kushtagi	524	...	121	51,769	99	− 10·2	
Jagirs, &c.	1,011	2	640	311,671	163	+ 12·7	
District total	4,879	7	1,267	675,813	138	+ 8·9	16,998

Castes and occupations.

The most numerous caste in the District is that of the agricultural Kāpus, numbering 181,100, two-thirds of whom are Lingāyats. Kommaras or potters number 104,100; Bedars, 72,000; Sālas or weavers, 30,500; and Upparas, 30,100, of whom 17,700 are extractors of salt from saline earth. The Dhers number 18,200, and the Chamārs or workers in leather, 14,600. The number of persons directly engaged in agriculture is about 66 per cent. of the total.

Christian missions.

At Mudgal there is a Roman Catholic mission, which was established about 1557, during the reign of the Adil Shāhis of Bijāpur, who granted lands to the mission and exempted them from taxes. The mission is one of the oldest in India, and is said to have been established by priests dispatched from Goa by St. Francis Xavier. The native Christian population of the District in 1901 was 524, of whom 481 were Roman Catholics.

General agricultural conditions.

The larger portion of the District is composed of *masab*, a mixture of reddish and white sandy soils, interspersed with *regar* or black soil and *kharab*. In contrast to the Sindhnūr *tāluk*, in which *regar* predominates and *rabi* crops are extensively grown, the soils of the remaining five *tāluks* are chiefly *masab*, and are used for *kharīf* crops. White *jowār*, gram, wheat, cotton, and linseed are the chief *rabi* crops, being raised on the *regar*; while red *jowār*, *bājra*, *tuar* and other pulses, and sesamum are sown in the *masab* as *kharīf* crops. The *kharab* soils are utilized for garden produce, and require heavy manuring. The alluvial soils in the valleys of the rivers also produce *rabi* crops, and are very fertile.

Chief agricultural

The tenure of land is mainly *ryotwāri*. In 1901, out of a total area of 2,968 square miles comprised in the *khālsa* and 'crown' lands, 2,205 were cultivated, 22 being irrigated, while 124 were cultivable waste and fallows, 130 were forests, and 509 were not available for cultivation. The staple food of the people consists of *jowār*, *bājra*, and *kangni*, produced from 42, 10, and 8 per cent. respectively of the net area cropped. Cotton was grown on 303 and wheat on 39 square miles. Sugar-cane is raised in small quantities with well-irrigation in all the *tāluks*, and in the Gangāwati *tāluk* it is irrigated from the Tungabhadra channel. statistics and principal crops.

In 1888, when the District was settled, there were 331 square miles of unoccupied land, but in 1901 only 124 square miles remained unoccupied. The ryots have done nothing to improve the cultivation by the introduction of new varieties of seed or better agricultural implements.

Cattle, &c. No special breed of cattle is characteristic of the District. Those in use are strong and well suited for ordinary agricultural work, but not for deep ploughing, for which bullocks have to be imported. Up to 1887 Arab stallions were maintained for breeding purposes, but owing to the hot climate breeding operations were not successful. Ponies, sheep, and goats of the ordinary kind are kept.

Irrigation. In the Gangāwati *tāluk* there is some wet cultivation supplied by an old channel 9 miles long, taking off from the Tungabhadra. The total irrigated area in the District is only 22 square miles, supplied by this channel and by wells, of which there are 1,404. Tanks number 89, large and small, but they are used for drinking purposes only. There is great scope for extensive irrigation in the District; and surveys and estimates have been completed for the two Kistna channels and the Bennūr project, which would cost more than 20 lakhs and irrigate 107 square miles, yielding a revenue of about 11¼ lakhs. The repair of the large tank at Kachkanūr will cost 2¼ lakhs, and it is estimated that it will irrigate 27,170 acres, yielding a revenue of nearly 2¼ lakhs.

Forests. The District has 130 square miles of unprotected forests in the Shāhpur and Sūrāpur *tāluks*, and on the Yamnigadh hills in the Gangāwati *tāluk*.

Minerals. The most important mineral is gold, obtained from auriferous quartz. The mines in the Raichūr *doāb* were leased in 1894 to the Hyderābād Deccan Company, but are not being worked now. Laminated limestone like the Shāhābād stone is found and worked in the Shāhpur, Sūrāpur, and Kushtagi *tāluks*.

Arts and manufactures. There is no important industry in the District. Coarse cotton cloth, *dhotīs*, and *sārīs* are woven in decreasing quantities, as mill-made cloth is imported at cheaper rates. Blankets are manufactured by the shepherds from the wool of their sheep, and sold at from Rs. 2 to Rs. 4 apiece. Wooden toys are made at Kanakgiri in the Gangāwati *tāluk*.

Commerce. The chief exports are *jowār* and other cereals, pulse, cotton, oilseeds, chillies, jaggery, tobacco, *tarvar* bark, hides, bones, and horns. The principal imports consist of salt, salted fish, opium, spices, gold and silver, copper and brass vessels, refined sugar, iron, kerosene oil, yarn, raw silk, and silk, cotton, and woollen stuffs.

There are five commercial centres in the District—Rangampet in Sūrāpur, Mudgal and Maski in Lingsugur, Sindhnur, and Gangāwati—from which the whole of the imported articles are distributed to different parts. Besides these, 37 weekly markets are held at various places. The trading castes are the Komatis and Mārwāris, who do banking business also.

Railways and roads. The south-west corner of the District is crossed by the Southern Mahratta Railway. The total length of gravelled roads is 219 miles, all under the Public Works department. The principal routes are: Lingsugūr to Pāmankalūr (11 miles), to Sūrāpur (30), to Jantgal (59), and Sūrāpur to Nailkal (27).

Famine. In 1793 and 1803 the District was visited by two great famines known as the *dogibarā* or 'skull' famine and *rāgibarā* or *rāgi* famine, when people and cattle died by thousands. *Jowār* in 1793 sold at two seers per rupee and *rāgi* in 1803 at the same price. The District suffered in 1814, 1819, 1831, and 1866 from famines more or less severe, but worse than all these was that of 1877–8, the effects of which were felt far and wide. Thousands of persons lost their lives, or emigrated to other regions, and many villages were deserted. The rainfall in 1876 was 10 inches, and in 1877 only 2·4 inches, and *rabi* and *kharīf* crops in both years entirely failed. More than 100,000 persons died during this famine, cholera and small-pox being responsible for a large number. These figures refer only to the four *tāluks* of which the District was then composed. More than 75 per cent. of the cattle died for want of water and fodder. In 1892 there was scarcity, and in 1897 there was famine which cost the State 3 lakhs. The great famine of 1900 did not affect the District beyond causing scarcity.

District subdivisions and staff. The District is divided into three subdivisions. One consists of the two *Sarf-i-khās* or 'crown' *tāluks* of Shāhpur and Sūrāpur, under the Second Tālukdār; the second consists of the Lingsugūr *tāluk* only, under the Third Tālukdār; and the remaining three *tāluks* are under the First Tālukdār. There is a *tahsīldār* in each *tāluk*.

The *Nāzim-i-Dīwāni*, or District Civil Judge, presides over the District civil court. There are five subordinate civil courts: those of the *tahsīldārs* of Lingsugūr, Gangāwati, Kushtagi, and Sindhnūr, and that of a Munsif for the *tāluks* of Shāhpur and Sūrāpur. The First Tālukdār is the chief magistrate of the District, and the *Nāzim-i-Dīwāni* is also a joint-magistrate, exercising magisterial powers during the absence of the First Tālukdār from head-quarters. The Second and Third Tālukdārs and the six *tahsīldārs* exercise second and third-class magisterial powers. There is little serious crime in ordinary years, but in adverse seasons dacoities and cattle and grain thefts increase in proportion to the severity of the season. Civil and criminal justice.

Nothing is known of the revenue history of the District beyond the fact that lands were formerly leased on contract. This system was abolished in 1866, and a light rate was fixed per *bīgha* (¾ acre) according to the nature of the land. The revenue survey was completed in 1888, and assessments were fixed for fifteen years. The survey showed that the cultivated area had increased by 29½ per cent. The enhancement of revenue was Rs. 33,600, or nearly 3½ per cent., the demand having risen from 9·8 to 10·2 lakhs. The average assessment on 'dry' land is 12 annas (maximum Rs. 1–10, minimum one anna), and on 'wet' land Rs. 7–8 (maximum Rs. 15, minimum Rs. 1–8). Land revenue.

The land revenue and the total revenue of the District are shown below, in thousands of rupees:—

	1881.	1891.	1901.	1903.
Land revenue . .	6,83	11,90	11,07	11,90
Total revenue . .	9,06	15,71	14,95	15,80

Since 1887 a cess of one anna in the rupee on the land revenue has been levied for local purposes, of which a quarter, or Rs. 17,000, is set apart for public works. The District board at Lingsugūr is presided over by the First Tālukdār, and there are *tāluk* boards at the head-quarters of the six *tāluks*. Local government.

The First Tālukdār is the head of the District police, with a Superintendent (*Mohtamim*) as his executive deputy. Under him are 7 inspectors, 73 subordinate officers, 420 constables, and 25 mounted police. These are distributed among 26 *thānas* and 27 outposts, and also guard the District treasury Police and jails.

and the jail. The District jail is in the village of Karkal, near the head-quarters; prisoners whose terms exceed six months are transferred to the Central jail at Gulbarga. There are lock-ups in the six *tāluk* offices.

Education. The proportion of persons in 1901 who were able to read and write was 2·5 per cent. (4 males and 0·1 females). The first State school in the District was opened in 1869, and board schools were opened in 1896. The total number of pupils under instruction in 1881, 1891, 1901, and 1903 was 775, 1,990, 3,010, and 3,070 respectively. In 1903 there were 29 primary and 3 middle schools, with 130 girls under instruction. The total amount spent on education was Rs. 20,525, of which the State contributed Rs. 13,600. Of the total, 69 per cent. was spent on primary schools. The fee receipts in 1901 amounted to Rs. 1,076.

Medical. There are three dispensaries, with a total accommodation for 12 in-patients. The number of cases treated in 1901 was 18,669, including 43 in-patients, and the number of operations performed was 516. The total expenditure was Rs. 7,226.

The number of cases successfully vaccinated in 1901 was 2,583, or 3·87 per 1,000 of population.

Boundaries, configuration, and hill and river systems. **Osmānābād District** (formerly called Naldrug).—District in the west of the Hyderābād State, bounded by the Bombay Districts of Ahmadnagar and Sholāpur on the north, west, and south; by Bhīr and Bīdar Districts on the north and east; by the Akalkot State of Bombay on the south; and by Gulbarga District on the south-east. It encloses the detached Bārsi *tāluk* of Sholāpur District, and lies between 17° 35′ and 18° 40′ N. and 75° 16′ and 76° 40′ E., with a total area of 4,010 square miles; but the area of the *khālsa* and *Sarf-i-khās* ('crown') lands is only 2,627 square miles, the rest being *paigāh* and *jāgīr*. A range of hills, which enters the District at the north-west corner from Ahmadnagar, and continues to the south-east, divides it into two portions: a plateau to the north-east and east, and lowlands to the west, south-west, and south. The *tāluks* of Wāsi, Owsa, Kalam, and parts of Tuljāpur, Osmānābād, and Naldrug are situated on the plateau; the remainder of the District on the lowlands. The general slope of the plateau is from south-west to north-east. The land rises from Tuljāpur towards Osmānābād; thence it begins to descend gradually towards the north-east, terminating in the valley of the Mānjra river.

The most important river is the MĀNJRA, which runs due east along the northern boundary as far as the north-eastern corner of the Owsa *tāluk*, where it takes a southerly direction before entering Bīdar District. Its length in Osmānābād is about 58 miles. Other streams which traverse portions of the District are the Sīna and its tributary the Kherī, the Tirna, and the Borna, which all run in a south-easterly direction, the Sīna forming part of the boundary between Osmānābād and Bhīr District.

The geological formation is the Deccan trap. There is no forest in the District, and the trees that are found consist of *babūl* (*Acacia arabica*), *nīm*, mango, and several species of *Ficus*. Geology and botany.

The country, being devoid of forests, contains no large game of any note; but antelope and hares are found in small numbers, as are also wolves, hyenas, and wild hog. Among game-birds, partridges, quail, and wild pigeons are common; and where there is a tank, wild duck may be seen during the cold season. Fauna.

Climatically, the District may be divided into three portions: the first, containing the Naldrug and Owsa *tāluks*, is hot but dry; the second, consisting of Tuljāpur and Osmānābād, is cool and somewhat damp; while the third comprises Wāsi, Kalam, and Parenda, the climate being humid. Generally speaking, the temperature of the plateau is much pleasanter than that of the plain. Climate and temperature.

The annual rainfall for the twenty-one years ending 1901 averaged 33 inches. The amount received in 1897 (14 inches) and in 1899 (20 inches) was abnormally scanty, and resulted in the great famine of 1900. Rainfall.

The District has been under Muhammadan rule since the beginning of the fourteenth century, when it was annexed to the empire of Delhi by Alā-ud-dīn Khiljī. On the foundation of the Bahmani kingdom, it fell to that power, and when that monarchy in turn dissolved, to the Sultāns of Ahmadnagar and Bijāpur. The conquest of the Deccan by Aurangzeb reunited it to Delhi, till the foundation of the Hyderābād State in the early part of the eighteenth century. It was ceded to the British Government with the Raichūr *doāb* under the treaty of 1853, but was restored to the Nizām in 1860. History.

The District contains six places of archaeological interest. The fort of NALDRUG, a fortified town on the Bori river, and the head-quarters of the *tāluk* of that name, belonged to a Hindu Rājā during the fourteenth century. The Jāma Masjid in the Owsa *tāluk* is built in the Bijāpur style of architecture, with a dome and façade of cusped arches. Groups of caves Archaeology.

known as the Dābar Lena, Chamār Lena, and Lāchandar Lena lie around the town of OSMĀNĀBĀD (Dhārāseo), the first-mentioned group being Jain and Vaishnava excavations. Roughly the caves may be assigned to the period A.D. 500 to 650. Hasangaon, 40 miles north-west of Naldrug, contains two large caves in a solitary hill, which were Brāhmanical rock shrines. PARENDA, an old fortress, 64 miles north-west of Naldrug, was erected by Mahmūd Gāvān, the celebrated minister of the Bahmani Sultān, in the fifteenth century. TULJĀPUR, a town 20 miles north-west of Naldrug, is a famous place of Hindu pilgrimage, and contains a temple dedicated to the goddess Bhavāni. There are very interesting Buddhist remains at THAIR (Ter), 12 miles north-east of Osmānābād, which has been identified as the site of Tagara, a city of great antiquity mentioned by Ptolemy.

Population. The number of towns and villages in the District, including the large *jāgīrs*, is 866. The population at the last three enumerations was: (1881) 543,402, (1891) 649,272, and (1901) 535,027. The towns are OSMĀNĀBĀD, the head-quarters, TULJĀPUR, THAIR, OWSA, LĀTŪR, and MORAM. About 89 per cent. of the population are Hindus, and 84 per cent. of them speak Marāthī.

The following table exhibits the principal statistics of population according to the Census of 1901:—

Tâluk.	Area in square miles.	Number of		Population.	Population per square mile.	Percentage of variation in population between 1891 and 1901.	Number of persons able to read and write.
		Towns.	Villages.				
Osmānābād	380	2	78	72,176	189	− 16.5	Not available.
Kalam	303	...	70	38,030	125	− 27.1	
Wāsi	342	...	78	47,484	138	− 26.9	
Owsa	370	2	104	61,436	166	− 19.4	
Tuljāpur	403	1	71	55,385	137	− 16.2	
Naldrug	353	1	57	53,487	151	− 8.1	
Parenda	476	...	106	56,912	119	− 16.9	
Jāgīrs, &c.	1,383	...	296	150,117	118	− 16.4	
District total	4,010	6	860	535,027	133	− 17.4	16,579

In 1905 Wāsi was merged in Kalam, and Naldrug in Tuljāpur. In its present form the District thus consists of only five *tāluks*—OSMĀNĀBĀD, KALAM, TULJĀPUR, OWSA, and PARENDA—besides the two large *paigāh ilākas* of Ganjoti and Lohārā, and the *jāgīrs* of Bhūm and Wālwad.

Castes and occupations. The most numerous caste is that of the cultivating Kāpus (Telugu) or Kunbīs (Marāthā), who number 205,000, or 38 per cent. of the total. The Dhangars or shepherds number 28,700; the Mahārs or village menials, about 51,000; and the Māngs or Chamārs, leather-workers, 36,000. The Vānīs or trading castes number 42,000 altogether, and the Brāhmans 18,000. The population directly engaged in agriculture is 310,000, or nearly 58 per cent. of the total.

Christians in 1901 numbered 50, all of whom were natives.

General agricultural conditions.

The entire District is situated in the trap area, and most of its soil consists of the fertile *regar* or black cotton soil, interspersed with red and white or sandy soils. In the *tāluks* of Osmānābād, Kalam, Wāsi, and Parenda the black cotton soil predominates, favouring the cultivation of *rabi* or cold-season crops to a larger extent than in the remaining *tāluks*, where reddish and sandy soils are met with to a greater extent, producing chiefly the *kharīf* or rainy season crops. Next to the *regar* in fertility is the *masab* or mixture of white and reddish soils, and last comes the *kharab* or sandy soil. *Regar* produces white *jowār*, gram, wheat, and cotton; in the *masab* soils yellow *jowār*, *bājra*, and pulse are grown, while the *kharab* is generally utilized for garden produce, which needs heavy manuring in order to produce a good crop, the soil being naturally poor. The soils at the foot of the range of hills running across the District are especially fertile, containing the rain-washed detrital matter from the rocks above, and having all the properties of alluvium.

Chief agricultural statistics and principal crops.

The tenure of lands is mainly *ryotwāri*. In 1901, out of a total area of 2,627 square miles of *khālsa* and 'crown' lands, 1,813 were cultivated, of which only 76 were irrigated. Cultivable waste and fallows occupied 648 square miles, while 166 were not available for cultivation. The staple food-grain is *jowār*, grown on 70 per cent. of the net area cropped. Wheat, rice, and *bājra* are next in importance, the areas under each being respectively 75, 37, and 29 square miles. Cotton is grown in all the *tāluks*, and the total area occupied by it is about 56 square miles. Sugar-cane is raised in small quantities with well-irrigation, the area under this crop being slightly less than 10 square miles.

Since the last settlement in 1883, which resulted in the taking up of all the available lands by the ryots, no extension of holdings has been possible. The ryots have shown no interest in the introduction of new varieties of seed or of improved agricultural implements.

Cattle, &c.

No particular breed of cattle is characteristic of the District, but those found are strong and robust, and well suited for deep ploughing, which is essential to the heavy loamy and argillaceous soils prevalent. Sheep and goats of the common kind are reared. Ordinary ponies are to be had for from Rs. 20 to Rs. 30; but the better sort, well-known for their staying powers and sure-footedness, fetch as much as Rs. 100. For some years past the State has kept two Arab stallions at Osmānābād and one at Parenda, for the purpose of improving the local breed.

Irrigation. The irrigated area amounts to only about 76 square miles, supplied by wells, of which 8,800 are in good repair. Such tanks as exist are used for drinking purposes only, while the beds of the rivers are too low to permit of their water being used for cultivation.

Minerals. There are no minerals of any economic value, beyond the ordinary granite and basaltic rock, used in building and road-metalling. Near Katri, Kāmta, and Wadgaon in the Osmānābād *tāluk*, reddish earth is found, which is used by the Hindus for plastering floors.

Arts and manufactures. No important industry is carried on in the District. Coarse cotton cloth and *dhotīs*, *sārīs*, and *cholīs* used to be manufactured locally, but for some years past cloth of all kinds and yarn have been imported at cheaper rates. The shepherds usually manufacture blankets from the wool of their sheep, which are sold at from Rs. 2 to Rs. 3 apiece. At Lātūr in the Owsa *tāluk*, which is a large trade centre, a small ginning mill was erected in 1889, and two more have been started since 1901. There are no regular tanneries, but the Chamārs generally prepare leather for the water-buckets largely used for irrigation purposes.

Commerce. The chief exports consist of *jowār*, other cereals and pulses, cotton, oilseeds and oil, chillies, cattle, sheep, bones and horns, tobacco, leather, and *tarvar* bark. The principal imports are salt, salted fish, opium, spices, gold and silver, copper and brass utensils, refined sugar, iron, kerosene oil, sulphur, raw silk, and silk and cotton cloth of all kinds.

The chief centre of commerce is Lātūr, from which almost the whole of the imported articles are distributed throughout the District. Osmānābād is next in importance. The principal trading castes are the Vānīs, Mārwāris, Komatis, and Bhātias, who also engage in banking business. In all the *tāluks* weekly markets are held, where a brisk trade is carried on.

Railways. The Great Indian Peninsula Railway line passes through a minute portion of the *tāluk* of Tuljāpur. Bārsi, in the Bombay District of Sholāpur, on the Bārsi Light Railway, is the nearest station to the District head-quarters, from which it is 32 miles distant. There are two stations on the same line at the villages of Sendṛi and Uptai in the Parenda *tāluk*.

Roads. The total length of roads in the District is 272 miles, of which 144 miles are metalled and 128 miles unmetalled. The principal roads are: Lātūr to Doki, Yermala to Amba in Bhīr District, Bārsi to Sholāpur, Osmānābād to Tāndulwādi, Parenda to Bārsi, and Naldrug to Tāndulwādi.

Famine. No reliable records exist of any famines prior to the restoration of the District by the British in 1860, with the exception of what has been said by Colonel Meadows Taylor, in his *Story of My Life*, regarding the distress that prevailed during 1854–5 owing to the influx of famine-stricken people from the adjoining tracts. The great famine of 1877–8 affected one *tāluk* only, while in 1896–7 a portion of the District suffered. In 1897 the local rainfall was less than half the usual quantity, and in 1899 less than two-thirds; and the District, which had suffered from previous failure of crops, was among those most severely affected during the famine of 1900. Both the *kharīf* and the *rabi* crops failed, and at one time about one-fifth of the total population were in receipt of relief. An attack of cholera supervened, and the Census of 1901 showed a decrease of 17·3 per cent. in the population. The District also lost about 40 per cent. of its cattle, and the total cost of the famine to the State amounted to 22 lakhs.

District subdivisions and staff. The District forms two subdivisions: one comprising the *tāluks* of Kalam, Owsa, and Parenda, under the Second Tālukdār; and the other consisting of the *tāluks* of Osmānābād and Tuljāpur, under the Third Tālukdār, the First Tālukdār having a general supervision over the work of all his subordinates. Each *tāluk* is under a *tahsīldār*.

Civil and criminal justice. The District civil court is presided over by a Judge styled the *Nāzim-i-Dīwāni*. The subordinate civil courts are those of the *tahsīldārs* of Osmānābād, Tuljāpur, and Parenda, and of a Munsif for the *tāluks* of Owsa and Kalam. The First Tālukdār is the chief magistrate, and the District Civil Judge is also a joint-magistrate, who exercises powers as such in the absence of the First Tālukdār from head-quarters. The Second and Third Tālukdārs and the *tahsīldārs* exercise magisterial powers of the second and third class. Serious crime is not heavy in ordinary years, but in times of scarcity dacoities and cattle-thefts increase in proportion to the severity of the season.

Land revenue

Nothing is known of the revenue history of the District, beyond the fact that Malik Ambar's revenue system was in force from the beginning of the seventeenth century. His settlement was based upon an actual survey of the lands, and upon the productiveness of the soil. Villages were formerly leased by the State to revenue farmers, who received 1½ annas per rupee for collection. So far as is known, the revenue has always been collected in money and never in kind. In 1866 the subdivisions of the District were formed, though they have been much altered since by frequent transfers. In 1883 a revenue survey was completed, and an assessment fixed for thirty years. The rates fixed approximated to those in the adjoining Bombay Districts of Ahmadnagar and Sholāpur. The enhancement of revenue which resulted from the survey was 1·2 lakhs, or over 11 per cent., the revenue having risen from 10·22 to 11·4 lakhs. The average assessment on 'dry' land is R. 1 (maximum Rs. 2, minimum R. 0-1), and on 'wet' land Rs. 3 (maximum Rs. 5, minimum R. 1).

The land revenue and total revenue of the District for a series of years are given below, in thousands of rupees:—

	1881.	1891.	1901.	1903.
Land revenue . .	10,21	11,67	11,80	11,77
Total revenue . .	10,41	12,79	22,19	12,71

Local and municipal government.

Since 1888 a local cess of one anna in the rupee has been levied on land revenue for local purposes. Boards have been formed in every *tāluk*, except Osmānābād, consisting of official and non-official members, with the *tahsīldārs* as chairmen. A District board with the First Tālukdār as president supervises the working of the *tāluk* boards, as well as the Osmānābād municipality. A small conservancy establishment is maintained at all the *tāluk* head-quarters. The local cess in 1901 yielded Rs. 87,500, one-fourth of which was set apart for local works and the municipal establishments.

Police and jails.

The First Tālukdār is the head of the police, with a Superintendent (*Mohtamim*) as his executive deputy. Under him are 8 inspectors, 41 subordinate officers, 376 constables, and 35 mounted police. These are distributed among 16 police stations, and guard the *tāluk* treasuries. A small special police establishment, called the *rakhwāli*, guards carts carrying merchandise, and any cattle or animals that bivouac at certain appointed places. This force is paid out of funds collected from the cartmen and owners of cattle at fixed rates. There is a District jail at Osmānābād, besides lock-ups in the outlying *tāluks*. Only short-term prisoners are now kept in the District jail, those whose terms exceed six months being sent to the Central jail at Gulbarga.

Osmanābād occupies a fairly high position as regards the literacy of its population, of whom 3·1 per cent. (6 males and 0·12 females) could read and write in 1901. There were 44 public educational institutions in 1903, of which 12 were State and 32 local board schools. The number of pupils under instruction in 1881, 1891, 1901, and 1903 was 947, 2,055, 3,407, and 2,839 respectively, including 74 girls in 1903. No information is available regarding private schools. Of the 12 schools managed by the Educational department, 3 were girls' schools with 77 pupils, and 5 were secondary boys' schools. The first State school was opened in 1866, and the local board schools were started after the establishment of the local boards in 1888. The total amount spent on education in 1901 was Rs. 26,000, of which Rs. 16,600 was met from State funds and the remainder from Local funds. Of the total 52 per cent. was devoted to primary schools. The fee receipts for the year were Rs. 1,102. Education.

The District has one hospital and three dispensaries, with accommodation for 40 in-patients. In 1901, 23,900 cases were treated, of whom 104 were in-patients; and 391 operations were performed. The expenditure was Rs. 10,800, of which Rs. 9,400 was paid by the State, and the balance by the local boards. Medical.

In 1901 the number of persons successfully vaccinated was 1,516, or 3 per 1,000 of the population. Vaccination is gaining favour with the people, though slowly.

Osmānābād Tāluk.—'Crown' *tāluk* in the centre of Osmānābād District, Hyderābād State, formerly known as Dhārāseo. The area, including *jāgīrs*, is 417 square miles; and the population in 1901 was 77,533, compared with 92,829 in 1891, the decrease being due to the famine of 1900. It contains two towns, OSMĀNĀBĀD (population, 10,607), the head-quarters of the District and *tāluk*, and THAIR (7,327); and 87 villages, of which 9 are *jāgīr*. The land revenue in 1901 was 1·5 lakhs. Osmānābād is composed wholly of *regar* or black cotton soil.

Kalam.—'Crown' *tāluk* in the north of Osmānābād District, Hyderābād State. The population in 1901 was 38,030, and the area 303 square miles; but in 1905 the Wāsi *tāluk* was incorporated in it. The total area is now 658 square miles, of which the population in 1901 was 87,701, compared with

120,081 in 1891, the decrease being due to the famine of 1900. The Mānjra river separates the *tāluk* from Bhīr District on the north, and the soil is chiefly *regar*, with some alluvium. It contains 151 villages, and yields a land revenue of 3·7 lakhs. The *jāgīr tāluks* of Bhūm and Wālwad lie to the west with 31 and 13 villages, and populations (1901) of 11,416 and 6,997 respectively. Their areas are about 143 and 61 square miles.

Wāsi.—'Crown' *tāluk* in the north of Osmānābād District, Hyderābād State, which was absorbed in the Kalam *tāluk* in 1905. The population in 1901, including *jāgīrs*, was 49,671, and the area 355 square miles. The land revenue was 1·9 lakhs.

Owsa Tāluk (*Ausa*).—Eastern *tāluk* of Osmānābād District, Hyderābād State, with an area of 478 square miles. The population in 1901, including *jāgīrs*, was 71,365, compared with 88,484 in 1891, the decrease being due to the famine of 1900. The *tāluk* has two towns, OWSA (population, 6,026), the head-quarters, and LĀTŪR (10,479), a great commercial centre; and 130 villages, of which 26 are *jāgīr*. The Mānjra river separates it on the north from Bhīr and on the east from Bīdar District. Near the village of Gharosa, 11 miles east of Owsa, is a small range of hills. The land revenue in 1901 was 1·7 lakhs.

Tuljāpur Tāluk.—Western *tāluk* of Osmānābād District, Hyderābād State. The population in 1901, including *jāgīrs*, was 58,415 and the area was 411 square miles; but in 1905 the Naldrug *tāluk* was added to it. The combined area is now 781 square miles, of which the population in 1901 was 114,750, compared with 121,799 in 1891, the decrease being due to the famine of 1900. The *tāluk* contains two towns, TULJĀPUR (population, 6,612), the head-quarters, and MORAM (5,692); and 134 villages, of which 6 are *jāgīr*. The land revenue in 1901 was 3 lakhs. The *paigāh tāluks* of Lohārā, with 126 villages and a population of 60,936, and of Ganjoti with 76 villages and a population of 44,644, are situated in this *tāluk*. Their areas are 610 and 361 square miles respectively.

Naldrug Tāluk.—A *tāluk* formerly in the south of Osmānābād District, Hyderābād State, amalgamated with the Tuljāpur *tāluk* in 1905. The population in 1901, including *jāgīrs*, was 56,335, the area was 370 square miles, and the land revenue was 1·3 lakhs.

Parenda Tāluk.—'Crown' *tāluk* in the west of Osmānābād District, Hyderābād State, with an area of 501 square miles. The population in 1901, including *jāgīrs*, was 59,685, compared with 71,860 in 1891, the decrease being due to the famine of 1900. The *tāluk* contains 112 villages, of which 6 are *jāgīr*; and Parend (population, 3,655) is the head-quarters. The land revenue in 1901 was 1·8 lakhs. The soil is chiefly *regar* or black cotton soil.

Lātūr.—Town in the Owsa *tāluk* of Osmānābād District, Hyderābād State, situated in 18° 25′ N. and 76° 35′ E. Population (1901), 10,479. Lātūr is a great centre of the cotton and grain trade in communication with Bārsi railway station, 64 miles distant. It has three ginning factories, a British sub-post office, and a State post office, as well as a vernacular school and a travellers' bungalow.

Moram.—Town in the Tuljāpur *tāluk* of Osmānābād District, Hyderābād State, situated in 17° 47′ N. and 76° 29′ E. Population (1901), 5,692. Large quantities of grain and jaggery are exported via Sholāpur and Akalkot. Two weekly markets are held—one on Sundays for general trade, and the other on Mondays for the sale of cloth only. A new bazar, Osmānganj, is under construction. Moram contains a school.

Naldrug Village.—Village in the Tuljāpur *tāluk* of Osmānābād District, Hyderābād State, situated in 17° 49′ N. and 76° 29′ E. Population (1901), 4,111. The fort of Naldrug is situated above the ravine of the Bori river, and is one of the best fortified and most picturesque places in the Deccan. Before the Muhammadan invasion in the fourteenth century it belonged to a local Rājā, probably a vassal of the Chālukyas. It fell to the Bahmani dynasty, who built the stone fortifications. After the division of the Bahmani kingdom in 1482, it was seized by the Adil Shāhis of Bijāpur, and was a bone of contention between them and the Ahmadnagar Sultāns. Alī Adil Shāh in 1558 not only added to the fortifications, but erected a dam across the Bori, which afforded a constant supply of water to the garrison.

Osmānābād Town.—Head-quarters of the District and *tāluk* of the same name, Hyderābād State, situated in 18° 11′ N. and 76° 3′ E., 43 miles north of Sholāpur and 32 miles east of Bārsī. Population (1901), 10,607. It lies in the Bālāghāt, and was formerly known as Dhārāseo. The offices of the First, Second, and Third Tālukdārs, the District engineer, Customs Superintendent, and the District civil court are all located here. Besides these, Osmānābād contains several schools, a State and a British sub-post office, and a dispensary. While the District was temporarily ceded to the British, from 1853 to 1860, the head-quarters were removed here from Naldrug, owing to the healthy climate of the place. It is a great centre of trade. Two miles north-east of the town is a group of seven caves, four of which are Jain, while the others are probably Vaishnava.

Owsa Town (*Ausa*).—Head-quarters of the *tāluk* of the same name in Osmānābād District, Hyderābād State, situated in 18° 15′ N. and 77° 30′ E. Population (1901), 6,026. Malik Ambar, the Nizām Shāhi minister, captured the fort here and named it Ambarpur, which was corrupted into Amrāpur. The fort is square in shape, surrounded by a double wall and a moat all round, and is said to have been built by the Bijāpur kings. It contains a large gun, 18 feet long, with the name of Nizām Shāh engraved on it. Most of the old buildings are in ruins, but an extensive underground building measures 76 by 50 feet, the roof of which forms the bottom of a large cistern. An old mosque was built during Aurangzeb's viceroyalty of the Deccan, as appears from an inscription it bears. The town is a flourishing centre of the grain trade, the exports being sent to Sholāpur and Bārsi.

Parenda Village.—Head-quarters of the *tāluk* of the same name in Osmānābād District, Hyderābād State, situated in 18° 16′ N. and 75° 27′ E. Population (1901), 3,655. The fort, erected by Mahmūd Gāvān, the celebrated Bahmani minister, contains several large guns mounted on bastions. Parenda was the capital of the Nizām Shāhis for a short time after the capture of Ahmadnagar by the Mughals in 1605. It was besieged unsuccessfully by Shāh Jahān's general in 1630. It was, however, reduced by Aurangzeb during his viceroyalty of the Deccan. The fortifications are in good order, but the old town is in ruins. Numerous ruins in the neighbourhood and the fort testify to the former populousness of the place. It now possesses a *tahsīl* and police inspector's office, a customs-house, a school, and a *tāluk* post office.

Thair (*Ter*).—Town in the District and *tāluk* of Osmānābād, Hyderābād State, situated in 18° 19′ N. and 76° 9′ E., on the Tirna river, 12 miles north-east of Osmānābād. Population (1901), 7,327. There are some very interesting remains, said to be connected with the ancient city of Tagara. It contains a police station and a school, and is composed of twelve *wādīs* or hamlets, being really an overgrown village. A project is under consideration for the construction of a canal from the river close by.

[J. F. Fleet, *Journal, Royal Asiatic Society* (1901); H. Cousens, *Archaeological Survey of India, Annual Report* (1902–3), p. 195.]

Tuljāpur Town.—Head-quarters of the *tāluk* of the same name in Osmānābād District, Hyderābād State, situated in 18° 1′ N. and 76° 5′ E., 28 miles from Sholāpur and 14 from Osmānābād. Population (1901), 6,612. It contains a police inspector's office, a customs-house, a dispensary, a *tāluk* post office, a travellers' bungalow, and a school. Tuljāpur is a centre of trade. In a ravine at the foot of the hill is the temple of Tulja Bhavāni, which is visited by Hindus from all parts of India, especially on the full moon of the Dasara festival, when a great *jātra* is held. It is said to have been built by the Rājās of Sātāra and Kolhāpur. A weekly market is held here on Tuesdays.

Raichūr District[1].—District in the Gulbarga Division of Hyderābād State, adjoining Mahbūbnagar and Gulbarga, which bound it east and north, and the Madras Districts of Bellary and Kurnool in the south, from which it is separated by the Tungabhadra river. Before the extensive changes made in 1905, referred to below, it lay between 15° 50′ and 16° 54′ N. and 76° 50′ and 78° 15′ E., and had an area of 3,604 square miles, *khālsa* lands covering 2,319 square miles and the rest being *samasthāns* and *jāgīrs*. Boundaries, configuration, and hill and river systems.

A range of hills traverses the Yādgīr *tāluk* from west to east for a length of 20 miles, and enters the Seram and Kodangal *tāluks* of Gulbarga District in the north-east. There are three other ranges, one extending from the north-west of Raichūr towards Yergara for 15 miles, another in the Raichūr and Mānvi *tāluks* 10 miles long, and the third 19 miles long in the south of the District in the Raichūr and Alampur *tāluks*. These really form a single range, extending for nearly 60 miles from the north-west of Raichūr to Alampur, with two breaks. The general slope of the country is from the north-west towards the south-east.

The most important river is the Kistna, which enters the Deodrug *tāluk* and flows for a distance of 130 miles in a south-easterly direction. The Tungabhadra forms the southern boundary up to the point of its confluence with the Kistna in the Alampur *tāluk*. The Bhīma enters the Yādgīr *tāluk*, and falls into the Kistna 16 miles north of Raichūr.

The District is occupied principally by Archaean gneiss, including, near its western boundary, some bands of crystalline schists known as the Dhārwār series, which contain auriferous quartz veins. At the extreme east, the triangular area above Geology.

[1] This article, except where otherwise stated, describes the District as it stood before the changes made in 1905.

the confluence of the Kistna and Tungabhadra is occupied by rocks of the Kurnool series. The Dhārwārs and the Kurnools are fully described in the publications of the Geological Survey of India, the former by R. B. Foote (*Records*, vols. xxi, part ii, and xxii, part i), the latter by W. King (*Memoirs*, vol. viii, part i).

Botany. The most important trees are teak, ebony, *bījāsāl* (*Pterocarpus Marsupium*), *nallāmaddi* (*Terminalia tomentosa*), *eppa* (*Hardwickia binata*), *tarvar* (*Cassia auriculata*), mango, tamarind, *nīm*, and species of *Ficus*.

Fauna. No large game is found, owing to the absence of forests; but in the hills leopards, bears, hyenas, and wolves are met with occasionally. Among game-birds, partridges and quail, and near the tanks and on the rivers wild duck, teal, and other water-fowl, may be seen.

Climate, temperature, and rainfall. The District is generally healthy from October to the end of May, but during the rains ague and fever prevail. The parts bordering the rivers are damp. The temperature in May rises to 111°, but the nights are cool, and in December it falls to 70° F. The annual rainfall during the twenty-one years ending 1901 averaged 25·37 inches.

History. Before the Muhammadan conquest, Raichūr was part of the Warangal kingdom, and it became subject to Vijayanagar when that power was established early in the fourteenth century. After Muhammad bin Tughlak's death, it fell to the Bahmanis, then to the Adil Shāhis of Bijāpur. After the conquest of Bijāpur by Aurangzeb, it was united to Delhi, but was separated from the empire on the foundation of the Hyderābād State. Under the treaty of 1853 it was 'assigned' to the British, but was restored to the Nizām in 1860.

Archaeology. The principal antiquities are found in or near the fort of Raichūr, which is said to have been built by Gore Gangaya Ruddivārū, the minister of the Rājā of Warangal between 1294 and 1301. The District also contains the old forts of DEODRUG, YĀDGĪR, Alampur, and Malliābād, besides numerous temples and mosques.

Population. The number of towns and villages in the District, including *jāgīrs* and two large *samasthāns*, is 899. The population at the last three enumerations was: (1881) 398,782, (1891) 512,455, and (1901) 509,249. The chief towns are now RAICHŪR, GADWĀL, KOPPAL, MUDGAL, DEODRUG, KALLŪR, and MĀNVI. Hindus form 90 per cent. of the total population; 51 per cent. of the people speak Telugu, 37 per cent. Kanarese, and 9 per cent. Urdū.

The following table shows the chief statistics of population in 1901:—

Tāluk.	Area in square miles.	Number of Towns.	Number of Villages.	Population.	Population per square mile.	Percentage of variation in population between 1891 and 1901.	Number of persons able to read and write.
Raichūr	441	1	110	88,741	201	+ 5.6	Not available.
Yādgīr	268	1	50	36,075	134	− 31.0	
Alampur	179	...	42	29,294	163	+ 10.8	
Yergara	358	1	77	59,463	166	+ 9.1	
Mānvi	559	1	137	69,306	124	+ 20.3	
Deodrug	514	1	151	76,491	148	+ 2.5	
Jāgīrs, &c.	1,285	1	326	149,879	116	+ 2.9	
District total	3,604	6	893	509,249	141	− 0.7	10,872

In 1905 Yergara was divided between the adjoining *tāluks* of Mānvi, Raichūr, and Deodrug, and Yādgīr was transferred to Gulbarga District. On the other hand, Lingsugūr, Gangāwati, Kushtagi, and Sindhnūr were added to Raichūr from the broken-up Lingsugūr District. In its present form the District comprises eight *tāluks*—Raichūr, Lingsugūr, Mānvi, Alampur, Deodrug, Gangāwati, Kushtagi, and Sindhnūr—besides the *samasthāns* of Gadwāl and Amarchinta, and the two *jāgīr tāluks* of Koppal and Yelbarga belonging to the Sālār Jang family.

Castes and occupations. The most numerous caste in the District is that of the cultivating Kāpus, numbering 72,900, of whom 53,300 are Lingāyats. Almost equal to them are the hunting Bedars, numbering 72,600. The number of persons directly engaged in agriculture is 56 per cent. of the total. Of the 276 Christians in 1901, 237 were natives.

General agricultural conditions. Raichūr is situated in the metamorphic and trap regions, and its varieties of soil are *regar*, *masab*, *milwa*, and reddish or lateritic. The last-mentioned soil is much prized, and so are also the *regar* and *milwa*; but the *masab* is a very poor soil, and needs water and heavy manuring. *Regar* predominates in the Raichūr, Mānvi, and Deodrug *tāluks*, where *rabi* crops are extensively raised, while reddish and *milwa* soils are used for *kharīf* crops. In the reddish and *milwa* soils a moderate fall of 12 to 15 inches of rain is sufficient to mature the crop, while *regar* needs 25 to 30 inches.

Chief agricultural statistics and principal crops. The tenure of land is mainly *ryotwāri*. In 1901, 1,670 square miles were cultivated, out of a total area of 2,319 square miles of *khālsa* land. The remainder included 127 square miles of cultivable waste and fallows, 120 of forest, and 402 not available for cultivation. Only 36 square miles were irrigated.

The staple food-crops are *jowār* and *bājra*, produced from 781 and 141 square miles of land respectively, or 47 and 8 per cent. of the net area cropped. Cotton was grown on 285 square miles, distributed over all the *tāluks*, while rice and oilseeds covered 33 and 77 square miles.

Since the settlement in 1891, the value of land has increased, and almost the whole of the available area has been taken up, and little extension is now possible. No steps have been taken to improve cultivation by the introduction of new varieties of seed or better agricultural implements.

Cattle, &c. The cattle are of the ordinary kind, but are strong and well suited for deep ploughing. There is no special breed of ponies, sheep, or goats. In the town of Raichūr, a weekly market is held, where cattle, ponies, and sheep are sold. At the annual fair at Gadwāl, a large trade is done in cattle. The District contains numerous grazing areas.

Irrigation. The total irrigated area is only about 36 square miles, which is supplied by 234 tanks and 4,804 wells, all in good repair. In the Yergara *tāluk*, a channel 9 miles long from the Tungabhadra river supplies most of the tanks. Estimates amounting to Rs. 60,000 for improving this channel are awaiting sanction, and, when completed, it will irrigate a very large extent of land. The largest tank is at Kanjpalli, 2 miles from Yergara, the dam of which is 2 miles long and about 40 feet high.

Forests. A small 'reserved' forest, 70 square miles in area, is situated in the Yādgīr *tāluk*, and about 50 square miles are covered with protected and unprotected forests, making a total of 120 square miles. Teak, ebony, rosewood, *bījāsāl* (*Pterocarpus Marsupium*), *nallāmaddi* (*Terminalia tomentosa*), *eppa* (*Hardwickia binata*), sandal-wood, *sendra* (*Acacia Catechu*), and bamboos are found in the 'reserved' tract.

Minerals. The most important mineral is the auriferous quartz, found in the Mānvi and Deodrug *tāluks*, near the villages of Topaldodi and Wandalli, which was worked by the Deccan Mining Company. Operations have recently slackened at Wandalli and altogether stopped at Topaldodi. Laminated limestone like the Shāhābād stone is also found in Yādgīr, and talc in the Deodrug *tāluk*.

Arts and manufactures. There is no important hand industry in the District. Coarse cotton *dhotīs* and *sārīs* are woven everywhere. In the Alampur *tāluk* *shatranjīs* and printed floorcloths are manufactured, while in the Yādgīr *tāluk* printed screens and tablecloths and furniture and wooden toys are made. Raichūr town is noted for its gilt and coloured soft native slippers, which are exported far and wide, and also for its fancy earthen goblets and drinking vessels.

Four cotton-presses, three at Raichūr and one at Yādgīr, employed 275 hands and pressed 7,426 tons of cotton in 1901; and an oil and another ginning and pressing factory are under construction. A tannery at Raichūr turns out 500 skins per day, and employs 60 persons. The skins and hides are sent to Bombay, Madras, and Cawnpore. Nitre and salt are prepared in small quantities by lixiviating saline earth; the salt is bitter and is used in making pickles. There is also a distillery at Raichūr.

The principal exports consist of *jowār* and other food-grains, linseed, castor-seed, sesamum, leather and hides, bones and horns, *tarvar* bark, and cotton. The chief imports are salt and salted fish, opium, coco-nuts, refined sugar, kerosene oil, sulphur, camphor, spices, mill-made cloth, yarn, raw silk, and silk and woollen stuffs. Commerce.

Raichūr town is a centre of commerce, and since the opening of the railway in 1871 it has grown in importance and supports a large commercial population. The trading castes consist of Baljawārs, Lingāyat Komatis, and Mārwāris, who also do a large banking business.

The town of Raichūr is the junction of the Great Indian Peninsula and the Madras Railways, which cross the District from north to south for 62 miles, with eight stations in the District. Railways.

There are altogether 182 miles of roads, of which 84 miles are gravelled, and are maintained by the Public Works department, the others being ordinary fair-weather roads. The latter lead from Raichūr town to Alampur (60 miles), to Deodrug (34), and to Mānvi (24). The metalled roads are the Deosugūr road (13), Raichūr to Wandalli gold-mines (43), the Yergara road (10), and the Raichūr-Lingsugūr road (18 miles). Most of these roads now serve as railway feeders. There are 32 fords and ferries on the Kistna, the Tungabhadra, and the Bhīma, at some of which boats are kept, while at others coracles are used for carrying people and goods across. Roads.

From old records it appears that this District was the scene of much distress in 1804, 1819, 1833, 1846, 1856, and 1877–8. The effects of the famine of 1846 were felt beyond the borders; but the severest disaster was that of 1877–8, Famine.

which devastated many villages and caused immense distress both in Raichūr and in the surrounding Districts of Hyderābād State and of the Bombay and Madras Presidencies. The *kharīf* and *rabi* crops both failed during these two years and grain could not be obtained. As an indication of distress, it is reported that gold sold at Rs. 6 or Rs. 7 per tola, i.e. at one-fourth its usual price, and many people sold their children. The State spent large sums of money on relief works and poor-houses to alleviate the distress; but, notwithstanding this, many perished, and numerous villages were depopulated, while cattle died by thousands for want of fodder and water. In 1897 some distress prevailed, but timely rain in June relieved the pressure by cheapening food-grains.

District subdivisions and staff. The District is divided into three subdivisions: one comprising the *tāluks* of Lingsugūr, Gangāwati, and Kushtagi, under a Second Tālukdār; the second comprising the *tāluks* of Sindhnūr, Deodrug, and Mānvi, under a Third Tālukdār; and the third comprising Raichūr and Alampur, under another Third Tālukdār. The First Tālukdār exercises a general supervision over the work of his subordinates. Each *tāluk* is under a *tahsīldār*.

Civil and criminal justice. The District civil court is presided over by the *Nāzim-i-Dīwāni*, or District Civil Judge, and the *tahsīldārs* sit as subordinate civil courts. The *Nāzim-i-Dīwāni* is a joint-magistrate, exercising magisterial powers during the absence of the First Tālukdār from head-quarters. The Second and Third Tālukdārs and the *tahsīldārs* exercise second and third-class magisterial powers. Serious crime is not heavy in ordinary years, but cattle-thefts and dacoities fluctuate according to the degree of severity of the season.

Land revenue. The revenue system of Malik Ambar appears to have been adopted in the beginning of the seventeenth century. Subsequently villages were let on contract, after fixing the revenue according to the nature of the lands, and the contractors received $1\frac{1}{2}$ annas per rupee as commission. The *ryotwāri* system, with cash payments, was introduced in 1866. In 1888 the Deodrug and Mānvi *tāluks* were surveyed and settled for fourteen years; and the remaining *tāluks* were settled in 1891, also for the same period. From the survey it was found that the cultivated area had increased by 271 square miles, or 19·6 per cent., and the enhancement of revenue was Rs. 53,821, or 5·6 per cent. The average assessment on 'dry' land is R. 0–12 (maximum Rs. 3, minimum R. 0–2), and on 'wet' land Rs. 5 (maximum Rs. 12, minimum Rs. 2).

The land revenue and the total revenue of the District are given below, in thousands of rupees :—

	1881.	1891.	1901.	1903.
Land revenue . .	11,51	12,23	11,60	11,94
Total revenue . .	15,01	23,34	19,82	22,62

Owing to the changes of area made in 1905, the land revenue demand is now about 18·4 lakhs.

Local and municipal government. The District board, in addition to its own work, manages the Raichūr municipality and also supervises the working of the *tāluk* boards, which have been formed in every *tāluk* except Raichūr. Of the total cess, five-twelfths are set apart for local and municipal works, yielding Rs. 25,000 in 1901. In addition, a sum of Rs. 33,000 was contributed from other miscellaneous sources to meet the expenditure in that year, which was Rs. 58,000.

Police and jails. The First Tālukdār is the head of the police, with a Superintendent (*Mohtamim*) as his executive deputy. Under the latter are 7 inspectors, 53 subordinate officers, 398 constables, and 25 mounted police, distributed among 25 *thānas* and an equal number of outposts. Besides the regular police, there are 1,696 rural policemen. The District jail is at Raichūr town, and lock-ups are maintained in the five outlying *tāluks*. The District jail can accommodate only 100 convicts, but prisoners whose terms exceed six months are transferred to the Central jail at Gulbarga.

Education. In 1901 the proportion of persons in the District able to read and write was 2·1 per cent. (4·1 males and 0·15 females). The total number of pupils under instruction in 1881, 1891, 1901, and 1903 was 269, 1,255, 2,771, and 2,679 respectively. In 1903 there were 31 primary and 2 middle schools, and the number of girls under instruction was 94. The amount expended on education was Rs. 16,600, of which the State contributed Rs. 10,700 and the remainder was met by the local boards. About 53 per cent. of the total was devoted to primary schools. The total fee receipts amounted to Rs. 1,119.

Medical. The District has 5 dispensaries, with accommodation for 14 in-patients. The total number of cases treated in 1901 was 30,535 out-patients and 124 in-patients, and 1,153 operations were performed. The expenditure was Rs. 14,800, of which Rs. 13,500 was paid by the State and the balance from Local funds. There are two dispensaries in the two *samasthāns* of Gadwāl and Amarchinta on the model of the State dispensaries.

In 1901 five vaccinators were engaged in the work of vaccination, and 3,096 persons were successfully vaccinated, or 6·08 per 1,000 of the population.

Raichūr Tāluk.—*Tāluk* in Raichūr District, Hyderābād State, with an area of 526 square miles, including *jāgīrs*. The population in 1901 was 94,695, compared with 89,782 in 1891. It had one town, RAICHŪR (population, 22,165), the head-quarters of the District and *tāluk*; and 128 villages, of which 18 are *jāgīr*. In 1905 the *tāluk* was enlarged by the addition of part of Yergara. The Kistna river separates it from Mahbūbnagar District in the north. The land revenue in 1901 was 2·6 lakhs. The soils are chiefly alluvial, *regar*, and sandy. The two *samāsthans* of GADWĀL and AMARCHINTA lie to the east and north-east of this *tāluk*, with populations of 96,491 and 34,147, areas of about 864 and 190 square miles, and 214 and 68 villages respectively. The former contains one town, GADWĀL (population, 10,195).

Alampur.—South-eastern *tāluk* of Raichūr District, Hyderābād State, with an area of 184 square miles, including *jāgīrs*. The population in 1901 was 30,222, compared with 27,271 in 1891. The *tāluk* has 43 villages, of which one is *jāgīr*; and Alampur (population, 4,182) is the head-quarters. The Kistna river separates it from Mahbūbnagar District on the north, and the Tungabhadra from the Madras District of Kurnool on the south. The confluence of these two rivers is situated in the extreme east of the *tāluk*. In 1901 the land revenue was 1·2 lakhs. The soils are alluvial and *regar* in the south, and sandy in the west.

Mānvi Tāluk.—*Tāluk* in Raichūr District, Hyderābād State, with an area of 573 square miles, including *jāgīrs*. The population in 1901 was 70,773, compared with 58,828 in 1891. It contained one town, MĀNVI (population, 6,253), the head-quarters; and 140 villages, of which 3 are *jāgīr*. In 1905 part of the Yergara *tāluk* was incorporated in Mānvi. It is separated from the Madras District of Kurnool in the south by the Tungabhadra river. The land revenue in 1901 was 2 lakhs. The soil is chiefly *regar* or alluvial.

Sindhnūr Tāluk.—*Tāluk* in Raichūr District, Hyderābād State, with an area of 621 square miles, including *jāgīrs*. The population in 1901 was 65,434, compared with 49,776 in 1891. The *tāluk* contains one town, SINDHNŪR (population, 5,242), the head-quarters; and 126 villages, of which 61 are *jāgīr*. It is separated on the south-east from the Madras District of Bellary by the Tungabhadra river. The land revenue in 1901 was 2·5 lakhs.

Gangāwati Tāluk.—*Tāluk* in Raichūr District, Hyderābād State, with an area of 517 square miles, including *jāgīrs*. The population in 1901 was 65,010, compared with 55,097 in 1891. The *tāluk* contains one town, GANGĀWATI (population, 6,245), the head-quarters; and 140 villages, of which 37 are *jāgīr*. The *samasthān* of Anegundi, comprising 12 villages with a population of 4,295, is included in this *tāluk*. The Tungabhadra river separates it from the Madras District of Bellary on the south-east. The land revenue in 1901 was 1·8 lakhs. The soil includes alluvial, black cotton, and sandy varieties. The *jāgīr tāluk* of Koppal, belonging to the Sālār Jang family, is situated to the west of this *tāluk*. It has an area of 513 square miles, and a population of 85,033, and 152 villages, besides one town, KOPPAL (population, 8,903), the head-quarters.

Kushtagi.—*Tāluk* in Raichūr District, Hyderābād State, with an area of 796 square miles, including *jāgīrs*. The population in 1901 was 95,797, compared with 106,625 in 1891. The *tāluk* contains 236 villages, of which 115 are *jāgīr*; and Kushtagi (population, 3,433) is the head-quarters. The land revenue in 1901 was 1·6 lakhs. Kushtagi is composed chiefly of black cotton soil. The *jāgīr tāluk* of Yelbarga, belonging to the Sālār Jang family, lies to the south-west of this *tāluk*. It has an area of 480 square miles and a population of 67,016, dwelling in 101 villages.

Lingsugūr Tāluk.—*Tāluk* in Raichūr District, Hyderābād State, with an area of 703 square miles, including *jāgīrs*. The population in 1901 was 87,547, compared with 73,063 in 1891. It contains two towns, LINGSUGŪR (population, 5,161) and MUDGAL (7,729), the *tāluk* head-quarters; and 180 villages, of which 86 are *jāgīr*. The *samasthān* of Gurgunta, consisting of 38 villages, with a population of 19,937, is included in this *tāluk*. The Kistna river enters the State at Opanhāl in the west and flows in a north-easterly direction. The land revenue in 1901 was 1·6 lakhs.

Deodrug Tāluk.—*Tāluk* in Raichūr District, Hyderābād State, with an area of 531 square miles, including *jāgīrs*. The population in 1901 was 78,280, compared with 76,306 in 1891. It has one town, DEODRUG (population, 6,773), the head-quarters; and 155 villages, of which 4 are *jāgīr*. In 1905 part of the Yergara *tāluk* was added to Deodrug. The Kistna river flows through the north and west of the *tāluk*. The land revenue in 1901 was 1·7 lakhs. The soils are mostly *regar* and alluvial.

Anegundi.—Old town and fortress in Raichūr District, Hyderābād State, situated in 15° 21′ N. and 76° 30′ E., on the left bank of the Tungabhadra. Population (1901), 2,266. It is the seat of the Rājās of Anegundi, who are lineal descendants of the kings of Vijayanagar. Anegundi and Vijayanagar on the opposite bank are popularly identified with the Kishkhinda of the Rāmāyana. The Vijayanagar dynasty ruled from 1336 to 1565, when it was overthrown by an alliance of the Muhammadan Sultāns of the Deccan. Anegundi means 'elephant pit,' being the place where the elephants of the Vijayanagar kings were kept.

Deodrug Town.—Head-quarters of the *tāluk* of the same name in Raichūr District, Hyderābād State, situated in 16° 25′ N. and 76° 56′ E., 34 miles west of Raichūr town and 4 miles south of the Kistna. Population (1901), 6,773. Deodrug contains an old fort enclosed on all sides except the west by hills, and was the stronghold of the *poligārs* of the Bedār tribe, who were so powerful that the first of the Nizāms sought their alliance. The *tahsīl* and police inspector's offices, a dispensary, one State and six local board schools are located here. To the north of the town is a hill containing talc.

Gadwāl.—Head-quarters of the *samasthān* of the same name in Raichūr District, Hyderābād State, situated in 16° 14′ N. and 77° 13′ E., 35 miles east of Raichūr town. Population (1901), 10,195.

Gangāwati Town.—Head-quarters of the *tāluk* of the same name in Raichūr District, Hyderābād State, situated in 15° 26′ N. and 76° 32′ E., 5 miles north of Anegundi. Two miles east of it flows the Tungabhadra river. Population (1901), 6,245. The town contains a school, a dispensary, a post office, and two old temples. It is a commercial centre, largely exporting grain and jaggery. A weekly market is held on Sundays.

Kallūr.—Town in the Raichūr *tāluk* of Raichūr District, Hyderābād State, situated in 16° 9′ N. and 77° 13′ E., 10 miles west of Raichūr town. Population (1901), 6,456. It has three temples built of stone, all in good preservation, and two mosques.

Koppal.—Old hill-fort and town in Raichūr District, Hyderābād State, situated in 15° 21′ N. and 76° 10′ E., on the Southern Mahratta Railway. Population (1901), 8,903. It was occupied in 1786 by Tipū Sultān, who had the lower fortress rebuilt by his French engineers. It was besieged by the British and the Nizām's forces for six months in 1790, before it was finally carried. During the Mutiny of 1857, Bhīm Rao, a rebel, obtained possession of it, but was slain with many others of his party, and the rest surrendered. The fortifications consist of two forts; the upper fort is situated on the lofty and insulated summit of a hill, about 400 feet above the plain. Sir John Malcolm described it as the strongest place he had seen in India. It is now the chief town in a *jāgīr* of the Sālār Jang family, and contains a State post office and a vernacular school maintained by the estate.

Lingsugūr Town.—Town in Raichūr District, Hyderābād State, situated in 16° 7′ N. and 76° 3′ E. Population (1901), including the Mahbūb Bāzār, 5,161. It was the head-quarters of Lingsugūr District till 1905, and contains the usual offices, a middle school, a dispensary, the District jail, a State post office, and a British post office. Two weekly markets are held, on Saturdays and Sundays. The Mahbūb Bāzār, 2 miles north of the town, was the site of a cantonment while the District was held by the British from 1853 to 1860.

Mānvi Town.—Head-quarters of the *tāluk* of the same name in Raichūr District, Hyderābād State, situated in 15° 59′ N. and 77° 3′ E. Population (1901), 6,253. It contains temples of Mārothi, Rāmasimha, and Venkateshwara, and a Jāma Masjid. Opposite the temple of Mārothi, which is erected on a hill to the west of the town, is a large block of stone bearing a lengthy Kanarese inscription. Another stone bearing an inscription stands near a well in the fort, which is now in ruins.

Mudgal.—Head-quarters of the Lingsugūr *tāluk*, Raichūr District, Hyderābād State, situated in 16° 1′ N. and 76° 26′ E. Population (1901), 7,729, of whom 4,753 were Hindus, 2,593 Musalmāns, and 380 Christians. The fort was the seat of the Yādava governors of Deogiri in 1250. It came successively into the possession of the Rājās of Warangal, the Bahmani and Bijāpur Sultāns, and lastly it fell to Aurangzeb. There is a small Roman Catholic colony in the town, whose ancestors were originally converted by one of St. Francis Xavier's missionaries from Goa. The church was built at an early date and contains a picture of the Madonna. Mudgal has two schools, one of which is supported by the mission, a post office, and an *Ashūr-khāna*, where the Muharram ceremony is held with great *éclat* in the presence of thousands of pilgrims.

Raichūr Town.—Head-quarters of the District and *tāluk*

of the same name in Hyderābād State, situated in 16° 12′ N. and 77° 21′ E. Population (1901), 22,165, of whom 16,249 were Hindus, 5,664 Musalmāns, and 186 Christians. According to an inscription in the fort on a huge stone 42 by 3 feet, it was built by Gore Gangaya Ruddivāru in 1294. The country round Raichūr was the battle-ground of the ancient Hindu and Jain dynasties, as well as of the Musalmān and Hindu kingdoms of Gulbarga and Vijayanagar. After the decline of the Bahmani power towards the close of the fifteenth century, it formed part of the Bijāpur kingdom. Upon the subjugation of Bijāpur and Golconda by Aurangzeb, Raichūr was garrisoned by the Mughals. A short distance from the west gate of the fort are the remains of a strongly built palace, now utilized as a jail. The town is the junction of the Madras and the Great Indian Peninsula Railways, 351 miles from Madras and 444 miles from Bombay. The fortifications form a square of large stones 12 feet long by 3 feet thick, laid on one another without any cementing material. They consist of two walls, an inner and an outer, and are surrounded on three sides by a deep ditch, while on the fourth or southern side there is a hill. The outer fortifications and the gateways were constructed by Ibrāhīm Adil Shāh about 1549. The inner fort has two gateways and the outer three. The fort contains an old gun over 20 feet long. Outside the eastern gate is a mosque having a single minaret 240 feet high and 30 feet in circumference, with a winding staircase, which was built in 1503 during the reign of Mahmūd Shāh Bahmani. A good view of the surrounding country is obtained from the top of this minaret. The Jāma Masjid in the town was built in 1618. Raichūr has three cotton-presses, a tannery, and a distillery, and is a rising commercial centre.

Sindhnūr Town.—Head-quarters of the *tāluk* of the same name in Raichūr District, Hyderābād State, situated in 15° 47′ N. and 76° 46′ E. Population (1901), 5,242. The town contains a post office and a school. Country cloth, grain, and especially cotton are largely exported. Half a mile from the town is a stone mosque said to have been erected during Aurangzeb's reign.

Boundaries, configuration, and hill and river systems.

Bīdar District.—District in the Gulbarga Division of Hyderābād State, lying between 17° 30′ and 18° 51′ N. and 76° 30′ and 77° 51′ E., with a total area of 4,168 square miles, of which 2,120 square miles are *jāgīr*[1]. It is bounded by Nānder

[1] These figures relate to the District before the alterations made in 1905; see paragraph on Population.

District and the *paigāh* estates of Nawāb Sir Vikār-ul-Umarā, on the north; by the *paigāh* estates of Nawāb Sir Khurshed Jāh, on the east and south; and by the Districts of Bhīr and Osmānābād and the *paigāh* and Kalyāni *jāgīrs*, on the west.

From Khānāpur, 8 miles west of Bīdar, a range of low laterite hills, forming a plateau which terminates towards the north above the valley of the Mānjra, extends due east as far as Sadāseopet in Medak District; otherwise the country is almost flat, with a gentle slope towards the east.

Besides the Mānjra, the largest river in the District, which enters it from Osmānābād, and runs almost due east, there are ten minor streams: the Ghirni and Bahnār, both tributaries of the Mānjra; the Tiru, Urgi, Reondi, Manmuri, Lendi, Tirna, Madhura, and Kāranja. The Mānjra is the only perennial river, all the others running dry during the summer months. None of these rivers is utilized for irrigation purposes.

The District is occupied almost entirely by the Deccan trap, the underlying gneiss appearing along its eastern border. **Geology.**

Bīdar is noted for its healthy climate. The waters of the lateritic region are chalybeate, and possess tonic properties. The southern half of the District being a high plateau about 2,350 feet above the sea, and well drained, the climate is very dry and healthy. The temperature is much lower here and in the west than towards the east. The western and northern *tāluks* are generally more favoured as regards rain than the southern and eastern. The annual rainfall averages about 37 inches. In 1899 and 1900 it was scanty, the latter being a famine year. **Climate and rainfall.**

The history of the District commences with the capture of the capital by Muhammad bin Tughlak in 1321. In 1347 Bahman Shāh Gangū, the first Bahmani king of Gulbarga, took Bīdar. In 1430 Ahmad Shāh Wali Bahmani founded the modern town, built the fort, and removed his capital here from Gulbarga. On the dissolution of the Bahmani kingdom, the District fell to the Barīd Shāhis of Bīdar, who reigned from 1492 to 1609; afterwards it was included in the Adil Shāhi kingdom of Bijāpur. The city was plundered by Malik Ambar, the Nizām Shāhi minister of Ahmadnagar in 1624, but was recovered by the king of Bijāpur, and remained part of his realm till about 1656, when Aurangzeb took it. The District was included in the Hyderābād State on its foundation early in the eighteenth century. **History.**

Archaeology.

The District contains numerous relics of its palmy days, prominent among them being the fort of Bīdar, which is surrounded by a wall and ditch. Though the fortifications and battlemented walls are very strong and are still well preserved, the old palaces are more or less decayed. On the bastions are a number of guns, formed of bars of metal welded together and bound by hoops. Bīdar contains many ruined palaces and mosques, among the latter being two large mosques known as the Jāma Masjid, a handsome building, and the 'sixteen-pillared' mosque. Outside the town and to the west of it are the tombs of the Barīd Shāhi dynasty. The tombs of twelve Bahmani kings lie to the north-east of the town. Numerous ruins of temples, caves, and mosques are to be found near KALYĀNI, the capital of the Chālukyas, and at the villages of Nilanga, Karūsa, Kaulās, Nārāyanpur, Sākol, Sirūri, Sītāpur, and Tiprath.

Population.

The number of towns and villages in the District, including large *ilākās* and *jāgīrs*, is 1,464. The population at the last three enumerations was: (1881) 788,827, (1891) 901,984, and (1901) 766,129. The decrease during the last decade was due chiefly to famine, but partly to the transfer of the Jūkal *tāluk*, with a population of 15,789, to Atrāf-i-balda District. The head-quarters are at BĪDAR, the other towns being KALYĀNI, HOMNĀBĀD, KOHĪR, UDGĪR, BHĀLKI, and ALIKHER. More than 86 per cent. of the population were Hindus, 14 per cent. being Musalmāns, with only 15 Christians. The District lies at the junction of three linguistic divisions, and about 34 per cent. of the people speak Marāthī, 35 per cent. Kanarese, more than 16 per cent. Telugu, and about 15 per cent. Urdū.

The following table gives the chief statistics of population in 1901:—

Tāluk.	Area in square miles.	Number of Towns.	Number of Villages.	Population.	Population per square mile.	Percentage of variation in population between 1891 and 1901.	Number of persons able to read and write.
Bīdar	114	1	46	29,005	254	− 0·5	Not available.
Kārāmūngi	150	...	57	31,412	209	− 7·3	
Aurād	158	...	54	16,330	103	− 24·0	
Kohīr	147	1	42	32,041	217	− 0·3	
Nilanga	248	...	63	39,830	160	− 17·5	
Udgīr	544	1	153	78,642	144	− 16·7	
Varvāl-Rājūra	687	...	211	74,637	109	− 41·2	
Jāgīrs, &c.	2,120	4	831	464,232	219	− 15·3	
District total	4,168	7	1,457	766,129	181	− 15·1	14,564

In 1905 the Kohīr *tāluk* was merged in Bīdar, and Aurād in Kārāmūngi, while minor changes have been made in the Udgīr, Nilanga, and Varvāl-Rājūra *tāluks*. The District in its present form comprises five *tāluks*—BĪDAR, KĀRĀMŪNGI, NILANGA, UDGĪR, and VARVĀL-RĀJŪRA. It was formerly part of the Bīdar Division.

Castes and occupations. The most numerous caste is that of the agriculturist Kāpus or Kunbīs, 113,800, besides other agricultural castes, numbering 71,000, including 28,000 Munnūrs. The Baniās, or the trading and money-lending caste, number 13,000. Next come the Dhangars or shepherds, 52,000. The Mahārs and Māngs number 68,000 and 60,000 respectively; the former work as agricultural labourers and the latter in leather. The Velmas number 32,000. The number of persons directly engaged in agriculture is 54 per cent. of the total. There were only four native Christians in 1901.

General agricultural conditions. The soils of the District consist of *regar* or black cotton soil, and *masab* or red soil. The *regar* is generally met with in basins, valleys, and hollows, while the *masab* or red soil is found in high country. The *regar* is derived from schistose and gneissose rock (trap), and the red soil from laterite; both are very fertile.

Chief agricultural statistics and principal crops. The tenure of lands is entirely *ryotwāri*. *Khālsa* and 'crown' lands covered 2,048 square miles in 1901, of which 1,788 were cultivated, while 51 were fallows and cultivable waste, 20 were forests, and 189 were not available for cultivation. The staple food-crop consists of the various kinds of *jowār*, grown on 44 per cent. of the net area cropped. Next come wheat, rice, and *bājra*, the areas under which were 91, 50, and 2 square miles respectively. Rice is grown in all the *tāluks* except Kohīr. The area under pulses of different kinds was 159 square miles.

Cattle, &c. There is no special breed of cattle, but those reared locally are sufficient for the needs of the cultivators. Marāthā ponies sell for from Rs. 40 to Rs. 200, and the State maintains two Arab stallions at Bīdar for the purpose of improving the breed. Sheep and goats of the ordinary kind are reared.

Irrigation. The area irrigated is only about 34 square miles, distributed as follows: canals and channels supply 4 square miles, wells 28, and other sources 2. Though there are eight tanks and ponds, they are used, with one exception, for drinking purposes only. The chief supply of water is derived from wells, of which there are 2,980.

Forests. The District contains no 'reserved' or 'protected' forests, but there are 20 square miles of unprotected forests.

Minerals. The minerals found are soapstone, red ochre, and a gypsum-like mineral, the last being used for plastering flat roofs to make them waterproof. Blocks of red and yellow laterite and black basalt are generally used for building purposes. The latter is largely utilized for tombstones and takes a very good polish.

Arts and manufactures. Bīdar town is celebrated for its *bidri* ware, to which it has given its name. This consists of an alloy of copper, lead, tin, and zinc, inlaid with silver and occasionally gold. *Hukkas*, *pāndans* (betel-boxes), tumblers and goblets, washing basins and ewers, and other vessels are made of this ware. Unfortunately the industry is dying out, owing to want of support. Some fine specimens of this work were made for presentation to His Royal Highness the Prince of Wales (His present Majesty) in 1875, and others have been sent to various exhibitions from time to time. Some embroidery and needlework is also prepared. Ordinary coarse cotton cloth and *sārīs*, &c., formerly manufactured to a considerable extent, are being gradually displaced by the importation of cheaper mill-made cloths. Black blankets made by the Dhangars (shepherds) fetch from Rs. 1-8 to Rs. 6 apiece. Formerly several sugar refineries existed in the District, but the importation of cheap refined sugar has ruined the local manufacture.

Commerce. The principal exports are *jowār* and other food-grains, cotton, oil, chillies, oilseeds, sheep, jaggery, tobacco, and horns. The chief imports consist of hardware, salt, salted fish, opium, gold and silver, copper, brass and copper vessels, refined sugar, iron, mineral oil, sulphur, raw silk, and all kinds of woollen, silk, and cotton fabrics. The centre of trade is the town of BĪDAR. HOMNĀBĀD, which was once the chief market, has lost its importance since the opening of the Nizām's State Railway. The principal trading castes are the Vānīs, Komatis, and Baljawārs, who are also money-lenders. Weekly markets are held in different parts of the District. A great horse and cattle fair used to be held annually at MĀLEGAON, in November and December, which lasted for a whole month. Upwards of 4,000 horses and ponies were sold at the last fair in 1897, but it has not been held since the outbreak of plague.

Roads. There is no line of railway in Bīdar. The metalled road from Osmānābād to Hyderābād passes through the District, and is lined on both sides with avenues of acacia.

Famine. The famine of 1876-8 affected Bīdar only slightly, but the

District suffered severely from that of 1899–1900. The rainfall in 1899 was only 15 inches, while prior to that year there had also been droughts. Six relief works were opened in the *tāluks* of Varvāl-Rājūra, Udgīr, and Nilanga, which suffered the most, the highest daily attendance being 29,262. The out-turn of the *kharīf* and *rabi* crops was about 28 per cent., while the early rice crop yielded 37 per cent., and the late or *tābi* crop was a total failure. The population at the Census of 1901 showed a decrease of 15 per cent., largely due to famine, while the loss of cattle was estimated at more than one-half. The total cost of the famine amounted to nearly 3 lakhs.

District subdivisions and staff.

There are two subdivisions in the District. One, consisting of the *tāluks* of Udgīr, Varvāl-Rājūra, and Nilanga, is in charge of the Second Tālukdār; and the other, comprising the *tāluks* of Bīdar and Kārāmūngi, is under the Third Tālukdār, the First Tālukdār exercising a general supervision over their work. Each *tāluk* is under a *tahsīldār*.

Civil and criminal justice.

The District civil court is under a Civil Judge styled the *Nāzim-i-Dīwāni*. There are seven subordinate civil courts, each under a *tahsīldār*. The First Tālukdār is the chief magistrate of the District, and the Civil Judge is also a joint-magistrate, who exercises powers during the absence of the First Tālukdār from head-quarters. The Second and Third Tālukdārs and the *tahsīldārs* exercise second and third-class magisterial powers. There is not much serious crime in ordinary years; dacoities vary according to the state of the season.

Land revenue.

No information is available regarding the revenue history of the District. According to the old system, villages were farmed out to contractors who received $1\frac{1}{2}$ annas per rupee for collection. In 1866 this system was abolished throughout the Nizām's Dominions, and administration by District officials was introduced. In 1885 the District was surveyed and settled for fifteen years. The average assessment on 'dry' land is Rs. 2 (maximum Rs. 3, minimum Rs. 1–4), and on 'wet' land Rs. 8 (maximum Rs. 15, minimum Rs. 2–8).

The land revenue and the total revenue of the District are given below, in thousands of rupees:—

	1881.	1891.	1901.	1903.
Land revenue .	10,04	10,96	10,94	10,22
Total revenue .	13,24	15,54	15,30	13,89

Local boards and

A local cess of one anna per rupee is levied on the land revenue, three pies of which are set apart for local purposes.

municipalities. There is a District board at Bīdar, and six *tāluk* boards have also been formed. The District board supervises the working of the *tāluk* boards as well as that of the municipality of Bīdar. The total expenditure of these boards in 1901 was Rs. 12,200. There is a small conservancy establishment at each of the *tāluk* head-quarters.

Police and jails. The First Tālukdār is the head of the District police, with a Superintendent (*Mohtamim*) as his executive deputy. There are 27 police stations in the District; and the force consists of 446 constables, 75 subordinate officers, and 52 mounted police under 7 inspectors. There is also a small special police force called *Rakhwāli*. The District jail at Bīdar has accommodation for 100 prisoners, but those with sentences of upwards of six months were until recently transferred to the Central jail at Nizāmābād.

Education. The District takes a low position as regards literacy, only 1·9 per cent. (3·7 males and 0·6 females) of the population being able to read and write in 1901. The total number of pupils under instruction in 1881, 1891, 1901, and 1903 was 655, 2,849, 2,742, and 2,559 respectively. In 1903 there were 30 primary and 2 middle schools and one high school, with 304 girls under instruction. The total expenditure on education in that year amounted to Rs. 25,800, of which Rs. 4,365 was contributed by the local boards, Rs. 12,857 by the State, and Rs. 1,560 from school fees.

Medical. There are four dispensaries, including one *yunāni*, in the District, with accommodation for 12 in-patients. In 1901 the number of cases treated in all these dispensaries was 34,900, of whom 194 were in-patients. The number of operations performed was 503, and the total expenditure was Rs. 11,248.

In 1901 only 1,773 persons were successfully vaccinated, representing 2·3 per 1,000 of the population.

Bīdar Tāluk.—*Tāluk* in Bīdar District, Hyderābād State. The population in 1901, including *jāgīrs*, was 105,392, and the area was 487 square miles. In 1891 the population was 105,781. These figures include the totals for the Kohīr *tāluk*, merged in Bīdar in 1905, which had an area of 236 square miles and a population in 1901 of 52,558. The *tāluk* contains two towns, Bīdar (population, 11,367), the head-quarters of the District and *tāluk*, and Kohīr (6,379), besides 177 villages, of which 89 are *jāgīr*. The land revenue in 1901 was 1·6 lakhs. The *tāluk* is situated on a plateau, composed mainly of lateritic soil, and is crossed by the Mānjra river. The *paigāh tāluks* of Chincholi (population, 42,971; villages, 47), Ekeli (population, 24,324; villages, 53), and Chitgopa (population, 80,929; villages, 93), and the *jāgīr* of Kalyāni (population, 36,205; villages, 72) adjoin this *tāluk*. KALYĀNI (population, 11,191), HOMNĀBĀD (7,136), and ALIKHER (5,740) are the chief towns in the Kalyāni *jāgīr* and Chincholi *tāluk*.

Kārāmūngi.—'Crown' *tāluk* in Bīdar District, Hyderābād State. The population in 1901, including *jāgīrs*, was 51,808, and the area was 362 square miles. In 1891 the population had been 60,341, the decrease being due to the famine of 1899–1900. The *tāluk* contains 130 villages, of which 19 are *jāgīr*; and Janwāda (population, 2,165) is the head-quarters. Since 1905 the *tāluk* has included the old *tāluk* of Aurād, which had an area of 189 square miles, a population in 1901 of 19,301, and 65 villages. The land revenue in 1901 was 1·7 lakhs. The Mānjra river flows through the *tāluk*. The *paigāh tāluk* of Nārāyankher (population, 42,972) lies south of this *tāluk*, and consists of 106 villages. Farther south again is the *paigāh tāluk* of Hasanābād (population, 21,563), with 45 villages.

Nilanga.—*Tāluk* in Bīdar District, Hyderābād State, with an area of 315 square miles. The population in 1901, including *jāgīrs*, was 48,002. In 1891 the population had been 59,148, the decrease being due to the famine of 1899–1900. The *tāluk* has 89 villages, of which 26 are *jāgīr*; and Nilanga (population, 3,343) is the head-quarters. The land revenue in 1901 was 1·6 lakhs. In 1905 the *tāluk* received a few villages from the Varvāl-Rājūra *tāluk*. Nilanga is composed chiefly of *regar* or black cotton soil. South and east lie the three *paigāh tāluks* of Partābpur, Bhālki, and Ghorwādi (population, 42,761, 20,784, and 35,178), containing 63, 21, and 56 villages respectively. BHĀLKI (5,788), the only town, is situated in the *paigāh tāluk* of the same name.

Udgīr Tāluk.—*Tāluk* in Bīdar District, Hyderābād State. The population in 1901, including *jāgīrs*, was 101,228, and the area was 681 square miles. In 1891 the population had been 121,467, the decrease being due to the famine of 1899–1900. The *tāluk* contains one town, UDGĪR (population, 5,984), the head-quarters; and 207 villages, of which 54 are *jāgīr*. The land revenue in 1901 was 3·1 lakhs. The soils are chiefly *regar* or black cotton soil and some laterite. In 1905 some villages were transferred to the Deglūr *tāluk* of Nānder District, while other villages were added from Varvāl-Rājūra.

The *jāgīr tāluk* of Mirag, with a population in 1901 of 21,734, containing 45 villages, lies between this *taluk* and the Bīdar *tāluk*.

Varvāl-Rājura.—*Tāluk* in Bīdar District, Hyderābād State. The population in 1901, including *jāgīrs*, was 87,503, and the area was 772 square miles. In 1891 the population had been 148,805, the decrease being due to the famine of 1899–1900. The *tāluk* contains 244 villages, of which 33 are *jāgīr*; and Varvāl-Rājūra (population, 3,998) is the head-quarters. The land revenue in 1901 was 3 lakhs. The Mānjra river flows through the southern portion of the *tāluk*, which is composed of black cotton soil. In 1905 the *tāluk* was reduced by the transfer of some villages to Udgīr and Nilanga.

Alikher.—Head-quarters of the *paigāh tāluk* of Chincholi, Bīdar District, Hyderābād State, situated in 17° 51′ N. and 77° 17′ E., 21 miles north of the Mānjra river. Population (1901), 5,740.

Bhālki.—Head-quarters of the *paigāh tāluk* of the same name in Bīdar District, Hyderābād State, situated in 18° 3′ N. and 77° 12′ E., about 9 miles east of the confluence of the Kāranja with the Mānjra. Population (1901), 5,788.

Bīdar Town.—Head-quarters of Bīdar District, Hyderābād State, situated in 17° 55′ N. and 77° 32′ E., on an elevated and healthy plateau 2,330 feet above the sea. The population has increased during the last twenty years: (1881) 9,730, (1891) 11,315, and (1901) 11,367. According to local tradition, the Kākatīya Rājās of Warangal endowed a temple of Mahādeo which existed here, and a town sprang up in its vicinity in the middle of the thirteenth century, which became the capital of a large province. Ulugh Khān, afterwards Muhammad bin Tughlak, besieged and took it in 1321; but subsequently, when the governors of the Deccan rebelled, Alā-ud-dīn Hasan, the founder of the Bahmani dynasty, annexed the town to his new kingdom in 1347. Ahmad Shāh Wali, the tenth Bahmani king, founded the modern city and built the fort, removing his court here from GULBARGA in 1430. Bīdar continued to be the capital of the Bahmani kings until the extinction of that dynasty, when Amīr Barīd founded an independent State in 1492. Amīr Barīd ruled over Bīdar and the surrounding country, and was succeeded by his son Alī Barīd, in 1538, who was the first to assume the title of Shāh and died in 1582. Three other kings, Ibrāhīm, Kāsim Barīd, and Mirza Alī Barīd, followed, the last of whom assumed the title of Amīr Barīd II. This short-lived dynasty became extinct when Amīr Barīd II was made a prisoner and sent to Bijāpur by Ibrahīm Adil Shāh. In 1624 the Nizām Shāhi troops under Malik Ambar attacked and plundered Bīdar, but it was retaken by the Bijāpur king. In 1656 Aurangzeb besieged and took Bīdar, changing its name to Zafarābād. The town remained in the possession of the Mughals till the first of the Nizāms declared his independence, early in the eighteenth century.

The town of Bīdar must have been of great extent in its prosperous days, as appears from its palaces, mosques, and other buildings. Among these may be mentioned the great *madrasa* or college built by Mahmūd Gāvān, the Bahmani minister, which is now in ruins, the Jāma Masjid, and the Sola Khamba or 'sixteen-pillared' mosque. The last of these is in the citadel, which also contains the ruined Rang Mahal or 'coloured palace,' the remains of a mint, a Turkish bath, an arsenal, and several powder magazines. The fortifications and battlemented walls of this place are very strong, and are still well preserved. On its numerous bastions pieces of ordnance are mounted, some of very large size; one of them is specially remarkable as having been brought here from Bijāpur. West of the town are the tombs of Alī Barīd, Kāsim Barīd, and others of the same dynasty, while twelve tombs of the Bahmani kings are situated to the north-east in the village of Ashtūr. Most of the old buildings in the fort are now used as offices.

Bīdar is the chief trade centre of the District, and has given its name to a class of metal-work made of an alloy of copper, lead, tin, and zinc, inlaid with silver or gold. This industry is, however, not very flourishing.

Homnābād.—Town in the *paigāh tāluk* of Chincholi, Bīdar District, Hyderābād State, situated in 17° 47′ N. and 77° 08′ E. Population (1901), 7,136. It has declined considerably in prosperity since the opening of the Nizām's State Railway, which has diverted trade.

Kalyāni.—A *jāgīr* town in Bīdar District, Hyderābād State, situated in 17° 53′ N. and 76° 57′ E., 36 miles west of Bīdar town. Population (1901), 11,191. About the middle of the eleventh century Someshwar I made Kalyāni the capital of the Chālukyan kingdom. A hundred years later the power was usurped by Bijjala Kalachuri, the commander-in-chief, and before the close of the twelfth century the Chālukya power was at an end. While Kalyāni remained a great capital, it was noted as the residence of Vijnāneshwar, the author of the treatise on law known as the *Mitākshara*, and of Basava, who founded the Lingāyat sect. Further particulars about Basava and the Lingāyats will be found in the article on Mysore State. The Kalachuris were succeeded by the Yādavas of Deogiri (DAULATĀBĀD); and after the establishment of the Bahmani dynasty, Kalyāni passed into their possession in the fourteenth century, and subsequently into that of Bijāpur. The Mughals sacked it in 1653. In 1656 Aurangzeb invested the fortress, which surrendered after an heroic defence. During the contests which followed the decline of Chālukyan power, and the struggles between various Muhammadan rulers, the magnificent temples which once adorned the place were demolished or converted into mosques.

Kohīr.—Town in the District and *tāluk* of Bīdar, Hyderābād State, situated in 17° 36′ N. and 77° 43′ E., 24 miles south-east of Bīdar town. Population (1901), 6,379. It contains the tombs of two well-known Musalmān saints, besides numerous mosques; the Jāma Masjid, erected during the reign of the Bahmani kings, is a building of note. The town contains a middle and girls' school, a post office, and the police inspector's office. Kohīr is celebrated for its mangoes.

Mālegaon.—A *jāgīr* village in the north-east of Bīdar District, Hyderābād State, situated in 18° 41′ N. and 76° 58′ E. Population (1901), 270. It was once celebrated for its annual horse fair, where upwards of 4,000 horses and ponies were disposed of at prices ranging up to Rs. 700. Piece-goods, cloth of all kinds, hardware, &c., were among other things exposed for sale. Owing to plague and famine the fair has not been held since 1897.

Udgīr Town.—Head-quarters of the *tāluk* of the same name in Bīdar District, Hyderābād State, situated in 18° 24′ N. and 77° 7′ E. Population (1901), 5,984. The fort belonged to the Bijāpur kings, and was besieged by Shāh Jahān's general in 1635, and surrendered to him. In 1760 a great battle was fought here between the Nizām and the Marāthās. Nizām Salābat Jang and his brother occupied Udgīr with 7,000 cavalry, but were surrounded by 60,000 Marāthās. Desperate fighting continued for days, and the Nizām was forced to agree to the terms of peace imposed by the Marāthās. The fort was built about 1493, and has a ditch all round. Two palaces are situated inside, and two outside, but all are in ruins.

ESTATES

Paigāh Estates.—A group of estates in Hyderābād State, comprising 23 *tāluks* dispersed over the Districts of Bīdar, Nander, Osmānābād, Gulbarga, Medak, Atrāf-i-balda, and Nizāmābād, and a few scattered villages in Aurangābād, Warangal, Mahbūbnagar, and Nalgonda. They consist of 1,273 villages and towns, with an aggregate area of 4,134 square miles and a total revenue of about 40 lakhs. These estates belong to the representatives of three deceased noblemen, Sir Asmān Jāh, Sir Khurshed Jāh, and Sir Vikār-ul-Umarā. The following table shows details of the estates according to the Census of 1901:—

Names.	Number of *tāluks*.	Area in square miles.	Number of villages.	Population, 1901.
Sir Asmān Jāh	7	1,232	396	265,194
Sir Khurshed Jāh	8	1,512	468	268,902
Sir Vikār-ul-Umarā	8	1,390	409	240,315
Total	23	4,134	1,273	774,411

The history of the Hyderābād *paigāh* nobles dates back to the reign of Akbar. Mullā Jalāl-ud-dīn, the founder of the family, came to Shikohābād from Lahore during the reign of that emperor. His son, Muhammad Bahā-ud-dīn Khān, was appointed head of the treasury at Akbarābād (Agra) in Aurangzeb's reign. Muhammad Abul-Khair Khān, the founder's grandson, attracted the attention of Nawāb Asaf Jāh, with whom he came to the Deccan, and, after having served as deputy-Sūbahdār of Mālwā, finally settled at Hyderābād. In 1743 he was sent against Bāpu Naik, a Marāthā chief, who was levying *chauth* in these territories, and defeated him. Subsequently he held the deputy-Sūbahdārship of Khāndesh and Aurangābād. He died at Burhānpur in 1749, leaving an only son, Abul Fateh Khān, who received the title of Tegh Jang from Nawāb Nizām Alī Khān. Further distinctions and titles were bestowed upon him, among them being that of

Shams-ul-Umarā, which became the family title. He commanded 10,000 cavalry, which formed the beginning of the *paigāh* forces, for the maintenance of which the estates were originally granted. Abul Fateh Khān died at Pāngal while accompanying the expedition against Tipū, and was succeeded by his son, Muhammad Fakhr-ud-dīn Khān, who received his grandfather's name of Abul-Khair Khān. In 1800 he married a daughter of the Nizām, and thus the family became allied for the first time to the ruling house of Hyderābād. In 1827 the title of Amīr-i-Kabīr, or 'premier noble,' was bestowed upon him. Fakhr-ud-dīn Khān was a great patron of learning, and a good mathematician, being the author of *Sitta-i-shamsia*, a work on physics, mechanics, astronomy, &c. He built the Jahān-numā and many other palaces, and died in 1855, leaving five sons.

The third son, Rafī-ud-dīn Khān, who succeeded his father as Amīr-i-Kabīr, was appointed co-regent with Sir Sālār Jang on the death of the Nizām Afzal-ud-daula Bahādur in 1869, the present Nizām being then only three years old. This office he held till his death in 1877, when his younger brother Rashīd-ud-dīn Khān succeeded him as co-regent, receiving the titles of Shams-ul-Umarā and Amīr-i-Kabīr. The *paigāh jāgīrs* and estates were subsequently divided between two branches of the family, one represented by Sir Asmān Jāh, a grandson of Fakhr-ud-dīn Khān, and the other by Rashīd-ud-dīn Khān, who died in 1881, leaving two sons, Sir Khurshed Jāh and Sir Vikār-ul-Umarā.

When the present Nizām attained his majority, he conferred the title of Amīr-i-Akbar on Sir Asmān Jāh. This nobleman became minister of Hyderābād in 1888, and after six years of office retired in 1893, being succeeded as minister by Sir Vikār-ul-Umarā. Sir Asmān Jāh died in 1898, leaving an only son, Nawāb Muīn-ud-dīn Khān Bahādur, who is now the sole representative of this branch of the family. Sir Vikār-ul-Umarā resigned the office of minister in 1901, and died early in 1902, leaving two sons, Nawāb Sultān-ul-mulk Bahādur and Nawāb Walī-ud-dīn Khān Bahādur. Sir Khurshed Jāh, who survived his brother for only a year, has also left two sons, Nawāb Shams-ul-mulk Zafar Jang Bahādur and Nawāb Imām Jang Bahādur.

Sālār Jang Estate.—An estate comprising six *tāluks* situated in various Districts of the Hyderābād State. It consists of 333 villages, and has an area of 1,486 square miles, with a population (1901) of 180,150. The *tāluks* are Kosgi in

Gulbarga, Ajanta in Aurangābād, Koppal and Yelbarga in Raichūr, Dundgal in Medak, and Raigir in Nalgonda. The total revenue is 8·2 lakhs.

The present representative of the family is Nawāb Sālār Jang, grandson of the late Sir Sālār Jang, G.C.S.I., the great minister of the Nizām[1]. The family claim descent from Shaikh Owais of Karan, who lived in the time of the Prophet. Shaikh Owais the second, his tenth descendant, came to India during the reign of Ali Adil Shāh (1656–72), and settled in Bijāpur, where his son, Shaikh Muhammad Alī, married the daughter of Mullā Ahmad Nawāyet[2], minister of the Bijāpur kingdom, by whom he had two sons who rose to high rank. Mullā Ahmad having joined the imperial service about 1665, his successor ill-treated the two brothers, who eventually left Bijāpur during the reign of Sikandar Adil Shāh and entered the service of Aurangzeb. One of these, Shaikh Muhammad Bākar by name, was appointed Dīwān of Thal-kokan, and after retiring from active work settled at Aurangābād, where he died in 1715. His son, Shaikh Muhammad Takī, served under Aurangzeb, Bahādur Shāh, and Farrukhsiyar. Asaf Jāh, the viceroy of the Deccan, appointed him commander of the garrisons of all his forts. Shams-ud-dīn Muhammad Haidar, son of Muhammad Takī, continued in the service of Asaf Jāh, and was promoted by his successors. Under Salābat Jang his command was raised to 7,000 foot and 7,000 horse, and he received the title of Munīr-ul-mulk, with the appointment of head steward. He was subsequently made Dīwān of the Deccan *Sūbahs*, and finally retired to Aurangābād, of which city he was governor.

He left two sons, the elder of whom, Safdar Khān Ghayūr Jang, was appointed Dīwān of the Deccan *Sūbahs* in 1782, with the title of Ashja-ul-mulk. The third son of Ghayūr Jang, from whom the present members of the family are directly descended, was Alī Zamān, Munīr-ul-mulk II. After his death his eldest son became the third Munīr-ul-mulk, and was married successively to two daughters of Mīr Alam (Saiyid Abul Kasim). Mīr Alam, who was thus the maternal great-grandfather of Sir Sālār Jang, belonged to the Nūria Saiyids of Shustar in Persia. His father, Saiyid Razzāk, came to India when quite young, and settled at Hyderābād, where Nizām Alī Khān bestowed *jāgīrs* upon him. Mīr Alam acted as

[1] *Memoirs of Sir Sālār Jang*, by Syed Hossain Bilgrami (1883).

[2] Vide *History of Nawayets*, by Nawāb Aziz Jang, published at Hyderābād, 1313 Fasli (1904).

vakīl between the British envoy and the Hyderābād minister in 1784. Two years later he went to Calcutta as the Nizām's representative, and in 1791 he was sent to Lord Cornwallis to discuss the peace proposals between Tipū Sultān and the allies. He commanded the Nizām's troops in the campaign of 1799 against Tipū, and in 1804 was made minister after the death of Azam ul Umarā. After his death in 1808, he was succeeded as minister by his son-in-law, Munīr-ul-mulk III.

Sir Sālār Jang, the grandson of Munīr-ul-mulk III, succeeded his uncle Siraj-ul-mulk of Hyderābād in 1853. For thirty years the story of his life is the history of the HYDERĀBĀD STATE, to the article on which reference should be made. For his eminent services he was made G.C.S.I., and during a visit to England in 1876 he received the D.C.L. degree at Oxford and the freedom of the City of London. In 1884 the Nizām appointed the elder son of Sir Sālār Jang as minister, who, however, resigned in 1887, and died two years later, leaving an infant son, Nawāb Yūsuf Alī Khān Bahādur Sālār Jang, who is now the only direct representative of this distinguished family.

Amarchinta (or Atmākūr).—A *samasthān* or tributary estate in the east of Raichūr District, Hyderābād State, consisting of 69 villages, with Atmākūr (population, 2,330) as its headquarters. It has an area of 190 square miles, and a population (1901) of 34,147. The total revenue is 1·4 lakhs, and the tribute paid to the Nizām is Rs. 6,363. Amarchinta is an old *samasthān*, but no historical records are available. The fort of Atmākūr, the residence of the Rājā, is in a good state of preservation. The Kistna river flows along the southern boundary, separating Amarchinta from the Gadwāl *samasthān*; its waters are not available for irrigation, owing to the height of the river banks. Amarchinta and Atmākūr are noted for fine muslins of excellent quality, woven in the shape of handkerchiefs, *dhotīs*, and turbans with gold and silk borders.

Gadwāl Samasthān (or Keshavnagar).—A *samasthān* or tributary estate in the east of Raichūr District, Hyderābād State. It contains one town, GADWĀL (population, 10,195), and 214 villages, and has an area of 864 square miles, with a population (1901) of 968,491. The total revenue is 3 lakhs, and the tribute paid to the Nizām is Rs. 86,840. Gadwāl existed long before the foundation of the Hyderābād State. It formerly issued its own coin, which is still current in Raichūr District. Nothing is known regarding the early history of the *samasthān*. The fort at Gadwāl town, the residence of the present Rājā, was commenced about 1703, and completed in 1710 by Rājā Somtādari. The present Rājā is a minor, and the estate has been under the control of the Court of Wards since 1902. The Kistna and Tungabhadra water the northern and southern portions of the *samasthān*, and the land bordering on these rivers, being alluvial, is very fertile. The remaining portion consists of *masab* land and uncultivable waste. Most of the cultivation is of the 'dry-crop' description. There being very few tanks, little 'wet' cultivation is possible, and well-irrigation is carried on only to a limited extent. Silk *sāris*, scarfs, turbans, and *dhotīs* with gold borders of a superior kind are manufactured at Gadwāl town. Ten factories are at work, and about 2 lakhs' worth of these articles is exported annually to Hyderābād, Secunderābād, Raichūr, and other places in the neighbourhood.

Jatpol.—A *samasthān* or tributary estate in the south of Mahbūbnagar District, Hyderābād State, consisting of 89 villages, with an area of 191 square miles, and a population (1901) of 31,613. The total revenue is 1·9 lakhs, and the tribute paid to the Nizām is Rs. 73,537.

From inscriptions it appears that in 1243 Annapota Nāyadu took possession of the estate, and captured PANGAL and other forts. His dominions extended on the east as far as Srisil, on the west to Kotta and Sugūr, now belonging to the Wanparti *samasthān*, on the north to Devarkonda, and on the south they were bounded by the Kistna river. His descendants ruled for several centuries. In the last quarter of the eighteenth century Rājā Jagannāth Rao, having no male issue, adopted Lachma Rao, a scion of the Rao family of Pākhāl. In 1831 Lachma Rao obtained the Jatpol *pargana* from the Nizām on a fixed rental of Rs. 70,000. The present Rājā, Venkata Lachma Rao, who is a younger brother of the Rājā of Venkatagiri in the Madras Presidency, also succeeded by adoption. He has cleared off debts amounting to nearly 2 lakhs, with which the estate was encumbered. The Rājā resides at Kolhāpur (population, 2,204), though until eighty years ago Jatpol was the head-quarters.

Pāloncha.—A *samasthān* or tributary estate in the south-east of Warangal District, Hyderābād State, consisting of six sub-*tāluks*, with an area of about 800 square miles, and a population (1901) of 38,742. The revenue is said to be only Rs. 70,000, and the tribute paid to the Nizām is Rs. 45,875. The estate further receives an annual sum of Rs. 4,716 as *deshmukh's* fees from the Nizām, and the Rājā owns the estates of Bhadrāchalam and Rekapalli in the Godāvari District of Madras.

The estate appears to have existed before the reign of Pratāp Rudra of Warangal, who conferred the title of Ashwarao on the Rājā in appreciation of the latter's horsemanship, *ashwa* in Sanskrit meaning 'horse.' After the capture of Warangal by the Musalmāns, the king of Delhi bestowed the *parganas* of Hasanabad and Sankargiri (Paloncha) upon Anappa Ashwarao in 1324, and these remained in possession of the family for eighteen generations till 1698. In 1769 Narsinha Ashwarao was killed in battle by Zafar-ud-daula, who plundered the Rājā's treasury and took possession of all the documents and ancient *sanads* engraved on copper-plates. In 1798 the Nizām granted a *sanad* to Venkatrām Ashwarao, with the stipulation that he should maintain 2,000 cavalry and 3,000 foot soldiers; but this condition did not long remain in force. Internal feuds and dissensions between the two principal branches of the family now commenced and continued till 1858, when Sir Sālār Jang, the minister of Hyderābād, put an end to them by granting a fresh *sanad* to Rājā Sītārām Chandra. At the same time the two *tāluks* of Bhadrāchalam and Rekapalli, situated along the left bank of the Godāvari, were taken over by the British Government. The Rājā, who had contracted heavy debts and had mortgaged the *samasthān* to a banker, died without issue. The banker collected the revenue of the State for twelve years, and at the end of that period filed a suit and obtained a decree for 6 lakhs. The Nizām paid the banker 3 lakhs in cash, sanctioned the transfer of the two *tāluks* of Mallūr and Ramanjavaram in lieu of the balance, and confiscated the estate. The Rājā's mother died in 1875, but before her death she had adopted the present Rājā, who was her daughter's son. After a prolonged inquiry, the British Government restored the two *tāluks* of Bhadrāchalam and Rekapalli to the Rājā, who also received 6 *tāluks* from the Nizām on payment of the 3 lakhs advanced to the banker. From 1324 to the present time twenty-eight Rājās have ruled in succession. Pāloncha was originally the head-quarters of the *samasthān*, after which Bhadrāchalam was for some time the residence of the Rājā, but Ashwaraopet has now become the capital.

The *samasthān* is very unhealthy and malarious, owing to a large portion of it being covered with thick jungle. The Godāvari river crosses it from north-west to south-east, dividing it into two portions, that along the right being in the Hyderābād State, and that along the left in the Madras Presidency. The bed of the river is so deep that its waters cannot be used for irrigation.

Wanparti.—A *samasthān* or tributary estate in the south-west of Mahbūbnagar District, Hyderābād State. The villages number 124, and are scattered over the Nāgar Karnūl, Jedcherla, Mahbūbnagar, Kalvakurti, and Amrābād *tāluks* of Mahbūbnagar District. The area is about 450 square miles, and the population in 1901 was 62,197. The revenue is 1·5 lakhs, and the tribute paid to the Nizām is Rs. 76,883. Up to 1727 Sugūr was the seat of the Rājā, and gave its name to the *samasthān*, but subsequently Wanparti was selected as the capital. The Kistna river flows through the south-western portion for a distance of 16 miles, but owing to the depth of the bed its waters are not utilized for irrigation. The town of Wanparti contains an oil-mill for extracting castor oil, which is exported to Raichūr and also to Kurnool in the Madras Presidency. Cloth and *sārīs* both of cotton and silk are made here, but their texture is not so fine as those of Amarchinta and Gadwāl.

INDEX

G.

H.

I.

L.

M.

R.

Pimpalner
Amalner
Jalgaon
Bhusawal
Malkapur
Akot
Dhulia
Pachora
Khamgaon
Akola
Surgana
Malegaon
Buldana
Chalisgaon
Ajanta
Chandor
Manmad
Assaye
Nasik
Ellora
Basim
Vaijapur
AURANGABAD
Aurangabad
Jalna
Kadirabad
Hingoli
Sangamner
Nevasa
Godavari R.
Paithan
PARBHANI
Rahuri
Basmat
Manwat
Pathri
Parbhani
Nander
Ahmadnagar
Mazalgaon
Sonepet
NANDER
Sirur
Gangakher
Shrigonda
Mominabad
Malegaon
Latur
Udgir
Karmala
OSMANABAD
Parenda
Osmanabad
Phalton
Kalyani
Bidar
Pandharpur
Sholapur
Homnabad
Akalkot
Gulbarga
Jath
Bijapur
Sangli
Miraj
Kolhapur
Shahabad
Wadi
Sagar
Jamkhandi
Bagewadi
Deodrug
Bagalkot
Lingsugur
Raichur
RAICHUR
Ramdurg
Manvi
Belgaum
Khanapur
Sindhnur
Adoni
Dharwar
Gadag
Kampli
Hubli
Bellary
Sandur
Guntakal
Savanur
Harpanahalli
Longitude East of Greenwich

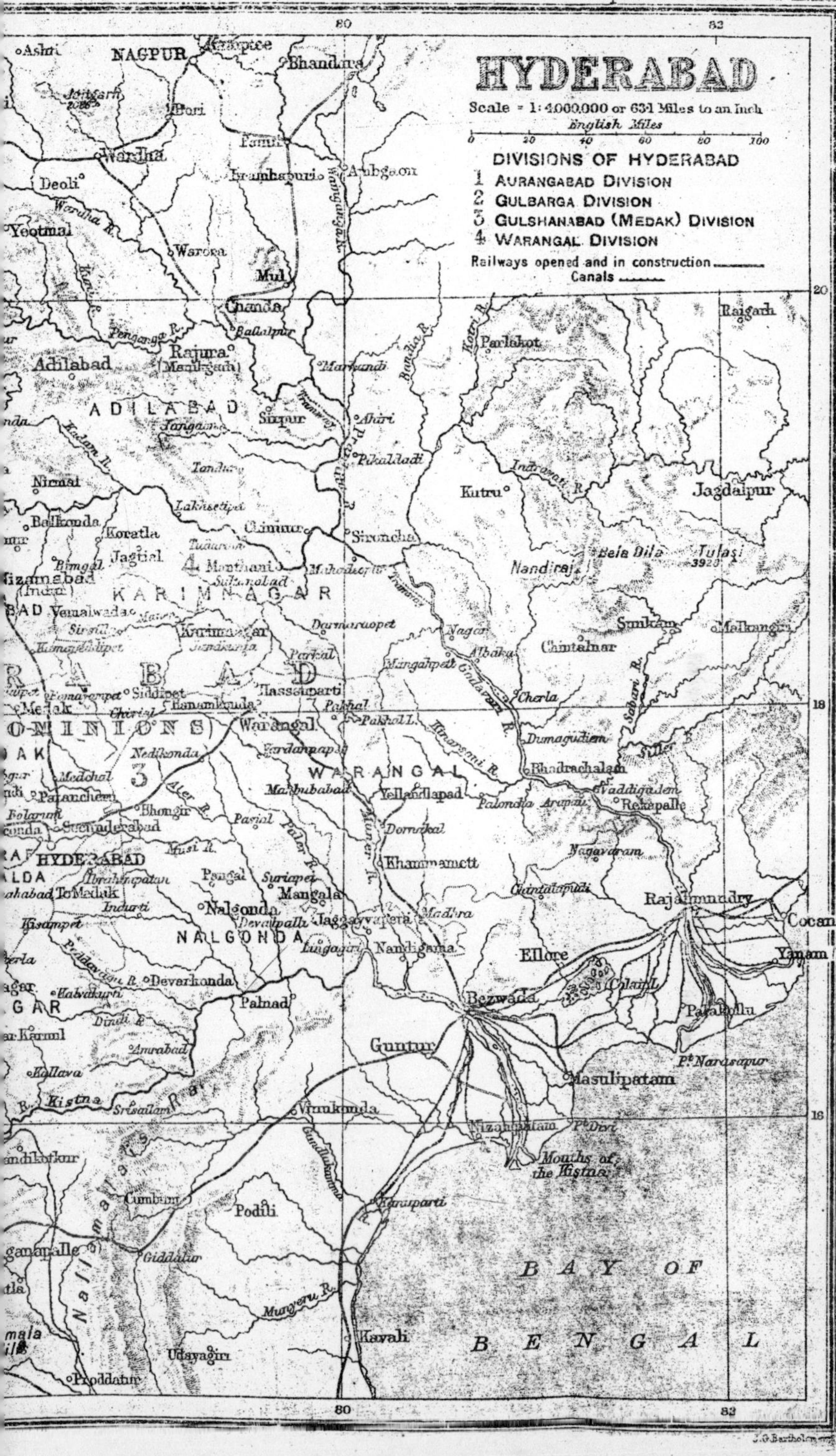
HYDERABAD
Scale = 1:4000,000 or 63.1 Miles to an Inch
English Miles
0 20 40 60 80 100
DIVISIONS OF HYDERABAD
1 AURANGABAD DIVISION
2 GULBARGA DIVISION
3 GULSHANABAD (MEDAK) DIVISION
4 WARANGAL DIVISION
Railways opened and in construction
Canals
BAY OF
BENGAL